# Zion on the Hudson

# Zion on the Hudson

## DUTCH NEW YORK AND NEW JERSEY IN THE AGE OF REVIVALS

FIRTH HARING FABEND ⁊59

Rutgers University Press
*New Brunswick, New Jersey, and London*

**Library of Congress Cataloging-in-Publication Data**

Fabend, Firth Haring
    Zion on the Hudson : Dutch New York and New Jersey in the age of
revivals / Firth Haring Fabend.
       p.  cm.
    Includes bibliographical references (p.   ) and index.
    ISBN 0–8135–2771–6 (alk. paper)
    1. Dutch Americans—New York—Religion. 2. Dutch Americans—New
Jersey—Religion. 3. Reformed Church—New York—History—19th
century. 4. Reformed Church—New Jersey—History—19th century.
5. Dutch Americans—New York—History—19th century. 6. Dutch
Americans—New Jersey—History—19th century. 7. New York—Church
history—19th century. 8. New Jersey—Church history—19th century.
I. Title.
BX9498.D87A4 2000
285.7'747'089.9.1—dc21                                           99–43168
                                                       CIP

British Cataloging-in-Publication data for this book is available from the British Library

Manufactured in the United States of America

*For Hugh, William, and Ione Elizabeth*

# CONTENTS

# FIGURES

# TABLES

# PREFACE

Two questions intrigued me as I set out to write *Zion on the Hudson*. Why did Dutchness persist in New York and New Jersey for so long after immigration had ceased? What eventually caused it to disappear? These questions, of course, raised an underlying question: What is meant by Dutchness? I have tried to answer the last question in chapter 1. It has taken all ten chapters to answer the first two questions.

Once into the sources, I realized that the persistence of Dutchness in New York and New Jersey appeared to be related to the religious beliefs settlers had brought with them from the Reformation Netherlands. Moreover, it was related in ways that became increasingly complicated over time, not only by the convulsive social change taking place in the country but by certain developments on the religious scene that raised difficult challenges for the Reformed Dutch Church, the primary institution the Dutch established in America. (The name of this church has gone through many permutations over the centuries. Here it is referred to as the Reformed Dutch Church and also, less formally, as simply the Reformed Church or the Dutch Church. Its official name since 1867 has been the Reformed Church in America.)

I also soon realized that I was not alone in my interest in the Dutch contributions to the history of the United States. Indeed, I found myself party to a lively national and transatlantic debate. On the one side were those who argued that the English legacy to U.S. history and the formation of American identity was all-important, and the contributions of other European nations, including the Netherlands, insignificant at best. To these historians, evidence of a durable "Dutchness," for instance, was nothing more than a nostalgic cultural vestige. On the other side were those who protested that the Dutch influence on U.S. cultural, social, economic, and political institutions had been, if not actually repressed, certainly overlooked and underestimated.

Historians on the Dutch side of the divide labored under a severe handicap. For while the colonial history of New England and the Chesapeake (Maryland and Virginia)—and thus perforce the British legacy to U.S. history and culture—has been explored, analyzed, and interpreted to its microcosms, the history of the Dutch colony in America, New Netherland, has been relatively ignored. This situation arose to some extent because few U.S. scholars read modern, much less seventeenth-century, Dutch. But it is also, many believe, an example of the phenomenon that those who win the war get to write the history.

Redressing the balance slowly but surely has been the occupation, over the last twenty years, of the New Netherland Project in Albany, New York, which under the direction of Charles T. Gehring has been translating and publishing the documents of the Dutch period in America—and in the process generating a body of work that will eventually set the Dutch legacy in its rightful perspective. To the efforts of Charles Gehring, to all those scholars who have delivered papers at the project's annual Rensselaerswyck Seminar, and to those Dutch, English, and U.S. historians who have been exploring "connecting cultures" and "miracles mirrored" (the short titles of important books), I owe my own education in the vast subject of cultural transmission.

*Zion on the Hudson* adds to the wide-ranging discussion sorting out the historical influences on American society by offering clear evidence that, at least in the area of religion, the theological ideas that the seventeenth-century Dutch settlers brought with them to the New World from the Reformation Netherlands were potent enough to color the religious culture, the social life, the educational institutions, the marrying patterns, and the child-rearing practices in their part of the New World for two centuries and more thereafter. In short, the decisions of the Synod of Dort in 1618–1619, at which the Reformed Dutch Church was officially launched, and the religious culture undergirding them, governed to a significant extent the social customs, mores, and way of life of the former Dutch culture areas of New Netherland to the end of the nineteenth century. They may still have force today.

# ACKNOWLEDGMENTS

Many kind and generous friends, acquaintances, and even total strangers have supported me with their encouragement and edified me with their stores of knowledge during the years that I researched and wrote (and re-wrote) *Zion on the Hudson*. I have long been grateful to Russell Gascro, Archivist of the Reformed Church in America, who smiled when he read my first outline and advised me to cut it by a couple of centuries. Patricia U. Bonomi, professor emerita of history at New York University, was, as she has been to me in the past, a good friend from prospectus in May 1992 to final draft in the summer of 1998, and I am grateful to her for her interest and her always cogent comments and direction. Another mentor and former professor, Paul R. Baker, read the whole first draft and gave me a boost in confidence when I most needed it.

Four Reformed theologians and historians, John W. Beardslee III, John W. Coakley, Eugene Heideman, and James R. Tanis, gave careful readings of the chapters in their spheres of interest and kindly guided me over the hard spots, saving me from many gaffes. It should be needless to say, but I say it anyway: any deficiencies that remain in these areas are none but my own.

With care and devotion, two historians, both skillful editors, read the whole manuscript not once but twice: my high school friend re-met in cyberspace, Richard B. Lyman, and my friend in Dutchness, David William Voorhees. As only they can really know, I am indebted to both of them for suggestions and improvements too numerous to count.

It is a pleasure to thank library personnel, particularly Renée S. House, Director of the Gardner A. Sage Library at the New Brunswick Theological Seminary, and her staff for their many kindnesses over the years, Carol Kinsey, Marsha Blake, and So Ae Lee especially. Ron Becker, Al King, Fernanda Perrone, and Edward Skipworth at Alexander Library, Rutgers

University, were indefatigable in helping me to find material in the rich Special Collections of that institution. Staffs of the New York State Library in Albany, the Rare Books and Manuscripts Room at the New York Public Library, the New Jersey Historical Society, the Albany Institute of History and Art, and the New-York Historical Society were invariably helpful. I am grateful to Tim Adriance, Robert Griffin, and Kevin Wright at the Bergen County Historical Society, Ruth Van Wagoner and her staff at the Bergen County Historical Archives, and Ken Schaffer at the Collegiate Church Archives, all of whom gave me unrestricted access to the collections in their charge. Ellen H. Fladger, Archivist at Union College in Schenectady, and librarians at Sprague Library, Montclair State University, the Johnson Free Public Library in Hackensack, and the New City Free Library in New City, New York, often helped me to locate pertinent material. The Montclair Public Library was patient in locating hard-to-find secondary sources through the interlibrary loan system, and William Dane at the Newark Public Library was very kind in allowing me access to his private precincts.

I am grateful once again to the Rutgers University Press editorial and production personnel for insisting on making "their" books the best they can be: Marilyn Campbell (the second time around), Helen Hsu, Sarah Blackwood, and especially Elizabeth Gilbert, to whose fastidious copyediting it was a pleasure to submit.

I thank also individuals other than those already mentioned who may not even remember the help, advice, direction, or encouragement they gave me along the way: Bob Brugger, Donald J. Bruggink, David Steven Cohen, James Corsaro, Joyce D. Goodfriend, Norman Kansfield, Walter H. Lippincott, Paul Mattingly, Mary Murrin, Donald Sinclair, and Wendell Tripp. To those I may have left out of this list, I apologize.

For research grants, I am grateful to the New Jersey Historical Commission, and for a subvention to offset the costs of publication, I especially thank the Society of Daughters of Holland Dames.

Parts of chapters 7, 8, and 10 have been published in a different form in *de Halve Maen* (the quarterly magazine of The Holland Society of New York), in *New York History*, the quarterly of the New York State Historical Association, and in Renée S. House and John W. Coakley, eds., *Patterns and Portraits: Women in the History of the Reformed Church in America* (Grand Rapids: Wm. B. Eerdmans Publishing Co., 1999). I am grateful for permission to use this material here.

Finally, I thank Carl for his support in all the indispensable ways that make reality of hopes, dreams, and plans.

*Zion on the Hudson*

# Introduction

*As a person of ancestry largely Dutch, I am proud to take my Dutch blood to a
Dutch church every Sunday, and as a minister of Christ I am proud to stand in this
pulpit and preach the same doctrines and use the same sacramental forms that have
been used on the soil of New York since New Amsterdam was a trading post.*
—The Reverend Henry Du Bois Mulford, Syracuse, N.Y., 1893

𝒜s English Puritans called the Massachusetts Bay Colony their "New Israel" or their "Citie sett upon a Hill," so Dutch Reformed Calvinists in New Netherland referred to their new home as their "Reformed Zion," a place as surely their own to practice their form of Protestantism as the Bay Colony was to the Puritans. And practice it they did. When the Reverend Henry Du Bois Mulford proclaimed his pride in his Dutchness from his Syracuse, New York, pulpit on a Sunday morning in October 1893, Reformed people had been practicing their faith in America for 269 years.

Although the Dutch came to the New World in the seventeenth century as explorers and traders in the service of the Dutch West India Company, religion soon followed, for it was accepted in the Netherlands that state and church were mutually benefited by advancing the "true Christian religion." (By the time of the Reformation, when Dutch Calvinists spoke of the "true" Christian religion, they referred to the doctrines and practices of the Reformed Dutch Church as established at the Synod of Dort in 1619.) The first permanent settlers to New Netherland, equipped with Psalm books, the Reformed creeds and confessions, and the Heidelberg Catechism, arrived in 1624, accompanied or at least soon followed by a lay pastor known as a *ziekentrooster*, or comforter of the sick. By 1628 an ordained Reformed Dutch minister had organized a congregation and was conducting worship services in a room constructed for the purpose over the horse-mill near the fort at the Battery (Exchange Square today). Three hundred years later, in the early 1900s, H. L. Mencken and other scholars found Dutch dialects still spoken within the boundaries of the original New Netherland, Dutch material culture and folkways abundantly evident, and the Reformed Dutch Church flourishing on the banks not only of the Hudson River, but all over New York and New Jersey, as well as in the Midwest.

There is, however, a paradox. Dutch culture and the Reformed faith appeared in the New World almost contemporaneously with Puritanism in New England. But three hundred years later, when H. L. Mencken estimated there to be some two hundred persons still speaking the Jersey Dutch dialect in Bergen and Rockland counties, the faith the settlers brought with them was the smallest of the mainstream Protestant denominations in America. It will be one of the objects of this book to consider why, when it was endowed with the myriad advantages of having been first on the ground in the seventeenth century, the Reformed Church, the dominant cultural institution of the Dutch in America, failed to become the dominant religion in the Middle Colonies, or even nearly as prominent as its sister Protestant faiths.

Competition provides one explanation. A plethora of sects clamored for attention and adherents in pluralistic colonial and postcolonial America, and, compared especially with the Anglican Church, the Reformed Dutch Church in its quest for survival, let alone dominance, received negligible financial and moral support from the mother church in the Netherlands. Also, the political takeover of New Netherland by the English in 1664 altered the expected course of Dutch hopes in the New World, while chronic divisions within the Reformed Church itself hampered its advancement throughout the eighteenth century.

But there is more to the matter than external competition, changes in political governance, and internal disunity. There is, this study will propose, a direct connection between the persistence of Dutchness in New York and New Jersey for hundreds of years after settlement and the small size of the Reformed Dutch denomination. By focusing on the beliefs and behavior of the clergy and laity of the Reformed Church in their Zion on the Hudson in the Second Great Awakening, and in its aftermath, the so-called evangelical age or age of revivals, this work explores the connection.

The first problem in a work that attempts to explain the persistence of Dutchness two hundred and more years after Dutch emigration to New York and New Jersey had basically ceased is to define Dutchness. In the 1820s, when this study begins, the Dutch can hardly be considered an immigrant people after two centuries in America. Yet it is clear that Dutch Americans at that time still regarded themselves in many ways as "apart," a people with a particular historical past struggling for identity and integrity in an increasingly populous and pluralistic society—and relying on their church as an instrument for remaining Dutch, but also for becoming American. What being Dutch meant in the nineteenth century is the subject of the first part of chapter 1.

The second problem is to explain why, in the age of revivals, those churches formed in the Reformation (the Presbyterian, Congregational, and Reformed predominantly) were averse to revivalism. Revival—renewal, rebirth, regeneration, resurrection—is the central trope of the Christian faith and its central goal. Christians expect revival. In the Psalmist's cry, "Wilt thou not revive us again, O Lord?," *again* is the significant word. Thus it is ironic that the religious revival in its colorful nineteenth-century manifestations did not come easily or naturally to every denomination or to every Christian. As they had been disturbed in the eighteenth century by the religious innovations of the First Great Awakening, churches built on orthodox Calvinist theology, and churchgoers instilled in it, were deeply troubled again in the nineteenth century by the new-style revivals, for these revivals, like their predecessors, were also undergirded by new interpretations of revered old doctrines.[1] This is the subject of chapter 2.

A third problem involves "getting at" the beliefs and behavior of a people. I have taken three approaches to this problem. One is to look at this amorphous mass of seemingly anonymous churchgoers via the complex relationship between ethnicity and religion.[2] The English takeover of New Netherland in 1664 had prompted many Dutch, especially those with large families and small reserves of arable land on an increasingly populous island, to leave Manhattan and make a second beginning in the hinterland west of the Hudson River, and they took their religion with them—as they did their sense of being strangers in a strange world, not once but twice. This perception of being a people in process, always pilgrims, always different, always uprooted as they trudged the bumpy road to the Kingdom, persisted into the nineteenth century.

But there is another way to see this journey. How ethnic peoples in our present multicultural society behave in the religious arena suggests that they use their churches creatively to ease their entrance into and advance their progress in their new surroundings. The theory that ethnic groups and the national churches and religions associated with them might be functionally future oriented, not anachronistically backward looking, as was once thought, can be applied to the Dutch experience in the seventeenth and eighteenth centuries.

When that experience is viewed in this light, it permits the Reformed Dutch Church and its adherents in nineteenth-century multicultural New York and New Jersey to be seen not primarily as defenders of Old World doctrines, standards, and traditions, as they usually have been. Rather, by regarding the church as a crucible, instead of as a fortress, forces in the denomination can be identified that worked within the crucible to produce structural and even doctrinal changes in the church, so that it might serve its needs and purposes in an American context.

Another approach for getting at the experience of the laity in a church known for its doctrinal conservatism is to explore lay beliefs and behavior in terms of theology—a tack well suited to this particular denomination, which traditionally thought of itself in terms of both Old Testament theology and New. With the models before them of the Exodus on the one hand and Christian millennialism on the other, Reformed Church adherents viewed themselves as God's people acting with special awareness of biblical promises for their survival, and of biblical prophecies of the advent of the Kingdom of God on earth. In this self-perception, the Reformed Church was buttressed by its sense of exceptionalism, the church devoted as no other to what it repeatedly referred to as the "purity of the doctrines as determined at Dort."[3]

A third approach is to try to get at beliefs and behavior by investigating that place where the people's religious life intersected with their secular life—the heartland of evangelicalism, a place whose contours and textures have been neglected.[4] We know that the religious culture of the evangelical era involved much more than Sunday worship, midweek Bible classes, Sabbath school, prayer groups, and meetings of the missionary society. But it is difficult to uncover what went on in that area where purely religious activities intersected with everyday life. About the laity, the "population labeled church members," we have in general indeed only the vaguest ideas.[5] What did they do when they left the pew? To discover the answer I not only have looked into the pew but have followed the occupants of the pews out into the world they lived in.

It is particularly important to do so with the Reformed Dutch, because it was both in the sanctuary and in the social arena outside of it that Dutchness was perpetuated generation after generation—and also where Dutchness finally met its master. Investigating the social life of Reformed Dutch churchgoers—a robust ethnicizing force in all the close-knit, face-to-face communities where the Reformed Church flourished—has rewarded close attention. Diaries and letters, both of laity and of clergy, as well as material published with the laity particularly in mind—including the denomination's weekly newspaper *The Christian Intelligencer*, Sabbath school curriculum material, and prescriptive guides for parents and teachers—afford insights into those intimate matters of everyday life often lost to view in the plethora of quantitative studies of American religion over the past several decades.

A fourth problem in writing about the Dutch in America is that certain well-established stereotypes must be overcome, the most pernicious being that Dutch Calvinism and Dutch culture succumbed to the colony's dominant English culture soon after the English takeover in the seventeenth century.[6] If they did, how are we to account for the vitality of the denomination in the nineteenth century—and for the clear persistence of Dutch ethnicity in that century? Either the stereotype is wanting, or "something happened."

This study will maintain that something happened. That something was the Second Great Awakening, beginning in the 1790s with a noted revival at Yale College and continuing more or less for fifty years, through the Panic of 1837 and its aftermath. If the Reformed Dutch Church seemed to succumb to English culture at the end of the seventeenth century, or to languish in the middle of the eighteenth century, it is clear that those states were not permanent ones. By the end of the eighteenth century, the denomination was on the move, and in the 1790s, as the Second Great Awakening was beginning to stir churched and unchurched alike, the Reformed leadership was producing a unique written constitution intended to guide the denomination into its new American future. It may be true that Dutch ethnic identity in New York and New Jersey had become less salient by 1740, but it did not end then, nor did it end in the Revolutionary period. It was alive and well in the middle of the nineteenth century, when the Dutch language was still taught to schoolchildren in New Brunswick, New Jersey, when Reformed clergymen wore gowns "in imitation of the Dutch Divines of Holland," and when a professor from the University of Utrecht visiting New York and New Jersey commented that "it was a pleasure to find the old Dutch ancestral customs maintained."[7] Such examples can be multiplied a thousandfold.

In their attitudes toward change, especially changes in the doctrines and forms determined at Dort, Reformed clergy and laity in the nineteenth century were divided, in general, along progressive/conservative lines. And Dutch ethnicity, instead of disappearing, was reinvigorated in the nineteenth century, this work will show, by a number of factors that may be counted on the conservative side of the ledger: continued loyalty to Dort and to Calvinist theology, a renewed interest in Dutch history and culture, the rise of the religious press, the influence of Rutgers College and New Brunswick Theological Seminary, and continuing patterns of land use that kept old communities in the original Dutch culture areas intact.

These factors were all related in one way or another to the Reformed Dutch Church's determination to honor its roots in Calvinism and its historic struggles in the Reformation. On the progressive side, however, another set of circumstances rooted in the broader culture thwarted these efforts, and the Reformed Dutch Church and its adherents, while on the one hand acting as fiduciaries of Dutch traditions and culture in diverse, pluralistic America, on the other reimagined those traditions and reworked that culture, so that in time they became a "new American thing," as William Carlos Williams would call the larger culture. The story, then, is one whose denouement is of eventual and inevitable Americanization, for in the fast-changing world of nineteenth-century America, Dutch efforts to maintain their own and their church's Dutch roots and cultural identity eventually became futile, and both church and people ended by adapting to the conditions of the changing times.

They adapted, in the style of the day, to a large extent in public. This is significant, because in doing so they were entering the mainstream and becoming American in spirit as well as in name.

Here the narrative conveys a parallel story, that of the evangelical age itself. As *Zion on the Hudson* relates the experience of Dutch Calvinists in nineteenth-century New York and New Jersey, it tells it perforce against the background of the unfolding age of revivals, a story now mostly forgotten, although it took place to a great extent in public and was minutely reported in the public press.

It is at a metaphorical door, in fact, a construct between indoors and outdoors, prayer closet and parlor, private worship and public, that the reader of this book will stand, looking in, into pious hearts and minds where religion sank its deepest roots, and looking out into the streets and fields and auditoriums where so much of religion took place in the nineteenth century. In private, Reformed Dutch people attempted to teach their children the rudiments of their faith in their homes, confronted themselves in their diaries and journals as they recorded their spiritual struggles, doubts, and unbelief, and retired to pray in secret over the state of their souls and that of the souls of their loved ones.

But in public, along with thousands of their pious fellow evangelicals, they also flocked to crowded revival meetings in the open air, to Sunday school picnics attended by a thousand children and adults, to public funerals on a scale unimaginable today, to weddings so crowded some could barely see the heads of the bride and groom over the spectators. In droves they joined an array of moral reform societies and benevolent associations and missionary organizations, all determined to make the whole world a Christian place. On Decoration Day, they gathered in cemeteries en masse with evangelicals of their sister persuasions to dress the graves and pray over the dead. In the fashion of the day, they even learned to die in public, with dozens of onlookers assembled around their deathbeds to hear their dying words, to catch perhaps a gasping phrase hailing the first glimpse of paradise.

Ministers published their sermons by the thousands, and Reformed evangelicals by the thousands read not only the sermons of their own clergymen but also those of other denominations. In this way, they came to be able, like their fellow Christians in all branches of the evangelical world, to debate with ease arcane theological points in the columns of the religious press. In time, they also came to be able to think of themselves as more American than Dutch, and finally as not Dutch at all—or as one of them put it, as no more like their Dutch progenitors than a windmill was like a steam engine.

This fresh look at the religious culture of New York and New Jersey in the nineteenth century will reveal that it, too, was no more like anything that had gone before than the eighteenth-century world of the Dutch Pietist minister Theodorus Jacobus Frelinghuysen resembled the world of the evangelical preacher Charles G. Finney in the flamboyant age of revivals.[8]

*Zion on the Hudson* concludes with the suggestion that even a denomination as formalist and doctrinally conservative as the eastern branch of the Reformed Dutch Church sincerely believed itself to be was obliged to rethink itself in order to survive. In the social tumult and revivalistic atmosphere of nineteenth-century America, it adapted in spite of itself to the evolving religious needs and desires of its own membership. Although change sometimes occurred at a glacial pace, it occurred because of a progressive, forward-looking, and Americanizing element within the ranks of both clergy and laity.

As this work describes the efforts of the Dutch in nineteenth-century New York and New Jersey to preserve the standards of their church while developing a taste for a new kind of theology and a preference for an American identity, it will, finally, document how Dutchness, at the end of the nineteenth century, at last became only a historical memory in New York and New Jersey.[9]

CHAPTER 1

# Being Dutch and Being
# the Reformed Dutch Church

*So many of the best Yankees of New-England are becoming Dutchmen . . . that we seem to be
progressing backwards toward the time when the Pilgrim Fathers forsook the bondage of their
own country for a home, and freedom, and peace in Holland.*
—Christian Intelligencer, May 27, 1858

"Being Dutch" could mean a number
of different things in nineteenth-century New York and New Jersey. In fact,
being Dutch then was even more complicated than it had been in the seventeenth century, when it was already complicated enough. In the seventeenth century, some Dutch in what they thought of as their Reformed Zion
on the Hudson had been born to Dutch parents in the Netherlands and were
reared there. They were Dutch by birth. But studies have indicated that only
about half of the total population of New Netherland fell into this category.[1]
The other half came directly from places outside the Netherlands—in order of their importance: from various German cities, states, duchies, and
principalities, from France and the Spanish Netherlands (Belgium today),
and from Scandinavia. A small percentage of the total came from other parts
of continental Europe, from the British Isles, and from Africa.

Further complicating the definition of being Dutch is the fact that in
the Netherlands itself in the seventeenth century the population was also
only about half Dutch. It has been estimated that, in the seventeenth century, half a million of the total Netherlandish population of two million were
permanent immigrants who had originally migrated there from other parts
of Europe for economic, religious, or political reasons. In addition, another
class of transient migrants employed in the Dutch army, the merchant fleets,
and as migrant seasonal labor vastly increased this proportion.[2] It is not
known how many of these people, especially the permanent settlers, learned
to speak Dutch, married Dutch persons, and affiliated with the Reformed Dutch Church or another active church (Roman Catholic, Lutheran,
and Mennonite were the other prominent faiths), but it is known that some

of them eventually emigrated to New Netherland. Although they obviously continued to remember their own original cultural norms, mores, customs, and patterns of thought and behavior—and brought these with them to the New World—they also had absorbed Dutch ways. They may be thought of as Dutch by circumstance.

Still other inhabitants of New Netherland were completely non-Dutch people with no history of a sojourn in the Netherlands, and thus with no firsthand acquaintance with Dutch culture and customs. Yet, in the New World they chose to identify themselves with Dutch customs, language, religion, and philosophical outlook—to situate themselves, as it were, under the umbrella of cultural Dutchness. These have been called "ethnicizers" or "Batavianizers"—a term shortly to be explained. They saw a reason for aligning with the Dutch before the English came, and, when the English took over, they saw a reason to take sides in the inevitable tensions and ambiguities that resulted from the change in administrations. Their reasons were likely rooted in the appeal of characteristics often associated with the Dutch: tolerance, openness, the value placed on civic concord, pragmatism, charity, humanism, love of liberty, literacy, the relatively enlightened Dutch attitude toward women, and the perceived merits of Dutch law over English law.[3] These New Netherlanders may be considered Dutch by choice.

Finally, another component of the New Netherland population considered itself Dutch because of its affiliation with the Reformed Dutch Church, which was the only officially recognized church in New Netherland. Other religions were tolerated, nevertheless, if they were discreet, and a practice that had previously developed in Reformation Europe now appeared in New Netherland and expanded in New York: people identified themselves and others by the national origins of the church with which they affiliated—the Dutch Church, the French Church, the English Church, and so on—regardless of their own national origins. If an Englishman was allied with the Dutch Church, he identified himself as Dutch and was considered so by others.

This practice expanded after the English takeover of New Netherland and the organization of other national churches in New York and continued into the nineteenth century. Evidence for it is abundant, as when a layman signed himself, for instance, "An English Dutchman" in a letter to the Reformed Church publication *The Christian Intelligencer*. In other cases that illustrate this practice, a Reformed Dutch clergyman claimed that "some of our very best Dutchmen were reared in other communions"; a Congregational minister noted that a "great many Congregational Christians have come to be Reformed Dutchmen when they came to New York"; and a Reformed minister described a colleague as "lineally of Scotch and of Huguenot descent, having no blood connection with Holland, and yet he was a Dutchman in the best sense of the word, and the best of Dutchmen."[4]

This curious verbal classification, blending the national or ethnic and the religious, suggests that, for some, identifying with any particular national past and particular national culture was a plastic, protean process able to take on new shapes with new circumstances, mean whatever it seemed to mean. One could "be Dutch" by calling oneself Dutch, by embracing supposed Dutch values and Dutch institutions, and in general by behaving in what one imagined to be a Dutch manner.[5]

The verbal blending also suggests that, in New Netherland, as in the Netherlands in the seventeenth century, ethnicity was understood differently from the way it is today. In a Europe of fluid boundaries and fluctuating borders, of ever-migrating populations, of a polyglot and multicultural United Republic of the Netherlands, but one with an officially privileged church, "ethnicity" was less consequential and religion more so. In New Netherland, which reproduced similar linguistic and religious conditions (eighteen languages were said to be spoken in New Amsterdam, and the Reformed Dutch Church was the only officially recognized church), the same observation can be made. Copious personal testimony indicates that those "born into" the Reformed Dutch Church, as well as those outsiders who chose to affiliate with it, admired it not for ethnic or sociocultural reasons or reasons of national pride, but for religious reasons: they believed it to be the "purest" of all Christian churches—that is, the church that prided itself on most closely adhering to the biblical model affirmed at Dort.

At the same time, for non-Dutch persons, the very eclectic, verging on the ecumenical nature of the Reformed Church's roots may have been a factor in its appeal: its oldest confession of faith was written in 1559 by Guido de Bres, a Belgian. Its chief catechism was composed in Heidelberg, Germany, by Germans (in 1566). Its liturgy was the work of a Pole and a Frenchman, Jan Laski and John Calvin. And the five Canons of Dort (1619) were formulated by a synod with wide international representation. In America, its first two elders, Peter Minuit and Jan Huyck, had formerly served as elders in the French Reformed Church in the German city of Wesel; and already in the seventeenth century, the Dutch Church in New Jersey had absorbed a nascent French Huguenot church. The American translator of its standards from Dutch into English, John Henry Livingston, was of Scottish-American background. And over the life of the church in this country, and mainly in the eastern branch of the church, six hundred clergy have been received into it from other denominations. Most astonishing, it has been discovered that the liturgy used in the Reformed Dutch Church in America since 1767 was based on an English translation of an

older Dutch liturgy made for English Puritans worshiping in the Netherlands in the seventeenth century, not a translation of the liturgy as agreed
upon at Dort in 1619. In 1885 the Reformed minister George S. Bishop
observed that in some sense the Reformed Dutch Church was never really
Dutch at all.[6]

After New Netherland was relinquished to the English in 1674, at the
conclusion of a series of three Anglo-Dutch wars, and in the face of the
confusing political and social discontinuities this change brought with it,
some New Netherlanders chose to Anglicize, while others "Batavianized."
The historian John Murrin has commented that it probably took the takeover "and the social and political pressures that it generated to give [the
heterogeneous peoples of New Netherland] a self-conscious 'Dutch' identity, with England providing an alternative and a counterpoint." The fall of
New Netherland did not initiate a process of easy assimilation to English
cultural values, he maintains. "Instead it magnified, perhaps even created
for many people, intense Dutch loyalties among the vanquished."[7]

In developing a working definition of Dutchness, and in trying to describe it as it evolved in nineteenth-century New York and New Jersey, the
words "magnified" and "created" in this description of the process of
Batavianization are operative. But, first, what is that process, and what are
its origins?

The original Batavians, according to Tacitus, were a tribe of early Germanic peoples settled around present-day Leiden. Just as the "ancient"
Highland culture of Scotland, the Druidic history of Wales, and the "thousand-
year pageantry and grandeur" of the British monarchy were created out of
whole cloth by British chroniclers in the late nineteenth and early twentieth centuries (with some Saxon and medieval exceptions), so did the Dutch
invent their own history and identity, basing it on the character of the Batavi,
as described by Tacitus and elaborated by others. The original Batavianizers
were the Dutch people themselves in the sixteenth century, who by that
time probably had not a corpuscle of Batavian blood in their veins.[8]

The Batavi were supposedly a simple, sturdy, freedom-loving, moral
people who rose in A.D. 69 and 70 against their corrupt, slothful, and immoral Roman rulers. In an early Continental example of self-invention, or
national character–building, or the invention of tradition, the Dutch began
to regard themselves as the descendants of these ancient Batavians by 1517.
In that year, historical chronicles based on medieval romances and Tacitus's
*Germania* were published in the *Divisiekroniek*, a "mingling of fact and
fancy, fable and documented history" so popular that it went through fifty-
three editions in the Netherlands as a school history text.[9]

The evolution of the Batavian myth from which the Dutch people invented themselves has been traced from the *Divisiekroniek* in 1517 through Hugo Grotius's *Book of the Ancient Republic of Batavia* in 1610 through the propagandistic history of the Netherlands of Romeyn de Hooghe in 1706, which went to great lengths to distinguish the Dutch from the other nations of Europe. Basing his description of Dutch national character on the slender facts in Tacitus, De Hooghe wove a picture of the Dutch as thrifty and modest, fiercely opposed to sovereigns "concentrated in one head," and oriented toward commerce, not show and rank. In short, De Hooghe "magnified" and "created" a virtuous Dutchness for the Dutch. De Hooghe's Dutch women, like their supposed mothers in Batavia, were industrious and chaste, their menfolk frugal, punctilious, and hard working. Although these cliches were often out of alignment with reality, they were passed on to the nineteenth century in anecdotal lore, in popular history such as John L. Motley's best-selling *Rise of the Dutch Republic*, and in the historical reportage of Reformed clergy in the *Christian Intelligencer*.[10]

A repetition of or variation on this same process took place in seventeenth-century New York, again in Revolutionary and postrevolutionary New York and New Jersey, and yet again in nineteenth-century New York and New Jersey. In these periods, Dutch and Dutchophile alike, upstaged and overshadowed first by English and later by Yankees on the one hand and threatened by waves of immigrants from Catholic Europe on the other, hunkered under the protective umbrella of a comfortable ethnic old-stock church and ethnic identity they could call their own, even if it wasn't.

The tendency of Dutch Americans, neo-Dutch, pseudo-Dutch, and Dutchophiles to Batavianize that was noticed in seventeenth-century New Netherland neither disappeared nor did it cease to be linked to a certain hostility to England, politically and culturally. It resurfaced after the Revolution in some rural parts of the Dutch culture areas of New York and New Jersey in the persistence of the Dutch language, or dialects of it, in the continued building of earlier house forms, in the enduring preference for old foodways, in the revival or reinvigoration of sentimental elements of the material culture of patria, the fatherland, and most of all in devotion to the doctrines and traditions of the Reformed Dutch Church.[11]

In the nineteenth century, Batavianization made another and final appearance in a sentimental harking back to Dutch history and an idealizing of things Dutch that was animated by the Reformed Church weekly newspaper's accounts of brave little Holland in its struggle against fierce Catholic Spain and on the glories of the Netherlands in its Golden Age. Other factors intensified this tendency: Rutgers College and New Brunswick Theological Seminary, for instance, actively promoted a sense of themselves as imbued with Dutch roots and a specific Dutch orientation. Linked, as we will see, to the Reformed Dutch Church's fidelity to the theology, doctrine, and church order laid down at the Synod of Dort two centuries before, the tendency to Batavianize was an important agent in causing Dutchness to persist in New York and New Jersey until the end of the nineteenth century.[12]

Dutchness is here defined then as a loyalty to the distinctive qualities attached, or presumed to be attached, to what is, or is presumed to be, the Dutch national character and culture.

One last complication must be aired: a definitive description of Dutchness is probably forever beyond our grasp because of the fact that the discrete geographical regions within the Netherlands all had their own ancient distinct and distinctive cultural traditions and folkways. This said, it also bears noting that by the nineteenth century Dutch Americans in general did not appreciate this nicety. By then, Dutchness in America had become something all its own.

*I*f being Dutch in America was complicated, being the Reformed Dutch Church in America in its first two centuries was even more so. From its planting in New Amsterdam in 1628, it was to follow a path of adversity and obstacles that seemed to know no end. In fact, the Reformed Church followed two paths simultaneously, and discord and strife were almost always their names.[13]

The Reformed Dutch Church in America took its form of government, as well as its doctrines and liturgy, from the mother church as established at Dort. The basic structural unit, the congregation, was made up of communicants led by a minister or *domine* (also spelled *dominie*). Every congregation had a consistory, formed of the minister and a number of elders and deacons, chosen from the laity. The consistory was the governing body of the congregation, with elders responsible for ecclesiastical discipline and deacons for the maintenance of the church property and the needs of the poor and infirm. The Classis of Amsterdam in the Province and Synod of North Holland supervised the congregations in North America until around 1800, when they were permitted to govern themselves in regional classes to which they sent representatives twice a year. (The role of the classis is spelled out in chapter 5.) Finally, in a General Synod once a year the ministers of all the congregations, each accompanied by an elder, met together to take up denominational matters, but this too did not happen in the New World with any regularity until around 1800.

In its infancy, the Reformed Church in New Netherland was hampered by a shortage of ministers willing to serve in the American wilderness, and by a population more interested in the rough-and-ready world of fur trading on the frontier than in Psalm books and sermons in settled communities. Over the centuries, these two difficulties would never be overcome. There was a chronic shortage of Reformed ministers, even in the highest-growth period of the denomination, 1850–1860, and churches were never as full or congregations as faithful as their leaders would like.

From the beginning through the Revolutionary War period, the Reformed Church weathered crisis after crisis. In the seventeenth century, these included most prominently the English takeover in 1664 of New Netherland, where for some forty years the Reformed Church had enjoyed the privileged status of a quasi-official church. Although permitted by the Articles of Surrender and the Duke's Laws of 1665 to maintain that status by the new rulers of the colony, the church found that it was increasingly forced to defend itself against English attempts to undermine it to the advantage of the Anglican Church. Moreover, it had to worry about the incursions of Roman Catholicism in this era of King James II, who had appointed a Roman Catholic, Thomas Dongan, to govern the Dutch colony.[14]

At the time of the English takeover, some Dutch showed themselves willing if not eager to compromise with the English, causing a deep fissure between them and "loyal" Dutch. A quarter-century later, in the governmental crisis known as Leisler's Rebellion in 1689, open division in the Reformed Dutch Church broke out again between those who sided with Jacob Leisler and those who cooperated with and played up to their new English rulers. Among the English Party at this time were some of the same people who had been willing to deal with the English a generation earlier, at the time of the political and administrative takeover of the colony. Old resentments now found a seat in a new generation.

The first Reformed Dutch ministers to New Netherland at the beginning of the Dutch period were Pietists. (The first lay pastor, Bastiaen Krol, was a Pietist, as were the first ordained minister, Jonas Michaelius, and his successor Everardus Bogardus.)[15] If at the beginning, there was only Pietism, in time more formalistic ministers were sent from the Netherlands, allowing the Reformed Dutch in New York and New Jersey a choice in religious styles—a menu from which to select how they wanted to worship, but also a recipe for the factionalism and divisiveness that came to haunt the denomination for centuries.

In the Leislerian period, the appeal and strength of Dutch Pietism increased, exacerbating the political strife and discord in now-English New York between Pietists and orthodox, progressives and traditionalists. Some believers were attracted to the personal religion preached by the Pietist Reformed Dutch minister Guiliam Bertholf, known as the "itinerating apostle of New Jersey," and by his colleagues Bernhardus Freeman and Cornelius Van Santvoord, all three of whom openly supported Jacob Leisler. Others, often anti-Leislerian, preferred "orthodox" or traditional modes of worship as practiced by the more formalist ministers who occupied pulpits in Manhattan and on western Long Island.[16]

The term *orthodox* is used to describe the more conservative in theological thought, but orthodox and Pietist aligned themselves on opposite sides of the political fence in the 1680s as well, although it is important to note that both sides adhered to historic Reformed positions and doctrines. Simply put, the warm personal tone of the Heidelberg Catechism, and its downplaying of the harsher doctrines of classic Calvinism, appealed to Pietists, while the orthodox preferred to follow the traditional liturgy, with its set prayers and fixed, familiar forms, and its predestinarian philosophy.[17]

Each style of worship inevitably begot its proponents and detractors, both styles persisted simultaneously, and each style continued well into the nineteenth century to attract churchgoers according to their temperaments and their ecclesiological preferences and desires. To reduce this enduring pattern to its most basic terms, one style of worship and set of beliefs attracted those open to change—the progressives; the other attracted those opposed to change—the conservatives or traditionalists. Attitudes toward change were not, however, constants that defined two ever-present parties within the church over time. Rather, in each new era, and with each new issue, progressives and conservatives took up sides, with progressives on one issue sometimes becoming conservatives on another.

Dutch Pietism emphasized a simple experiential piety and godly living on the part of each individual, sometimes called personal holiness. At the heart of the Pietist movement in the Netherlands, the historian James R. Tanis has noted, "was the struggle against apathy and indifference and the fostering of a vital and precise Christianity among fully committed believers."[18] "Precise Christianity" spurned the forms of organized religion. The liturgy, the creeds, set prayers, even the Lord's Prayer were in the view of Pietists intercessionary measures not needed in a Christian's efforts to approach God.

Aside from their objection to the recitation of memorized prayers and rote liturgical forms, several other major points distinguished the Pietists from the orthodox. One of these was the question of a conversion experience (sometimes called regeneration or spiritual rebirth) and "the fruits of the new life in the individual"—that is, continued spiritual growth after regeneration.[19] For the orthodox, faith was a necessary condition for salvation. For Pietists, faith was necessary but not sufficient. Spiritual rebirth or regeneration, the "putting on of the new man in Christ," was vital.

Pietists took this line of reasoning even further. Besides claiming that a personal conversion experience or the "new birth" was necessary for receiving the Kingdom, they also insisted it was necessary for receiving the sacrament of communion—and for administering it. Going even beyond this, they did not hesitate to identify in public those ordained ministers whose souls, in their opinion, were not regenerate. Naturally, their outspoken views and judgmental attitudes were unpopular with clergymen of a more traditional stripe, who felt they had a right to hope they were in a state of grace by virtue of their faith in Christ's saving blood and by living lives of daily rectitude.

If the Pietist idea that ministers as well as laypeople must experience a regenerative warming of their hearts for Christ was an unwelcome one to the traditional clergy, so was Pietism's inherent democratic bias. In practice, the idea of a priesthood of all believers was repugnant to those highly educated and traditionalist ministers who believed their training and ordination set them above and apart from the common herd. Such ideas had sown discord between church establishment and Pietists in the Netherlands, and they did so as well in New York and New Jersey after Bertholf, Freeman, and Van Santvoord began to attract followings.

While these men were still active in the ministry, a variant of Pietism arrived in New York and New Jersey in 1720, when the Reverend Theodorus Jacobus Frelinghuysen was called to four pastorless congregations in the Raritan Valley. Frelinghuysen, German by birth, was brought up in the Reformed Dutch Church in that part of western Germany that culturally was almost interchangeable with the eastern Netherlands. The crucial influences on him were clergy and theologians involved in the so-called Nadere Reformatie (Further Reformation) in the Netherlands, including Gisbertus Voetius, Willem Teellinck, Hermanus Witsius, the a Brakels (father and son), Johannes d'Outrein, Abraham Hellenbroek, Jodocus Lodenstein, and Jacobus Koelman (most of whom had also influenced the theological beliefs of Bertholf, Freeman, and Van Santvoord). Frelinghuysen's rather narrow variety of Calvinistic Pietism, as expressed in the Frisian Catechism that he used, insisted on a regenerative experience that would result not only in holy living but in the desire for excruciatingly precise moral conduct on the part of the reborn individual.[20]

As we will see in chapter 2, because of their emphasis on a degree of human agency in the salvation process, seventeenth-century Pietists, whether of the Bertholf or the Frelinghuysen variety, were accused by the formalistic ministers and laity of harboring liberalizing (that is, "Arminian") tendencies, the debate over which in the Netherlands had engendered the Synod of Dort in 1618. The controversy over human agency, or human ability, was to survive into the nineteenth century and in fact to govern the path of the Reformed Dutch Church as it worked out an accommodation to revivalism and as it waded into the rising tide of denominationalism.

$\mathcal{F}$or over a century, Frelinghuysen has enjoyed a growing reputation as the "forerunner," the "herald," the "prophet," and even the "father" of the Great Awakening in New Jersey—even, it has been written, the father of the Great Awakening in all of colonial America, preparing hearts and minds for the charismatic Gilbert Tennent in the late 1720s and for George Whitefield in 1739. A closer look at the actual history of his reputation by one scholar within the Reformed denomination suggests, however, that Frelinghuysen caused not an awakening, but "only a disaffection" in his congregations that resulted in a debilitating eighteen-year feud.[21]

It is not necessary here to recount the details of the feud between the minister and his congregations. Briefly, the substantive grievances against him were based on his disregard of proper Reformed usages and his insistence that his brand of Pietism was "*the* theology of the Reformed Church, rather than simply one strand among others, and a minority one at that."[22] What is pertinent, in the present context, is the challenge to this minister mounted by members of his flocks, for the defiant actions of the laity in the 1720s set the stage for the conflict in the next two generations over the American Dutch Church's relationship to the mother church in the Netherlands, and in the long and fierce debate over giving up the Dutch language for preaching.

To sum up, if all of the Calvinistic churches in the American colonies—Congregational, Presbyterian, and Reformed—were to be radically shaken and shaped by the Pietistic preaching, teaching, and writing of the seventeenth- and eighteenth-century Reformed Dutch clergy, as scholars believe,[23] it was not Frelinghuysen but his seventeenth-century predecessors in the field, Krol, Michaelius, and Bogardus, and later notably Guiliam Bertholf, who must be credited with first bringing personal religion and a taste for enthusiastic preaching and evolving theological interpretation to New York and New Jersey. By emphasizing the Heidelberg Catechism, which downplayed the harsh doctrines of predestination and reprobation as outlined in the Canons of Dort, these first Pietists were conveying a new idea to the New World, that personal holiness involved taking personal moral responsibility for one's conduct and even for one's personal relationship to God—a novel and doctrinally daring idea for Calvinist preachers to advocate.[24]

But in other major ways that resonate down through the centuries, Frelinghuysen left an important mark on the Reformed Dutch Church and beyond it. His innovative preaching techniques were appropriated and popularized by the Presbyterian minister Gilbert Tennent, and word of them reached both Jonathan Edwards and the revivalist George Whitefield. Frelinghuysen's disregard of denominational boundaries anticipated the ecumenism of the evangelical revivals in the nineteenth century. (He scandalized conservatives by permitting both Tennent, a Presbyterian, and Whitefield, an Anglican, to preach and pray in English in his churches, and by holding private conventicles open to committed Christians, no matter what their formal church affiliation.) He supported the idea of an American coetus, or ecclesiastical assembly within the Reformed Church, independent of the mother church, that could examine and ordain ministers on American soil, and he subscribed to a plan for an academy to train them. Most important, he influenced a generation of young Americans, including his own sons, to take up the Reformed ministry, educating them in his Pietist beliefs and examining and ordaining a number of them. These men and others they in turn prepared for the pulpit doggedly pursued, until they were successful, the idea of an academy on American soil where men could be properly educated for the Reformed pulpit. And these same forward-looking clergymen, with their "spirit of independency," uniformly championed the Patriot cause in the Revolution.[25]

*T*he crises in the Reformed Dutch Church multiplied throughout the eighteenth century. In the middle of the century, a rancorous dispute over the introduction of the English language into preaching resounded in the congregations of New York City for ten years. Support for an American classis fully independent of Amsterdam was declared in 1755, causing a break in relations for seventeen years between the progressive coetus faction and the conservative "conferentie" faction. So severe was this breach that Reformed scholars believe it nearly caused the demise of the denomination itself, and it undoubtedly inhibited its growth. The rift between coetus and conferentie deepened in the Revolutionary period, with progressives or Americanizers among both laity and clergy taking up the call for independence and the conservative conferentie adherents, a much smaller number, remaining loyal to Britain.

In this series of seemingly endless conflicts, the Reformed laity never behaved like the deferential population tightly controlled by a rigidly traditionalist clergy operating under unvarying rules of church order that some within the Reformed leadership wanted them to be. Rather, Reformed lay people of both progressive and conservative outlook repeatedly asserted themselves against their clergymen and made decisions and took actions regarding their own worship life not indicated or expected by official Reformed understandings.

In the Leislerian years at the end of the seventeenth century, for instance, those of progressive/Pietist leanings refused en masse to attend worship, receive communion, or pay the salaries of ministers who had opposed Leisler. Likewise, in the Raritan troubles fomented by Frelinghuysen's authoritarian dictates, conservatives among his parishioners shunned his services and withheld their contributions to his salary. They also successfully banded together to challenge him by appealing to the highest level of the denomination with authority over them—the Classis of Amsterdam in the Netherlands. The same pattern can be seen in the coetus/conferentie split, with both progressives and conservatives defying pressure from the Classis of Amsterdam to reconcile their differences. In the language wars of the 1750s and 1760s, the pro-Dutch forces, slighting the advice of the classis to agree to English preaching in the interests of attracting members, took the pro-English side to court—and lost. And the coetus faction, despite intense pressure from conservatives among the clergy and the laity to desist from attempting to organize a training academy in America, finally secured in 1766 a charter for Queen's College (Rutgers University today).[26]

Two centuries of lay activity in such issues as these prepared the ground and acted as a model for continued lay action in the nineteenth century when Reformed doctrine was confronted by a new wave of liberal ideas and provocative new styles of worship—that is, when being the Reformed Dutch Church meant being loyal to the past while attempting at the same time to deal with changing times and new ideas. As the institution gradually Americanized, knowledge of past tribulations and past victories no doubt gave strength to each new generation.

But this is not the whole story; there is a wider significance to the process that was taking place within this ethnic and ethnicized denomination. The Reformed Church's arduous process of change over the centuries parallels and illuminates the same process that was taking place in the society at large, as Americans painfully broke away from their political and cultural connections to the Old World and, on native grounds, as Alfred Kazin called it, forged a new literature, new music, new art, new philosophies, new ways of relating to God, a whole new culture. The Americanization of the Reformed Dutch Church is the story in miniature of the Americanization of America.

# CHAPTER 2

# *"So Like Heaven"*

## THE SYNOD OF DORT

*If man is an animal suspended in webs of significance he himself has spun,*
*culture is those webs.*
—Clifford Geertz, 1966

𝒯he Puritans in New England and the Pietists and orthodox in New Netherland were transplanted Europeans. A century later, some of the most prominent figures of America's Great Awakening (circa 1740) were of European birth and culture. But the leading lights of the Second Great Awakening, beginning in 1790 at Yale College with Timothy Dwight, peaking in the 1830s under Charles G. Finney, and continuing on a crest well into the latter half of the nineteenth century under such clergymen as the Reformed minister Thomas De Witt Talmage, whose fiery evangelical sermons were read weekly by twenty million people, were home-grown Americans advancing styles of worship adapted to American geographic, demographic, and economic and social conditions.

Even so, an event that had taken place in early seventeenth-century Holland, the Synod of Dort, dictated the course of revivalism in the United States in the nineteenth century, as controversies over the doctrines set out in the five famous Canons of Dort served to precipitate Old Light/New Light schisms and secessions in the Presbyterian, the Congregational, and, as we shall see, the Reformed Dutch Church.

The web of nineteenth-century religious culture in which all branches of the Reformed faith were suspended was spun at the Synod of Dort in 1618–1619. Of those branches—in England, Scotland, Germany, France, Switzerland, and the Netherlands—the web held none more closely in its intricacies than the Reformed Dutch Church as it evolved in America.[1] (See figure 1.)

The Synod of Dort was an international assembly of theologians, ecclesiastics, and Dutch political officials that convened on November 13,

FIGURE 1. It was standing room only when the Synod of Dort (1618–1619) was in session. In the foreground are the spectators who daily thronged to hear the discussions. Johannes Bogerman presided at a table at the far end of the room. At the table in the center of the room the Remonstrants, or Arminians, were seated. The delegates from England, Scotland, Germany, and Switzerland sat in the benches on the right. If the French Protestants had been allowed to attend, they would have sat in the empty seats, upper right. The Dutch delegates occupied the benches on the left and to either side of the entrance. *Courtesy Prentenkabinet, Leiden University.*

1618, in the city of Dordrecht, under the auspices of the States General of the Netherlands. The purpose of the meeting was to settle certain doctrinal matters that were troubling Protestantism, particularly in the Netherlands, and particularly certain points of John Calvin's theology—or rather his disciple Theodore Beza's interpretation of it.

In brief, the followers of the Leiden University theology professor Jacobus Arminius (1560–1609), who himself had died nine years before the synod convened, disputed Beza's interpretation of Calvin's doctrines of total depravity and predestination (man was so hopelessly sinful that nothing could save him but God's grace). The Arminians also disputed as too harsh Beza's interpretation of the doctrines of unconditional election (man had no role whatsoever in his own salvation); of limited atonement (Christ died for the elect, not for all); and of irresistible grace (one could do nothing to obtain grace on one's own, for God alone determined who would receive it, nor could one reject it if it was offered). In place of Calvin's predestinarian doctrines, the Arminians, or Remonstrants, as they were also called, advanced doctrines of universal grace and freedom of the will.[2] As the church historian Philip Schaff summed up the dilemma of the synod, the Arminians were posing the "problem of the ages, which again and again has baffled the ken of theologians and philosophers, and will do so to the end of time: the relation of divine sovereignty and human responsibility."[3]

Thirty-nine Dutch, Belgic, and French pastors and eighteen elders were named delegates, nineteen Presbyterian delegates came from Reformed churches in other parts of the Continent, including Germany and Switzerland, five delegates were sent by James I of England, and one represented the Church of Scotland. At the last minute, Louis XIV prohibited the delegates appointed by the Reformed Church of France from attending. The matters addressed at the synod, in addition to the vexing doctrinal questions, included the degree of control the state should have over the church.[4]

By far the most problematic theological issue at Dort, which was intertwined with the doctrine of election or predestination, was reprobation: Did God choose only a few elect humans for salvation, and consign the rest of humanity to hell? And if so, the Arminians asked, how could a loving God be so indifferent to his own creation? Other knotty issues included whether Calvinist doctrine made God in effect the author of sin, and whether it put limits on God's grace by suggesting that it was not sufficient to save untold multitudes from hell. The Calvinists, or Counter-Remonstrants, rejected the Arminians' attempt to water down Calvin's doctrines, on the grounds that everything they said violated what was clearly found in Scripture. The Arminians parried with the proposition that Scripture should be approached rationally, with new tools of biblical criticism.

After fifty-seven indecisive sessions, the Arminians were ejected from the Synod, and Arminian ministers, of whom there were some two hundred, were prohibited from preaching and were actually banished from the Netherlands. The remaining delegates in another ninety-seven sessions drew up the five Canons of Dort, which came down on the conservative side of the above doctrinal questions forever. Or so they supposed.

The appealing ideas of universal grace and freedom of the will were not, however, so easily suppressed, and within six years public desire to hear them had enabled the Arminians to return to their pulpits and their pews. Further, the English, Scottish, and German Reformed churches did not bind themselves, as did the strict Dutch Calvinists, to the system of scholastic Calvinism represented by the Canons of Dort. Schaff notes that these churches treated the canons with respect, but "did not clothe them with the same symbolical authority" as did the Dutch. Within a generation, English Congregationalists and the Presbyterian Church of Scotland had subtly altered the Dort formulas in some essentials by adopting, respectively, the Savoy Declaration and the Westminster Confession of Faith; the Church of England continued to adhere to its original Thirty-nine Articles and the Book of Common Prayer; and the German Reformed Church ended by insisting on having no binding symbol "but the free untrammeled" Heidelberg Catechism, which downplayed predestinarian thought.[5] Nevertheless, the Synod of Dort came to provide a common platform for a large segment of Reformed Protestantism that in the nineteenth century grew painfully aware of the challenges of new religious ideas that were reviving for debate some of the seventeenth-century doctrinal conundrums.

The main theological question thought to have been settled forever at Dort—but that is discussed in some quarters to this day—can be distilled to this: is man able to affect in any small way his own salvation? The answer Dort affirmed was a resounding *no*, followed by an equivocal *but*. *No*, man's will was ineffective in changing his eternal status as God had preordained or foreseen it. *But* he should not despair, but keep working toward his salvation anyway. God's ways are unknowable and unsearchable. Because he exists not in time but in eternity, which is a difficult if not impossible concept for man to comprehend, God may have a divine strategy that he has not revealed to us, because our insufficient minds could not comprehend it anyway. God is sovereign and omnipotent and can bring about any result he desires. As a triune God, he has seen fit to atone for our sins by his death, and he has sent his Holy Spirit to us to comfort, console, and lead us to repent and to seek communion with him. Even though God is the one and only and omnipotent agent in salvation, we are solely responsible for our own sins, Calvinist theory goes, for God has given us the ability to know good from evil and the will to choose between them. We must repent of our sins, absolve God from all blame for them, and desist from trying to understand the unsearchable secrets of the divine mind.[6]

As Calvin had recommended in his *Institutes*, the theologians and clergymen at the Synod of Dort approached the questions and ramifications of the doctrines of election and predestination with great caution, because of the incomprehensibility of these ideas to the minds of mortals. Taking their cue from Calvin, those at the synod advised against trying to understand the doctrines. God is ineffable, and it is not for man to pry into his ways, they warned. To do so is to risk unbelief, despair to the point of suicide, and fatal neglect of the ordinary means of grace: prayer, preaching, the sacraments (particularly Holy Communion), Bible study, and meditation.

Despite these admonitions, however, prying into God's mysterious ways proved to be irresistible. The public latched onto, and proceeded to worry to the bone, the most difficult and harshest of the canons—those relating to election, reprobation, and limited atonement—ignoring the advice that one not intrude into the divine mind, but rather repent, have faith, follow the law, and trust in the saving power of Christ and the Holy Spirit.

In the nineteenth century, when Calvinism faced new attack from liberal theologies, all but the most orthodox of Protestants came to think of the Canons of Dort not only as unnecessarily harsh and inflexible, but perhaps even as having been misinterpreted in the first place. Some of the most orthodox, however, were found within the Reformed Dutch Church in America, and they cherished Dort and its historical associations with the Reformation in the Netherlands beyond compare. To this day, the Reformed Church in America has not officially disavowed Dort, although the Reformed Church in the Netherlands did so early in the nineteenth century.

As the Dutch in America wove the intricate fabric of their religious culture, Dort came to be the central fiber: the most laden with meaning, the most fraught with emotion and import, the most unifying, and the most divisive. Just as we cannot understand nineteenth-century religious culture in general without understanding the significance of Calvin's theology for all of the Reformed denominations, so we cannot understand the history of the Dutch in America without understanding the resonance and power of Dort.

The Reformed minister George W. Bethune said it succinctly in a sermon in 1836: The Synod of Dort "edified the entire Protestant world." No less a figure than an Episcopal bishop who had been present at it, Bethune wrote, described it as a place "so like heaven that he would love to dwell there forever," and the very walls and portals of hell were said to have trembled while the synod was in progress. A participating Presbyterian divine called it an "assembly as excellent and pious as any since the days of the Apostles" themselves. And a nineteenth-century historian of the church wrote that long after the city of Dordrecht "shall have disappeared from the face of the earth, its name shall be regarded as one of the most important in the annals of ecclesiastical history."[7]

Although the Reformed Dutch Church can trace its roots to the sixteenth century in Switzerland, under the reformer Zwingli, it was at Dort that it was officially born, so to speak. Staying on for an additional twenty-five sessions after the other participants had left, the Dutch theologians agreed, in the Post-Acta, upon Dutch translations of the Apostles' Creed, the Nicene Creed, the Athanasian Creed, the Belgic Confession, and the Heidelberg Catechism. And here also they settled matters sublime and mundane relating to church ordinances, church visitation, the call to ministerial office, adult baptism, festival days, hymns, profanity, Sabbath observance, standards of schoolmasters, visitation of the sick, foreign missions, the liturgy, ministers' salaries, a new translation of the Bible into Dutch, known to history as the Staten-Bijbel, and so on. These particularly Dutch characteristics of the Reformed Church came to be cherished in the New World as beloved—and, for some as time went by, increasingly sacrosanct—reminders of the mother church, the fatherland, and the long and bloody struggle of the Dutch provinces to free themselves from the yoke of Catholic Spain.

Progressive elements within the eastern American Reformed Dutch Church in the nineteenth century ventured to tolerate diversity of opinion on some of the doctrinal matters that had been laid down at Dort, but their devotion to what they believed was the purity of that doctrine soon brought conservatives or "Ultras" into sharp conflict with progressives.[8] The conservative mind within this denomination held such sway, in fact, that even at the end of the nineteenth century the Reverend William J. R. Taylor could declare that Reformed theology was "literally and essentially the same as it was in the beginning," that is, at Dort. "Those Standards, gleaming in the sun-light of the Inspired Word," he stated, "will not be lowered to any 'Banner with a strange device' of the 'New Theology of to-day or to-morrow.'"

With the role of the denomination's theological seminary at New Brunswick, New Jersey, in mind, Taylor continued: "Our whole scheme of doctrine, our history and the spiritual life of the Church, are firmly set against every phase of that Rationalism which has well nigh emptied the Protestant Churches of Germany, and almost driven Calvinism out of Calvin's City, and unsettled the foundation of the Mother Church in Holland, and made the Heidelberg Catechism as a stranger in the city whose name it bears. Against this modern 'Zeit Geist' . . . [the seminary] stands with open doors to all who will abide under her venerated banners; but over those open doors, guarded by the Canons of Dordrecht, the Spirit of the Reformed Church in America has written 'No room for trimmers nor for traitors here!'"[9]

Taylor's view did not represent the leading edge in the denomination. In nineteenth-century New York and New Jersey, the farsighted within the Reformed Dutch Church could see that revival religion and evangelical culture brought with it opportunities for local growth, participation in society's moral improvement, the church's westward expansion, ecumenical unity, and foreign mission. Those of progressive outlook trusted that, in entering into the *Zeitgeist* that Taylor and his fellow thinkers so abhorred, the Reformed Church might finally find the route to completing its long, slow process of Americanization, and shed at last its Dutch image and foreign coloration, which many by this time acknowledged had become detrimental to its progress.

The thirst for religion that gripped Americans in the nineteenth century stirred in them deep anxieties about their eternal fate, their life after death. For untold millions, the salvation of their souls was the ultimate goal of their lives. As they had in the Great Awakening in the eighteenth century, the hopeful in the Second Great Awakening earnestly looked to their clergymen for answers to the burning question "What must I do to be saved?," a question first asked of Paul and Silas by the jailer at Philippi (Acts 16:30) and repeated by generations since.

The short answer, the one Paul and Silas had given to this famous question, was "Believe in the Lord Jesus Christ, and you will be saved, you and your household." But over nineteen centuries of theology, the answer to this question had become much longer and much more complicated, and it posed especially thorny problems for those Calvinist ministers committed to doctrines that insisted on God's omnipotence in deciding who would be saved and who would not.

In short, allegiance to Calvinism, particularly to the Canons of Dort, did not permit orthodox clergymen to stray into the thickets introduced by Unitarianism, Methodism, the New Divinity, New Light, New School, and New Side doctrines, or the New Measures advocated by the revivalist Finney, all of which emphasized man's ability, indeed responsibility, to work toward his own eternal happiness. The short, sweet answer of Paul and Silas had been rendered inadequate by interpretations of Scripture that found ample support in the Bible for man's total depravity and total "inability" to affect his own eternal destination in any way, as well as for the doctrines of predestination, election, and the limited atonement of Christ.[10]

Even so, the idea of some level of human agency in the work of salvation was not new to Reformed believers. The Canons of Dort clearly stated that those who are not certain of their salvation should "diligently persevere in the use of means . . . [for] a merciful God has promised that He will not quench the smoking flax, nor break the bruised reed." In other words, far from condemning efforts on one's own behalf toward one's relationship to the Savior, Dort had advocated that the hopeful Christian should intentionally make use of the means of grace as he climbed his metaphorical ladder to heaven.[11]

The Reformed Church was put off by revivalism as conceived by Finney, because his New Measures came up against another venerable tradition in this denomination that all things should be "done decently and in good order." The means of grace were to be used, indeed; but they were to be the ordinary means, prescribed in the Bible, in the catechism, and in the Canons of Dort: faithful preaching, use of the sacraments, regular worship, prayer, meditation, Bible study, and good works. No New Measures such as Finney advocated were needed to replace them.

Finney's innovative methods included "protracted meetings," lasting from dawn to dusk for days, or for evening for weeks on end, in which the conversion of sinners was the main objective. Finney's adherents went from door to door each day to extend personal invitations to the unconverted to these meetings, which were characterized by group prayer, vivid and wrenching personal testimonies of sin and salvation, and the anxious bench, where the worried unconverted thought likely to be susceptible to exhortation were invited to sit to hear prayers on their behalf. The personal testimonies and Finney's flamboyant and exciting preaching brought the assembly to peaks of emotion, with converted and unconverted alike sobbing and fainting and rolling on the floor. The inquiry room, where the anxious sinner could go to ask his or her faith questions, and the card of intention, in which the sinner proclaimed a desire to be saved, were among the New Measures popularized by this revivalist, the most charismatic figure of his day. Reformed Dutch, whether orthodox or Pietist, may have believed that the individual must work toward his own spiritual growth, but they also believed that the human will could not, in the end, influence the workings of the divine will by a circus of shouting and emoting and carrying on—which is what the nineteenth-century revival often seemed to be. (See figure 2.)

In addition to engendering doctrinal disputes and controversy over means, revivals were problematic in the nineteenth century because they gave rise to what can be thought of as the problem of dry bones rising— a "political" almost as much as a theological dilemma. This metaphor comes

FIGURE 2. Revival meetings, often held outdoors, sometimes got out of hand. *Picture Collection, The Branch Libraries, The New York Public Library.*

from the powerful revival narrative in Ezekiel, in which God made his everlasting covenant with his chosen people, their dry bones came to life, and they "stood on their feet, an exceeding great army." Lay people empowered by the revivalist's idea that they are at least somewhat in charge of their own spiritual destinies can also come to life and stand on their feet, and in doing so they cause customary relations between clergy and laity to alter, lines of authority to blur, traditional power bases to erode, usual procedures and polities to be discarded. In short, they threaten clerical expectations and denominational influence, direction, and control.

The most resonant image of nineteenth-century America is not a Cheyenne brave pursuing a buffalo herd over the prairie, or a boatload of immigrants arriving in New York Harbor, or a Union soldier on the field at Antietam, but a fiery evangelical preacher exhorting a swooning crowd to repent and be saved. In fact, many historians of American religion regard the religious revival as the defining factor of nineteenth-century American life. And many, no matter how they account for it, view the evolution of evangelical culture as the single most important development of that century, including the Civil War. From the energies unleashed in the Second Great Awakening, beginning in the 1790s, grew the missionary movement, the moral reform movement, the temperance movement, and abolition. From the roots of this great religious revival sprang and bloomed also the "benevolent empire," the ecumenical associations of pious Protestant churchmen and -women who joined together in a thousand societies to fulfill what evangelicals regarded as American's millennial destiny as a saved and saving nation. Ultimately, at the end of the century, the irrepressible impulse to make the world a better place gave rise to the social gospel movement. As one historian has put it, evangelical religion "made Americans the most religious people in the world, molded them into a unified, pietistic-perfectionist nation, and spurred them on to those heights of social reform, missionary endeavor, and imperialistic expansionism which constitute the moving forces" of American history.[12]

Another historian has chosen an apt metaphor to describe the atmosphere of nineteenth-century America: so religious were the northern states in that era, George Marsden has written, that they differed little in that respect from the states in the Bible belt in the South today. Then, "virtually the whole United States was a Bible belt" caught up in the spirit of revivalism.[13]

Neither of these descriptions, however, hints at the ambivalence of traditional Christians toward the revivals, particularly toward the notion of human ability or human agency, the idea that man could play a role in his own salvation by desiring it, and by consciously using religious revivals to bring it about. Calvinists believed that a revival of spiritual interest, whether on the individual or on the community scale, was the result of divine intervention, a miracle on which they had no more effect than they had in producing an earthquake. It was unavailing, indeed, it was heretical, to use the means advocated by popular nineteenth-century evangelists like Finney to promote one's own spiritual regeneration—or anyone else's.

Other departures from Calvinist doctrine underlay the theological innovations abroad in nineteenth-century America, and disputes over doctrine flared into schisms as the Second Great Awakening peaked in the 1820s and 1830s. It is familiar knowledge that over such issues Congregationalists and Presbyterians split into Old Lights and New Lights, Old School and New School, but it is less well known that the Reformed Dutch Church was also scathed by them. In 1822 the General Synod of the church was charged with condoning "faulty" doctrine for not having sufficiently chastised a minister who had suggested that Christ's atoning death was sufficient to save all mankind from hell, not just those predestined for salvation by God, as orthodox Calvinism would have it.

In the secession that followed this controversy, thirteen congregations in New York and New Jersey broke off from the main body of the Reformed Dutch Church to form the True Reformed Dutch Church; a further nine congregations were seriously divided; between nine and thirty-one were weakened; and thirteen ministers (12.5 percent of the total Reformed clergy at the time) either seceded or were suspended.[14] In a denomination consisting in 1826 of 181 congregations, for a maximum of 53 congregations (or 29 percent) to be affected constituted a sizable disaster.

The seceders have often been represented as bitter cranks and diehard spoilers, but repercussions of the Secession of 1822 were felt by the Reformed Dutch Church for the rest of the nineteenth century, and thus the secession cannot be so easily discounted. Although the leaders of the denomination chose officially to regard the Secession of 1822 as a passing annoyance, it was in fact much more than that. The secession led to an immediate pamphlet war that went on for the rest of the decade, and the havoc it wrought in some areas of the denomination was not forgotten for a century, if then. Perhaps the most serious consequence occurred in 1857, when another secession, reviving the 1822 charges, took place in Reformed churches in the Midwest. Led by strict Dutch Calvinists who had emigrated to the United States from the Netherlands beginning in 1846, the Secession of 1857 culminated in the formation of the Christian Reformed Church, and over time it was strengthened by adherents dissatisfied with the ongoing Americanization in the main body, by remnants of the 1822 secession, and eventually by Reformed congregations unhappy with the denomination's hands-off position on Freemasonry.[15] Were it not for these two secessions, the Reformed Church in America would be a larger, stronger denomination today.

Undergirded by charges of doctrinal liberalization that were, in fact, inaccurate, the 1822 secession occurred just at the time when denominational leaders were finally coming to grips with the need for some toleration of new doctrinal interpretations. Because both sides strenuously and publicly insisted on their orthodoxy and their faithfulness to Dort, the secession not only managed to diminish the denomination numerically; it also emphasized the denomination's basic conservatism and its foreign image as Dutch and Dort-bound. Thus it was a severe setback to modernization—that is, Americanization—just as its leadership had begun to acknowledge Dutchness as an impediment to the denomination's expansion.

What to do? Although the denominational leadership publicly glossed over the damage done by the secession to the church's public image, it took stock of the damage and rallied to counteract it on several fronts. First, in the area of education, it decided in 1822 to concentrate on building up its two main institutions of higher education, as well as to start supporting the burgeoning Sunday school movement. Second, in the same year it hailed the formation by a number of pious individuals of the Missionary Society of the Reformed Dutch Church, which over the course of its short life of eleven years was to collect funds that aided about a hundred start-up churches and frontier outposts and 130 missionaries. Third, it supported with equal enthusiasm this Missionary Society's decision to launch a monthly publication, *The Magazine of the Reformed Dutch Church*, designed to appeal to the membership of the denomination as well as to attract new members outside of the Dutch population. And fourth, it encouraged its members to get involved in the new benevolent and moral reform societies that were beginning to sprout up everywhere in the evangelical era. In every direction that it attempted to move forward, however, powerful conservative voices within the denomination attempted, often successfully, to hold it back, keeping it tied to Dort.

# CHAPTER 3

# *The 1820s*

## ARRAYING FOR A NEW CENTURY

*Mr. Editor, what a presage of the future is afforded to the great mass of Society by the*
*infant schools, the free schools, the sabbath schools, the Bible, and Missionary, and*
*Tract Societies . . . ! Who can resist the conviction that a way is preparing for*
*brighter and better days to man upon earth!*
—Magazine of the Reformed Dutch Church, December 1828

*I*n the 1820s, as the Reformed Dutch Church's third century in America began, its leadership recognized that the denomination was in danger of falling by the wayside. It was losing ground in relation not only to its fellow Reformed denominations, the Presbyterian and the Congregational, but also to the newer evangelical Methodists and Baptists, who were making daily headway in converting cities and hinterland alike to their versions of Protestantism. Roman Catholicism was a threat of a different order, but a real one that would alter the old Puritan/Pietist religious culture forever.

More immediately, the pamphlet war being waged over the Secession of 1822, the lawsuits over disputed church property, the suicide of Reformed minister Peter Froeligh (son of the secession's leader, Solomon Froeligh), and a series of well-publicized secessions from the secession itself were cause for alarm. The merciless attention paid by the press to all of these issues and events entertained an onlooking world only too ready to find amusement at the trouble in paradise, and it was feared that the spotlight on the denomination's long history of internal strife was not only discouraging its membership but also turning away prospective members.

Although the secession was the straw that could have broken the camel's back, it did not. But to recoup the real losses in numbers and in the church's public image that it had caused, as well as to hope to prosper on the fast-changing evangelical scene, particularly vis-à-vis denominations directly competing with it for adherents, action was imperative. The denomination now took steps in three directions to ensure its viability: in education, in public relations, and in the rising field of moral reform and benevolent work.

The most prominent figure in the denomination in 1822 was the Reverend Dr. John Henry Livingston (1746–1825). Since 1784 he had been head of two educational institutions long affiliated with the denomination: Queen's College, first chartered in 1766, and its sister institution, known simply as the "Professorate," a training school for ministerial candidates. Eventually, Queen's College was to evolve into Rutgers University, and the Professorate became the New Brunswick Theological Seminary, the first graduate school of theology in the United States.

Livingston was held in the highest regard in the Reformed Dutch Church for having healed, with his 1771 Plan of Union, the coetus-conferentie conflict that had riven the denomination for seventeen years, for translating and editing the Dutch standards of the denomination and combining them into the denomination's first American constitution in 1793, for his role in developing a theology of world mission, and for his long association with the Professorate and with Queen's College.[1]

Livingston's sterling reputation was also based on his doctor of divinity degree from the University of Utrecht, which put him squarely in the spiritual tradition of the Voetians who had made that university the seat of Dutch Pietism, or heart religion, in the seventeenth century, and of their American proponents: the Pietist ministers Michaelius, Bogardus, Bertholf, Freeman, Van Santvoord, and T. J. Frelinghuysen and the latter's sons and students in the eighteenth century. As such, he himself had inspired generations of ministerial students with the story of his own spiritual rebirth and his witness to the importance of experiential religion.

Needless to say, however, with this background, and with his talent for healing controversy and for avoiding obstacles that could engender it, Livingston was no advocate of New Measures revivalism or the doctrinal innovations of the nineteenth century that underlay them. He could say with confidence that the seceders in 1822 were mistaken in accusing the Reformed Church of faulty doctrine and lax discipline, much less of tolerating trendy new measures to win heavenly crowns. But even so he and others among his more progressive Reformed Church colleagues were well aware of the need for a new look at old doctrines. They preached, for instance, that nothing in the Scriptures forbade the hope that unbaptized infants could be saved, that a merciful and omnipotent God was not incapable of saving the heathen, and that it was quite within the realm of possibility that the greatest part of mankind would be saved in the end by a loving Creator—all faulty doctrines in the eyes of the ultraorthodox within the denomination and of the hard-core predestinarian secessionists.

In 1822, just when the unnerving accusations of Solomon Froeligh and company, and the subsequent secession, were disturbing the ever fragile peace of the denomination, Livingston persuaded the General Synod to enlist a team of prominent laymen to raise an endowment to ensure the future stability of both Queen's College and the Professorate, both of which had from the start been on shaky financial ground. The finance drive was a success, and by the time of Livingston's death three years later in 1825, a committee of six, three trustees and three persons appointed by the General Synod of the denomination, was charged with supervising Queen's, now called Rutgers College; the Professorate, now to be known as the New Brunswick Theological Seminary; a preparatory school; and four faculty. Thirty students were enrolled in the college that year and nineteen in the seminary.[2] (See figure 3.)

In retrospect, the decision to maintain the old ties between the college and seminary at this time, instead of letting the two go their separate ways, was a fateful one, because it reemphasized their common origins in a specific group ancestry and thus reinforced the sense Reformed people already harbored that they were historically different and culturally distinct from other Americans. In other words, the decision sent out a clear signal that the denomination's Dutch roots were too important to it to abandon, even as it concurrently struggled to shed the negative effects of its foreign image.

Rutgers and the New Brunswick Theological Seminary maintained their formal ties until 1867, and the close relationship that evolved between them in their first century together cannot be understated. They were truly one womb and cradle to generations of Reformed clergymen and laymen, and the traditions and history associated with them are indivisible from the religious culture of the denomination. These two institutions were thus potent factors in the process of ethnicization as it continued to evolve—and in the persistence of Dutchness in New York and New Jersey.

The womb was fragile and the cradle uncushioned, but a "home feeling" was consciously cultivated that came to be cherished by students, parents, faculty, and clergy alike. Rutgers' interests, wrote the *Intelligencer* in 1850, "lie very near many hearts, . . . and it is . . . desirable that every . . . form of influence should be employed . . . to invest [the college] with endearing associations, and to awaken a 'home feeling' and a sense of responsibility respecting it."[3]

To develop this home feeling, a traditional sense of ethnicity was intentionally nurtured, a past-oriented identification, a collective memory, a special history, a consciousness of kind—in short, those characteristics that make up a sense of a distinctive peoplehood, the essence of ethnicity. Its home feeling was a potent force in attracting to both the college and the

FIGURE 3. Until 1856, "Old Queens," constructed in 1811, was still housing the seminary, the college, the preparatory school, and four faculty families. *Courtesy Special Collections and University Archives, Rutgers University Libraries.*

seminary young men from Reformed families all over the Dutch culture areas in New York and New Jersey.

This home feeling for the institutions at New Brunswick was advanced by Reformed clergymen in their parishes and was eagerly received by parents desirous of sending their sons to a place where all that was needed for the "training of the sons of the Church for the service of the Church" would be afforded. At New Brunswick, they could be sure, their sons were guaranteed a grounding in the divine verities of Reformed doctrine and immersion in a "superior spiritual culture" that would be immediately familiar to them, because they had been exposed to it and rooted in it in their homes and in their home churches.[4]

The home feeling, or sense of a distinctive history and significant origins, was still alive in 1884, a hundred years after the founding of the seminary, as is apparent in the addresses at the centennial celebration that year. Parental imagery welcomed returning graduates to their "spiritual birthplace and home" ("Let the warm, maternal heart that throbs with undying love for all her children, bid you a tender, tearful, affectionate welcome"), and the "fathers" were extolled for their efforts in having created that birthplace a century before.[5] It was a birthplace where Dutchness could reign and no one would question it. Rather, all rejoiced in it.

The affective significance of Rutgers and the New Brunswick Seminary to the denomination is clear in the attitude toward commencement. From their pulpits and in their family visitation, Reformed preachers urged their flocks to attend the commencement exercises, so as to learn more about the college and to be moved to support it. As commencement approached, advertisements for transportation to it appeared in the *Intelligencer*, with the New-Jersey Railroad Company offering special rates as an enticement: from New York City for one dollar; from Newark, 75 cents; from Elizabethtown, 65 and a half cents; from Rahway, 50 cents. Because evening events made an overnight stay necessary, trains were scheduled to make the return trip in the morning at 5:00 and 7:30 A.M.

On commencement day, 1850, "perambulations" of strangers poured out of the railroad depot and milled in the streets of New Brunswick. Throngs of wagons, carriages, and vehicles of every kind surged in from the country, and the streets were filled with immense numbers "wending their way to the loved institution our Church has caused to be founded there."[6] (See figure 4.)

An elaborate procession began to assemble on the Rutgers campus early in the morning. Led by the janitor, next in order came the freshmen, sophomore, and junior classes, the candidates for the B.A., and the students of theology, law, and medicine. These were followed by candidates for the M.A., professors of other colleges, the Rutgers faculty, the board of superintendents, the governor of New Jersey, the chief justice and the attorney general of the state, the trustees of the college, clergy and strangers of distinction, members of the state legislature, officers of the army and navy, and finally the general citizenry.

From the campus, the procession wound its way to the First Reformed Church, where with prayers, the salutatory address, senior orations, the valedictory, and music—in ceremonies lasting all day—degrees and honorary degrees, D.D.s, D.L.s, and M.D.s were conferred. The capacious sanctuary was crowded to overflowing. Afterward, a collation was held in the college museum nearby, to which everyone walked from the church. In 1845, at an evening levee at President Hasbrouck's house during commencement week, "Youth, Beauty and Learning were all represented"; and such civilities, commented the *Intelligencer*, "polish a society and give expression and nobility to the human mind."[7] It was not lost on anyone that they also presented an occasion for Reformed youth and Reformed beauty to acquaint themselves with each other with an eye to future alliances.

As late as 1884, when Rutgers had been fully independent and nonsectarian for some years, the two institutions were still spoken of in terms straight out of Dort as "indissolubly one . . . in the purposing mind [of the] Reformed Church . . . to glorify God by training the sons of the Church."[8]

# OLD RUTGERS COMMENCEMENT.

Another year has roll'd around ;
Again we hear the joyful sound
Of Rutgers' old and sweet-toned bell,
Telling the sure and welcome knell
To study hard of Greek and Latin,
And now the moths and worms can fatten
On " Napier's Bones" and Attic salt,
And rats and mice may run and vault
Up stairs and down in Rutgers College
And cram their mouths brim full of knowledge.
The blue Symplagadies no more,
Will crush the ships upon their shore,
The Argonautic band, from Greece,
Will no more seek the golden fleece ;
And Homer's heroes, who they say,
Wore hair as long as Charley May,
Will no more tread the bloody path
They trod for old Achilles' wrath,
And " Jessie's" black-board now will stand
Wash'd clean and smooth with soap and sand ;
Old Time has brought commencement day
And soon the " de'il will be to pay."

To Brunswick town is hurrying now,
The D. D. with his reverend brow ;
The M. D. leaves his drachms and scruples
To see and hear old Rutgers' pupils ;
The Lawyers leave " assault and batter"
And come to see their Alma Mater ;
The judge puts on his youngest wig,
And comes to town to eat roast pig ;
And woman with her eye of light
Will grace the gallery to-night,
Whilst Juniors, Sophs, and Seniors too,
Will drink mint-juleps till they're blue,
And in the church there'll be a jam,
All packed in tight as they can cram,
Whilst hundreds, standing at the door,
Will find no use in knocking more ;

And those who get within the church
Will laugh at those left in the lurch,
And those who could not quite get in,
Will say those in are smothering ;
And orators, with silv'ry tongues,
Will strain and stretch their labouring lungs ;
Use action, trope, and flaming figure
To make the sense and sound grow bigger ;
Whilst belles and beaux will laugh and chatter
(The sense and sound to them no matter)
Until they hear a comic chap,
And then the boys will stamp and clap ;
And then you'l see the little dears
Laugh till their eyes are fill'd with tears ;
The faculty will look around,
And frowning, try to drown the sound,
And " Sleepy John" roused from his rest,
Will loudly cry, " *Quid rei est.*"
'Tis vain, they'll only laugh the more,
And Fresh and Sophs will stamp and roar ;
Thus will they do 'till " Benediction,"
Their capers begg'ring all description.

Old Rutgers mourn ! commencement day
Will tear thy offspring far away
From thy fond shelter and abode,
And they must tread the rugged road
Of this rough world with toil and labour,
For *Quis-que suæ, fortunæ faber ;*
Oh ! may the guardian of the right
Protect them in the weary fight.

And may Philoclias' brilliant star,
Up glory's firmament afar,
Light those she sheds her halo o'er,
Their motto still " *Excelsior.*"
And *Peithesophia ! !* may that name
Ne'er lack a son to prove *her fame*
On his escutcheon bearing high
In honours path PI KAPA PHI.

FIGURE 4. Commencement at Rutgers College and the New Brunswick Seminary gave rise to fond poems and humorous burlesques. The church where all were "packed in tight" while hundreds milled about outside was the First Reformed Dutch Church on Bayard Street. *Courtesy Special Collections and University Archives, Rutgers University Libraries.*

In a second step on the education front, the denomination finally recognized in the 1820s the value of the Sunday school in educating children in the tenets of the faith when it affiliated in 1824 with the new American Sunday School Union (ASSU). Although this was not the Reformed Dutch Church's first excursion into ecumenical activity—missionary work was the first, in the 1790s—it was a departure for it to unite with other Protestants in a cooperative effort that involved tailoring its educational program to suit a group consensus. But for some at least, of greater urgency now even than strict devotion to its Dortish polity and purity was to participate with its sister evangelical denominations in a concerted all-out approach to the religious education of the rising generation.

Like all Christian churches, the Dutch Church viewed the religious education of children as a sacred mandate from Jesus. Because children were precious to Jesus ("Suffer the little children to come unto me"), children were precious to evangelicals. Indeed, they were not only the future of the church, they were the stuff of the Kingdom itself. And for all evangelicals, the religious education of children was an undertaking that involved immersing them so thoroughly in the gospel message that they would not only become good and useful Christians on earth; they would repent of their sins, come to know Jesus as their personal Redeemer—and thus be assured a place in heaven when they died. In pursuit of this goal, it was to the Sabbath school (or Sunday school, as it was also called) with its armies of teachers, its vast array of curriculum material, and its popular social activities, that evangelicals turned. A vital engine in a far-reaching and pervasive endeavor to carry out what they perceived as America's mission as a redeemer nation, the Sabbath school became a major tool for evangelical clergymen in bringing their congregations to an awareness of the necessity for personal salvation and the importance of being good and doing good.

Although parents, particularly mothers, were the church's main ally in the effort to convert children to the cross, the role of Sabbath schools took on increasing importance, once their efficacy was apparent. Spurned at first by both parents and clergy, Sabbath schools eventually came to be valued by many as "the most influential preparatory agency for accomplishing Gospel work which a minister can employ."[9]

The first such schools in America were geared to both adults and children, and their first mission was to teach illiterates to read, but they reached out also to the middle-class churchgoing child, to the literate but unchurched, and to the immigrant, especially in the cities. It was a novel idea when in 1791 Isabella Graham opened a Sunday school class in New York "for girls and misses," but her example was soon bettered by her daughter

Joanna Bethune, who later that year opened the first regular Sabbath school in the city for poor and neglected street children of both sexes. The efforts of Graham and Bethune soon resulted in the formation of the Female Union for the Promotion of Sabbath-schools, under the direction of a group of pious ladies, many of whom were active in the Reformed churches in lower Manhattan.[10]

Initially, ministers opposed the Sabbath school as an infringement by the laity on the preacher's right to catechize, as well as on the grounds that suitable teachers would never be found and that the work of teaching on Sunday profaned the Sabbath. Parents, in agreement, added that it was an encroachment on their parental prerogative as well, that too much religion made children overly serious and morose, and that it was cruel to confine children in a stuffy room on Sunday when they could be free to roam outdoors.

The first Sunday school in the Reformed Dutch Church was begun in 1799 in New Brunswick by Mrs. Ira Condict, wife of the minister of the First Reformed Church, in partnership with Dina van den Bergh, a ruling power in the congregation as the widow of two of its former most revered ministers, T. J. Frelinghuysen, Jr., and Jacobus Hardenbergh. By 1819 the New Brunswick Sunday school enrolled more than a hundred white and forty-three black scholars. Despite its popularity and the prestige of its founders, however, indifference to it on the part of "some of the best Christian people" in the community continued for many years, one of the objections being that it fostered "independency" in a denomination that prided itself on the "good order secured by presbyterial government" at Dort. (When the school's enrollment began to dwindle in the 1820s, over a temporary personnel problem, the superintendent expressed his fear to the Reverend Samuel Blanchard How that it might die. "Let it die," was How's advice.)

Even though this school ended by flourishing, no official acknowledgment of this method of educating children in the faith can be found in the records of the Reformed Dutch Church until 1824, when the General Synod finally endorsed Sabbath schools as "mighty instruments for the advancement of the Kingdom" and entered into relationship with the ASSU. The Sunday school movement grew by leaps and bounds. By 1830, six thousand schools belonged to the American Sunday School Union, with sixty thousand teachers and four hundred thousand students. It was a powerful instrument not only of religious education but of the socialization and "civilization" of the illiterate and of immigrants, and of homogenization, and Americanization, too, as it brought the old-line ethnic churches into common cause with new denominations.[11]

In a third area that involved education, the Reformed Dutch Church was not so late to come. The education of women had always been a priority for this denomination. As had been true in the Netherlands longer than elsewhere in Europe, the influence of educated women on the formation of good character and good citizens was given particular emphasis. In the commercial hubs of the Dutch provinces even in the fourteenth century, literacy and numeracy were indispensable to economic survival, let alone advancement. And a literate and numerate populace was also vital to a society where church and state had a mutual interest in encouraging order, concord, and Christian values. Schools in the Dutch Republic were regarded as "like gardens, where the love of God and respect for legal authority must be transplanted into the young," regardless of their gender.[12] The French scholar Joseph Scaliger in 1593 was astonished to find that in Holland even servant girls could read.[13]

The foremost school of the time for young women in New York City and a favorite of Reformed families was founded in 1827 by the Reformed minister Isaac Ferris. The Rutgers Female Institute, modeled on the famed Albany Female Academy, at first met opposition. "Many doubts were expressed as to the feasibility even as to the need of such an institution," Ferris recalled later. But he prevailed in convincing a cadre of influential men that the establishment of separate schools for females had produced a "marvelous improvement" in their learning. "The cobweb notions about female capacity to acquire the higher studies have been swept away," he wrote, "and with them . . . the kindred notions of the inutility of mental culture to a female."[14] At Ferris's urging an association of stockholders formed and pledged to raise $30,000 for a building. The shares were $100 each, and $16,400 was immediately subscribed by 103 gentlemen of the city. The Institute, which was never officially a part of the Reformed Church per se, although it was enthusiastically admired by it, was incorporated by the Regents of the University of the State of New York. Fifteen men sat on its first board.[15]

The school opened at Madison Street, one door east of Clinton Street, in April 1839. The Rutgers Female Institute was nonsectarian, though "Christian principle will be the grand base of our superstructure, and the cement of the whole." With such a prominent Reformed clergyman at its helm, however, Reformed parents could be sure that their daughters would feel right at home—and be safe from proselytizing influences. The school immediately attracted many young women from well-known families in the Reformed community.[16]

From its inception, the Rutgers Female Institute had a practical aim. It dealt with education "as a matter of real importance and not of theory.

It secure[d] serious work on the part of all engaged, [and aimed] at train-ing the mind as well as furnishing the memory." Ferris took pride in the fact that the institute carried advancing students "up through the moral, metaphysical, and mathematical study of most of our best institutions for males" and that it had from the beginning granted free room, board, and tuition to young ladies of slender means wishing to train as teachers. He was convinced that the institution was contributing to the public good.

By the time Ferris left the institute in 1856 to become chancellor of the University of the City of New York (today's New York University), the institute had enrolled more than 4,000 young women, 250 of whom were graduated with honor to positions of influence and usefulness. Their edu-cation, Ferris said in his farewell address, was a "passport to everywhere." Although not everyone agreed with Isaac Ferris that a woman's education in the nineteenth century was a passport to anywhere, much less every-where, for Reformed women education would prove to be one of the pass-ports out of Dutchness into a new American ethnicity.

*I*n 1822 the Reformed Church took another significant step into the brave new world that was evangelical America through its ready embrace of a proposal by the Missionary Society of the Reformed Dutch Church, formed that year, to publish a magazine aimed at the lay reader. This publication, church leaders hoped, would burnish the denomination's image, increase its opportunities to charm its own shaky membership, and attract potential new adherents. It was called *The Magazine of the Reformed Dutch Church,* and it began publication in 1826 as a monthly. *The Christian Intelligencer,* the weekly newspaper that succeeded the *Magazine* in 1830, was to be an influential agent in expediting the final stages in the Americanization of the denomination and the Dutch community in nineteenth-century New York and New Jersey. At the same time, ironically, it retarded that process.

The time was more than ripe by 1826 for the Reformed Dutch Church to produce its own entry in the growing field of religious newspapers.[17] In long-settled areas like New York and New Jersey, where the Reformed Church flourished, literacy had become widespread, offering new oppor-tunities for disseminating the evangelistic message, the New Testament's Good News. As the editors pointed out in introducing their publication in April 1826, the age was marked by the diffusion of knowledge among all classes of men. "[Knowledge] is no longer confined to the wealthier part of society, and to scholars. . . . [Today, it] begins to shed its light even over the labouring part of the community." Church leadership imagined the simple cottager, after the labors of the day, retiring to his fireside to read and study, and it seized that image to offer to its members, as the other evangelical denominations had already begun to do, a periodical they could call their own.[18]

The stated goals of the *Magazine* were to advance the missionary cause abroad and at home, shape the minds and morals of every member of the church, defend the doctrines of the gospel as expressed "in purity and precision in the canons and decrees of the Synod of Dort," and acquaint the rising generation with the history of the Reformed Church in the Netherlands.[19] Laced with lengthy and erudite treatises on the Reformation history of the church and on Calvinist theology as laid down at Dort, an important goal of the *Magazine* was to convey to its readers the glories of the Netherlands in its Golden Age and the Dutch people's heroic military and political struggles against Catholic Spain in the sixteenth century. It is ironic, however, that in introducing readers to forgotten chapters in Dutch history, the publication, so intent on joining the American mainstream, actually rekindled Dutchness.

Initially, the *Magazine* did not meet with a good reception. In the first year of its existence, it had 1,750 subscribers. This averaged out to only 10 subscriptions per congregation, and some congregations had no subscribers. (Copies no doubt circulated hand to hand among a larger group.) The editors urged ministers and consistories to support the publication more vigorously. Its low price, only $1.50 per year, placed it "within the power of every family to become possessed of this record of Evangelical truth," they pointed out, ignoring the fact that price was not the stumbling block.

The stumbling block was the mixed signals the editors were sending. On the one hand, they deplored the liberalizing tendencies of the day with regard to doctrine, but on the other they advocated an ecumenical approach to mission strategies, moral reform efforts, benevolence work, and Sabbath schools, thus managing to displease both conservatives and progressives simultaneously. For many in the Reformed Church, especially in the early decades of the nineteenth century, anything that smacked of ecumenism threatened the "purity" of the church as formulated at the Synod of Dort. But for progressives, the Great Commandment, to preach the gospel to every living creature, was *the* urgent challenge of the century, more urgent than unswerving devotion to Dort. The *Magazine*, and after 1830 the *Intelligencer*, were aggressively pro-mission. This explains why some could view the publication as showing a "tremendous opposition to liberalism," while others viewed it as "characterized by a truly liberal spirit."[20]

In the second year of publication, the editors attempted to increase subscriptions by appealing not only to the laborer reading by his cottage fireside, but also to his wife and children. In June 1827 there first appeared a female correspondent, Amanda, whose recurrent philosophical reflections were designed to attract women readers. Soon, poems such as "Where art thou, my mother?" by A. R. of New Jersey and tales of pious children successfully resisting the wickedness of the world became regular features, as they did in the papers of other denominations and even in the secular press as well.

Cajoling reluctant subscribers with the admission that "We endeavor . . . to do our best . . . to mix the useful with the pleasant, . . . to please your taste and offer food for your minds," the editors introduced in the third volume, for 1828–1829, reviews of "pleasant and instructive books" for children and "useful religious stories" designed to appeal to women. Even so, subscriptions did not meet expectations. "Is it possible," the editors scolded, "that there can exist a Dutch family . . . who can yet grudge twelve shillings a year . . . to support the only religious publication of . . . [our] Church?"

In 1830 the editors took a fresh look at the *Magazine* and tried a new approach to publication. Convinced that the increasing taste for reading must be satisfied by ever more "religious intelligence" and other matter designed to conduce its readers to virtue—and also considering that it had become perhaps a little too secular for some tastes in its news and editorial columns—it found a new editor and gave itself a new name, *The Christian Intelligencer*. It switched from monthly to weekly publication, became a newspaper instead of a magazine, went in size from a small to a large (folio) format—the same as the popular New York *Observer*, a Presbyterian paper—and adopted a larger, more legible typeface. It did not alter its stated goals, but rather reaffirmed them as devoted to the mission effort, "to the cause of Evangelical truth, and vital godliness generally, and particularly to the domestic concerns, and the best interest of the Reformed Dutch Church's own 'household of faith.'"

The government did not charge postage on periodicals sent through the mail from one publisher to another at this time, so editors of both the religious and the secular press eagerly exchanged their publications, postage free, with other national and with British editors. Also, international copyright law did not exist until the Bern Convention of 1887, and although some regulations came into effect in 1845, editors cheerfully pirated one another's news and views, sometimes with attribution, sometimes without. In this way, information and ideas filtered from the British papers, which in turn picked up news from Continental papers, on through to the American press. Thus the *Intelligencer*, in reprinting substantial amounts of political and diplomatic news from around the world, functioned as an important agent of cultural transmission and of modernization by bringing that intelligence into even very isolated rural hamlets in the Dutch culture areas. In the same way, it conveyed current religious thought and practice directly into the parlors of Reformed households. It had the effect, eventually, of enfolding the members of those households in a larger community defined not by the narrow, parochial concerns of an ethnic church, but unified in the great effort of the era, the transcendent common evangelical cause of saving America for Christ.

This earnest evangelical publication found its way into Reformed households via a network of agents made up of clergymen and elders. By 1832, eighteen agents worked New Jersey and thirty-three, New York. Little Falls, Pompton, Montville, English Neighborhood, Belleville, Paterson, Tappan, and Tarrytown had agents. It was not until 1835, nine years after the *Magazine* began, that Acquackanonck, Pascack, Schraalenbergh, and Hackensack acquired agents willing to distribute copies to subscribers, collect payments and arrears, and sign up new subscribers. The seat of the 1822 secession, these were the most conservative Dutch communities in New Jersey and those where the old ways lingered longest. In these ultra-conservative communities, apparently, even such a religious novelty as a denominational newspaper was suspect.

Although the *Intelligencer* was careful to espouse the doctrines of the church as formulated at the Synod of Dort in the Netherlands two hundred years before, in political matters it was emphatically pro-American, even nationalistic. The editors praised the paper and the religious press in general as of the "first importance among human instrumentalities" to the advancement of the Redeemer's Kingdom, next to a competent, faithful, self-sacrificing ministry. But, like good Jacksonians, they also celebrated American political and juridical institutions: "By [them] religion, liberty, and laws / Exert their influence and advance their cause." As one editor put it at midcentury, the newspaper was ever marked "by a fervent desire to make American liberty the fond mother of intelligence, virtue, industry and order." It was consistent with its patriotism, of course, that it openly encouraged the last holdouts for maintaining the Dutch language as the language of the pulpit to give up and adjust to English.[21]

𝐹inally, in its determination to join the American mainstream, the leadership of the Reformed Church embraced the "benevolent empire," where usefulness in all its glory flourished. The idea of usefulness, also called sanctification, consumed the evangelical mind in the nineteenth century. Sanctification was the process by which one was set free from sin, by God's grace, after which the Holy Spirit inspired one to wish to be good, do good, and serve the Kingdom by being "useful" to the Lord. Like personal holiness, usefulness or sanctification was the result of conversion and its fruits, and thus it was a term fraught with anxiety, for if one was not impelled to be useful to society, one was not, perhaps, truly saved.[22]

Under the influence of the concept of sanctification or usefulness, Protestantism became a mighty force for social change. Evangelicals on fire to prepare the world both physically and spiritually as a place fit for Christ's return—and perhaps prompted at the same time by a desire to corroborate or test the authenticity of their own state of grace—flocked to join voluntary societies. In *An Errand of Mercy*, the historian Charles I. Foster compiled a list of 158 moral reform, benevolent, charitable, and missionary societies, asylums, commissions, unions, associations, and auxiliaries that flourished in America in the evangelical age. The list, he notes, is by no means exhaustive. This is a major understatement. The list would contain thousands of names if every such organization in every town and city in America were remembered.[23]

By the end of the decade of the 1820s, leading Reformed Dutch clergy and laymen were sitting on the boards of all the major organizations united in this effort to make the world a better place: the American Sunday School Union, the Lord's Day Alliance, the American Tract Society, the American Bible Society, and the primary missionary societies, to name just a few.

Reformed women also played important hands-on roles in the everyday work of improving the world not only in these organizations but in many that they organized of their own. In their desire to be useful, they had early on—by 1810 at least—approached their clergymen to allow them to convene Dorcas societies, far-reaching do-gooding agencies named after a woman of the Bible. (Dorcas, who was raised from the dead by the disciple Peter, was "full of good works and acts of charity." A tunic-maker, she is the original sewing woman of the faith [Acts 9:36–41].) The minutes of a Dorcas Society organized in New Brunswick in 1813, in the Reverend John H. Livingston's First Reformed Dutch Church, reveal that women understood a benefit not only to society but to themselves from participating in benevolent activity: "Few individuals possess the means of doing good on an extensive scale, but by uniting with others the aggregate produced may be considerable. . . . By uniting in a benevolent undertaking the ties of society are strengthen'd, for while we co-operate in carrying relief and comfort to the afflicted, we learn to love each other, and all the best affections are called into exercise."[24]

If local problems and contemporary trends were weaning the Dutch away from their insularity and their attachment to Dort, for many within the denomination this was an unwelcome development. The Synod of Dort may have been described as "so like heaven," but, for many, departing from Dort was edging too near hell. Reformed Church efforts in the 1820s to join the mainstream of American religious culture represented giant steps forward by an ethnic denomination that for two hundred years had looked to its Dutch antecedents to define its institutional integrity. But by 1830, it had become apparent that these efforts were in trouble as the old tensions between progressives and conservatives were restated in the terms of the nineteenth century's new dilemmas.

# CHAPTER 4

# *"Our Reformed Zion,"*
# *1830–1860*

*The good work [in Harlingen, N.J., 1831] began in the outskirts of the congregation, and traveled in toward the center. Its progress was rapid, and soon the whole mass was brought under the solemn and awakening influence of the Holy Spirit. . . . Those who had long been impenitent and careless were aroused from the torpor of years, and constrained to cry out from the depths of their aching hearts, "What must I do to be saved?"*
—John A. Todd, 1860

*I*n every area where progressives attempted to modernize the Reformed Dutch Church—particularly, as this chapter will show, in the areas of education, ecumenical action, and public relations—they met with stiff opposition from the Ultras, old-school men who found all change abhorrent and who were determined to maintain the integrity of their Reformed Zion just as they firmly believed it had been conceived at Dort. In one area, however, progressives and conservatives shared concern for departures from Dort. This was in the matter of revivals, for in this they had to treat with innovations in received doctrine, not new insights into Scripture, and not merely updates of strategy, novel directions in policy, or modifications in worship style.

*B*y the 1830s Protestant America had realized that something drastic had to be done to civilize, socialize, and Christianize the Great Unwashed—the hordes of Roman Catholic and "heathen" immigrants flooding into the country. The modern religious revival with its New Measures as introduced in the 1820s by the evangelist Charles Grandison Finney was conceded to be an effective means by which Americans could be taught to rise up and seek salvation for themselves, their family, and their friends and neighbors, and then turn their attention to helping the rest of benighted humanity. Indeed, in the main revival decades of the century, revivals went hand in hand not only with the spread of a liberalized, Arminianized theology but also with such humanitarian concerns as were expressed in the moral reform movement, the benevolent empire of interdenominational cooperation, and the development of missionary strategies, both at home and abroad.

But first a dilemma inherent in the Finney-style revival had to be overcome. All of the Calvinist faiths represented at the international synod in Dordrecht in 1618–1619 had subscribed to the five Canons of Dort: total depravity, unconditional election, limited atonement, the irresistibility of grace, and the perseverance of the saints. Now, two centuries later, the dilemma faced by these same Calvinist churches was how to reconcile the doctrines of Dort with departures from those doctrines. If human beings were totally depraved and utterly incapable of helping themselves, and if only an elect predestined by God was to be saved, how could the orthodox Calvinist minister in good faith encourage them to hope they had a chance of saving themselves by participating in religious revivals?

By about 1830 a response had been articulated to this problem: God had created man with reason, or common sense, and God expected man to believe in the saving grace of Jesus Christ. If he believed, he would be saved, and well-managed revivals could teach him what to believe and how to believe it. To many ordinary churchgoers, as well as to many clergymen, the comforting answer of Paul and Silas to their jailer, "Believe in the Lord Jesus Christ, and you will be saved, you and your household," had become far more palatable than the notion of a wrathful God consigning millions of uninformed heathens and millions of hapless would-be faithful to hell for all eternity.

The new methods for saving souls popularized by Finney—the protracted meeting, the anxious seat, lay participation, extemporaneous prayer, public prayer meetings, women speaking and even praying in public— shocked Calvinists, especially Reformed Dutch people used to doing things "decently and in good order," as Dort had specified. The Finney-style revival meeting, designed and scheduled, managed and manipulated, tended to produce unseemly displays of emotion in the attenders and, too often, short-lived results. On the one hand, the traditional Reformed view was that revivals were miracles of God, "interpositions of Divine power," with which people had nothing to do, and had no part in producing, anymore than they had a part in producing thunder and lightning. All they could do if they wished for spiritual revival was to listen to faithful preaching, pray, receive the sacraments, study, believe, wait, and hope.

On the other hand, the Reformed Dutch had been acquainted with "heart" religion long before Finney came upon the scene—as early as the seventeenth century by those Dutch Pietist ministers who had brought the ideas of the Further Reformation to New York and New Jersey. Although there was resistance to Finney's innovations, many in the denomination welcomed them. Nor was it lost upon denominational leaders that the revival churches, particularly the Methodist, were flourishing. People wanted revivals, and in the long run expediency—perhaps even the future of the denomination—made it imperative that the innovations in some way be accommodated.

Among the Reformed Dutch, accommodation was achieved by making a distinction between the genuine revival and the spurious revival. In 1837, one of the most important revival years of the nineteenth century, the Reverend John Gray, minister of the Schodack Reformed Church in Rensselaer County, New York, preached a sermon on the "Prerequisites for, and how to obtain a genuine revival of religion." A genuine revival, Gray told his congregation, must begin in the hearts of the members of the congregation. Don't send for a certain Mr. or Dr. to bring about a revival. A man with the latest techniques may be able to "effect an excitement, but an excitement is not a revival and cannot work any [lasting moral change]." Rather, "Ask—what is the state of my heart? Am I a child of God, or an heir of hell? Am I maturing for heaven, or ripening for destruction?" Ask "What is the state of my household? Is it a house for God? How much is the Bible read? How often? How much is it believed? Obeyed? Is there an Altar to God in my house around which morning and evening you gather?"[1]

Gray, whose own preaching was described as "Tender yet bold, self-forgetful yet urgent . . . a right-down earnest tugging to get his hearers up to the cross," rejected the New Measures and managed revival, but at the same time, mindful of Article 16 of the first Canon of Dort, he did not repudiate human ability, or human agency, in bringing about a true revival. Indeed, he emphasized that human agency was instrumental in the event. An ardent supplicant for an extraordinary and general outpouring of the Holy Spirit, he exhorted his congregation to draw near to God in "fervent, agonizing prayer" and to "travail as in birth for salvation." Good works were important, too: a congregation's behavior, both in and out of church, must be acceptable to the Holy Spirit. They must never expect a revival while they "lounged on the crutches of sloth" or "reclined on the pillow of carnal security," or existed only to find fault, or to spread the flames of jealousy and discord in the church.

The prevailing line of reasoning in the denomination came to be that spiritual revival was essential for the survival of the church, and if it did not occur spontaneously, a little help was in order to bring it about. In an essay read in 1837 before the Society of Inquiry at "Rutger's [*sic*] Theological Seminary" and printed in the *Intelligencer*, the speaker described a genuine revival as one in which the Holy Spirit is in charge, and a deep solemnity pervades: "People's hearts melt, tender affection sweetens human relations, and love and humility mark all." But the church does not always seek the Holy Spirit, this speaker pointed out, and then religion declines. Thus, he concluded, revivals are absolutely necessary to ensure that genuine piety does not die—and the church with it.[2]

The revival that took place in the Harlingen Reformed Church in 1831, the same year that Finney was electrifying Rochester, New York, with his novel formulas for converting sinners, was considered genuine. It took place without benefit of New Measures, but with concerted human effort: by the congregation, student ministers from nearby Princeton, a "manly and practical" Reformed minister, John F. Schermerhorn, brought in for the duration, and finally the old minister, Peter Labagh, for the arduous postrevival work of keeping the people's "new born zeal from plunging them into error."[3]

The "good work began in the outskirts of the congregation, and traveled in toward the center. Its progress was rapid, and soon the whole mass was brought under the solemn and awakening influence of the Holy Spirit. Prayer meetings were held at private houses . . . almost every evening. . . . There was an unseen but mighty power hovering over the community. . . . Those who had long been impenitent and careless, were aroused from the torpor of years, and constrained to cry out from the depths of their aching hearts, 'What must I do to be saved?'"

Special services were scheduled in the church for three days in succession. At the close of the service each day, those anxious about their souls were invited to meet in the consistory chamber for religious conversation. The revival lasted all summer. Young people met together in private places for prayer. Hardened skeptics called on the Lord. Farmers left their plows and went to church. In his old age, a lawyer who had participated in this particular revival as a young man described it: "The Lord came down in his glory, and affixed his seal to the labors of his servant [the Reverend Dr. Labagh]. While that merciful visitation was not ascribable, perhaps, to any specific and direct ministrations of the pastor, still, his wisdom and vigilance so guarded the use of the means of grace, as to attract the Saviour when he was passing that way." Most important, this revival inaugurated a new era in the Harlingen Church. Church membership grew and grew active. "The tone of piety was deepened." Sunday schools flourished, contributions rose, men responded to the call to consistory, and the church was renewed, enlarged, and strengthened on every level.

The Great Revival of 1837 in New Brunswick, which even diehard Ultras like the Reverend Dr. Samuel B. How agreed was genuine, actually began in the Baptist Church in that city in the autumn of 1836, again with human agency in the form of two students from Hamilton Seminary, though not with any flashy New Measures. "A cheering work of Grace is in progress," S.L.B. Baldwin reported in the spring of 1837, "and 60 persons were admitted into the Baptist Church on Sunday. The Presbyterians have also caught the holy fire."[4] (See figure 5.)

In its ecumenicity, this revival was typical of the era. David D. Demarest, a student that year, recalled that all the churches in New Brunswick participated in it, and all were opened for services every evening of the week, "the pastors [not any itinerant evangelists] keeping charge of the services and themselves preaching . . . and setting forth the nature of guilt and of sin, need of pardon, the inability of the sinner, the need of renewal of the spirit." Inquiry meetings were held for those interested in instruction, but "there was no call to rise for prayers, no resort to the anxious seat, no counting of converts, no distributing of [intention] cards, no acceptance of a wish to be a Christian as evidence of conversion. The aim was to convict of sin and to create a sense of the need of the Savior and to expose all subterfuges and bring the sinner to Christ as his only hope and refuge. There were many converts and very few failed to remain steadfast through life"—again, the certain mark of a genuine revival.[5]

Hundreds were "affected with a religious awe" when the Great Revival peaked. "Religious meetings were thronged" in May 1837. "Sabbath days were seasons of refreshing, conversions were multiplied, and the entire population was moved by the Spirit of God." The Reverend Dr. Richard H. Steele, a successor to How in the same pulpit a generation later, emphasized that in that revival "no new measures or novel doctrines were resorted to in order to feed a mere excitement." Only the ordinary and established means of grace were employed, and religious meetings were held only for prayer and preaching. "There was no disorder, no confusion, no wild, misguided zeal. . . . All was serious, solemn, calm, devout, and at times deeply affecting."[6]

Even forty years later, the Great Revival of 1837 was minutely remembered: it had been, to one eyewitness, the greatest outpouring of the Holy Spirit on New Jersey since the days of George Whitefield. "Many hundreds of souls were born again." The churches were greatly strengthened and enlarged by it, more than by any other revival in the history of the state, he went on. There were prayer meetings every morning at 5:00 A.M. and preaching every night of the week in all the churches of the community. The power of holy, inspiring song "went up like the sound of many waters." Prayer was offered everywhere: "in unusual places—in workshops, in garrets, in every shady place or grove was heard the supplicating cry for pardon, and thanksgiving for the sweet joy of sins forgiven. Seeking Christ appeared to be the whole business of the people; little else was talked

...LY FREDONIAN.

NEW-BRUNSWICK

JOHN F. BABCOCK, } EDITOR AND PROPRIETOR.

MONDAY, JULY 11, 1881.

## THE TORNADO OF 1835.

### DESTRUCTION OF LIFE AND PROPERTY IN NEW-BRUNSWICK.

It is very common for our older citizens to refer to the Tornado which swept through this City on the 19th day of June, 1835—over forty-six years ago—and to the great destruction of life and property in the then comparatively small town. Many marvelous stories of wonderful escapes, etc., have been frequently related to us, which the lapse of time have rendered impossible to verify or contradict. A few days since LEWIS STOUT, Esq., brought to our office a well-preserved copy of an EXTRA FREDONIAN, which was published on Wednesday, June 24, 1835, on the fifth day after the disaster—a fact, by the way, which fully illustrates the general character of newspaper enterprise in those days, when the people were satisfied with weeks and days, instead of hours, in obtaining news of important events, local and otherwise. This EXTRA FREDONIAN contained a very full account of the disaster, which we copy in full for the information of the readers of the FREDONIAN of this day. No doubt our readers will read it with interest, preserve it carefully, and forty-five or fifty years hence some one will present it to the then Editor of the FREDONIAN to be again copied in its columns, and so hand it down to future generations. The story of the disaster reads as follows :

#### AWFUL VISITATION.

"The Lord hath his way in the whirlwind and in the storm, and the clouds are as the dust of his feet."

FRIDAY, the 19th day of June, 1835, is a day long to be remembered in this devoted city, for a heart-rending scene of desolation and mourning. At about 5 o'clock in the afternoon of that day, we were visited by one of the most terrific and destructive tornadoes ever experienced on this continent, and rarely equalled any where. It approached the city from the North West, and bore the appearance of an immense conical volume of black smoke, filled with flakes of fire from some burning building, and greatly agitated by the air. The universal impression, in the lower part of the city, was, that the upper part was on fire. Nearly the whole population, consequently, were in motion—those that were in a condition to do service making their way towards the apparent scene of conflagration, and the remainder anxious to ascertain where such a raging fire was. In a few minutes, the fearful truth was manifested, that an irresistible whirlwind was bearing away houses and barns and trees, and hurling them high into the air, producing an awfully sublime spectacle, and a scene of confusion and desolation, which it would be in vain to attempt to describe. From mere instinct—reasoning was out of the question—every one sought a shelter; but providentially many did not reach the buildings, which a moment afterwards were

heaps of ruins, and would have crushed them in the fall. Among those, however, who did reach what they vainly hoped was a place of security, were Judge Booraem, Clerk of Middlesex, and his son Henry, aged 23, who, with two or three other gentlemen, left the Clerk's Office on the first alarm of fire. When they reached George-street, they were apprised that it was a tornado, and not a fire, which they had to encounter, and they separated—Judge Booraem and his son, and one other, taking a southern direction to escape the storm, and the others a northern. Judge B. and his son got in front of the store of Mr. Little, on the corner of George and Schureman streets, which was crushed in an instant afterwards, seriously hurting Judge B. and mortally wounding his son Henry. The latter was borne home senseless, and died in about four hours. The former is doing well. Near the same place, and probably by the fall of the same building, a son of N. D. Baird was killed on the spot, the upper part of his head being literally taken off. Farther down town, in Schureman-street, a widow lady of the name of Van Arsdalen, was killed in the street by the falling timber. These are the only deaths we have heard of, though a great many were more or less hurt.

Mrs. Harrison's son, a small boy, badly wounded.

A child of Jeptha Cheesman dangerously hurt.

Miss Anna Booraem, from New-York, dangerously hurt.

Two sons, small boys, of Henry Frazee, considerably injured.

Dr. Van Deursen's son, small boy, slightly injured.

James Bishop, Jr., slightly hurt.

A child of Otis D. Stowart had his arm broken.

Nicholas Wyckoff dangerously hurt.

Lewis Drake badly injured.

Henry Cook seriously hurt.

Two sons of J. C. Ackerman, small boys, one seriously injured, the other slightly.

Richard Van Arsdallen slightly hurt.

Levi Lewis much bruised.

Two men in the employ of Richard Voorhees, badly wounded.

We have also the story of a lad 10 or 12 years old, the son of Wm. O. Dunham, being taken up from his father's door at the corner of George and New streets, and carried over the tops of trees and houses at least a quarter of a mile, and landed, with only a slight bruise, on the edge of the river! We believe this marvellous story has no other foundation, than that the boy was impelled by the wind to run down the street towards the river, and was finally thrown down on the wharf. It is beyond our faith to suppose that he could be whirled through the air that distance and come down not only alive, but almost unhurt ! Parts of houses and other articles known to have been thrown that distance were shivered to atoms.

There are doubtless others who were more or less injured, whose names we have not heard.

Notwithstanding the deaths thus produced, it may still be considered a providential circumstance that the alarm of fire was given—as several workshops and other buildings were crushed to atoms, which, but for the alarm, would have been filled with inmates, who could hardly have escaped death.

The tornado occupied a width varying from one hundred to two hundred yards, now contracting and then expanding, and had an undulating as well as whirling motion, striking the earth with great force, and tearing up the largest and most firmly rooted trees, or twisting them off, and then rebounding, taking off the roofs and upper stories of the strongest buildings, and passing over here and there one with scarcely any damage. Its course was southeast to the head of Schureman-street, and east down that street to the river, crossing the river, uprooting or scathing every tree and shrub that it touched, and pursuing its way about the same direction to the village of Piscataway, two miles distant, injuring

---

FIGURE 5. The Great Revival in New Brunswick in 1837 was fueled in part by the Great Tornado of 1835, thought by many to have been an "awful visitation" of the Lord's for their sinful ways. *Courtesy Special Collections and University Archives, Rutgers University Libraries.*

of. . . . If ever there was a genuine work of grace since the day of Pentecost, this was one."[7]

The distinction between genuine revivals and spurious revivals became central to Reformed thinking. The Reverend How had been at the center of the 1837 revival in New Brunswick. But ten years later, when another revival occurred in that town, he wrote to a former parishioner that "there has been such a spirit abroad in many of the churches, such a fondness for the new measures, . . . so many spurious revivals, . . . [and] such a fondness for our new doctrines, that I have kept myself very much at home." The kind of "spurious" revival from which How recoiled was the Finney type, scheduled in advance, advertised and promoted, and foreseen and managed with quasi-scientific precision from the personal invitation on to the anxious bench to the card of intention.[8]

The Reformed minister and professor of pastoral theology at New Brunswick, James Spencer Cannon, writing on the role and duties of the Reformed minister, declared in 1853 that it was the minister's obvious duty to use every proper means at his disposal to bring about a revival when he noticed a decline in religion. But the operative word was "proper," and this involved "public and faithful preaching of the Word," collecting the pious into "praying societies," and reading such works as Baxter's *Call to the Unconverted.* It did not involve exciting hoopla.

As for protracted meetings, their acceptability depended, Cannon cautioned, on how they were conducted. Some protracted meetings—such as those "at which regular agents in creating certain excitements are employed—are fraught with great evils, exhibit the art of man in place of the power of the Holy Spirit; substitute slavish fear for faith, and leave the awakened like cakes half turned; call women to pray publicly, and make the boldest hypocrites the prominent men in the Church."[9]

Reformed clergymen lamented the spurious revival on numerous grounds, a primary one being that its desired effects were often short lived. "The Reformed Dutch Church is no foe to revivals," the Reverend David D. Demarest wrote in 1856. "She has often experienced days of power, but at the same time she has ever guarded against spurious excitements. . . . A certain form of preaching, with multiplied [that is, protracted] meetings, and nicely-adapted machinery, is certain to accomplish the work, and turn out converts by scores. [But] it is . . . sad to witness the desolating effects of it on the Church. . . . How different the work, where God's living truth is the basis, and the outpoured Spirit is the agent, and many feel the arrow from the Divine quiver, and retire to weep in secret places, and enter into deliberate and solemn covenant with God! These are the seasons to be wished and prayed for, seasons of God's visits to His heritage, owning and blessing His appointed means of grace."[10]

In Hudson, New York, where he served a Reformed Church during the years 1852–1865, Demarest took a strong stand against what he deemed dangerous measures in promoting and carrying on revivals. The local Methodists had procured an evangelist "who understood his business well, and under whose peculiar and skillful methods, large congregations and large numbers of converts were obtained." But when some of Demarest's congregation became uneasy at the prospect of losing ground to the Methodists and suggested that the Reformed Church also sponsor a revival, "open its doors nightly to hold our own people," Demarest refused. He could not compete, he wrote, with one who was master of an art of which he knew nothing. "I would only have an audience of a few standbyes while those who enjoyed the sort of thing that they got at the Methodist Church would continue to go there. All we would gain would be that we would be a laughing stock, labelled old fogies, impotently trying to stem a rushing tide." The Methodists got four hundred converts, but only a very small number of them "reported for membership after the probation of six months was ended." Demarest, who had been a student in New Brunswick during the Great Revival there in 1837, had the satisfaction of "losing nothing but gaining much" in Hudson's spurious revival.[11]

The spurious revival, in the form of the protracted camp meeting held out of doors and lasting for days or even a week, was deplored as much for its carnival atmosphere as for its transitory results. As one observer put it in 1845, with hundreds and thousands of all ages, sexes, and characters dwelling in the woods together, night and day, for a whole week, "It is plainly impossible that the duties, restraints, proprieties, and delicacies of ordinary society should be observed." Such meetings furnished opportunities for the "vile" to come from the gambling dens and grog shops and houses of infamy in the city to practice their arts on the unwary. The innocent come only to meet the Lord, he wrote, but meet the tempter instead and in too many cases return home corrupted and disgraced. Even revival meetings held in churches sometimes became disordered with folly and fanaticism, but much worse, in this writer's view, were the tent meeting and the "ring" (the area in front of the platform where leaders sang hymns and began to pray) and the "uproar more distracting than the orgies of a heathen divinity."[12] (See figure 6.)

This was the "dry bones rising" problem. Normal order and control were challenged and decorum thrown to the winds. And when the bones belonged to blacks, an even dimmer view was taken of the activities, especially when whole congregations deserted their churches "to go and see the sights." In a letter to the *Intelligencer* headlined "Colored Camp Meeting at Tarrytown," a Reformed layman, signing himself "A.B.," described

FIGURE 6. Setting up police headquarters on camp-meeting grounds was meant to forestall unruliness and crime. *Picture Collection, The Branch Libraries, The New York Public Library.*

such an encampment at Beekman Woods, a square-mile grove of oaks, maples, and hickories forming a canopy over sixty or seventy "snowy white" tents, a preacher's platform, and seats for as many as three thousand. Here, among their cooking fires, groups of men and women gathered in close and animated conversation or worship. A chorus of a hundred voices sang, the infirm and aged looked on from their tents, youth strolled around or wandered off into the woods. In front of the platform was the "ring." Before long, A.B. was startled to hear the "shrieks and shouts of some forty or fifty shrill and penetrating voices . . . [all] speaking at once . . . [shouting] 'Amen,' 'glory,' 'Hosannah,' 'bless God,' 'Jesus,' . . . mingled in one loud yell. . . . There was leaping, and dancing, and clapping of hands, and frightful contortions of body and limbs."

In the center of this "wild and frenzied multitude," A.B. witnessed females, prostrate, rolling upon the ground. "One large, lusty creature, was floundering like a huge porpoise. . . . Others were lying . . . insensible, some in one position, some in another." This went on for hours, excitement increasing as the hour for preaching approached. When it did, through the preacher's whole discourse "he was cheered with the loud shouts of those within the ring [whom] . . . he raised to such a fury of excitement that they all sprung onto their feet, and danced, and jumped, and whirled, and screamed, and clapped, as if pandemonium itself had been on earth." A.B. left the meeting asking himself what such exhibitions had to do with the holy name of religion.[13]

No wonder A.B. found this camp meeting shocking. Only a few years earlier, the General Synod's idea of a revival had been a decorous time set apart—whenever religion was in a low and declining state—prior to the periodic administration of the Lord's Supper, for special humiliation and prayer, after which it could be hoped that faithful preaching would produce an outpouring of the Holy Spirit upon the congregation. But the General Synod's notions of revivals were evolving. By 1860 it had recognized the effectiveness of the modern, scheduled, managed revival to the extent that it even left the subject of uniting with other denominations in them to the judgment of individual ministers and consistories, though care should be taken, it cautioned, "that our doctrinal standards and our usages be not impaired."[14]

*E*ven if the Reformed Church was able to come to terms with nineteenth-century revivalism, in almost every other area where Reformed progressives seemed to move away from Dort, they met the stone wall of Ultra resistance, and the sticking point was always the same: the impairment of Reformed doctrinal standards and usages, and the neglect of Rutgers, the seminary, the Reformed Dutch Church Missionary Society, and the Heidelberg Catechism for institutions with an ecumenical allure. "Let the Church know this, and mark it distinctly," the Ultras in charge of the *Magazine* put it in 1828, "We do favour all the charities of the day. We do embark heartily in the grand and holy [missionary] enterprise, at home and abroad. But we do it in our own cautious prudent Dutch way. We are fostering and sustaining, first of all, our own cause, our own home affairs. . . . Those men who oppose us,—who oppose the *Magazine*, who go fully and headlong into the Eastern policy, and mingle with the Hopkinsian and Independent interests . . . [they] overlook and starve their own Institutions, . . . neglect the Theological Seminary, and the Missionary Society of the Reformed Dutch Church . . . while they pour out their riches in the lap of the Theologians of the East."[15]

The anxiety aroused by the prospect of weakening the ancient ties to Dort can be traced in a number of controversies in the nineteenth century in which the more conservative Dutch tended to insist on Dort—in the process heightening the image of the denomination as different, narrow, foreign. One of the areas most fraught with dissension was whether the Reformed Church should cooperate with other denominations in the American Sunday School Union, or whether it should maintain control over the curriculum—that is, over the means of transmitting the doctrines of Dort— by way of an auxiliary union comprising solely Sunday schools of Reformed Dutch congregations. On the battleground of the Sunday school, progressives and conservatives met head on.

Sunday schools had been widely resisted at their inception as encroaching on clerical and parental prerogatives. The first official reference to them in the Acts and Proceedings of the General Synod of the Reformed Dutch Church does not occur until 1824, a generation after their appearance within the denomination. Now enthusiastically endorsing them as mighty instruments for the advancement of the Kingdom, progressives within the General Synod exhorted ministers and churches to organize schools in their own congregations and to involve themselves with the newly formed American Sunday School Union.

It was the policy of the ASSU that all the main evangelical denominations be represented on its Board of Directors, and that all members of the board agree on all of the tracts and books it published. By 1830 the ASSU had issued over six million copies of Sunday school works, two hundred bound volumes for libraries, a teachers' magazine, and two other periodicals. Ministers in all the evangelical denominations "cheerfully contributed some of their best work" to its publications, and many of these works "delighted readers" for more than a generation.[16] ASSU publications such as *The American Sunday-School Magazine, The Infant Magazine, The Youth's Friend, The Sunday-School Journal, The Youth's Penny Gazette, The Sunday-School Banner, The Sunday-School Gazette,* and *The Child's World* were all were regularly excerpted in the *Christian Intelligencer.*

As noted in chapter 2, within six years of the formation of the ASSU, six thousand schools belonged to it, with sixty thousand teachers and four hundred thousand students. In 1833 alone, 2,607 teachers and 6,121 scholars professed Christ. By 1835, the Sunday school was so popular with once-skeptical parents that the Reformed minister Isaac Ferris lamented that though "great things have been accomplished by it, . . . still greater would it accomplish, were it not that it has been left to work alone, and been made the substitute for parental instruction."[17]

Within the Reformed Church, enthusiasm for Sunday schools was strong by this time, but support for participation in the American Sunday School Union was divided along familiar conservative/progressive lines. Shortly after the formation of the union in 1824, two factions arose in the Dutch Church—one supporting participation in the union and endorsing the literature published by it, and the other cautioning against the threat these represented to the "purity" of Reformed doctrine. "To eulogize Sunday schools," wrote the Reformed minister Abraham Messler, "would be something like praising the sun. . . . It is surprising that they were not thought of sooner." Yet, he warned, it was important that the officers of the church carefully supervise these "nurseries of piety" and not leave them to lay teachers, well-meaning parents, and decision makers, however pious, of other denominations.[18] The Ultras were not inclined to sacrifice the doctrine as formulated at Dort to the evangelical ideal of ecumenical endeavor.

To those in their Reformed Zion who insisted on the "good old way," newfangled ideas of church unity, unions of interdenominational Sunday schools, and associations of denominations whose goal was to publish a generic body of pious literature for children were not acceptable. The voice of this party was loud and clear: Dort would inevitably be diminished by engaging in such cooperative activities. These men, clergy and laity alike, demanded that the Reformed Church use only its own publications, especially in its Sabbath schools. "Though we may be called *Ultras,* and *Bigots,* because we are not . . . prepared to abandon our Catechisms," one clergyman wrote in 1830, "if it be *Ultraism* and *Bigotry,* to be attached to the Church of our Fathers, and to instruct our children in a knowledge of those doctrines . . . we rejoice to bear these epithets."[19]

In 1828, powerful Ultras set up an independent society calling itself the Sabbath School Union of the Reformed Dutch Church, its purpose "to bring the Sabbath Schools more immediately under the supervision & direction of the officers of the churches . . . and to influence the children . . . to commit to memory the catechism approved by our own church." This group, which included some of the most prominent members of the clergy, agitated for twelve years until the General Synod finally agreed to establish a Board of Managers to support and oversee its efforts—which included publishing its own curriculum material, and its own hymn book, spelling book, and primer.[20]

By 1848, nearly every Reformed Dutch Church had a Sabbath school, and ten thousand children were under the care of this Board of Managers. "We [in the Reformed Dutch Church] are no bigots—no exclusives; we say God speed to all evangelical Christians," the Reverend Isaac Ferris wrote that year. "We extend the right hand of fellowship to all the branches of the great Presbyterian family . . . for we belong to them . . . —yet we have our preferences for our own goodly heritage."[21] Many, including the Reverend James Romeyn, felt the same way: "We assert the right . . . to guard . . . and to cultivate this seedplot . . . of the Church's hope of perpetuation and enlargement. . . . Strangers have no business in our heritage, save to admire [and to assist . . . but as to supervising our institutions], 'show us your commission!' "[22]

Interestingly, however, six years later (1854), when there were 434 Sunday schools in the denomination, only 167 of these had affiliated with the Synod's board, suggesting that many member churches questioned the wisdom of a separatist policy and preferred the ecumenical approach. The board itself was obliged to wonder whether to disband and relinquish the whole field to the American Sunday School Union, or to take measures to render itself more efficient. But the conservative element won the day. As the board put it, "It is the duty of the Church to feed her own lambs. The American Sunday School Union is doing a grand work, and the country needs it, but it is anomalous for our own schools to report to it. . . . Synod must take action to give efficiency to our own Board."[23]

The conservatives could not win the war, however, for the rich culture that was growing up around the Sabbath school proved to be more appealing than the narrower, parochial attractions of Dort. This culture involved on the one hand religious education, character building, and citizen shaping—and on the other the social interaction of like-minded people on an unprecedented scale in the schools' elaborate annual anniversary commemorations, gargantuan-sized picnics, Fourth of July and Christmas celebrations, and musical evenings and "entertainments."

Saving children's souls was always the prime goal of the Sunday school, but forming a common moral culture that all children could relate to, and relate to one another through, was not far behind. A child "civilized by the discipline of a Sabbath School, with its memory stored with the Bible, . . . and neat and cleanly in its person becomes doubly interesting to its parents and doubly useful. . . . It can read, it has stores of knowledge, it has acquired good manners . . . , it is fitter for trade or for servitude; . . . it is the very opposite of that uncouth, uncivilized barbarian that it was when it . . . first felt a teacher's care."[24] (See figure 7.)

Although some Sabbath schools in the Reformed Church, as in other evangelical churches, limited membership to their own denomination, in others students and teachers mixed ecumenically within the school as well as at social events. Under the conceptual umbrella of the wider Sunday school, in these schools, children of recent immigrants and children of old-time settlers, children of the rich, the middling, and the poor, and urban children and rural children, were gathered, as it were, into one nursery of piety, one commodious cradle of good character, rocking toward heaven. At least that was the ideal. As the decades passed, however, it was clear that it was not the reality, as we shall see in chapter 7.

Their ecumenicity was also part of the appeal of the social activities of the schools, particularly the annual Sunday school picnic, usually held at the end of the summer. On August 29, 1860, most of rural Rockland County, it seemed, "was in commotion," all going to the Sunday school picnic at Tallman's Station, about fourteen miles west of Piermont on the New York and Erie Railroad. The cars, one participant wrote, were "loaded with human beings, cars so full, so crowded, such squeezing, such hanging on . . . It reminded me of a swarm of bees on an apple-tree." At Spring Valley, a happy throng met the train. "You ought to have been there to see the unloading of the precious freight. Did you ever see [a picture of] Noah's ark, with its inmates leaving? We were all of the two-legged tribe, yet I think the scampering must have been somewhat similar." A multitude of two thousand assembled, he added, and "it was a lovely sight to gaze upon the unity that prevailed. A Methodist presided, a Baptist prayed, a Lutheran, a Dutch Reformed, and a Methodist addressed the audience, and spoke of the benefits of Sabbath-school instruction. . . . Although a Dutchman [myself], and not used to shouting in meeting, I felt like making the woods resound with a hearty 'God-speed the day when the walls [between denominations] shall lie low in the dust.'"[25]

*A* number of institutions peculiar to the evangelical era, no longer remembered but immensely popular in the religious culture of the nineteenth century, had an effect in loosening the ties that kept the Dutch confined inside their own culture: of these the annual Visitations in the churches, the annual Anniversaries, and singing schools were the most effective.

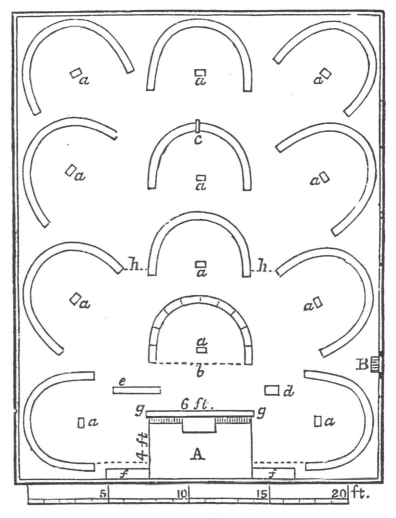

A. Superintendent's desk.   B. Door.

*a.* Teacher's seat with desk.   *d.* The stove.   *e.* Bench for new pupils.   *ff.* Book cases.   *gg.* Seats for visiters. *hh.* Passages eighteen inches wide.

Benches ten inches wide, and made into two parts, united with a hinge as at *c.* They will seat ten pupils.

The seats should average twelve inches from the floor.

FIGURE 7. Such manuals as *Teacher Taught. An Humble Attempt to Make the Path of the Sunday-School Teacher Straight and Plain* attempted to leave no question of procedures or processes unanswered. This manual was published by the American Sunday School Union. *Courtesy Gardner A. Sage Library, New Brunswick Theological Seminary.*

The Visitations, which took place each year in January, may be likened to a marathon revival whose main purpose was to "wake up and warm the affections of the Christian's heart," to kindle zeal in his breast, to edify the whole church. They were intended to function as a sacred festival, such as those that attracted the faithful to Jerusalem. For decades, they were a highlight of the church year.

In the classis to which the New York Reformed churches belonged, this widely publicized and well-attended annual happening constituted a rigorous schedule of church services, twice every weekday for three consecutive weeks in January, at 3:00 in the afternoon and again at 7:00 in the evening. In every Reformed Dutch church in the city during this period, revolving teams of three ministers visited one another's churches, where great crowds came out to hear them preach. Never, wrote the *Intelligencer* in 1840, "has a greater appearance of solemnity been witnessed."[26] A second purpose of the Visitations was to bring those who labored in the Lord's vineyard into close fellowship with one another and to render them more intimately acquainted with the spiritual condition of one another's flocks as they united in supplication for the welfare of the whole church.[27]

For the Reformed Dutch Church, a third purpose was to emphasize the Reformedness of the church, by focusing on its unique doctrinal heritage. But because other denominations held their Visitations at the same time, the event also had a significant unifying effect, integrating Protestants of many different confessions in the knowledge of their common interests. At the same time, it emphasized their American origins, for the Visitations were one of the innovations that separated the churches in America from their Old World origins and customs. When Dutch Calvinist seceders from the Reformed Church in the Netherlands arrived in New York in 1846, they found their American counterparts to be very different from themselves, and one of the ways they were different was that they had begun to adopt such novelties of American revival culture as the Visitations.[28]

Public demonstrations of piety known as the Anniversaries, also unique to nineteenth-century evangelical culture, took off in a burst of energy with the advent of settled weather. The month of May was "Anniversary Week." Beginning in the early 1820s, Anniversary Week, modeled on British precedent, grew up around the annual meeting in New York City of the American Bible Society and came to involve the annual meetings of scores of evangelical societies and associations—and eventually the national conventions of these organizations in what has been likened to a kind of evangelical convention circuit. Like the classical Visitations in January, the annual Anniversaries in May were for fifty years an integral and much beloved part of the era's religious culture. Their eventual demise was long and loudly lamented.

By 1834 in New York, this evangelical convention circuit was operating at full tilt, its meetings attended by hundreds of clergy and many thousands of laymen who poured into the city from outlying towns and counties in every direction.[29] In lower Manhattan, in the Chatham Street Chapel (a theater converted to a sanctuary, where Charles G. Finney was installed as minister in 1832), and later, when a larger venue was needed, in the Broadway Tabernacle, the "ablest men in the land . . . sat together on a common platform" and heard one after another of their colleagues' reports on the state of the scores of do-gooding organizations they represented. The May meetings were looked forward to as a "great reunion of all who spent their time and energies in the cause of the Maker," and as "men of thrilling eloquence" reported on their societies' achievements during the past year, "united and sympathetic audience[s were moved] to tears," the *Intelligencer* reported in 1860.[30]

The frenetic activities of Anniversary Week ran clergymen ragged. In May 1853, the Reverend Paul D. Van Cleef, senior minister of the Second Reformed Church of Jersey City, wrote in his diary that on May 9 he officiated at the anniversary of the Jersey City Sabbath School Association, which was attended by over a thousand children from three Reformed Dutch, two Presbyterian, the Baptist, and the Methodist Sunday schools in that city. That evening, he attended the Anniversary of the Seamen's Friends Society, and over the course of the week he was present at the Anniversaries of the American and Foreign Christian Missionary Society, the American Tract Society, the American Bible Society, the American Board of Commissioners of Foreign Missions, and the Sabbath School Board of the Reformed Dutch Church. In between he attended numerous prayer meetings and lectures, hurrying by ferry back to Jersey City to officiate at a funeral and to attend his consistory's annual meeting, in addition to fitting in his usual pastoral calls. An enterprising physician placed an ad in the *Intelligencer* apprising overextended ministers like Van Cleef "Afflicted by Debility and Bronchitis" that, during the Anniversaries, they might consult him for relief. "By means of a body-brace and appropriate directions," they would usually be able to continue their labor with increased vigor and comfort," he claimed.[31]

The practice of housing out-of-town clergy and laymen in private homes during Anniversary Week took place on a massive scale all over the city. In 1835, an English clergyman estimated that there must have been from three hundred to four hundred ministers in New York for the meetings, "but I believe none were necessitated to sojourn at hotel or lodging house." A central committee organized the arrangements and the logistics. At first, Dodd's Bookstore in the Old Brick Chapel served as headquarters. Later, the vestibule of the Broadway Tabernacle became the "clerical exchange"—the meeting place where old friends and colleagues greeted one another, exchanged news and gossip, and arranged their schedules and housing. Upon registration, each attendee was assigned a family to lodge with while in the city, and handed a map and a program of events. "The ancient hospitality of the Dutch remained, and few came to New-York who were not made welcome to a home," the *Intelligencer* reported. "Meetings were crowded. Society succeeded to society in the Tabernacle, and crowded houses attended almost every speaker."[32] Host families kept open house every evening during the week, allowing their temporary boarders to visit with one another long after the daytime activities were concluded.

The Broadway Tabernacle, an enormous round, domed structure on Worth Street east of Broadway, was the "centre of emotion and interest." Because of its central location, those who made up the audiences during the Protestant Holy Week, as it was called, even those who straggled in from the country, could find it without difficulty. For businessmen, too, its downtown location was convenient, and many wandered in during the day to spend an hour or two listening to the speakers on the spacious rostrum. Ample galleries circling the rostrum accommodated thousands of hearers.[33] (See figure 8.)

In 1850, when the custom of Anniversary Week was at its peak, twenty-six different societies held their national conventions or annual meetings during the second and third weeks of May. For those unable to attend, the religious press reported the proceedings at length, reproducing verbatim the lengthy annual reports of the various societies, so that those at home could partake of the excitement and follow the progress of the evangelical agendas so dear to their hearts. In an age when Protestants of every denomination shared the common goal of saving the world from sin and remaking society in the image of the Kingdom of Heaven on earth, thrilling indeed were personal witnesses of progress. For many within the Reformed Church, a denomination that still felt its outsider status, participation in the Anniversaries was a unifying and integrating experience that allowed them to enter upon a broad river of harmonious fellow feeling with their counterparts in other denominations—a de-ethnicizing experience, in short, that rendered labels and sectarian distinctions at least momentarily superfluous.

The singing school was a third institution popular with evangelicals that had a similar effect. Calvinists were ambivalent about church music, which they associated with Roman Catholicism. Charles Deshler, born in

FIGURE 8. Thousands of evangelicals thronged lower Manhattan during Anniversary Week every year. The Broadway Tabernacle, site of their main meetings, was erected for Charles Grandison Finney in 1836, and to his specifications, but he preached in it for only one year. © *Collection of The New-York Historical Society.*

1819, describing New Brunswick in his boyhood in the 1820s and 1830s, remembered that the Dutch Church had neither choir nor organ. A precentor, "who, when the hymn or psalm was given out, stood tuning-fork in hand on the low platform at the base of the pulpit steps, and after first sounding the little instrument, held it to his ear, 'took the pitch,' and led off the singing, which was heartily joined in by the congregation."[34] Deshler, as an Episcopalian child in Dutch New Brunswick, remembered being "repeatedly twitted by grown men" of the Reformed faith with the fact that the organ, the cross on the pulpit, the celebration of Christmas and Easter, and the dressing up of the church at those seasons were all alike 'rags of popery.'" In those days, only the "English church" had an organ.[35]

Attitudes toward church music began to change around 1830, and singing schools, "generally conducted by some peripatetic teacher from New York or Yankee-land," came into fashion as a mean of fostering and refining musical taste and of teaching congregations to read musical notation. At first, the Reformed Church frowned on singing schools, which usually led to the acquisition of an organ, not only because of the ancient association of organs with Roman Catholicism but because of the social context singing schools offered for an "infinite deal . . . of sparking, court- ing, flirting, and other by-play." Some conceded they were acceptable when, like revivals, they were managed correctly, but the editors of the *Christian Intelligencer* criticized them when they first emerged, convinced that they are "always unfavourable to the progress of vital piety."[36]

Not all singing schools were held on church property, and no doubt in these schools the music sung was more secular than religious. In the heavily Dutch Raritan Valley, country taverns were the destination of par- ties of young people in winter when singing schools, "one of the chief win- ter pleasures," were "got up" by young men and their allies, tavern keepers in the countryside:

> When there was good sleighing in winter these schools abound- ed . . . [and] Who, that has ever participated in these exhilarating rides [by sleigh] to the country singing schools, can ever forget them! First, there was the delicious excitement of preparation for them: the choice of fleet and stylish two and four horse team[s]; . . . the tucking in of the fair occupants; the arrangement of conge- nial . . . partners; the handing in of heated bricks . . . and small round cobblestones . . . to keep the hands warm; and then the rapid trot of the horses, the swift swing of the sleigh, the music of the bells . . . as they sped over the snow . . . the lights of the town sunk down in the distance and the occasional twinkle of some lighted farmhouse window sparkled into view; . . . and the merry unload- ing at the warm and cosy place of rendezvous.[37]

So popular were singing schools that by 1840 it was clear to the Re- formed clergy that they would have to come into tune, literally, with the times. The denomination's fuddy-duddy attitude toward the schools and in fact toward music itself, even church music, was emphasizing the old- fashioned image it needed to shed if it was to grow. Handily, the clergy rationalized by finding authority in the Bible for musical tutelage. "Attended singing school," wrote Paul Van Cleef. "Dr. How [of the First Reformed, New Brunswick] addressed the school on the importance of being able to excel in sacred music," the rationale being that singing "will be the em- ployment of saints in heaven to all Eternity." In the Somerville, New Jer- sey, Reformed Church, the Reverend Mr. Chambers also preached on the importance of sacred music, and to his sermon S.L.B. Baldwin assigned his highest accolade: "superbly excellent! sublimely grand!" Mr. Chambers "quoted several passages from the Old and New Testaments to prove the great importance of vocal and instrumental music in Divine worship," Baldwin added.[38]

By the 1850s, singing schools had proved to be too much of a good thing, for they had led to church choirs so vigorous that one correspondent to the *Intelligencer* proclaimed them a public nuisance. "Our choir lately has caught the choir disease," he wrote, "and are endeavoring to monopolize that part of the service and to 'make a show of themselves.'" The choir was, according to this writer, not remarkable for its voices, sang so that only about once in three months could one make out the words, started singing before the service, took up too much of the pastor's allotted time, introduced new tunes, sang when the congregation should be singing, and generally robbed the congregation of the "Christian's privilege of praising God with songs and psalms."[39]

He was not alone in his displeasure. "The fact is, some Church music is a combination of discordant sounds, uttered with vigor so vociferous that . . . the only thing that commends it is its heartiness," lamented another correspondent who longed for the old days, when the precentor stood in front and sang and the people followed. The Reverend Thomas De Witt Talmage also deplored the choir as an institution, because it had preempted the people's role. Today, he wrote, in 1875, the congregation barely knows any of the tunes the choir sings—which is to the choir's liking, he added, "for there is nothing more annoying to the choir than to have some new-born soul break out in song just as they are drawing a note out to an exquisite fineness. . . . What right have people to sing who know nothing about rhythmics, melodics, dynamics?" he asked sarcastically.[40]

The solution was: more singing schools. Every church or group of churches should have a permanent singing school led by a competent instructor, advised another letter writer, and the "whole land would soon resound with . . . melodious and harmonious heavings" besides which the "sentimental warblings of the modern and fashionable quartette" would pale. "The attempts to sing by congregations where not one in fifty knows the tune are a burlesque," he added, recommending the Fulton Street Reformed Dutch Church, "where they have free and open weekly singing meetings, [and] hundreds sing in beautiful tune."[41]

Indeed, when a true professional took hold of a church choir, the results could be highly satisfactory to clergy, choir, and congregation—and to the surrounding community. Such was the case when the Reverend Chester D. Hartranft became minister of the Second Reformed Church in New Brunswick and also Doctor of Music at Rutgers College. He at once took charge of the music of the church, created a choir, moved the organ from the rear of the church to the chancel, and built choir stalls accommodating fifty or more singers. Here he taught the best of sacred music to adults and trained the children and youth in the finest music, carols, and chorales. "In those days," one observer wrote, "family discipline was such . . . that assembly en masse for a rehearsal on Saturday afternoon was possible," and for many services, especially on Sunday evenings, the Second Reformed Church was often filled to overflowing.[42]

Within four years, Hartranft had organized a townwide choral society made up of 185 singers from all the churches in the town, and a community orchestra, which he conducted, and which attracted professional musicians from New York who reported they had never been led by a better conductor. Finally, he founded the New Brunswick Conservatory of Music, whose professors were the leading names of the day and which became for some years one of the foremost schools of music in the United States.

*B*y midcentury, the efforts of the Dutch Church to enter into the ecumenical spirit of the century had enabled it to make significant progress in shedding its foreign image. Even so, resistance to ecumenical activity was still strong, and Dutchness continued alive and well. A professor from the University of Utrecht visiting New York and New Jersey in 1850 commented that "it was a pleasure to find the old Dutch ancestral customs maintained." In fact, so "Dutchlike" were manners and material culture in New York and New Jersey that more than one traveler to the Netherlands seemed to think the cultural influence flowed eastward: "Customs . . . take deep root in Holland," one wrote, "and one sees many usages which are known in Bergen and Somerset [counties in New Jersey]. . . . Amsterdam and Rotterdam are all over like Chatham Street [in Manhattan] and South street [in Philadelphia] combined."[43]

It is ironic that the persistence of Dutchness can be accounted for in part by the very public-relations effort that had been mounted to erase the denomination's foreign image. Although church leaders intended both the denomination's *Magazine* and its successor the *Christian Intelligencer* to be instruments in the Americanization of its members, they adopted a policy of publishing extended historical discourses on the golden age of Dutch history, Dutch contributions to American political and cultural history, and the heroic struggle of the Dutch people against feudalism, Spain, England, and Roman Catholicism that had the opposite effect and that actually revealed instead the denomination's ambivalence about giving up its Dutch heritage.

William Smith's 1755 *History of New York* and a number of succeeding histories restored the all-but-forgotten Dutch role in the colonial period to public attention.[44] But the publication in 1809 of Washington Irving's popular lampoon *A History of New York* by "Diedrich Knickerbocker" distorted this role out of all recognition, leading the *Intelligencer* to attempt to set the record straight again. This was particularly important now that it was also becoming apparent that, in the emergent public school system, only the British version of America's history was being taught, the Dutch contribution suppressed.

Dutch pride had been offended by the English before. After the English takeover of New Netherland in the seventeenth century, one historian has written, "seething antagonisms born of national pride and prejudice did not ebb easily." Outrage at the English resurfaced a century later at the time of the Revolution, especially in Manhattan and in that part of the so-called neutral ground of the Revolution, the heavily Dutch Hackensack Valley. Here, sentiments were anything but neutral as the British army and its Tory sympathizers cut a savage swath, looting, burning, and foraging with special fury, forcing the local inhabitants to choose, in one historian's words, between loyalty to American principles and loyalty to the British crown. And resentment rose again in the nineteenth century as English culture became ever more dominant in America, and as the English version of America's origins became accepted wisdom. The first volume of George Bancroft's violently anti-British *History of the United States* was published in 1834 and included a chapter on New Netherland, but it did not appreciably affect in a positive manner the way Dutch contributions to American history were taught to children. "Yankee boasting . . . is disgusting to those with a proper regard for the truth of history," the *Intelligencer* fumed in 1856, reminding its readers that the English, "far from being pioneers in the cause of civil and religious liberty . . . were but poor copyists of manners, laws, and institutions" that had existed in Holland long before England dreamed of them.[45]

Washington Irving's satire, with its caricature of the typical Dutchman as a complacent, pipe-smoking "butter-box," added fuel to Dutch resentment during the entire nineteenth century. In a preface to a new and revised edition of the *History* in 1864, the author apologized for the mischief his work had wrought, all in good fun, he protested. But in 1896, nearly nine decades after its original appearance, a historian and genealogist of the Dutch, Teunis Bergen, could still recall that "my grandfather would not have [this work] in the house, and his son, my father, held to the same idea, and whenever we wished to make him mad we would get a new edition of [it] . . . and put it on the table, and it would go into the fire in five minutes, . . . because they said in a few years it will be quoted as history, and it has been . . . by the New Englanders."[46]

Dutch and Dutchophiles in the nineteenth century seem never to have wearied of trying to set the record straight, and the editors of the *Intelligencer* seem never to have lost an opportunity to report on their efforts. At a dinner given by the New England Society in 1875, one John De Vries Prout and the Reformed minister the Reverend Dirck Broek felt "patronized" by the Yankees when, during the toasts, the various Yankee speakers "with the[ir] usual ignorance of history" alluded to their forefathers' proud accomplishments in the New World. Every speaker, Prout reported, acknowledged the honest but vain attempt of the Dutch to colonize New York, Holland's little "page" in American history, and her "pluck" against foreign foes, but "a stranger would have concluded that . . . our whole country in her institutions . . . government, free worship, [and] public schools . . . had its roots in Connecticut and drew from her all she has become."[47]

When the New Englanders had finished congratulating themselves, the Reverend Mr. Broek rose to disabuse them of their misapprehensions. New York was a trading colony eleven years before the Pilgrims landed on Plymouth Rock, he reminded them. Freedom to worship God was rather the Pilgrims' freedom to prevent others from worshiping as they pleased. Dutch New York was a place of refuge for the persecuted of New England. Popular education and the American form of government derived from Holland, not New England. In Holland the poorest classes corresponded to the middle class in England. And after the exchange of New Netherland for Surinam (Guiana) in 1674, the New Amsterdam Dutch "moved to the richest regions on the Hudson, Mohawk, and Raritan rivers," where they flourished with no thanks to the English.

In informing readers of the Dutch point of view regarding America's origins, and America's debts to Dutch ideology and principles, this sort of historical reportage on the part of the *Intelligencer* was intended to heighten the laity's love for and pride in its Dutch past.[48] But in retrospect it can be seen to have had an unintended and undesired effect: it invigorated Dutchness—among Dutch Americans and would-be Dutch, or Dutchophiles, alike. In short, in reacquainting readers with what were often highly romanticized versions of Dutch history, the *Intelligencer*'s historical coverage seems to have influenced nineteenth-century Dutch Americans and those Dutchophiles sympathetic to them to "magnify" or even to "create" their Dutchness anew.

The *Intelligencer*'s ambivalence is demonstrated in editor William Craig Brownlee's saga of the fictional Hans Van Benschooten, which encouraged the Dutch to let go of the past, but at the same time clearly revealed the leadership's hesitation at abandoning Dutch roots—particularly the doctrines of Dort and the language of the forefathers.[49] For half a cen-

tury, Hans, a Hackensack Valley patriarch, had listened to the "sound doctrines of the good Reformed Church in his own native Dutch." Now, in
1826, fifty years after the Declaration of Independence, Hans finally ad-
mits that times are changing and that English must become the prevailing
language of the country. The admission grieves him: "It does oppress my
old heart to think of it: there is neither justice, nor reason in requiring such
a sacrifice from me." But finally, at the urging of his wife, Hans "looks
over the house of God crowded with the happy inhabitants of his valley;
and at the rising generation . . . and thinks of the current language of his
adopted country . . . and [even] the Domine fluently speaking that language," and his regrets gradually subside. "We are all Americans—happy
Americans," he concludes; "the language of the majority must prevail."

Still, as if to avoid alienating his conservative readers, Brownlee al-
lows Hans to continue to use Dutch at home for morning and evening
prayers and for the "earnest cravings of the divine benediction" on his
household at every meal of the day. Though his children cannot follow "every one of the divine sentences" in the chapters he reads from the Dutch
Bible twice a day, and though his own wife's Dutch is getting rusty, "they
must yield to him in this one thing: At my own fireside . . . I will continue
to pronounce . . . the sacred doctrines . . . in my own language."

Brownlee had a dual purpose in writing the saga of Hans Van
Benschooten, for besides emphasizing the benefits of literacy in English,
he could interlard it with heavy doses of Reformed thinking: the perils of
Sabbath breaking, for instance; the error of failing to imbue children's minds
at an early age with the pure doctrines of Dort; and the dangers in omitting any parts of the Heidelberg Catechism in the course of its annual recitation and explication from the pulpit. He made a connection, in short,
between Hans's linguistic dilemma and the standards of Dort, for particularly egregious in the author's mind was to omit, as some ministers were
daring to do in the 1820s, those few sections of the catechism touching
upon the subject of predestination. In linking Hans's abiding preference for
the Dutch of the Staten-Bijbel (the translation of the Bible published at the
direction of the delegates at Dort) and the theology and doctrines agreed
upon at Dort, Brownlee put his finger on the heart of the matter for the
most conservative elements in the Reformed Dutch Church in America:
Dort was in danger of being undermined. Hans was so important in the
crusade to preserve the "good old way" that Brownlee reprised him in 1837
in a work published for youth.[50]

The linguistic connection has its roots in 1619. After Dort, the proceedings of the synod were translated into Latin (1620), then Dutch, the
approved Dutch wordings of the canons and the Post-Acta were circulated

among the people, and a new translation of the Bible into Dutch—the 1637 Staten-Bijbel—was undertaken. Because they were based strictly on Holy Scripture, the words of the Canons of Dort and the new Dutch-language Bible—first the Latin words and then the Dutch words—quickly took on a sacred quality: they were hallowed, godly, inviolable. And it was because they were still considered hallowed, godly, and inviolable two hundred years later that many Reformed churchgoers continued to believe it a "profanation" to hear prayer, to pray, to hear preaching, to preach, to read Scripture, to sing Psalms, to say the creeds and confessions, to hear the Catechism "in any other language than the good old Duch [*sic*] of their Fatherland."[51] The final word on God's Word had been received at Dort and translated into Dutch, and for the orthodox it was in Dutch that the Word must go on being received.

Hans could not have said it more clearly: The "fundamental doctrines [of Dort] . . . have been drawn from the word of God, and set down with clearness, and precision in our Heidelberg, [and] are read in our Churches every day. . . . And thus . . . the whole congregation sees . . . the outlines of the system of the Gospel, in their beautiful connexion, and order, exhibited each year; and from year to year. And thus, our people have every facility given to them . . . of knowing fully all the leading doctrines of the Gospel, as they have been transmitted from our early fathers, and are exhibited in our Canons, and articles of religion."[52]

This was 1837. The Reformed Dutch Church and its people, more than two hundred years after the church's establishment in New Amsterdam, were still reluctant to let go of their Dutch heritage. Decades would pass, generations would come and go, Rutgers College and New Brunswick Seminary would inculcate in hundreds of young men a love for their religious distinctiveness and their special history in Dutchness, and pew would follow pulpit in the custom of "marrying Dutch," before the Reformed Dutch in New York and New Jersey finally relinquished that past.

# CHAPTER 5

# *Pulpit and Pew*

## A PORTRAIT

*If the Dominie's sermons sometimes appear cold and spiritless,
is it because the pews are empty?*
—*Christian Intelligencer*, May 16, 1835

*W*ho were these people, and how did they got to be the way they were? This is easier to answer for the Reformed clergy than for the Reformed laity. The way members of the clergy were—profoundly pious, powerfully motivated to save souls and reform society, striving ever to glorify God in all they did—had to do with their own family background. Whether they came to the ministry through the Reformed Dutch Church or, as hundreds did, through one of the other Reformed denominations, they invariably came to it from a deeply pious family.

Evangelical parents hopeful of promoting their children's eternal happiness encouraged their sons to enter the ministry, which in the case of the Reformed Dutch usually meant to enter first Rutgers College and then go on to New Brunswick Seminary for professional training. (Union College in Schenectady, New York, had from its formation in 1795 maintained a close relation with the denomination and within its first century furnished more ministers to it than any other undergraduate institution, with the exception of Rutgers.) A calling to the pulpit was considered a strong indication of God's saving grace, and parents whose sons heard the call and answered yes, and whose daughters married such men, rejoiced that this hopeful sign of their eternal destination was writ on their children's foreheads.

In pious families, the nineteenth-century ministry was often a family affair, a career chosen by fathers, sons, grandsons, nephews, and brothers for generations. When the Reverend George W. Bethune wrote of the Reformed clergy in 1836 that "they are a band of brethren," his metaphor could be taken literally: hundreds of Reformed clergy in the nineteenth century were related by ties of blood and marriage. There is no doubt that this marrying pattern in the clergy was one of the major factors in the ongoing self-ethnicizing process in which Dutch Americans indulged, for it set, affirmed, and reaffirmed customs and patterns widely adopted by the laity also. "Marrying Dutch" was a phrase coined in earlier centuries to describe a person of non-Dutch background marrying into the Dutch cultural community. It can be used as well to describe the habit of nineteenth-century Reformed Dutch people of marrying within the denomination.

In the eastern branch of the Reformed Church, the tradition of sons following their fathers into the ministry originated with Theodorus Jacobus Frelinghuysen (fl. 1720–1746), all of whose five sons were ordained, and with the eighteenth-century minister brothers John Henry and John Mauritius Goetschius, whose two sons and a grandson followed in their footsteps. (Frelinghuysen also had two daughters, both of whom married clergymen.) The Reverend Alexander Proudfit's son and two grandsons became ministers, as did Thomas C. Strong's brother and four of his sons, three of William J. Thompson's sons, and Adrian Zwemer's four sons. (Zwemer was an 1849 emigrant to the Midwest. A daughter became a missionary to Amoy, China.)

In 1840 there were 164 active clergymen in the Reformed Church in New York and New Jersey; in 1850, 285; and in 1860, 381, and virtually every one of them seems to have had a close relative or in-law in the profession. In the middle decades of the nineteenth century, some sixty Reformed clergymen had one close relative (son, grandson, brother, nephew, or in-law) in the ministry—or in a few cases at least one who had intended to enter it, but died before ordination or while in seminary. Another fifty or so had upwards of three close male relatives in the profession. Statistics do not reveal how many daughters and sisters of clergymen married clergymen, and they are elusive as to how many daughters, wives, and sisters of clergymen entered the mission field, but the numbers seem likely to have been of a significant order.[1]

In the Blauvelt and the Bogardus/Bogart/Bogert families, eight clergymen in each are recorded in Corwin's *Manual*; in the Demarest family fourteen clergymen are listed. Corwin did not attempt to account for cousinships in these families, but in the case of Blauvelts and Demarests, all persons of these names are known to have been related in some degree as members of the same large families that had settled in New Netherland in the seventeenth century.

In the Romeyn family, the clergymen brothers Thomas, Sr., and Dirck had a total of six sons and two grandsons in the ministry. Two sons of a daughter of Thomas entered the pulpit—James R. Berry and Philip Berry— as did Francis N. Zabriskie, the son of another granddaughter. (Three additional Zabriskies listed in Corwin's *Manual* were probably members of this prominent Bergen County family.) In addition, one granddaughter of Thomas Romeyn married the Reverend Benjamin C. Taylor, minister at Jersey City for forty-two years, whose son and three grandsons became ministers. Four sons and one grandson of the Reformed clergyman James Van Neste Talmage became ministers, as did two sons and three grandsons of the Reverend Cornelius Vander Meulen. The Scudder family put all of the above in the shade. The Reverend John Scudder (1793–1855), a medical missionary to India, fathered ten children. Of his eight sons, seven were ordained (the eighth died while in college). Ten grandsons were ordained, and five granddaughters went into the mission field.

The rigorous college and seminary experience they endured in New Brunswick stood students in good stead for the rigors of the ministry, which according to one young clergyman, consisted of "constant and crushing pressure."[2] The office of a Minister, according to the 1833 Constitution of the Reformed Church, Article 15, Section 13, "is to persevere in prayer and the ministry of the Word; to dispense the sacraments; to watch over his brethren the Elders and Deacons, as well as over the whole congregation; and lastly, in conjunction with the Elders, to exercise Christian discipline, and to be careful that all things be done decently and in good order. Every minister must consider himself as wholly devoted to the Lord Jesus Christ in the service of the church; and shall faithfully fulfill the obligations of his call, in preaching, catechizing, and visiting his flock; and be instant in season and out of season; and by word and example always promote the spiritual welfare of his people."

This language only begins to describe the demands and complexity of the office. You are their teacher, one minister was told at his installation, to instruct your flock in the truths of the Gospel. You are their pastor, to feed them with knowledge. You are their watchman, to sound the alarm to sinners. You are their leader, to go before them in every Christian duty and virtue. You are their servant, to labor for them, and to minister unto them. And you are accountable in all of these to your consistory, and to the higher authorities of the Church, and finally to Him who is your Master and your Judge.[3]

Take heed to yourself, the charge continued: Set the Christian example. Watch over your own heart. Subject your spirit to the law of Christ. Be a man of prayer. And then take heed to your flock by preaching, catechizing the youth, administering the ordinances, exercising discipline, and family visitation. Maintain sound doctrine. Press the Gospel upon your hearers. Preach the law, comfort the saint, alarm the sinner, direct the inquiring soul, arouse the careless sleeper, pour oil and wine into the wounded spirit, and pierce with arrows of conviction the bold offender. Speak gently to the contrite soul, but thunder to the hardened sinner, and endeavor to convince all that you are their friend and seek to promote their eternal interests.

And even after all these assignments and admonitions, it continued: Attend to the children of the church. Give them your paternal affection and care, furnish them with suitable instruction, and carry them in your heart to the throne of grace. Use the keys of the Kingdom tenderly, yet faithfully. Admit to your communion and fellowship only those of a Christian spirit. Be patient with the weak, but never be afraid to do your duty. In your pastoral visits, become intimately acquainted with your flock, and in your intercourse with your people, be affable and kind and gentle. Be accessible to both rich and poor. And do not neglect the judicatories of the Church (classis and synod meetings). Give your heart and hand to benevolences, and excite a similar spirit among your people. And finally, cultivate and manifest fraternal affection and confidence toward your brothers in the ministry.

Even this lengthy charge does not adequately describe the awesome responsibilities of the office, which the Reverend Nicholas Marselus described on the twentieth anniversary of his ministry as the "most *important* and the most *difficult* of any that we can be called to sustain . . . *important*, because the salvation of multitudes depends upon it . . . and *difficult*, because it requires such self-denying habits." The office was so difficult, indeed, that no man would dare undertake it, "if he had not a promise of peculiar assistance in the discharge of it." In twenty years, the Reverend Dr. Marselus received 654 members, baptized 660 children and adults, married 748 men and women, hammered home the message that we are all guilty and depraved and condemned to eternal misery unless we repent and believe, and warned sinners about the terrors of hell, not always successfully. "Many . . . have derived no saving benefit from the repeated exhibitions of a crucified Saviour, and are yet . . . in the gall of bitterness, and the bonds of iniquity," he lamented.[4]

In his own recapitulation of a quarter-century in the ministry, another Reformed minister, Benjamin C. Taylor of Jersey City, noted in his journal that he had given 2,102 sermons, 1,974 lectures, and performed 757 funerals, and 88 special services. This totaled 4,833 services, or 193 services on average per year, or 3.7 per week. Taylor also noted that this figure did not include prayer meetings, monthly concerts for prayer, consistory, classis, and synod meetings, "Anniversary Week," Sabbath school, catechism classes, and Bible classes—much less the frequent meetings of various committees and organizations. The Reverend Gabriel Ludlow outdid all records. In 1871, summing up his career of fifty years' ministry in one congregation, a colleague estimated that this clergyman had preached 7,800 sermons at the rate of three a week, plus funerals, performed 500 marriages, and baptized 910 infants.[5]

Ministers longed for time from their myriad commitments to study and read and prepare their sermons, but as one noted, in addition to his parish duties, the "age required attendance at a dozen committees every week, thousands of letters to answer every year, evenings for "converzationes" and lectures, soirees, and public dinners—the result of the century's 'evangelistic and philanthropic zeal.'" The burden on them had become so heavy by 1855 that the YMCA, Bible, Tract, Sunday school, Temperance, and Missionary societies proposed scheduling their meetings on Tuesday and Friday evenings, so that not every evening in the week was taken up by the business of these organizations.[6]

Preaching the gospel was, of course, the minister's first duty, and this most did on average three times a week. One anonymous "city pastor" estimated that the "discourses pastors are called upon to deliver in a single year would make six volumes of 400 pages each." And this figure did not include addresses at prayer meetings, to Sunday schools, at funerals, and on other special occasions. In addition, this disgruntled clergyman went on, ministers were expected to visit their parishioners on a regular basis, a topic "congregations were more unreasonable about than any other." Yet, how, he asked, could one find time to visit every family as often as it demanded, in addition to calling on the sick, the afflicted, the aged, and the anxious as often as they might require? In one month, this clergyman preached 13 sermons, delivered 3 special addresses, attended 4 prayer meetings, officiated at 3 funerals, visited the Sunday school every week, conversed with 12 persons on the subject of personal religion, and made 158 calls. And because his parish was in a city, he was "besieged from morn to night by book-vendors, inventors, beggars, traveling lecturers, and pedlars of maps, patent medicines, and sewing-machines."[7]

No wonder ministers collected remedies "for clearing the voice." (Swallow a new egg before speaking. Dissolve a bit of borax the size of a pea in the mouth before using the voice. Put a piece of unslaked lime the size of an egg in a pitcher of water, together with a teaspoonful of camphor water; place on a low stool with a cloth or towel so arranged as to form a conduct to the face, and inhale.) Some remedies may have been more popular than others. Margaret Schenck Nevius's "Remedy for Clergyman's Sore Throat" included two or three glasses a day of a mixture of rock candy, the juice of four lemons, and a pint of bourbon. And no wonder that "A Village Pastor" urged ministers to pray for one another every Saturday evening, some time between eight and ten P.M., or that they banded together in pastoral associations to "beget the friendliness and sympathy each needs."[8]

In the light of his rigorous schedule and multitudinous duties and roles, the picture drawn by some historians of the nineteenth-century clergyman seems unrecognizable. Was he really a pale, frail, ladylike creature, emasculated by a loss of status and power to rising business interests and a populace more interested in making money than in winning heavenly crowns? Was he really increasingly obliged to join forces with his female parishioners in order to make any progress at all in his chosen work?[9]

In 1902, in the fourth edition of his *Manual*, E. T. Corwin expanded his biographical directory of Reformed ministers.[10] The picture that emerges is of an energetic clergy, deeply involved on the parish level in preaching and pastoral work, in teaching and publishing, in the leadership of ecumenical undertakings, reform organizations, and benevolent societies, in missionary activity, in synodical and classical affairs, and so on. They are described not at all in feminine terms but as solid, strong, clear-thinking, forceful, plain, and practical manly men, epitomes of "muscular" Christianity.

A random selection from the *Manual* illustrates: The Reverend Joseph F. Berg is depicted as of vigorous mind and commanding manner, a controversial figure who battled error with earnestness and power, an uncompromising enemy of Popery, ardent and energetic. The Reverend James Romeyn Berry had a commanding presence and noble qualities. He illustrated the virtues of a matured manhood, unwearying in his endeavors, forceful, and effective. The Reverend George W. Bethune, who achieved "almost world-wide fame" in preaching, was able to sway large audiences at his will. Courageous and faithful, the fear of men did not influence him. The Reverend Philip M. Brett was noted for his manly frankness. The Reverend Jacob Brodhead of tall, masculine frame, and clear, interesting, and impressive ideas, had control over crowds of hearers in Philadelphia unparalleled in the history of that city. Thousands wept on hearing him, and long-obdurate hearts broke in penitence.

The Reverend William Craig Brownlee had unusual strength of mind. An impressive, strong, principled preacher, he was devoted to the manly theology of Paul, Calvin, and Knox. Independent, a fearless leader, he was opinionated, controversial, and bold, a lion in public, though a lamb in private. The Reverend James Spencer Cannon was tall, erect, muscular, powerful. The Reverend Jacob Chamberlain, a missionary to India for twenty-five years, was singlehandedly responsible for a territory the size of Connecticut. A medical doctor as well as a doctor of divinity, he treated 30,000 patients in his first fourteen years. To extend his field, he made a 1,200-mile, four-month trek into the hinterland of India, never before penetrated by a missionary, to distribute Bibles and preach to the heathen.

The Reverend Talbot W. Chambers, despite delicate health, was mentally precocious and powerful in debate. He preached for fifty-seven years. He was an acknowledged leader in the councils of the denomination, more influential than any minister since John H. Livingston. Like many of his colleagues, he published hundreds of articles, editorials, sermons, and book reviews. Of the Reverend Ezra W. Collier, it could be said, "That was a man, every inch of him!" Isaac Ferris had a "majestic presence," a broad and well-balanced mind, great sagacity, a large stock of common sense, and administrative powers seldom equaled.

The alphabetical listings of the Reformed clergy in the 1902 *Manual* go on in this vein for 643 pages of fine print, surely giving reason to question the notion that the nineteenth-century minister was an enfeebled, sentimental, feminized shadow of his tough, stern, more theologically rigorous Puritan or Pietist forebear. It is rather the case that evangelical clergymen had gradually adopted a softer, more palatable version of seventeenth-century Calvinism by the middle of the nineteenth century, because they had come to interpret Scripture in a different way and/or to emphasize different aspects of it: salvation, many had come to believe, was offered to all of God's children, not to the chosen few. They saw their task as to make the way known not only to theologically sophisticated hearers and the long-churched, but to those who had never been inside a church or heard a single verse of Holy Writ. Such clergymen circumnavigated the Calvinistic stumbling blocks that had often discouraged the novice and the inquirer—such as divine election—in order to encourage them to investigate the possibilities of Christianity. Progressive-thinking Reformed Dutch clergymen could choose to accent the conciliatory qualities of the Heidelberg Catechism in explaining doctrine, rather than the harsh and often offputting matter in the Canons of Dort. In emphasizing the catechism rather than the canons, they could transmit accurate doctrine to their hearers, as well as comforting guidelines for daily living and personal spiritual growth.

Dedicated, persevering, caring pastors were much loved by their flocks, and their devotion to their mission was not lost on observant congregants, such as S.L.B. Baldwin in Somerville, New Jersey, who recorded that his minister, lame from a fall from his sleigh on the way to church, delivered his hour-long sermon standing on one leg, "being unaware of the extent of his injury," so intent was he on preaching the Word.[11]

The measure of another clergyman was taken at his funeral in the questions asked of his congregation: "Did you love him? Have you benefited by his toils among you? Has he often fed you with knowledge? Has he comforted you in your distress? Has he relieved your mind when burdened with sin? Was he the messenger of glad tidings when darkness and despair surrounded you? Has he been the instrument by which a new song of praise has been put into your mouth?"[12] In this and no doubt in the vast majority of instances, the answer to all of these questions was Yes, though not in all cases. When the Reverend W. J. Thompson left the churches of Ponds and Wyckoff in 1845, "Not one desired him to depart," which, according to a colleague, "can be said of few ministers when they leave a charge."[13]

$\mathcal{A}$ portrait of the Reformed laity is harder to draw. For one thing, there is no such handy *Manual* as Corwin's to describe them, and although their role and duties were also outlined in the Constitution of the denomination, information about how and if they played the role assigned to them and carried out its duties can be gleaned only by painstaking efforts.

In New York and New Jersey in the nineteenth century, Reformed Dutch congregations were scattered from the northern reaches of the Hudson Valley on both sides of the river, out into the Mohawk and Schoharie valleys of New York State, and down into southern New Jersey. In Geneva and Ithaca, New York, in Jamesville and Owasco, and as far west as Buffalo, Reformed congregations formed and flourished. From Brooklyn and Long Island, and all over Manhattan, in Columbia, Dutchess, Putnam, and Westchester counties on the east side of the Hudson, and west of it into the fertile agricultural valleys of the Hackensack, Pascack, Ramapo, Passaic, and Raritan valleys, they sprang up wherever the Dutch and their numerous descendants migrated. (See figures 9 and 10.)

It is clear from studying these far-flung congregations that their attachment to the Reformed religion and their efforts to retain their Dutch identity were far from the only forces that influenced their characteristics. Geography and demographics as well as local economic and political forces shaped the thinking and the behavior of both clergy and laity and rendered the Reformed Dutch in the Albany area, say, different in marked ways from their coreligionists in, say, the southern regions of the church. The Dutch in Albany, for instance, among whom it is often mistakenly thought that Dutch ways lingered longest, were in fact more progressive in their thinking than the Dutch in New Brunswick, with its college and its seminary, its strong component of intellectuals and theologians, and its easy access to Manhattan.

There are explanations for this. Albany's first priority had been commerce, not religion. From the days of the fur traders into the era of the steamboat and the railroad, mercantile interests, not religion, held sway upriver. Further, historically, Albany's trade was conducted on two fronts, up and down the Hudson with New York, but also east with Boston and England, whereas the bulk of New York's trade had been primarily with the Continent—no doubt a factor in causing Anglicization to be slower to take root in lower New York and New Jersey than upriver.

Also, the Dutch in the Albany Synod were physically closer to the liberating influences of the western frontier, such as the innovations taking place in the "burned-over district," as well as to more theologically liberal New England, and they accepted new interpretations of old theological ideas as they did the necessity for ecumenical missionary and benevolent activities more readily than did their counterparts in the southerly synods. One historian has commented, "new ideologies offered . . . various new ways of thinking that together eroded the authority of Calvinism as the world view best able to provide meaning to the people of Albany."[14]

In the farming communities in lower New York and New Jersey, religion had historically played a larger role in the lives of Reformed adherents than it did upriver. The establishment of the denomination's seminary in New Brunswick emphasized not only the centrality of religion in the southern region but also its devotion to Dort and to classic Calvinism. By midcentury, the seminary, in reaction to the new theologies that appealed to Albany, had come under the theological influence of rigid neo-Calvinistic thinking. It showed its conservativism by condoning a massive anti-popery campaign led by Joseph Berg, professor of didactic and polemic theology at the seminary—a campaign supported by the clergymen editors in charge of the *Christian Intelligencer* in Manhattan. In the words of one historian, the Synod of New York was at this time "egregiously provincial, anxious about the rumored excesses on the expanding frontier, and primarily concerned with purity in doctrine and practice."[15]

The Dutch in Bergen County, who had been among the first adventurously to branch out from Manhattan and settle the hinterland west of the Hudson after the English takeover in 1664, retained (or reinvented or reverted to) significant elements of their Dutchness long into the nineteenth century, and did so despite the fact that they were geographically close to metropolitan New York and its presumably broadening influences. At the same time, of course, the Hudson River and Highlands distanced them geographically from Manhattan, and did so until the twentieth century when the George Washington Bridge facilitated concourse. Dutch preaching was not abandoned until 1835 in Tappan, New York (Rockland County), and as noted earlier the Jersey Dutch dialect was still spoken in the early part of the twentieth century in Bergen and Rockland counties.

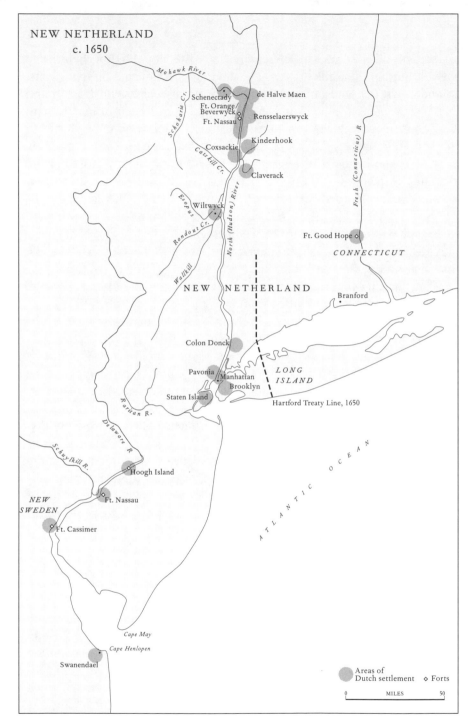

FIGURE 9. New Netherland, c. 1650. The population has been estimated as under ten thousand. *Map drawn by George Colbert.*

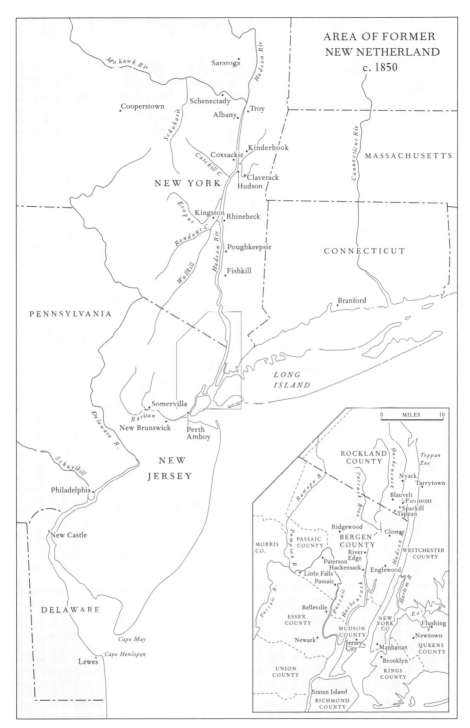

FIGURE 10. Area of Former New Netherland, c. 1850. In 1850, there were 281 Reformed Dutch churches in New York and New Jersey, with a membership of 110,275. *Map drawn by George Colbert.*

Geopolitical factors also account for this conservatism, for this area—the "neutral ground" of the Revolution—suffered more from British depredations during the conflict than virtually anywhere else in the colonies. Bergen and Rockland counties lay on the military route from New England through the Hudson Highlands to the South, and historians document a dozen major attacks there by the British army, as well as innumerable raids and forays by its sympathizers.[16] For generations after the War, the resulting anti-British sentiment fueled a partiality on the part of the local population for the "good old ways"—that is, the Dutch ways of their old Reformed Zion.

To sum up, *the* Dutch culture area in New York and New Jersey in the nineteenth century should be seen not as a monolithic block, but rather as comprising a number of differing culture regions spread out over a large and amorphous geographical area.

Still, as we seek to examine the religious culture, beliefs, and behavior of an ethnic and ethnicized population on its long-drawn-out journey toward a new American identity, a picture of those who made up these disparate branches of the Dutch community is called for. From statistics in the form of classis reports, we can begin to create such a picture.

In 1826, the Reformed Dutch Church consisted of twelve regional classes: eight in New York State (New York, Long Island, Albany, Ulster, Rensselaer, Washington, Poughkeepsie, and Montgomery); three in New Jersey (New Brunswick, Bergen, and Paramus); and one in Philadelphia. Fifty years later in 1876, there were thirty-three classes. (Five of these were in the Midwest and one in India and will not be considered in the following overview.) A classis in the Reformed Church is an ecclesiastical body made up of the minister and a delegated elder from each consistory within a geographical area. (As noted earlier, a consistory comprises the minister and elders and deacons of a particular congregation.) The classis is a mediating institution between the local churches and the General Synod, the main judicatory body of the denomination, which meets once annually. The Book of Church Order describes the relationship as such: "The local churches exist neither autonomously . . . nor as an expression of the General Synod, but in an intercongregational reality called classis."[17]

To classes is given the power to approve or disapprove calls to the ministry (the call being the sole right of the local consistory), to examine candidates for the ministry, to ordain ministers, to form new congregations, and to appoint delegates to the General Synod. In the nineteenth century, much emphasis was placed at the twice-yearly classis meetings in determining if correct doctrine was being preached in the member churches, if the Heidelberg Catechism was being duly explained on a regular basis from the pulpit, if family visitation was being performed, and so on. Typically, matters on the agenda at classis meetings included whether all pulpits in the classis were filled, whether all congregations were financially stable, whether salaries of all the ministers were current, buildings were in good repair, congregations were free of financial debt of consequence, and new or weak churches were steadily growing. Attendance and the progress of catechetical classes, Sunday schools, Bible study groups, and prayer meetings were always of concern, as were pastoral visitation, and whether contributions were cheerfully and generously given and peace and brotherly love were universally present. Inevitably, intemperance, the haunting by young men of taverns, and members' indifference commanded attention.[18]

Highly structured occasions lasting for at least two days, classis meetings were intended to develop the spiritual state of the member churches and to quicken the zeal of the whole body. At classis sessions, which rotated among congregations within the classis, it was hoped that narratives of revivals and conversions, the glory of pastoral accomplishments, Sabbath school successes, and even the grievances and reversals of the discouraged would produce a deep devotional interest in clergy and laity alike. Although their social aspects were secondary, the empathetic relations that grew out of them were designed to bond classis members together in love for church and community. Classis reports and minutes were promptly printed in the *Christian Intelligencer* and distributed in published form to the churches, so that those who did not attend the meetings (that is, the vast majority) could be kept informed of conditions in the various classes.

Each classis was obliged to require from every consistory in its jurisdiction a "statistical table filled up according to such formula as General Synod shall prescribe, accompanied with such remarks on the spiritual state of the congregation as they deem proper."[19] At its annual meeting, the General Synod received these statistical tables, which reported the number of member families within each congregation, the number of total persons in the congregation, the number in communion, and the number received on certificate (that is, from another congregation) and on confession (publicly describing their conversion experience and their commitment to the faith), and subsequently published them. Also reported were numbers dismissed (moving away), suspended (as a disciplinary measure), and deceased, and the number of infants and adults baptized. Some of these categories were dropped by 1850, and new categories were added to account for numbers of catechumens, Bible class attendees, and Sabbath school scholars, as table 5.1 indicates. Financial contributions to the operating budget of the churches and to the outreach program of the denomination were included by 1855. Collated and analyzed, these reports produce an overall picture of congregants and of the denomination as it grew.

TABLE 5.1    *The Reformed Laity, a Statistical Portrait, 1826–1870*

| | 1826 | 1840 | 1850 | 1855 | 1860 | 1865 | 1870 |
|---|---|---|---|---|---|---|---|
| Number of classes, NY and NJ | 12 | 19 | 22 | 25 | 26 | 27 | 27 |
| Number of churches | 181 | 240 | 281 | 329 | 365 | 368 | 382 |
| Number of pastors | 104 | 179 | 285 | 331 | 381 | 385 | 425 |
| Number of families | 9,521 | a | 23,365 | 27,900 | 30,903 | 31,169 | 33,901 |
| Potential communicants/family[b] | 19,042 | a | 46,730 | 55,800 | 61,806 | 62,338 | 67,802 |
| Total of the congregation | 47,491 | a | 110,275 | 126,172 | 137,848 | 155,221[c] | 168,826[c] |
| Joining on certificate | 220 | a | 1,084 | 1,397 | 1,645 | 1,502 | 1,510 |
| Joining on confession | 663 | a | 1,315 | 1,513 | 2,248 | 2,169 | 3,063 |
| Total in communion | 11,312 | a | 33,250 | 37,442 | 46,720 | 49,660 | 54,606 |
| Infants baptized | 1,390 | a | 1,983 | 2,343 | 3,317 | 2,779 | 2,413 |
| Adults baptized | 136 | a | 258 | 289 | 458 | 498 | 848 |
| Number of catechumens | d | d | 7,085 | 7,241 | 14,376 | 17,314 | 21,402 |
| Number in Bible classes | d | d | 4,144 | 5,317 | 11,394 | 14,059 | 20,326 |
| Number in Sabbath schools | d | d | 19,314 | 26,143 | 43,485 | 37,361 | 44,688 |
| Contributions | d | d | d | $77,322 | $389,753 | $514,775 | $1,103,290 |

SOURCE: *Acts and Proceedings of the General Synod of the Reformed Protestant Dutch Church of North America* (New York, years cited).
[a] Uneven reporting by classes makes totaling impossible.
[b] Arbitrary assignment of 2 per family.
[c] Estimated, based on average size of family (4.98) and number of families.
[d] These categories were not reported.

The statistics themselves are sketchy, however, for compliance with the reporting rules was cursory in many cases. In 1826, for instance, the Classis of Montgomery, the largest classis in the denomination that year with 34 congregations, made no report, even though 16 clergymen were serving these congregations. Still, of the 74 congregations (of a total of 181) that reported in the other 11 classes in 1826, it is possible to make some tentative observations.

A total of 9,521 families made up these eleven classes, with a combined total of 47,491 members. The average size of a family was 4.98, and it is presumed for the purposes of this discussion that a family consisted of two adults and 2.98 children, although of course actual families were quite diverse in makeup. (Baptized children were considered church members, even though they could not partake of the sacrament of Holy Communion until they had been confirmed and had made a profession of their faith to the consistory. This customarily occurred in their teenage years.) Of the 9,521 member families, 11,312 persons were "in communion" in 1826—more than one person per family, but far fewer than two per family. If the average family consisted of two adults and 2.98 children, either it was unusual for both adults in a family to partake of the sacrament, or in some families no member participated—hypotheses to be considered below.

Membership figures indicate that the denomination was growing, but slowly. Although only 40 percent of churches reported in 1826, and 77 congregations or 42 percent of the total lacked a minister, total membership was increasing, albeit very gradually. Joining the church in 1826 on profession of faith were 663 individuals; 220 joined on certificate, which means they transferred their membership from another church. This was nearly equal to the number, 242, who were officially "dismissed" to another denomination. Death accounted for another 241 removals. Infants baptized numbered 1,390; 136 adults were baptized, and no doubt these were among the individuals joining on profession. All in all, the picture is of a struggling body in which inflow and outflow of members was about equal, with a slight upward trend.

By 1840, the number of classes had grown from 12 to 19, and there were now 240 churches served by 179 clergymen. Only about three-quarters of these congregations bothered to report to the General Synod on the situation of their congregations, however, and even these figures are incomplete and thus not amenable to aggregate analysis. Some congregations failed to report at all. Some reported number of member families; some did not. Some reported number of families, but not number in communion. Clearly the General Synod had not yet been able to compel compliance with its reporting rules, reflecting the fact that the denomination, as an entity of authority, was still inchoate in 1840. It had not yet gathered its potential strength, nor had it been able to exercise the powers that it envisioned as its own. Other categories were spottily reported, making totaling impossible. But insights into the behavior of the men, women, and children in the congregations that reported fully can be gleaned, nevertheless.

In the important Classis of New York in 1840, for instance, the ministers in the so-called Collegiate churches preached in rotation in four different church buildings to 475 families, with an average family size of six (based on a total of the congregation of 2,850). (See table 5.2.) Communicants in these churches totaled 1,193, or nearly 3 per family, a figure higher than the 1826 total for the whole classis and higher than that in rural Tarrytown in 1840, for instance, where of 87 families, 123 individuals partook of the sacrament—or about 1.3 per family. Was this disparity due to greater religiosity in the urban churches? To more effective preaching? Or to some other factor? In two other city churches in 1840, the Market Street Reformed and the South Dutch Reformed, a combined total of 340

TABLE 5.2    *Classis of New York, Selected Congregations, 1840*

| Churches | Number of families | Total in congregation | Total communicants | Number in Bible classes | Number in Sabbath school |
|---|---|---|---|---|---|
| Collegiate | 475 | 2,850 | 1,193 | 120 | 450 |
| South Dutch | 120 | 700 | 176 | 50 | 150 |
| Market Street | 220 | 1,300 | 421 | 50 | 200 |
| Tompkinsville | 72 | 360 | 91 | a | 115 |
| Tarrytown | 87 | 435 | 123 | 20 | a |

SOURCE: See table 5.1.
a Not reported.

families consisting of 2,000 individuals were on the rolls (or an average of 5.8 per family). Of these 340 families, 597 persons communed—roughly 1.5 per family (half that in the Collegiate churches), whereas in rural Tompkinsville on Staten Island even fewer partook of the Lord's Supper that year (91 individuals out of 72 families)—that is, only slightly more than one person per family.

In the Collegiate churches, 120 of the 2,850 members of the four congregations reporting attended Bible classes; in Tarrytown, 20 individuals out of 435 total church population attended Bible classes—minuscule proportions both. It would seem, then, that the urban-rural disparity seen above in relation to communion cannot be attributed to a greater religious enthusiasm on the part of urban churchgoers as expressed in this case through a desire to know more about the Bible. The two city churches reported 50 in Bible classes, or fewer than 1 per family. The Tompkinsville Church reported none. Tompkinsville reported 115 in Sabbath school, however—more than one per family. The three city churches with a total of 815 families reported a total of 800 in Sabbath school, or about one person per family on average.

These seemingly low figures require explanation. If Reformed churchgoers were so pious, so concerned with their eternal fate, why did so relatively few of them avail themselves of Bible instruction, Sabbath school, and communion? Do the figures indicate incomplete or inaccurate reporting? Or are they symptomatic of apathy on the part of churchgoers unwilling to take the time to deepen their understanding of the tenets of their faith? If the latter, then the often-bitter criticisms of the laity by the clergy, to be aired in a moment, seem understandable. On the other hand, the skeptic would not be amiss in speculating that such pastoral criticisms represented not the actual reality that statistics might reveal, but rather the rhetorical breastbeating of a generation of preachers faintly echoing the

TABLE 5.3  *Ratio of Communicants to Number of Families,
All Classes, New York and New Jersey, 1850–1870*

| Years | Number of families | Number of communicants | Ratio |
|-------|--------------------|------------------------|-------|
| 1850 | 23,365 | 33,250 | 1.42 |
| 1855 | 27,900 | 37,442 | 1.34 |
| 1860 | 30,903 | 46,720 | 1.51 |
| 1865 | 31,169 | 49,660 | 1.59 |
| 1870 | 33,901 | 54,606 | 1.61 |

SOURCE: See table 5.1.

thunderous jeremaids of an earlier age. Is this so? Should they be viewed merely as nineteenth-century evangelical leaders' techniques for stirring their congregations to greater repentance, wider acceptance of the gospel message, fuller participation in the life of the church? Or do they in fact indicate an indifferent laity?

Compliance with the General Synod's reporting requirements improved over time. The figures regarding the ratio of communicants to families in the denomination remain low over the twenty years from 1850 to 1870, however, although the percentages of persons attending Bible classes and Sabbath schools rise steadily, as tables 5.3 and 5.4 indicate.

In 1850, the number of classes in New York and New Jersey had grown to 22, comprising 281 churches served by 285 ministers—an increase of 41 churches and 106 ministers in a decade. (This does not include the two classes in Illinois and Michigan, composed of recent immigrants from the Netherlands.) Families numbered 23,365; communicants 33,250—about 1.4 per family. (See table 5.1.) There were 7,085 catechumens, 4,144 persons in Bible classes, and 19,314 in Sabbath schools. To relate these figures to the number of member families, roughly one person in six families attended a Bible class, and slightly more than one per family a Sabbath school. Again, these are surprisingly low showings, considering the general impression one has of intense evangelical piety in this period and the dramatic increase in numbers of congregations and ministers over the decade 1840–1850.

In 1855, the denomination was still on the move—indeed, the 1850s was the decade of its greatest growth. There were now 329 churches in the core 25 eastern classes, with 331 ministers serving 27,900 families.[20] Total congregants were reported at 126,172, or an average of 4.5 persons per family. Communicants numbered 1.3 per family (37,442), seemingly a stable number over time. About one person in every five families availed himself or herself of Bible instruction (5,317). Sabbath school attendance

TABLE 5.4    *Attendance in Bible Class and Sabbath School,*
*All Classes, New York and New Jersey, 1850–1870*

|  | Number of families | Number in Bible class | Percentage | Number in Sabbath school | Percentage |
|------|------|------|------|------|------|
| 1850 | 23,365 | 4,144 | 17.7 | 19,314 | 82.7 |
| 1855 | 27,900 | 5,317 | 19.1 | 26,143 | 93.7 |
| 1860 | 30,903 | 11,394 | 36.9 | 43,485 | 140.7 |
| 1865 | 31,169 | 14,059 | 45.1 | 37,361 | 119.9 |
| 1870 | 33,901 | 20,326 | 60.0 | 44,688 | 131.8 |

SOURCE: See table 5.1.

remained stable, with just over one individual per family attending on average. Financial contributions averaged $2.77 per family.

The eastern classes numbered 26 in 1860, with a spurt in total congregations from 329 to 365, and a concomitant increase in clergy from 331 to 381. There were now 30,903 families in New York and New Jersey calling themselves Reformed Dutch, up 10.76 percent in five years, with a total membership of 137,848 (up 9.25 percent in five years)—average family size remaining constant. Of the membership, 46,720 were in communion, or roughly 1.5 per family. After decades of stability, this 15 percent increase in communicants requires explanation (forthcoming below). At the end of this decade of growth, there were more than twice as many catechumens as in 1850 (14,376 versus 7,085), and Sabbath schools enrolled 43,485 students or well over one per family (1.40). Financial contributions were way up, with an average family contribution of $3.91 for outreach and $12.61 for congregational purposes, $16.52 per year per family.

A decade later, in 1870, the statistics reveal 27 classes, 382 congregations, and 425 ministers serving 33,901 families. The number of communicants is up again by nearly 7 percent to 1.6 per family with 54,606 communing; catechumens number 21,402; Bible students 20,336; and Sabbath schools are up slightly with 44,688 students. Do rising figures suggest a healthy situation? Or do persistently low showings in relation to number of member families in the denomination indicate a listless attitude toward spiritual growth, an unspoken expectation that faith be effortless, or perhaps a desire to be aligned with a church for social reasons or reasons of appearances?

Also to be considered is what the statistics may conceal. Nonstatistical data gleaned from diaries and published church histories throw another light on these figures, indicating that in some families all or many members availed themselves of all the services of the church: sacramental, educational, and social. The low figures in the categories related to Bible class attendance, Sabbath school attendance, and communion strongly hint at the truth: many families hardly darkened the doors of the churches to which they belonged. They were members in name only, and considerations of social class may have been a factor, as chapter 7 will make clear.

Low figures for communion attendance may be accounted for in part by attitudes toward communion. The Reformed Church recognizes only two sacraments, baptism and Holy Communion. Baptism is normally performed upon infants, although adult baptism is not and was not in the nineteenth century at all uncommon. In 1870, for instance, 848 adults were baptized. But normally, baptism is a decision made for a child by his or her parents.

To partake of Holy Communion, in contrast, represents for a member of the Reformed Church a personal decision made by a baptized and confirmed person who has made a public profession of his or her faith before a consistory and who, prior to the celebration, has seriously considered his sins, repented of them, and believes them to be forgiven. These guidelines are still in effect, on paper, but the attitude toward communion has changed considerably. An informal survey suggests that today it is rare in a mainline Protestant denomination, including the Reformed Church in America in New York and New Jersey, that the sacrament is not taken when it is offered. Even though the Rules of Church Order as formulated at the Synod of Dort state that adult members of the church in full communion are bound to partake of the Lord's Supper, statistics reveal that in nineteenth-century New York and New Jersey, just the opposite was true: many did not take the sacrament when it was offered. (At the Synod of Dort in 1619, it was agreed that communion should be celebrated once every two months, including at Easter, Pentecost, and Christmas. This held until 1833, when the frequency was changed to at least twice a year, but preferably once a quarter.)

Writing on the history of the sacrament, the Reformed historian Daniel J. Meeter has attributed this to the fact that "late medieval penitential piety [was] transformed" after the Reformation by a "popular emphasis on 'worthiness' and a fear of profaning the Lord's Table."[21] An example may be found in the behavior of the eighteenth-century Pietist minister Theodorus Jacobus Frelinghuysen, who was so profoundly fearful of profaning the table that he actually refused to serve communion to parishioners he personally judged to be unworthy; he threatened on at least one occasion to physically bar those he considered unworthy from the table with his own body.

A glance at the language of the Reformed liturgy used in the nineteenth century makes clear that the emphasis on personal worthiness continued to be taken very seriously: "for he that eateth and drinketh unworthily, eateth and drinketh damnation to himself." The would-be communicant had not only a personal responsibilty to ascertain his own worthiness to receive the Supper; indeed, it was the duty of the consistory, following Article 32 of the 1793 Constitution, to make, prior to the celebration, "a faithful and solemn inquiry" as to whether any member of the church had departed from the faith or "in walk or conversation" had behaved in any way unworthy of it. Standards for admission to the table were high and were kept high, and offenders were rebuked, admonished, and if unrepentant barred from approaching it.[22]

In the liturgy's list of specific disqualifying offenses, it was probably not very difficult for an honest, soul-searching churchgoer to find his or her own failings. The list includes "all idolaters; all those who invoke deceased saints, angels, or other creatures; all those who worship images; all enchanters, diviners, charmers, and those who confide in such enchantments; all blasphemers; all those who are given to raise discord, sects, and mutiny, in church or state; all perjured persons; all those who are disobedient to their parents and superiors; all murderers, contentious persons, and those who live in hatred and envy against their neighbors; all adulterers, whoremongers, drunkards, thieves, usurers, robbers, gamesters, covetous; and all who lead offensive lives."[23]

The low figures reported for communicants in relation to the adult church membership in the nineteenth-century Reformed Dutch Church may indicate, therefore, not an indifference to this central sacrament of the faith on the part of the laity, but rather a complicated mix of awe at its seriousness and significance, honest self-doubt as to one's worthiness to receive it, and fear of divine retribution (drinking damnation unto oneself) if one were to receive it unworthily. Those confident to approach the table no doubt drew their trust from the reassuring passage of the liturgy that, once confessing and believing themselves forgiven, no remaining sin or infirmity could "hinder [anyone] from being received of God in mercy, and from being made worthy partakers of this heavenly meat and drink."

One final factor should be considered. In the nineteenth century, the emphasis in evangelical churches, including the Reformed, was on salvation, and the "great doctrinal topic of the pulpit was the way in which [Christ's] death was related to forgiveness of sin," as one theologian put it. The preached Word, the sermon, not the sacraments, was the center of the worship experience. Slightly rising statistics for Reformed communers over the decades suggest that, as the standards for admission to communion were relaxed, or rather as clergymen may have taken it upon themselves to omit some of the harsher liturgical language, more lay people may have felt freer to approach the table. Efforts to revise the Reformed liturgy were unavailing until a proposed revision in 1868 was finally approved and adopted in 1882.[24]

Taken together, hard data and soft, statistics and anecdotal material, both reveal and conceal a more complex institutional history than one or the other alone permits. What appear from statistics to be healthy growth and an increase in piety among the Reformed laity over time may be a reflection of a fading judgmentalism and a lowering of standards on the part of the leadership of the church. And, although a subset within the denomination may have increased in true piety and participation, the data, both statistical and anecdotal, suggest that real commitment to the church on the part of the larger membership was a constant concern.

$S$till, these explanations do not account for the relatively low ratio of Bible class and Sabbath school participation relative to total membership. Further, it is impossible to ignore, in the mutual criticisms of clergy and laity, dissatisfactions between them that may alone account for poor attendance and low interest on the part of the latter, and for a lackluster performance on the part of the clergy. Those Reformed churchgoers who constituted the ever watchful, ever faithful, ever involved hard core of the membership were severe taskmasters. Ultras among them held ministers strictly to the doctrines of Dort, and all, whether of traditional or progressive mind set, insisted on vibrant preaching, a warm and engaging manner, and high standards of personal conduct on the part of their clergymen. When displeased, they let their ministers whistle for their pay, as they had since the stressful era of Leisler's Rebellion in the seventeenth century, and when pleased they showered them with cash and expensive gifts.

Churchgoers made no bones about their distaste for long prayers, obscure vocabulary, ministers who did not follow the exact form of the church order, ministers who after a solemn sermon or prayer meeting were soon seen smiling jovially, ministers whose air, manner, and language suggested a greater eagerness to exhibit themselves than their Master. Laity complained of those whose prayers were too obscure for ordinary folk, prayers "protracted to an unendurable length" of twenty or twenty-five minutes, prayers that were "motley combinations of all that is technical, complicated, artificial, perplexed, and involved," and prayers that were "ostentatious exercises of mere memory."[25] Even Reformed ministers complained of one another's prayers: "We could not understand the doleful strain of a certain brother's prayer," wrote the Reverend Thomas De Witt Talmage in 1874, "until we found he composed it on a fast day during the yellow fever in 1821, and has been using it ever since." The reason congregations "have their heads bobbing about" during prayers, he wrote, is because the clergyman is too abstract in his petitions. He should "call the troubles of his people by their names." In other words, be specific and relevant, and they will listen. There are in the churches and in the ministry, he added, a "great many men who are dead, but have never had the common decency to get buried."[26]

The Ultras complained about ministers who dared to preach that Christ died for all (unlimited atonement)—an unacceptable departure from the Canons of Dort (or an unfortunate misinterpretation of them). The progressive sort complained about sermons monotonously based on the familiar questions and answers of the Heidelberg Catechism. The Reverend Dr. Talmage, who had attained a worldwide celebrity for his own "electric" preaching (it was estimated that his sermons, which were syndicated in 3,600 newspapers all over the world, were read weekly by 20 million people), wrote of a fellow domine that he had not prepared a new sermon in ten years and that his church was the last one Rip Van Winkle attended before getting drowsy.[27]

The most frequent charge against ministers was dry preaching. Sermons were a form of public entertainment for nineteenth-century evangelicals, who eagerly thronged those sanctuaries whose ministers best filled their desire to hear the Word explained. But more important, sermons met a deep desire on the part of the faithful for spiritual enlightenment. Sermons stirred their deepest emotions, satisfied their intellectual thirst for sacred knowledge, and inspired them to spiritual advancement and a higher Christian life. Of inferior, repetitious, dry, or doctrinally imprecise preaching, they were acutely disparaging. Although S.L.B. Baldwin noted that "almost everyone had forgotten it," the Reverend Mr. Chambers of the Somerville Reformed Church, on June 16, 1844, preached a sermon he had given four years previously, on June 14, 1840. "There was an improvement in its delivery," this alert parishioner commented.[28]

Mary Van Dyke of New Brunswick, while living in Washington, D.C., went to hear a Unitarian minister preach. He was young, handsome, and probably worldly wise, she wrote, but "whether heavenly wisdom belonged to him [was] not quite so apparent." A few months later, she heard a sermon at the Capitol: "Mr. G. is a pleasing speaker, a poetical writer, but does not preach sermons that make people cry out mightily for God's mercy."[29]

Paul Van Cleef, a student at New Brunswick Theological Seminary, "heard a Dr. Hagaman read a dry sermon from a dead man's dried brains in a very dry manner." And Garret Schenck, a Rutgers student, thought the illustrious Reverend Dr. Thomas De Witt "one of the most awkward men I ever saw in the pulpit. . . . His remarks though they showed a great fund of information were tedious." On another occasion, this young man wrote of the Reverend Dr. Samuel A. Van Vranken, professor of didactic theology in the seminary, "Sometimes he is affected to tears when his audience can see no cause for it. . . . It appears somewhat ridiculous when a minister sheds tears and his hearers are still unmoved." A Baptist minister whom this critic went to hear "is not a very easy writer or speaker . . . and is not I should think a man of much education."[30]

Cornelius L. Hardenbergh of New Brunswick, taking the waters in western New York, wrote to his sister that a Presbyterian preacher he had gone to hear was a man of some talent, "but his sermon was so entirely according to the mode of thinking taught in the Auburn School, that I confess it did not do me a great deal of good." (The sermon dwelt too much on human ability to suit this Calvinist, and not enough on the sacrifice of Christ on the cross—for him an unwelcome departure from Dort.)[31]

Maria Ferdon of Bergen County had nothing but scorn for "graceless prayers" and preaching that was "not gospel." The Reverend Mr. Blauvelt "certainly does pervert the Scripture," she noted in her diary; Mr. Fish's preaching was "no comfort"; Mr. Van Buskirk's was "no food for my soul"; Mr. Blauvelt "should never attempt to preach again"; some preachers were "dumb dogs," asleep in the gospel; a Methodist preacher was full of "very false doctrine."[32]

Maria's parents had been affiliated with the 1822 Secession, and she herself (born in 1827) maintained a lifelong connection to the secession ministers and their churches, but her diaries reveal her equally lifelong confusion over the doctrines involved. "Have no desire to hear the preaching they have in this church. Faith is not the way to be saved," she wrote on one occasion. She often "read Calvin again" to find answers to her spiritual questions, but she turned as well to the doctrines of John Wesley "on two-fold justification." Her "hungry and thirsty soul" longed for the "church of old and the good old way," and she yearned for gospel (that is, "talk of Jesus"), not legal (that is, doctrinal) preaching. Yet talk of Jesus left her feeling that her own salvation was "uncertain."

Dry preaching was not the only serious charge against the clergy. In 1842, the Reverend James Romeyn told the General Synod, in a thundering 55-page jeremiad subsequently published, that ministers had "let themselves be diverted from their pulpits to "wander into other than the gospel field." In short, the Reformed clergy was becoming secularized (for which one may also use in this case the term *Americanized*). An alarming number are unemployed, Romeyn reported, and others have allowed their pulpits to proclaim much besides "Christ crucified," that is, moral reform, the temperance cause, and so on. Some had left the ministry to head up agencies and institutions of "worldly enterprize [*sic*]," or become "wandering stars" on the lecture circuit instead of commissioned ambassadors of God. Even advertisements for "book pedlars," he noted with disgust, express a preference for a minister of the gospel—"a goodly prize we are valued at." Reformed ministers have allowed "reformed inebriates" to speak from the pulpit, while they sit in the pew "and the silver trumpet of the Gospel Jubilee is silent on the wall."[33]

During the week, ministers—in a totally un-Dortlike manner—neglected their duties, Romeyn went on, to "amuse or reform or persuade" on the podium, and their message was made up of statistics and anecdotes of a drunkard's misery and shame. Others lectured on literature, agriculture, or politics. "The battle is raging, and ministers in the Reformed Church, like Saul on Mount Gilboa, are leaning on their spears," he thundered. Instead, they must concentrate on preaching Christ. "Every other call should receive Nehemiah's reply, 'I am doing a great work and I cannot come down.' O Brethren," he concluded, "we are a consecrated band. We can discharge our office only by dwelling at the foot of the Cross," not out "amid our farms, inventions, speculations, business, bye-paths, cares collateral." Be overcome, he exhorted his colleagues, that you are "A minister! God has revealed his Son in [you]!"[34]

Turning the tables, in this same sermon, Romeyn made clear that the crisis he observed in the church was not to be laid only at the feet of clergymen. The crisis, he charged, was caused also by the falling away of interest in religion on the part of the laity. Like his minister, the Reformed churchgoer was becoming secularized—modernized or Americanized. A plethora of voluntary associations drew his attention away from God, and he could not help but be affected by the appalling laxity in morals, by fellow parishioners who changed denominational connections at the drop of a hat, and by the effect of Transcendentalism, whose "gilded, poisonous sentences" as pronounced on public platforms spread the "revolting form of Pantheism . . . that Mind is Deity."[35] To return to the question asked earlier, were such ministerial harangues as Romeyn's the ritualistic vestiges of seventeenth-century thunder, or were they genuine, reality-based laments over the indifference of their flocks and their own inefficacies in overcoming that indifference?

Attendance appears to have been a real and a perennial problem. Under the heading "Lord What Wilt Thou Have Me to Do?" the *Christian Intelligencer* published a long unsigned article (one among many), probably by one of its clergyman editors, exhorting churchgoers to attend worship on Sunday. ("Alas! who can survey, without shuddering, the half empty house of prayer on the Lord's Day afternoon, and the theatre crammed to suffocation to witness the licentious . . . exposures of an impudent danseuse?") As classis statistics reveal, church members neglected other obligations as well—whether intimidated by the standards of the faith, whether to spite a disappointing minister, or whether out of indifference to their faith is not clear. Do not fail to take communion, this article went on. Fulfill your social religious duties (the prayer meeting, Bible class, Sabbath school, and so on), and give more generously to the support of the church.[36] A printed recipe sarcastically advised those intent on "destroying a church" to absent themselves from one service every Sunday, or miss at least one in three. (If the minister "is not very strong, once in four times may answer.") Also, neglect the prayer and Bible class meetings, criticize the minister freely, praise him sparingly, find fault plentifully, and pray for him little or not at all. Withhold cooperation, give yourself no concern whether his salary is paid or not, and "never call on him socially, or allow him to think that his comfort or that of his family" is of any importance at all.[37]

Although we have a general impression of nineteenth-century evangelicals as pious, reverent, and devout, and although many of the faithful clearly were so, the clergy's criticisms of the laity, like their statistical portrait, reveal that many congregants were passive, indifferent, and even openly hostile. The celebrated Dr. De Witt was plagued by a certain parishioner who was in the habit of relieving the fatigue of the Sunday service by rising from his seat and sitting on the gallery railing with his back to the preacher. No doubt this man's behavior was unusual, but so frequently did "rules for the house of God" circulate in the press that there can be no doubt that some churchgoers needed to be instructed not only to be regular, punctual, and quiet, but also not to lounge about the church door, to take off their hats inside the sanctuary, and to leave them off for the duration of the service. Sleeping during the service was evidently a problem ("Few things are more unpleasant to a minister than to see eyes closed and heads nodding"). Fidgeting and "gazing about" were endemic. Don't take out your watch and twirl it on your watch chain. Don't take the census of the congregation, or count the number of panes in the window, or follow the movement of the flies. Finally, be prayerful, follow the text in the Bible, and *sing* the hymns, churchgoers were instructed.[38]

A great many churchgoers "regard God's sanctuary as an immense show-room for the display of millinery, dry goods, and jewelry," a Reformed Church periodical editorialized in 1865, while "others regard it as the place for *intellectual* criticism, where the minister is to be laid on the dissecting table and his gestures, sermon, and manner of reading the hymns are to be taken apart piecemeal." Many more look upon the house of God "as a huge dormitory, and each separate pew as a bed . . . for a comfortable nap, until the close of the sermon. . . . To the minister it is exceedingly annoying to know that while he is preaching . . . ETERNAL LIFE, [some] are fast asleep."[39]

In "The Battle of Pew and Pulpit," the Reverend Mr. Talmage summed up the mutual criticisms of clergy and congregation. The pew complains about the minister's enunciation and volume; the pulpit responds that the pew can't hear because he's thinking about other things. He comes to church only to rest, and looks half asleep. The pew complains the minister's sermons all sound alike. (Don't talk about stale things. Tell us the latest ideas instead.) The pulpit responds that the pew keeps him so poor, he can't buy the books necessary to keep him fresh. "Pay me my arrears, and pay what you subscribed to pay." The pew complains that the minister is too plain for this elegant place. (We want a minister who will "talk about heaven, and make no allusion to the other place.") The pulpit replies that the people want an "ecclesiastical scentbag, a heavenly nosegay," who won't bore them with Judgment Day and brimstone, or get them into a "tearing-down revival, where the people go shouting and twisting about." They prefer a revival "wrapped in ruffles," one so still that "nobody will know it is there."[40]

Never one to mince words, Talmage produced a list of his own rules for church behavior: shake hands, meet the people in the aisle, say a word of comfort to those in trouble, greet one another, don't be part of the coughing brigade, don't cough just when some practical truth is about to be uttered from the pulpit, don't have a coughing fit just as the contribution box arrives, pay attention during the prayers, creed, and Scripture readings, and don't concentrate on your neighbors' millinery.[41]

*I*n the early decades of their settlement, Dutch Reformed congregants in New Netherland may have been docile listeners and passive accepters of the Word: "Lay preaching was not encouraged; books of approved sermons were provided from which a layman [a *voorzanger* (official chorister) or *voorlezer* (lay reader)] could read if no ministers were available. In general . . . [the] atmosphere [was one] approaching paternalism, and the ordinary church member received his doctrine . . . from those above."[42] But a century in America had wrought enormous changes in the laity, because indeed more often than not no ministers had been available, and the people, thrown on their own resources, had become used to governing themselves in their churches, often without benefit of clergy.

In 1737, the Reformed Dutch Church, after more than a hundred years in America, could count only nineteen ordained clergymen to serve sixty-five congregations.[43] The chronic shortage of ministers meant that the laity, especially in rural areas, had developed a can-do attitude toward religion, as they met in one another's houses for worship and Bible study, led perhaps only by a neighbor acting as *voorlezer*. If they were fortunate enough to find an ordained minister to organize a proper church for them and serve it, even on a quarterly basis, as was a common arrangement, they had to rely on themselves for everything in between.

This combined with the history Reformed churchgoers had long enjoyed of being able to choose between styles of worship, Pietist or orthodox, and of the independence of mind they had developed in political matters between the Glorious Revolution in Leisler's time and the American Revolution, meant that ministerial authority, when it did come upon the scene, was often challenged. In fact, over the church's first two centuries in America, it was only by the leadership's determined use of the most delicate mechanisms of defense—avoidance, denial, rationalization, compensation, and compromise—that the denomination itself did not dissolve and disappear in the wake of its own internal conflicts over doctrine and the proper relationship between clergy and laity.

In the power struggle that often developed between an independent-minded laity and a clergyman trained to expect deference and respect from his congregation, the minister's salary was usually the bloodiest battleground. It was a battleground where the congregation had the upper hand, if not the moral high ground. And it was a battleground where the facts suggest a certain mean-spiritedness on the part of congregations that merit the criticisms directed at them.

"Do you love your Dominie?" asked the *Intelligencer* in 1835. If you do, then pay your part toward his salary, it scolded, "and pay it cheerfully, fully, and at the time it comes due." A few months later, "Senex" gave facts and figures. Some churches, he reported, with eighty to a hundred families, pay their minister a mere $500 per year—that is, five or six dollars per family, and even this paltry amount is not regularly paid. In another case, two congregations of eighty-five families joined in supporting a minister at $600 per year, or three dollars per family. Yet, Senex noted, these congregations contained many wealthy individuals, and in fact only the minister among them was poor. In October 1836, S.L.B. Baldwin, in his role as a deacon in the Somerville Reformed Church, went around the parish trying to collect the minister's salary. Of the $350 due, he took in $79.25. In April, he collected only $71 of the $350 due. "The present," he commented, "are perhaps the hardest times since the late War." Four years later, in the depression that had settled in after the Panic of 1837, Baldwin went out again to collect. "Most of the money handed in [$143.50] is uncurrent. It is now a hard time to collect salary, or anything else."[44]

In the 1845 New York City Census, reported in the *Intelligencer*, 279 clergymen of all denominations received an average of $950 per year in salary and benefits, but the figures are deceptive, because in reality "some receive $5000 or $6000, and others not so many hundreds."[45]

In 1860, the cost of living in a country parsonage for a minister salaried at $550 per year came to $646.37. His expenses (he had a wife and three children) were tallied as follows:

| | |
|---|---|
| Provisions | $148.57 |
| Clothing | 139.30 |
| Fuel and Lights | 24.98 |
| Hired Help | 63.77 |
| Travel, Benevolences, and Incidentals | 85.22 |
| Books, Paper, Postage | 33.11 |
| Cow and Horse Keeping | 82.44 |
| Repairing and Replacing Furniture | 18.98 |
| House Rent | 50.00 |

The deficit of $96.37 was made up by the yearly "donation-visit" of the congregation, the somewhat patronizing custom, smacking of a kind of noblesse oblige, in which the congregation bestowed food items and cash on its minister to make up for the deficiencies of his salary.

It was repeatedly pointed out to congregations that inadequate salaries deterred young men from entering the ministry, that ministers had a right to a comfortable maintenance, and that pastors, on their small salaries, were unable to lay aside anything for their widows and orphans, or for their own old age. But still the problem of low salaries persisted. In 1875, the outspoken Reverend Mr. Talmage attributed ministers' "lack of force and fire" to the lack of a nourishing diet. "Don't give your $800 per year minister an elegantly bound copy of *Calvin's Institutes* for Christmas," he wrote. "He is sound already on the doctrine of election, and it is a poor consolation if in this way you remind him that he has been foreordained to starve to death."[46]

Though some ministers were treated shabbily by some congregations and were severely taken to task for every fault and failing, imagined or real, both by their congregations and by their own colleagues, many were held in high esteem, and even loved, by their congregations. Funeral sermons, church histories, biographical accounts, obituaries, diaries, letters, and parishioners' fond testimonies offer convincing evidence of the strong bonds between pulpit and faithful. As one layman said of his minister, "His people are strongly attached to him and he to them. . . . [His] faithful and unwearied labors . . . for our spiritual good . . . [his] ardent piety . . . winning eloquence and transcendent talents, have commended him to our highest respect and warmest affections." And when Benjamin Taylor retired from the Reformed Church of Bergen, the consistory unanimously voted him emeritus. "He had been their pastor for 42 years, and there was never any discord between him and his people, and they both desired that he should remain among them till his death."[47]

On their side, ministers appreciated their faithful parishioners. "The relation . . . between a minister and his [congregation] . . . is among the most important . . . [and] the most tender ever constituted," one wrote. Another likened his feelings for a beloved "mother in Israel" in his congregation to those of his own mother: Traveling, "I rejoice," he wrote, "that I have a mother at Albany, who wishes me all the blessings which stirred in the bosom of my natural parent." And one young minister was so bereaved when a favorite parishioner died that he wrote "I Miss Thee," a 67-line poem to express his feelings for her:

> I miss thee at the house of prayer. Thy form
> That reverently leaned God's Word to hear,
> And thy bright eye upon the preacher fixed
> With thoughtful look, as if thy soul drank in
> With joy the message of eternal life— . . . [48]

CHAPTER 6

# A Good Year in Zion

*Almost all of the social life was interwoven with the church and church work. . . .*
*The families came together on holidays and feasted at weddings and birthdays, but aside*
*from that, social life was largely a matter of "calling" or visiting. Relatives came and*
*stayed on as long as they pleased, and clergymen were continually dropping in overnight.*
—John C. Van Dyke, 1889

$\mathcal{A}$ devotion to the Calvinism of the Synod of Dort, the efforts of the *Christian Intelligencer* to acquaint its readers with the history of the Reformed Church and the Dutch nation, the sense of a distinctive peoplehood that was nurtured at Rutgers and the New Brunswick Seminary, the marrying patterns of the clergy: all these were factors in causing Dutchness to persist in nineteenth-century New York and New Jersey.

One other element contributed in a major way to the endurance of Dutch ways and customs: the settlement patterns in the Dutch culture areas of New York and New Jersey. Here, in the seventeenth and eighteenth centuries, bands of New Netherland families united by ties of blood, marriage, friendship, religion, and even political leanings established themselves in neighborhoods of family farms that served as home to generations of their offspring. In such communities, by the third generation whole neighborhoods of farms owned by members of the same and related families had evolved, with grandparents, parents, children, aunts, uncles, cousins, and in-laws all living near one another on clusters of family farms along adjacent roads, all interacting year in and year out at home, at work, at church, at school, and in a social life of constant face-to-faceness.[1]

Inspired by an ideal of family coherence and based on a tradition long associated with the Netherlands—equal treatment of heirs—this settlement pattern provided family members with economic advantages as well as affective and moral ones and was perpetuated for centuries. Cornelius C. Vermeule described it in the nineteenth century:

> [In] those happy days and years at Raritan Landing, always the house on the hill was full of guests. The uncles, aunts and cousins

from New York often came. Neighbors and nearby relatives were there en-masse at times when the great tables groaned with good things and guests made the place their own. Up the valley there were reciprocal welcomes to the homes of old Piscataway families . . . and many others of old Somerset. The intimate families whose friendship reached back four or more generations covered the three counties, and the pulse of it all was the "river road," that ancient "road up 'Raritan" . . . surveyed two centuries before.[2]

Not only did the seventeenth-century surveyor's compass and cross affect one's social life and one's pool of marriage partners in the nineteenth century, they also resulted in patterns of social life that were inseparable from church life. It was as if land-use patterns set in the seventeenth and eighteenth centuries conspired with the Reformed Dutch Church to contain its members in past-oriented identifications well into the nineteenth century. From Albany to the Hackensack Valley to the Raritan Valley, in Manhattan, in Brooklyn—in every geographical area where the church flourished—its members' intensely active social lives centered around church-related activities, often as many as six or eight a week, and a diverse range of wholly secular pastimes, shared always with the same local people. The most valid observation one can make about social life in the Dutch culture areas of New York and New Jersey is that Reformed people mingled almost exclusively with others reared in the same religious culture as themselves. The result was, of course, that shared values, beliefs, mores, expectations, and customs were constantly buttressed in the multitudinous and intertwining activities of church year and secular year. Daily face-to-face contacts by the same people with the same people allowed Dutchness daily to reinvigorate itself.

Diaries kept by Reformed churchgoers, their correspondence, and the newspaper designed with them in mind, the *Christian Intelligencer*, make it clear that the religious culture of these communities was a mix of the religious and the secular so intertwined as to defy description of either as a separate entity. The diary of a bachelor farmer and Reformed Church adherent, Adriance Van Brunt of Brooklyn, illustrates. Adriance records in his diary, which he kept from June 1828 to March 1830, and which is representative, that in one typical week he attended Sunday worship in the morning at the Flatbush Reformed Church and a pious lecture in the afternoon. On Monday and Tuesday he attended church funerals, where he heard sermons on the imperative need for repentance and salvation. On Wednesday, he went to a meeting of the Educational Society in the Flatlands Reformed Dutch Church, on Thursday, Bible class at Jacob Bergen's, and on Friday, a prayer meeting at Abraham Vanderveer's.

His diary records also his regular attendance throughout the year at singing school, Sabbath school, and meetings of church committees and the Long Island Bible Society, as well as his activities collecting door-to-door for the missionary society, of which he was vice president, founding a Bible class, and serving as a deacon on the consistory. And it reveals how all of these purely church-related activities were integrated with his social life in an unflagging sequence of interactions with fellow evangelicals in the rural Brooklyn of the day: visits, parties, teas, sleighing, skating, even co-ed sleep-overs, with the men sharing beds upstairs after a late-night party and the ladies sleeping on chairs, couches, or the floor in the parlor below. Almost without exception, the surnames of Adriance's friends are the surnames of New Netherland families.[3]

In her diary for 1842, Margaret Schenck, age twenty-two, distinguishes between "parties"—events to which one sent or received a written or at least an oral invitation—and "visiting," or the informal dropping in on one's friends and relations without prior notice. That year, Margaret attended a prodigious number of parties, 196 in all, or nearly four per week. The partygivers and -goers all bore New Netherland names, or names known to be connected with the Reformed Dutch Church in her community—people who would have had family and church business to discuss with one another, the business of the workaday world, and purely social business.[4]

Likewise, the diary of John S. Nevius, Jr., for the summer of 1869, when he was twenty-one, describes making calls, going to church, and taking part in group outings with other young people, virtually every one of whom had a surname known to have been present in New Netherland and every one of whom was affiliated with one or another of the Reformed Dutch churches in the area. Throughout this busy summer, John attended church, went sailing, walked along the Raritan canal, and was invariably together with friends and neighbors who were sisters and brothers and cousins of each other. Always there were the old familiar names, and always the freedom young people were allowed in mixed company, and often an undercurrent of romance. Brought up together, these girls and boys were partial to one another, and many eventually married their childhood friends. John's friend Benjamin Smith, age fourteen, away at school, wrote to him in 1862 to say "you told me that I must be careful for fear I would fall in love with some of the girls out here but I guess there hant much danger. . . . The girls out here haint as pretty as our jersey girls."[5]

Besides engaging in a constant round of religious activities that are familiar today (Sunday worship, Sunday school, Bible study, prayer groups, and so on), Reformed churchgoers, like their counterparts in other evangelical denominations, participated in a range of religious activities peculiar to the nineteenth century, and now obsolete: the annual Visitations in January, the Anniversaries in May, monthly concerts of prayer, refreshings and seasons of grace, donation days, fast days, and days of humiliation and prayer, to name some of them. Woven in among these activities were religious occasions inspired by the rites of life's passage: weddings and funerals, clerical installations and ordinations, and new-church dedications, all of which comprised important threads in the fabric of daily life and, both in the country and in the city, offered additional opportunities to bring the same people into contact with one another many times a year.

The woof and warp of the evangelical social fabric was strengthened by the quasi-religious occasions that threaded through the seasons: church fairs, strawberry festivals, commencement at Rutgers and the seminary, and Sunday school picnics of a thousand and more frolickers combined a religious setting or activity with opportunities for pure socializing. Indeed, evangelicals had a term for these events: "social religion" was an umbrella that covered everything from prayer meetings in private homes, followed by refreshments and gossip, to Fourth of July ceremonies in which solemn and stirring sermons were succeeded by elaborate al fresco feasts and what one Reformed minister described as a "noisy carnival of rum and gunpowder."[6]

Finally, social life entailed prodigious amounts of calling or visiting. With no telephones to connect them, it was important for people craving news and company to make and receive literally hundreds of informal social calls and visits in the course of a year. When these and the scores of formal parties and occasions their diaries record are factored in, the problem of describing that arena where the inner spiritual life of individuals and the everyday social intercourse of evangelical communities intersected is evident.

An attempt to describe it involves noticing that the main events of the calendar year and the liturgical year fell into three distinct clusters. Some clustered around traditional holidays that were brought by immigrants from the Old World to the New and that underwent adaptation and modernization here. Another cluster was made up of those occasions and events related to the common political roots and shared civil religion of Americans. And a third had to do with all the myriad activities gathered under the rubric "social religion." By examining first how the Dutch in New York and New Jersey celebrated Christmas and the Fourth of July, and then how they socialized in and out of church, we can capture the general texture of evangelical social activities and the specific ways the lives and values of this Dutch-descended people were altered by their participation in them as the process of Americanization inexorably advanced.

$S$ince the Reformation, Protestants had approached Christmas with ambivalence. In the Netherlands, the Reformed Church considered its observance (as of Easter and Pentecost also) a Papist vestige and ruled in 1572 that ministers could allude to the events in the life of Christ that such days commemorated, but must discourage any festivities. Bowing to the people's persistence in celebrating these occasions, however, the National Synod, to keep the peace, ruled in 1586 that Christmas, Easter, and Pentecost could be observed as special festivals, but that communion should be administered on them to give them a solemnity otherwise lacking.

Because of the Reformed Church's ancient disapproval of Christmas celebration, pious Dutch in New York and New Jersey remained ambivalent about it well into the nineteenth century. They observed it, but solemnly, on the one hand, whereas on the other they continued to relish the rowdiness and revelry historically associated with it. In 1830, its first year of publication, the *Intelligencer* editors wished their patrons and readers a merry Christmas, "for a merry heart makes the countenance cheerful." But let us not be mistaken, they added: "God forbid that we should encourage the mirth and glee that proceed from levity, and sinful hilarity." They encouraged mirth produced by being filled with the Holy Spirit, not wine, and urged that Christmas week be a holy week, not a time "spent in chambering and in wantonness."[7] No other mention of Christmas appeared in the paper that year, no Christmas story for children, no Christmas poem or hymn, no advertising of Christmas gifts. Though a lack of mention does not mean the day was not celebrated, diary entries indicate that it was not set aside in any special way.

Nearly a generation later, in 1856, there was nothing on page one of the *Intelligencer* about Christmas, although publication day that week fell on December 25. A stern editorial appeared on page two. It is proper to observe the day, the editors advised, as long as it is clear that there is absolutely no evidence that December 25 is the anniversary of Christ's birth. "The corrupt Papal Church, in its wicked arrogance, has frequently undertaken to change times and customs, and that lying Church must be held responsible for making the observance of Christmas identical in time with a lascivious Pagan festival." (Nineteenth-century editors and readers were anything but politically correct.) A Christian conscience will find a Christian way to honor the day, they went on, but the public needs to be warned of a "growing disposition to turn it into a Bacchanalian revel."[8]

Advertisements appeared in this year, however, for "Holiday Presents," pianos and melodeons, music, books, games, puzzles, paper dolls and a paper doll family, and "elegant home furnishing goods." Christmas was on its way to becoming the commercialized annual event we know so well today, and the Reformed Dutch community was beginning to join into its materialistic celebration. Even so, many continued to observe the day piously, some three hundred years after the Reformation. S.L.B. Baldwin, the father of several small children, attended church and Sunday school as usual on Christmas morning, 1842, as well as church in the evening, and he spent the afternoon reading Sears's *Biography of Christ*, a seventy-page pamphlet on the millennium, a sermon by Reformed minister Dr. George W. Bethune, and a number of weighty articles in the *Intelligencer*.[9]

The folkways long proscribed by the church of celebrating the darkest days of the agricultural year—the days around Christmastime—with burlesques and masquerades, processions and promenades, inversions, rowdyism, and unruliness crossed the Atlantic and soon rendered the Christmas season in America a time of carnival and public misrule. In the same Dutch communities where some spent the day quietly, Christmas was often far from solemn as survivals of these ancient practices made their appearance. In Somerville, for instance, where Mr. Baldwin piously considered the millennium, a local bartender "got up some Christmas sport" on December 25, 1844, by producing a pig with a greased tail. "The person who should seize and hold the pig by the tail, was to have him." After a long chase in which the pig got out of its enclosure and ran down to the depot with the local bloods in hot pursuit, one John Stewart secured the prize and carried it off.[10] This "sport" is a variant on the Dutch Shrove Tuesday pastime known as Riding the Goose, practiced and outlawed both in the Netherlands and in New Netherland, in which young men on horseback attempted to grab onto a greased goose suspended from a rope and pull its head off.

Another Dutch folkway, one with roots in the citizens' militias popular in the Netherlands in the seventeenth-century, was still practiced on Christmas Day in "Dutch" Poughkeepsie in 1851: "A splendid company of soldiers paraded our streets. They called themselves the 'Fantasticals' or 'Fancy Light Guards,' and after marching through the village to the warlike tunes of a band of music, went to a field at some distance from the village to shoot at a target." Their costumes, H. L. Thomas wrote to Abraham Lansing in Albany, were "extremely gorgeous," each different. One wore a "hat of gigantic size and grotesque shape—and another having an artificial nose about four inches in length—a third a pair of pantaloons half red and half white."[11]

A fear of growing public misrule at Christmas by lower-class youths and workers was the main impetus for the domestication of the holiday and its promotion as a family event centered around children, gift giving, and activities best celebrated indoors. But as the holiday in its indoor, domesticated format gained in popularity, some tutelage in how it might be observed, especially in the churches, was needed. The *Intelligencer* obliged with articles such as one in 1856 titled "How They Keep Christmas at Tompkinsville." In this Staten Island Reformed Church, two enormous Christmas trees laden with seven hundred presents were set up on either side of the pulpit, and the Reverend Philip Milledoler Brett addressed the congregation on the symbolic significance of the tree, which had been introduced to Americans by German immigrants: its evergreen branches signified the undying love we should have for Jesus, he told them. After prayers, hymns, and a "brief but pointed address" by the Sunday school superintendent, silver medals were awarded to nine children who had memorized the most Bible verses, and gifts were distributed: portable inkstands, plated penholders, pencils, purses, scissors, cologne, and candies.[12]

The celebration of the day grew apace. In 1861, a "modern" Christmas at the Northwest Reformed Church on West 23rd Street in Manhattan amazed the older generation. The graceful columns of the church's mission room were transformed into "towering masses of evergreens and roses." The walls were draped in roses, evergreens, wreaths, and garlands, and the chandeliers, buried beneath floral treasures, seemed to have sprung from a bed of evergreens on the ceiling. They hung over the children like "some tropical exotic." The room seemed like a "fairy creation," an illusion enhanced by the "flitting about of numerous bewitching lady teachers." Two long tables spread the whole length of the room were "loaded with every thing that could please the eye and delight the palate," and the bounty was distributed in such quantities to the children that many a one "regretted that Christmas comes but once a year."[13]

In the Raritan Valley, things were done on a more modest scale. At Christmas in 1869, Catherine Low Hardenbergh, seventeen, of New Brunswick, helped decorate the church with simple boughs. Two days before Christmas, her father and brother brought greens home to trim the parlors. The girls made sprays to place over the pictures and wreaths to hang on both sides of the folding doors, and Catherine helped Aunty fry *olekoks*— Dutch doughnuts. At the last minute, on Christmas Eve Day, she shopped for simple gifts for family members (one modest gift per person), and on Christmas Day, which was a Saturday, she stayed at home to put the house in order, while the rest of the family went to church.[14]

In the upriver community of Kinderhook, New York, it was 1875 before the Reformed Church there introduced a Christmas tree and greens to the sanctuary, though the Reformed Church in Fishkill Landing, not far south, had two trees, presentation prizes for every Sunday school scholar, and a "substantial Christmas-box" for the pastor of $200. In Keyport, New York, in 1875, children of the Reformed Sunday school gathered in the church on Christmas Eve to greet Santa Claus, but there was no tree, only a large star made of evergreens and lighted with tapers arranged in back of the pulpit. And at the Montgomery, New York, Reformed Church, the Reverend Cornelius Brett allowed the sanctuary to be decorated with evergreens and a Christmas tree in front of the pulpit to be laden with dolls and fruit and toys for the younger children, books and pictures for the older, and confectionary for all. The old men of the congregation received boxes of chocolate cigars, and the pastor was presented with a silver salver and a pair of silver goblets.[15]

By 1875, the holiday had been accepted almost universally in Reformed congregations, and the Reverend William R. Duryee of the La Fayette Reformed Church in Jersey City could write to the *Intelligencer* that the man who doesn't enjoy it is a great sufferer. The editors gamely joined in the approbation with an editorial entitled "Merry Christmas." The following year, the *Intelligencer* had its usual Christmas editorial urging a properly decorous observance of the day, but it also ran two Christmas hymns, a Christmas poem, two Christmas stories, and a story and a song for children. And advertisements aplenty touted the wares of the season. When the staid editors of this denominational publication joined the rush to the Christmas tree, the holiday can be said to have finally received the Reformed Church's official sanction.[16]

Associated with Christmas in the Netherlands is St. Nicholas Day, December 6. St. Nicholas is a nonbiblical, never canonized, and perhaps nonexistent saint, but nevertheless a living international legend. Commonly believed to have flourished in the first half of the fourth century, St. Nicholas is the patron saint of Amsterdam. He has long been assumed to have been as well the patron saint of New Netherland and subsequently of New York, but this has been proved not to be the case. Assisted by his servant Black Peter (Zwarte Piet), in the Netherlands this folk figure appears on the eve of his day to fill children's shoes with treats. (As the Reformed Church everywhere in the world discouraged any celebration of this ambiguous, extrabiblical folk icon, it is most curious that in 1642 a church built inside the walls of the Fort on the Battery was called the Church of St. Nicholas.)

The biographer of St. Nicholas, Charles W. Jones, has reported that "*nobody* has ever found any contemporaneous evidence of a St. Nicholas cult in New York during the colonial period." Nor did Jones find a single reference to either Nicholas or Santa Claus in the twelve other American colonies. The earliest surviving colonial reference to *Sinte Klaas goed heylig*

*Man* (other than, presumably, to the church in the fort), appears in 1763, ninety-nine years after the English takeover of New Netherland. The "colonizing of North America and the Reformation concurred in time," Jones wrote in 1978, "and the American colonists were preponderantly reformers. Hence in the seventeenth and eighteenth century N[icholas] did not add to the American land or language."[17]

Although there is no evidence of a "cult" of St. Nicholas in New York and New Jersey, and he was certainly not the patron saint of the area, his legend did cross the Atlantic with the Dutch settlers, as the naming of the church in the fort indicates. But the legend apparently languished, for according to Jones, St. Nicholas was introduced to New York anew in 1804 by the founders of the New-York Historical Society. Santa Claus, his New World namesake and effigy, was invented five years later, in 1809, by Washington Irving in his satirical *History of New York*. Spurious nineteenth-century "biographies" of St. Nicholas, followed by spurious "histories" of his reign in New Netherland, all based on the spurious *History of New York*, account for the misapprehension.[18]

What is most extraordinary about the rebirth of St. Nicholas in New York and New Jersey, and the subsequent creation of the folk figure Sinte Klaas—and relevant to questions of ethnic persistence—is that the nineteenth century acted as if the two characters had been there forever, and the twentieth century believed it. An elaborate re-creation of Sinte Nicklaas's annual visit to eighteenth-century Bergen County is staged each year at the Steuben House in River Edge, for instance—a museum that is maintained by the New Jersey Division of Parks and Forestry and whose important furnishings and collections are owned by the Bergen County Historical Society. The earliest part of this historical house dates to 1713, and during the Revolution it served at times as military headquarters, intelligence post, and encampment ground. But if Charles W. Jones is correct, it never witnessed a celebration of St. Nicholas or Sinte Klaas prior to 1804/1809, when Dutch-descended families with a powerful desire to identify with their roots, and their Dutchophile friends and neighbors, seized upon the reintroduced legend and made it their own—a testament to the powerful human longing for group identity.

During the calendar year, American political history offered opportunities for nineteenth-century citizens to affirm their common roots on Washington's birthday, Lincoln's birthday, Decoration Day, and the Fourth of July. Nineteenth-century evangelicals did not draw a fine line between church and state, and these political and quasi-political occasions were mingled with church life in what was thought of as part of a natural whole:

Protestant and patriotic, moral and well intentioned, and accepted by all concerned with little thought to the First Amendment.

Contemporary political events also offered opportunities, such as days of fasting, humiliation, and prayer, for public worship, days when Americans of all ethnic and national backgrounds could recognize their common history and experience. Such a day was proclaimed in 1841 when President William Henry Harrison died in office. A student at the New Brunswick Theological Seminary described the solemn and respectful manner in which this occasion was observed. "The stores have all been closed and secular business suspended, and the people flocked to the house of God to humble themselves and confess their sins and ask for pardon. . . . What an interesting and solemn sight to see a whole nation in mourning for their head and father."[19] Such occasions renewed evangelicals in their common endeavors and bound them closer in knowledge of the filial respect and affection they believed they owed to their leaders, secular and spiritual. As they united Americans of all religious backgrounds in a fellow feeling, they reinforced the bonds that drew ethnic and ethnicized groups like the Dutch Americans out of their cultural cocoons and ever more surely into the mainstream culture.

The most important public event in the evangelical year was Independence Day. Because evangelicals believed with a certainty that America was God's chosen country, on the Fourth of July they celebrated not only civil independence but religious freedom as well. "There is a wondrous analogy . . . between the settlement of the descendants of Jacob in the land promised to Abraham, and the history of the United States of America," the *Intelligencer* editorialized in 1840. "The Fourth of July when the Declaration of Independence announced its cardinal self-evident truths . . . [is] the legitimate consequence of the landing of the . . . pilgrims, one hundred and fifty years previous. Religious and civil freedom are inseparable."[20]

It should be noted here that, in 1840, even the editors of the *Intelligencer* were still crediting the English with having brought political freedom to the New World via their religious beliefs. Twenty years later, however, Dutch Americans had resuscitated knowledge of their own near-forgotten role in America's origins, and clergymen now made a point of emphasizing that role. On the Fourth of July in 1860, for example, Montville, New Jersey, a Morris County stronghold of the Reformed Church, was described as a "place where the people know how to celebrate Independence in a sensible manner." An "immense army with banners, stepping to soul-stirring music" took possession of the grove and, "following a "manly reading" of the Declaration of Independence by one Reformed minister, another preached on "Protestant Christianity"—a version of

Protestantism pointedly not identical to the beliefs of the Puritans—as the source of America's free institutions. A third spoke at length on revolutions, drawing an instructive analogy between the revolt of the Dutch against Catholic Spain in the Reformation and the revolt of America against a tyrannical Britain. And a fourth, who had recently returned from a trip to the Netherlands, discoursed on "What I Saw in Holland," a paean to the ideals of liberty and tolerance in that country as transplanted to America by the original Dutch settlers.[21]

Church fairs and Sunday school picnics were often scheduled for the Fourth. In 1845, the "Ladies of Bergen Neck" advertised their annual event, which was a fund raiser for the purpose of aiding in the payment of the church debt and open to all. Bergen Neck's pleasant situation on the west shore of the Hudson River made it an attractive resort both to those in Manhattan and to those inland. "The place fixed upon is the parsonage premises, within a few rods of the wharf. Access can be had by the Steamer *Passaic*, from the foot of Barclay Street, at 10 o'clock A.M., by the Port Richmond boats, and by land from Jersey City, distant 7 miles, affording one of the most delightful rides in the vicinity of the city. A variety of fancy and useful articles will be offered for sale, besides a choice and plentiful supply of refreshments."[22]

The Fourth of July provided an occasion in many communities for a daylong display of civil religion and Bible religion as Sunday schools and local militia mingled from churchbells at sunrise to fireworks after sunset. In Readington, New Jersey, the bells rang at sunrise on July 4, 1844, to call the townsfolk to the bower in Mr. Ten Broeck's meadow. At 10:00 A.M., parade marshals, Sabbath school officials, and a military band led the assembled procession to the Reformed Church, where choir and military occupied the front gallery and schoolchildren the pews immediately in front of the pulpit. After the morning exercises, which consisted of singing, prayer, reports of the various Sunday schools in the community, the election of officers, and addresses, the assembled marched at noon from the church back to the bower, where they partook of refreshments and heard an address specifically directed to the children. Then all marched back to the church, again to the tunes of the band under the supervision of the marshals, the order of march being military, the Committee of Arrangements, aged men, clergy and speakers, children, ladies, and strangers and citizens generally. This time children sat in the galleries and the adults in the pews.

The afternoon service began with prayer, singing, a reading of the Declaration of Independence, martial music, a patriotic oration, more singing, suitable remarks by the pastor, additional singing, and the benediction, after which the military led all back to the bower, where a dinner was served under the trees. No intoxicating liquors were allowed at the tables. When the cloth was removed, the toasts began (drunk with pure cold water), and continued until dark, when the young men of the town put on a display of fireworks.[23] (See figure 11.)

Christmas and the Fourth of July were occasions on which the social fabric of Dutch communities was reinforced again and again by the repeated interaction of families, extended families, and neighbors. But they were also occasions that drew the Dutch out of their ethnic enclaves by connecting them to a wider ecumenical and national culture in which economic status, social class, civic involvement, and changing attitudes toward the role of women in American society, more than simply a devotion to particular religious doctrines or national backgrounds, were the characteristics by which Dutch Americans were increasingly identifying themselves.

*A*fter the Fourth of July, evangelicals could relax. Most churches closed their doors for a month or two in summer because of low attendance, and opened them "to the scrubbers, the white-washers and the painters," while both clergy and parishioners took refuge in the countryside. The Reverend Theodore L. Cuyler, pastor of the Market Street Reformed Dutch Church in Manhattan, looked forward to his summer vacation. "A year's labor in the city leaves one somewhat like a mill-stream in August," he wrote. "The dam is low and the water-wheel turns slowly. . . . There is a wear and tear in the life of a city pastor   an incessant interruption—a demand for extra labors on platforms and in committee rooms—and a constant whipping-up, as if he were an omnibus-horse. . . . New-York lives in a hurry."[24]

The hectic church year took a toll on the laity, too, judging from the activities of one Reformed deacon who, in a letter to the *Intelligencer*, attested that during the past year, he had heard 97 regular sermons, 62 written sermons, 35 ex tempore sermons, 43 addresses, 37 talks, and 21 "remarks," attended 17 funerals, 9 weddings, 16 sociables, 1 fair, 3 festivals, 45 Sunday school classes, and passed the plate 64 times, besides attending consistory meetings, visiting the poor, and working in the church office. For his well-deserved summer respite, he planned to go to Coney Island, he announced.[25]

The Reverend Thomas De Witt Talmage, whose weekly sermons were published without a break for more than 30 years in 3,600 different newspapers, was ambivalent about the practice of closing the church in the summer. This was "warm-weather religion," as he called it, when "pulpit and pew often get stupid together, and ardent devotion is adjourned until September." But there was danger in this, for "who can afford to lose two months out of each year, when the years are so short and so few? He who

# Fourth of July, 1865.

## SOMERSET COUNTY

### CELEBRATION

### In Frelinghuysen's Grove.

### Order of Exercises.

1. MUSIC by the Band.
2. INVOCATION by Rev. B. C. MORSE.
3. MUSIC.
4. PRAYER by Rev. Dr. J. F. MESICK.
5. READING the Declaration of Independence by SYLVESTER ROBINS, Esq.
6. MUSIC.
7. ADDRESS by Hon. F. J. FITHIAN, of N. York.
8. MUSIC.

Intermission of two hours, during which Dinner will be served to the Returned Soldiers and invited guests. Families and visitors will dine *a la Pic Nic.*

### AFTERNOON EXERCISES.

1. MUSIC by the Band.
2. ADDRESS by Rev. Dr. H. C. FISH, of Newark.
3. MUSIC.
4. ADDRESS by Rev. Dr. CHAMBERS, of N. York.
5. BENEDICTION by Rev. JAS. I. BOSWELL.

The exercises will commence at half past 10 o'clock precisely. In the evening a grand display of Fireworks will take place on High Street, Somerville.

☞ Accommodations for horses have been provided in the Grove.

"SOMERSET UNIONIST" PRINT.

FIGURE 11. This program for a Fourth of July celebration in Somerset County makes clear that the separation of church and state was not a sensitive issue in 1865. *Courtesy Special Collections and University Archives, Rutgers University Libraries.*

stops religious growth in July and August will require the next six months to get over it." Iniquity does not take a vacation in the summer, the Reverend Talmage warned his readers. ("The devil never leaves town.") If this was not enough to alarm them, he assured them that more people die in summer than at any other season of sun stroke, dysenteries, fevers, and choleras. "We cannot afford to die," he concluded, "when we are least alert and worshipful."[26]

The *Intelligencer* editors, of like mind, in 1845 published a list of fourteen rules for Christians preparing for their summer excursions: Never neglect to read, meditate, and pray; attend some place of worship on Sunday; never entertain or visit on Sunday; never travel on Sunday; carry tracts with you to distribute along the way, and so on. "Friend reader! Would it not be well to . . . paste [these rules] in the top of your trunk?"[27]

Although the list did not include a rule that Reformed Dutch people should summer together, they did. The Reverend Cuyler spent part of the summer of 1855 in Saratoga, which the Dutch, he wrote in his weekly column in the *Intelligencer*, had taken over. "Our clergy and laity seem to outnumber all others," he wrote. And he let his readers know that "We have no reason to be ashamed of our representatives. There is no dandyism among the gentlemen; but little dancing among the ladies. They are of the 'solid men' of Gotham, sound on 'Change [the Stock Exchange], and sound in church doctrine."[28]

Claverack, New York, in Columbia County, Dutch turf from the days of the patroons, became in the nineteenth century a favorite summer gathering place for Reformed clergy and laity, just as it had become the locale for one of their most successful educational establishments, Claverack Academy. The Reformed minister Elbert S. Porter, for many years the editor of the *Intelligencer*, spent his summers on his farm in Claverack. The village, he reported in 1870, was becoming with each succeeding summer more and more a favorite resort for families from the city. The "old, beautiful and embowered village" attracted the sort of people who did not care for the "frippery and dissipation of the fashionable places," including many Reformed clergymen who kept theology and literature on their tongues, while their hearts found "refreshment in genial walks through green pastures and beside still waters." Of his Brooklyn congregation, there were in July 1870 about a dozen families already ensconced, with thirty more expected, some to remain until autumn. If they could not afford a house of their own, these vacationers boarded at Claverack Academy, which advertised moderate prices and which welcomed children.[29]

In addition to Saratoga and Claverack, in New York State the favorite vacation places for Reformed clergy and laity were the Catskills, Ostego

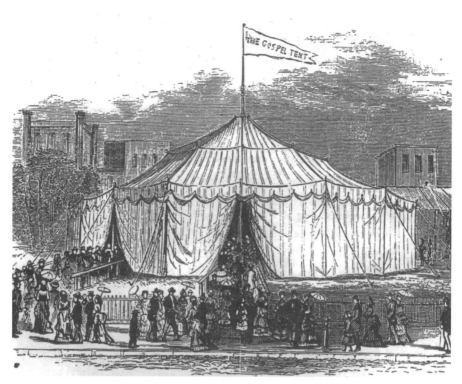

FIGURE 12.  Summertime was prime time for revivals. This one, in July 1876, was at today's busy Herald Square, the site of Macy's department store. *Courtesy Picture Collection, The Branch Libraries, The New York Public Library.*

County, especially Cooperstown, Hunter in Greene County, and the Adirondacks. In New Jersey, Perth Amboy on the Raritan Bay and, of course, the shore itself beckoned. The Raritan Beach Grove at Perth Amboy was favored for Sunday school picnics and church parties, because no intoxicating liquors were sold or permitted on the premises. The grove of stately pines, cedars, and oaks, situated on a bold bluff overlooking Raritan Bay and River, was a popular resort for generations of rural folk for twenty-five miles around Perth Amboy and was loved for the fresh and invigorating sea air and water and the beautiful vistas. Access by water was convenient, and the largest steamboats could land even at low tide.[30] (See figure 12.)

The steamboat and the locomotive brought new dimensions to summertime. From rural Rockland County, with its excellent train system, it was possible for Effie Blauvelt and her family to take the train to New York on a fine summer's day and board the Albany day boat to the town of "Catskills [*sic*]." They dined on the boat at midday, disembarked at Catskill at 3:30 P.M., hurried by stage to the West Shore Rail Road, and returned to West Nyack by train, all in the same day.[31]

But steamboats, in particular, had their drawbacks. Henry Gansevoort wrote to his mother in August 1853 that he found the noisy steamboat from Albany to New York uncomfortably hot, although it was endurable until the "witching hour of midnight when . . . the bedbugs and musquetoes [*sic*] were added to my other torments." The Reverend Cuyler commented that the steamer from Albany, the *New World*, was packed with 1,300 passengers, "like an omnibus on a rainy day." And when Elbert Herring of New York City and his wife Agnes Van Rensselaer visited her relatives in Albany in the summer of 1865, the return trip by steamboat was a nightmare with nearly 2,000 passengers, "and generally not of the superior class." The children all had "tremendous loud trumpets in their throats, with a propensity to use them almost constantly. . . . There was so much noise and confusion, so many doors and windows open, so many brats squealing, and so many Goths and Vandals coming in and going out" that it was impossible to enjoy the trip.[32]

Modest pleasures were close to home in the rural enclaves that had been settled by New Netherland families in the seventeenth century. Helen Verbryck Clark of Tappan, New York, a member of the Piermont Reformed Church, records in her diary the special place the Hudson River played in summer: she and her husband Cornelius took a row on the river of a summer's evening, on another sailed with friends, her son fished for tomcods off the dock at Piermont, Cornelius caught herring and a few shad to salt and some bass to eat fresh. He sailed with a friend down to Alpine and walked home over the Palisades. They drove on an August evening to the river at Hook Mountain, or on a Sunday hitched up the team and crossed the river by ferry to enjoy an outing in Central Park.[33]

As ever proliferating networks of railroads were chartered and built, Reformed folk in rural areas could enjoy rail service that linked them easily with local beauty spots and friends and relatives formerly visited only cumbrously by stage coach. The Camden and Amboy line first crossed New Jersey in 1833, and by 1838 it carried 165,000 passengers back and forth across the state.[34] By 1840, residents of Jersey City could travel by train to New Brunswick, Amboy, Trenton, and on to Philadelphia, and in that decade residents of the little hamlet of Blauveltville in today's Rockland County were served by two major railroad lines providing frequent service to the pier in Piermont, where they could proceed by boat to Manhattan. In 1841, they could travel west sixteen miles to Suffern and north to Goshen in Orange County.[35]

By 1848 a rail connection made it possible to travel directly from Jersey

City to Suffern. Local travel was expedited by spurs, connecting residents of little communities like Piermont, Sparkill, Orangeburg, Blauveltville, Nanuet, Spring Valley, Monsey, Tallman, and Suffern. The Jersey Midland Railroad operated between Ridgefield Park, New Jersey, and Tappan, New York, and as early as 1859, rural Rocklanders could travel directly from the little community of Sparkill to Jersey City.

The railroad facilitated pious as well as worldly activities. Evangelicals used the trains to get them to churches and revivals in distant communities. Maria Ferdon, from Bergen County, New Jersey, for instance, traveled frequently to Sharon, New York, near Albany, to visit her former pastor the Reverend Henry Bellenger and to attend the classis meetings there of the old secessionist congregations. In September 1866, Margaret Schenck and a group of eighteen New Brunswick friends and relations journeyed to Jerseyville, Illinois, and White Hall, Illinois, where Margaret's brother led a Reformed Dutch Church whose parishioners had migrated there from New Jersey. Although they were exhausted after their arduous five-day journey, they launched into the same activities they were accustomed to in New Jersey: they went to church and church events numerous times a week (including the Methodist, Presbyterian, and Baptist churches), and they visited. Margaret herself recorded paying and receiving more than two hundred visits during her five weeks in Illinois, or an average of nearly six visits a day.[36]

The diary of a young man from the Raritan area reveals much about the texture of social life and courting practices in Dutch New Jersey and illustrates also the seamless continuity between social life and religious life. It suggests as well that, certainly among young people, social behavior was not particularly inhibited by the pious counsels of their clergymen. Garretson Hageman of Middlebush, New Jersey, in Somerset County, attended the Millstone (later Harlingen) Reformed Dutch Church, and taught in its Sabbath school. He began a diary on his twenty-fifth birthday in 1869, and kept it for many years.

At twenty-five, Garretson's social life was flourishing, and he had scores of friends. In the supposedly staid and proper evangelical communities where they lived, Garretson and his friends drank, danced, stayed out late, and "romped and tussled" with each other in darkened parlors.[37] In general, they enjoyed a freedom from scrutiny that would have seemed quite natural to their ancestors in the Netherlands, where the "night-courting" of adolescents was in some provinces in the seventeenth century an accepted feature of coming of age, but perhaps shocking to those of cultural backgrounds where less freedom was permitted to the young.

On August 8, 1869, Garretson and friends, five couples in all, took a "party ride" to Washington Rock, a two-and-a-half-hour trip. There, after admiring the fine view of the agricultural valley below, New York City across the harbor, and the Atlantic Highlands, they had "dinner at two which done honor to the proprietor . . . champagne being among the drinkables." Toward nightfall the couples rode slowly on to Plainfield "where we had a little trot"—that is, they raced their horses beyond the allowed pace. They stopped at another hotel, where Garretson procured a smoked glass "to view the great eclipse," played billiards, had supper, and walked about the yard. At eight, they started for home, arriving at half-past ten. The outing, he wrote, gave "much bad feeling" to those who were not included, "it being reported that only those that were not engaged was envited [*sic*]." (This comment suggests a reverberation of the tradition in the Reformed Church in the Netherlands that, once a promise to marry had been given and the banns read in church, one was as good as married—and thus presumably less fun to be with, as one's favors now had to be reserved for one's betrothed.)

The next day, Garretson went to church in the morning, and in the afternoon called on Sadie, Belle, Anna, and Mary Voorhees, then went to Millstone to call on a friend, where he met two more friends and called on several more on the way home. On the tenth of the month, he was invited to the raising of Voorhees Garretson's horse barn, after which he went to Sadie Voorhees's to play croquet. After tea, he took Sadie and Lidi Suydam to Somerville to hear the singing. "Returned to hotel . . . and had some old Madeira and cake." The girls took the reins on the drive home; "we carried on dreadfull. . . . The [wagon] seat was small but it answered *good enough*[.] They pulled my ears. Each one took a hold of the one [ear] farthest from them it made me blush to have their arms so close to me, especially in such a position."

On August 20, Garretson and Lidi Suydam and another couple went to a party at Rocky Hill: "had very fine time [and] had introduction to . . . a great many other [girls]. Coming home . . . stopped at Rule's peach orchard & got hat full of peaches . . . reached home at 4 A.M., had a splendid time[.] Lidi promised me a kiss for every peach that I got her. I got her all I could find, you bet." Two days later, Garretson and Theodore Polhemus went to hear the Reverend Dr. Sears at Six Mile Run Reformed Church and afterward received "lots of invitations to dinner." After dinner he called on the Baird girls, Cassie Voorhees, and Mary Voorhees.

At a picnic in Hopewell a few days later, "the dancing was splendid, the floor was about 100 feet long and 45 feet wide." He "took a Brooklyn ladie to supper. danced every square dance with girls I have never seen before and perhaps will never see again. Reached home at 3:45 A.M." A few days later, he attended the Middlebush Sunday school picnic at Perth Amboy. "We had a splendid time arrived at 10 A.M. went a bathing before dinner, had good eating. after this we went a sailing up the river toward South River." He had a "splendid row" in a borrowed rowboat and "next went in bathing, then got up a party of 18 to sail to South Amboy." This day cost $1.15, and he got home early for once, at 9:15 P.M.

Garretson called on Belle and Anna Voorhees on August 31, and he "carried on high, they nearly gave me a thrashing which I deserved I know for I raised the d———." The next day, he and Theodore Polhemus took some girls to a fishing party in Mr. Garret Hageman's meadow: "We had a splendid time, went out rowing, [but] in showing [his] smartness" Garretson broke an oar. The owner "did not swear much. said not [a] damn bit more than expected. . . . All of our girls left us and went to party with some other gentlemen." Garretson, ever resourceful, found four new girls. "We had splendid dances . . . got home approx 3 [A.M.] well satisfied having received some sweet kisses."

In September, after planning for a week, Garretson organized a big party on September 24 "at Henry Polhemus's back place called 'Back House.'" In a state of great anticipation and excitement, he spent hours driving around the area inviting friends to the party, which unfortunately was not a complete success, for fewer than half of the hundred invitees appeared, and with difficulty Garretson had to extract a dollar extra a piece from the male guests to make up the pay for the musicians and the food and drink. Although his girl for the evening was Anna Voorhees, "Lidi Suydam said she would give me a kiss if I would find Will Wilson and get her fan [from him]. I found him in a jiffie, but did not take my pay then but I am going to have it *you bet*. Party ended at 2:15."

After church on November 7, Garretson talked with the girls, got into a horse race on the way home, and went to a friend's "grand Pa's" for dinner. "After dinner went to Millston[e] and called on a girl, who was not at home, then to another girl's, then to Blackwells Mills to call on two other girls, and finally to call on Anna and Belle Voorhees, where he found two other young men ensconced. "I made up my mind to see them leave first," he wrote. One left at nine o'clock, the other stayed till 11. "I got Anna in the back parlor and left Belle and him in the front parlor. he soon took the hint and left[,] Belle seeing him out." Belle did not come into the parlor again, but went upstairs to bed. "Then Anna and I had full possession [of both parlors] and we had a splendid evening together."

On December 9, he attended a singing meeting, where "we had a gay time I went upstairs to *help* the *girls* on with their shawls and hoods. *It is fun*. . . . Anna sat on my lap coming home." On December 21, there was a party at Henry Garretson's. "Very fashionable indeed, had one of the best times I think I ever had to any party." A fiddler played, and Garretson danced his first polka quadrille. He danced altogether with seven girls and "got home about three o'clock played out."

Christmas Eve found Garretson and his friends and aunt and uncle at a dance at Spencers' Hotel in Old Bridge. Here he was introduced "to a couple of young ladies and had a good dance with them Aunt Mariah she watched me closely." After escorting his aunt home, he went back to the hotel. "I asked some to dance without an introduction," he recorded proudly, although he also learned to his chagrin that one of his partners worked in the hotel as chambermaid. Nevertheless, he went "home to Aunt Mariah [at] 3 o'clock happy as a clam in high water."

The social whirl had no end. Two weeks later, Garretson escorted Sadie Voorhees to a party at Fred Voorhees's and danced with her plus nine named other young ladies "and several besides." Mrs. Voorhees provided the refreshments. "We boys found the music[.] broke up about 4 [A.M.]." Eight guests spent the night. "The girls slept in the same room in chairs and lounges and on the floor." The boys doubled up in beds upstairs. They got up at eight in the morning, breakfasted, had a chat, and started for home at about eleven.

$\mathcal{F}$un and games were by no means the sole province of young people in these lively communities, for everything from commencement at Rutgers and the seminary to adult birthdays, weddings, and silver and golden wedding anniversaries provided a reason for a party. At these affairs, laity and clergy were both well represented, mingling with one another on a social footing out of church as they did on a spiritual level within it. Indeed, there is little evidence of consciousness that the two realms might be incongruent. Nor is there any evidence of irony in the fact that the social affairs were often lavish, expensive, and bibulous. A clergyman might inveigh against the evils of drink from the pulpit, but it appears that the next evening might well find him and his flock clinking glasses at an elegant soiree.

Evangelicals, even at the height of the temperance movement, were not of one mind regarding the use of alcohol. Although the total-abstainer faction of the movement eventually emerged victorious nationally, New Jersey evangelicals favored educating society as to the evils of alcohol, and advocated moderation rather than abstinence—a position that may have been a legacy of the Dutch attitude toward alcohol, transmitted from the Netherlands. ("If there was any area where the Hollanders achieved European fame," according to one observer, "it was not their deep religious faith, but their taste for beer and wine.")[38]

A member of the New Brunswick Theological Seminary class of 1856 described a "large and brilliant party" given by Mr. and Mrs. Neilson, "an aristocratic name in this region," at what he called their baronial mansion a short distance from New Brunswick in June 1855. "The entertainment was gotten up in fine style, and consisted of ice cream, orange ice, charlotte russe, wine jelly, pine apple, lobster salad, and a host of other things too numerous to mention, besides lots of wine of different kinds. Indeed, . . . wine was more plenty[ful] than water." This student added, "You know the Maine liquor law was lost in this state by one vote." This elegant affair was attended by scores of Reformed lay people, as well as students and faculty of the seminary, and all the local clergymen and their wives.[39]

Judging from shopping lists, many pious Reformed folk, including women, were far from abstemious. On October 2, 1828, Adriance Van Brunt, now a deacon in the Flatbush Reformed Dutch Church in Brooklyn, purchased a half-dozen bottles of porter, a half-gallon of corn brandy, and a half-gallon of gin "for Jane and Sarah Marie," his unmarried sisters. A mere three weeks later, he restocked his stores with a half-dozen casks of porter, a half-gallon of Madeira wine, and a gallon of brandy.[40]

Believing alcohol to have certain health benefits, physicians prescribed drink for nursing mothers. There was a more informed view as well. When one New York doctor ordered a nursing woman to consume as much lager-beer and milk laced with brandy or rum as she could manage, her husband refused to allow her to drink either brew, for he had heard of a minister's wife "who had become a sot by the liquor prescribed while nursing her children." The mother who takes ale and beer "offers to her helpless babe a corrupted fountain, and she sows the seeds of disease in its blood. . . . [Moreover, Alcohol] benumb[s] the moral and spiritual nature of the mother, stimulate[s] the animal nature, and prepare[s] a heritage of depravity for the child."[41]

Despite the fact that they could not have been unaware of the dangers of alcohol in this era of the temperance movement, however, or of the social pressures mounting against it, drinking among the church-going Reformed Dutch clergy and laity in New York and New Jersey was an entrenched part of daily life. By 1850, temperance concerns had come to be a major theme of sermons and of editorials in the *Christian Intelligencer*, particularly as New Year's approached, for by midcentury evangelicals were in the habit of consuming vast amounts of alcohol as they greeted one another and the New Year. In both city and countryside, at each house where they stopped to pay their respects, young men were offered wines, cordials, and rum "freely as the air." Eating houses and bar rooms in New York City had begun to spread "free tables" on New Year's Day, and it was said that more drunkards were made that day than any other day or week in the year.

The editors of the *Intelligencer* reminded their readers that in the rosy wine lurked the tempter, Satan, and entreated their female readers, in particular, to refrain from offering intoxicating drinks to callers on New Year's. "The whole thing," they wrote, was, in fact, "in the hands of the ladies," for while the men of the house were out calling, their mothers, wives, sisters, and daughters were at home receiving callers and proffering refreshments to them. As call after call is made, the editors warned, and glass after glass is taken, "intoxication follows, and you [ladies] are responsible."[42]

Garret C. Schenck, a student at New Brunswick Theological Seminary, made New Year's calls in 1851 on Long Island in the morning and afternoon, and in Manhattan in the evening. "Wine was offered at almost every place," he wrote in his diary. But "we did not get at all drunk." Garret and his friend got to bed at two in the morning, having ridden thirty miles and walked five during the day.[43]

For young men, New Year's Day was an exciting occasion of freedom and excess. In 1870, "Ma had everything good [at noon] . . . and all ate hearty," Garretson Hageman wrote in his diary, after which meal he hitched up his horse and with his friend Theodore Polhemus went out calling. Belle and Annie Voorhees were at home and served them wine and good cake, then "Bell and I had a round I came out victorious." The two young men went on to the Reverend Dr. Sears's house, where they had cake and Adam's Ale. Then to Emma Boyd's for more cake. Then "to Alice Nevius [and] had lots of fun[.] had cake, apples, nuts, and lemonade all very fine." Then on to Mary Voorhees for jelly cake and wine and to Kate Van Doren's for cake, "wein," and apples, arriving back home at eleven in the evening.[44]

Weddings, which in the old days had taken place at home, were now performed in church and had become an important form of adult entertainment. By midcentury even the more liberal Reformed element was criticizing weddings for having become too lavish and too much of an expense. When the invitations to Cuyler Van Vechten's stylish wedding in Albany were given out, "it was generally understood that it was to be one of the most exclusive Church weddings ever known," Anna Lansing wrote to her brother Abraham in 1853. The doors of the church were to be shut and only the invited guests were to be admitted. But, she reported, there was such a crowd, and so many people pushed their way into the sanctuary, that she could not so much as see the tops of the bride and groom's heads and so left before the ceremony was over. "I have heard since that as Mr. Van Vechten had said it should be so very exclusive, the people had said it should not," she wrote. "So you see he had [to] submit to a public wedding after all."[45]

From Anna Lansing's intriguing and nuanced comment on this incident, we can infer that the uninvited members of the congregation and the community insisted on their right to enter their own church when and if they pleased. Its public role in their lives transcended any one individual's private considerations of class and snobbery. The community was resisting the impulse of the bride's family to transform an event—which some took to be an open and inclusive religious event—into a closed, exclusive one. It is worth remarking that here the usual salt-of-the-earth and down-to-earth image of the Dutch American is pictured in reverse, as if something in the materialistic midcentury air was encouraging a class spirit among them.

The lavish, no-expenses-barred Albany wedding of John Gould and Harriet Elmendorf, granddaughter of Solomon Van Rensselaer, was one of the highlights of the year 1878. To the reception at Cherry Hill in Albany (the estate of the Van Rensselaer family, descendants of the patroons), five hundred invitations were sent out, and for the reception two whole salmon à la mayonnaise, a boned and jellied turkey, six chicken salads, four lobster salads, and three hundred sandwiches were only the first five items on the caterer's long list of refreshments.[46]

This affluent family, with its mercantile background and connections, could well afford the expense of such a wedding. But things were done on a more modest scale on the farms of the Raritan Valley than in the fashionable precincts of the patroons, where "show," far from distrusted, was expected. Often, no meal was served at wedding receptions in the Raritan area, but only cakes and liquid refreshment, and guests numbered nearer fifty than five hundred. Even so, one can glimpse a competitive spirit in the comments on the tables: At Ann Voorhees's wedding reception, five kinds of cake were served, Alice Nevius reported to her brother; at Letticia Veghte's, six kinds; but at Matilda Beekman's, nine kinds.[47] And a materialistic spirit is evident in Garretson Hageman's account of the bride's presents at a wedding in 1870: a pair of gold earrings, a silver teaspoon, a silver ice pitcher, a sable collar and muff, three silver butter dishes, two pairs of earrings and breastpins, a sixty-piece set of china, silver berry spoons, a paper cutter, "and more," which Garretson estimated to be worth a thousand dollars in all.[48]

Although some wedding customs were changing according to evolving fashions, others persisted in an older mode with folkways remembered from the Old World. On the night of a wedding, it was an ancient custom, perhaps English in origin, to signify the event with bonfires, as diaries record over the decades. "Isaac P. Lindsley was married to-night to Aletta Vredenburgh. The boys had a bonfire in the street as usual on such occasions." And "Culver Baraclow was married at Kinderhook to a daughter of Dominie Van Dervoort. The infair is held at his mother's tonight, and the boys are burning tar barrels in front of the house."[49]

In Dutch-settled communities, the folk custom of the "home bringing," also called "infare," was offered by the groom's parents a day or sometimes a week after the wedding, and this was by invitation only as it involved the expense of a major feast. "John B. Veghte was married to Kate Dehart [on December 8] and yesterday they had the Home bringing to his fathers Mr. James Veghte's[.] they had a dinner party We was invited and they had about 50 strangers," reported his mother to son John S. Nevius, Jr., of New Brunswick. An ancient custom, the infare was observed in the Netherlands, as it was in one way or another throughout Europe and Britain. All ethnic groups and nationalities brought some variation of it with them to America, where it hybridized according to local circumstances. It is thought to have its roots in the rite of confarreation, by which the Romans constituted matrimony with the offering of a cake or bread made of farina or spelt.[50]

By the time of the Civil War, not only elaborate weddings but elaborate celebrations of wedding anniversaries were becoming quite the fashion. The guest list at a silver wedding anniversary in 1863 at Cherry Hill included Horatio Seymour, governor of New York, the well-known Reformed ministers Dr. Rufus W. Clark, Dr. Thomas E. Vermilye, and Dr. Isaac N. Wyckoff, and scores of friends, most having the familiar surnames of New Netherland. No expense was spared, and gifts included everything from a silver radish cup to a silver crumb scraper.[51]

The custom of lavish wedding anniversary celebrations caught on among less rarefied circles than Cherry Hill and began to be reported regularly in the *Intelligencer* after the Civil War. At the Reverend Elbert S. Porter's silver wedding anniversary in 1870, the young people of the congregation presented a "social musical entertainment" in the church, while in the parsonage a "happy company" of ladies prepared a "splendid supper" consisting of all the delicacies of the season. Members of the congregation surprised the minister and his wife with a six-piece silver set valued at nearly a thousand dollars, and a week later he and Mrs. Porter gave a "brilliant reception" for the congregation at which this silver set was displayed in a conspicuous place. A safe large enough to hold it was presented by a local safe-manufacturing company.[52]

Crowds, including all the neighboring ministers, gathered at the Harlingen, New Jersey, Reformed Church for the silver wedding of the Reverend John Gardner in June 1870. A bountiful repast for the "refreshment of the outer man . . . as is always done in Somerset County" was followed by the presentation of gifts: a silver tea set, silver coins, and "a beautiful buggy-wagon to ease the dominie's journeys through the congregation. . . . The dominie and juffrow" were overjoyed with the evidence of the love of their people.[53]

For some golden wedding anniversaries, fancy programs were printed up, along with hymns of praise especially written for the occasion by ministers and family members. Lavish feasts followed elaborate programs, and handsome and costly gifts were bestowed on couples who, fifty years before, had married with hardly any fanfare, expense, or publicity. Such occasions were reported in the *Intelligencer* and wittingly or not served several purposes: they reinforced the value society traditionally put on long, fruitful, happy marriages, of course. But they also communicated to a still culture-bound and ethnicized readership that their own church and lay leaders were accepting the values and customs of the mainstream consumer culture.

*A*t the beginning of the evangelical era, American society offered comparatively few "evil pastimes" to divert the pious from churchly pursuits. Most towns, even sizable ones, had no large halls or theaters, no opera, no concerts, no museums, no atheneums, and no scientific or literary associations to speak of. Churchgoing and visiting among family and neighbors were, as they had been since the seventeenth century, the chief diversions. By the 1830s social life was enlivened in many communities by the ubiquitous lottery and the annual appearance of the circus with its Negro minstrelsy, periodic horse racing, and recurrent visits from Indians who might encamp for a few weeks on the outskirts of towns—the women selling baskets in town, the men showing off their skill with bow and arrow— or from bands of wandering "Hungarians" who earned their living by singing and dancing and performing tricks and feats of strength.

Fires added their spontaneous excitement to the routine of the passing seasons, as did such natural phenomena as tornadoes, water spouts, eclipses, and the like, and there was nothing like a hanging to draw a crowd on a fine summer's day. The hanging of a New Brunswick–area murderer in the 1830s attracted to Gallows Hill a crowd of over twenty-five thousand, a large proportion of whom were women and children and no doubt— in that heavily Dutch-settled area—many of whom were pious Reformed churchgoers.

People hungered for diversion, however, and their wants increasingly came to be supplied by "panoramas," "moving dioramas," lecturers, traveling shows (featuring comic songs, monologues, and ventriloquism), traveling waxworks, freak shows, and eventually the genius of P. T. Barnum. In 1839, the *Democratic Republican Weekly New Era* advertised at the Masonic Hall in Manhattan a moving diorama, "a new scene called the Storm, being a Rural Landscape, with figures, cattle, etc., returning home, during which a storm arises, accompanied with terrific thunder and lightning." And at Peale's Museum one could take in "grand soirees magicale" by Monsieur Adrien, Jr., while at the American Museum on Broadway, Mr. Winchell was in town to give his inimitable descriptions of a landlord in trouble, as well as his Irish and Yankee characters and his famous Dutch Story in character. On exhibit the same evening, the advertisement promised, would be the Grand Cosmorama ("150 splendid views of all the principal cities and landscapes in the world").[54]

Traveling charlatans added to the attractions, or distractions. To the Somerville, New Jersey, courthouse came one Dr. Olcott in the summer of 1842. An "animal magnetism lecturer," Dr. Olcott performed "experiments in that comparatively new science," such as throwing a man into a magnetic slumber and then asking him such questions as "Who robbed Mr. Hedges' store?" Mr. Olcott "did not effect much," according to the always incisive S.L.B. Baldwin, and with public curiosity as to his repertoire soon satisfied, Mr. Olcott slipped out of town without paying the sheriff for the use of the courthouse.[55]

Cultural innovations that distracted their flocks' attention from religion were anathema to clergymen, of course, and by midcentury, with the growth of cities, the development of the theater and the opera, the style of increasingly elaborate parties and fancy balls, the influx of foreigners, and the disturbing proliferation of taverns and grog shops, the clergy had more to inveigh about than singing schools, lotteries, and horse racing.

Many came to the city, the editors of the *Intelligencer* warned, "with little or no inclination for worldly amusements, . . . but the melodious voice of some Madame or Signore" was difficult to resist. "How incompatible with the pleasures of religion, and the felicity of heaven are the opera and the theater, how easily the first glass leads to a thousand snares," the editors cautioned young men fresh from the country. "The winter is approaching, and the balls and promiscuous pleasure parties will issue their cards of invitation to the fashionable circle," but ask yourself, they urged, if your attendance will please God, grieve your parents, or bear reflection in a dying hour.[56]

Secular diversions multiplied. In 1850, Barnum's Chinese Museum at 539 Broadway, between Spring and Prince streets, had on view "a real Chinese Beauty with Feet Two and a Half Inches Long." Miss Pwan-Yekoo, the Chinese beauty, was seventeen years old, and part of her attraction may have been the composition of her entourage. Notwithstanding her tender years and her billing as belonging to a Chinese family of the highest respectability, Miss Pwan-Yekoo's traveling companions were a Professor

Soo-chime, thirty-two, his two young children, a male interpreter of eighteen, and a serving maid of twenty-three.[57]

Ministers found much to rail about in these years: "It was reported in a newspaper that church-members throng the performances of *Rachel* by the score! and that several clergymen were present *incognito*," fumed Reformed clergyman T. L. Cuyler in his weekly column in the *Intelligencer*. We "consistent Christians who are 'prejudiced against these traps of Satan' are sneered at, [but] while the Rachels are enacting their sham tragedies on the stage, I wonder how many soul-tragedies the Devil is . . . working out in the upper tiers . . . and the adjourning drinking saloons?"[58]

Everything from dancing to reading novels to buying chances at ladies' fairs was seen as diverting the attention of the people from holy pursuits, and Reformed dominies and pious laymen alike reproached "quill drivers" and "story spinners." They even questioned the propriety of what one letter writer called "ecclesiastical gambling": the popular practice of offering "lucky bags" and "ring cakes" and selling shares in fancy articles at church fairs and strawberry festivals. All of these and other apparatus invented by the devil are nothing more nor less than gambling and thus violate the laws of both God and man, one correspondent scolded.[59]

As attractive worldly diversions proliferated, Reformed lay people readily took them up. But many were also genuinely puzzled as to where to draw the line, and Reformed clergymen often found thoughtful allies among their female congregants. "H.E.B.," a woman in a Brooklyn Reformed Dutch congregation, who had a regular column in the *Intelligencer* in the 1850s, noted that many Christians who thought it "unquestionably wrong to attend the theatre, or the opera," nevertheless patronized the lecture rooms of the city museum and without compunction attended inferior, cheap dramas performed there. But what about dramas performed at home? she wondered. Are charades wrong? If so, then are riddles, puzzles, and conundrums wrong? Every sensible person condemns gambling, she wrote, but what about billiards, ninepins, whist, chess, backgammon, and drafts? Are these sinful? H.E.B. answered her own questions: The "narrow-minded, square-cornered Christian" says yes, she announced, for all these games "are the ABC of gambling."

As to dancing, H.E.B. was less definitive. Because Christ had not danced at the wedding at Cana, and because the Heidelberg Catechism, in answer to Question 109 on the Seventh Commandment, includes among forbidden activities "all unchaste actions, gestures, words, thoughts, desires, and whatever may entice thereto," dancing had been proscribed by the Reformed clergy in the Netherlands from the sixteenth century. Dancing was considered lewd, and "for devout church-members, the dance hall was an anti-church, a synagogue of Satan," A. T. Van Deursen writes.[60]

H.E.B. disagreed that dancing was sinful, because "even the Bible speaks of a 'time to dance.'" But it depended upon the circumstances, she ruled. It was permissible to "gambol in the field," to "dance on the green sward to the merry note of the farmer's violin, to waltz over the velvet carpets in the parlor, and to practice cotillions in the gymnasium in red flannel bloomers, but it was wrong to dance in ballrooms, with their attendant excitement, unwholesome viands, impure air, close, heated, gaslighted rooms, for these produce exhaustion, depression, and enervation." H.E.B.'s general rule was "whatever amusement will injure us, or injure others, is wrong."[61]

If they followed this rule, and sought amusement that would not injure themselves or others, even the most pious Reformed Dutch evangelicals had many choices in lively nineteenth-century New York and New Jersey. "A good day in Zion" for Reformed Dutch clergyman B. C. Taylor of New Brunswick was a Sabbath where he preached in the morning, attended the recitation of the Bible class in the afternoon, explained the recitation from the pulpit in the evening, and had large and attentive audiences on all three occasions.[62] But a good *year* in Zion, for many Reformed clergy and laity alike, had come to include more than piety and preaching. By the middle of the nineteenth century, a good year in Zion entailed more of modern America than it did of Dutch Calvinism.

# CHAPTER 7

# The Family

## A NURSERY OF GODLINESS

*Remember, parents, it is your special office to train your children in this way.*
*The Master has given you the work and clothed you with the requisite authority*
*to accomplish it. If you fail, no one can take your place.*
—Reformed Protestant Dutch Church, *Tracts*, no. 12, 1858

The potent forces that encouraged the ethnocentrism of Dutch Americans—the revival of interest in Dutch history through the reportage of the *Christian Intelligencer*, the enduring allegiance to Dort, the successful efforts of New Brunswick Seminary and of Rutgers to create a physical and psychological center of Dutchness in the heart of the former New Netherland, and geographical factors governing settlement patterns, social life, and marrying customs—were ultimately overcome by other equally powerful forces that shattered the Dutch sense of exceptionalism and impelled the Dutch out into the brave new world of Americanness. Among the most important of these agents was a concept of family captured in one of the thirty-four "golden maxims" of the Reformed Dutch Church's Lee Avenue Sabbath School in Brooklyn: "The family is a divine plantation, designed by God himself to be a nursery of religion and godliness."[1]

It was not a new concept. Christian churches had always stressed in their creeds and catechisms the responsibility of parents for the religious welfare of their children. What was new in the nineteenth century was the way in which the religious press appropriated the idea of the family as religious nursery and flooded the nation with veritable rivers of prescriptive literature from which pious parents imbibed the notion that they were the regents of God on earth to fulfill his will.

Genuine religious concerns for salvation on the one hand, tempered by the contemporary concern with the effects of unregulated immigration on the other, coincided with technological advances in printing and innovative new distribution methods to offer clergy and social leaders a golden opportunity to extend the gospel message while molding the American character into a moral and useful shape. For Reformed Dutch families breasting this tide of prescriptive literature, to find themselves in the same cultural currents as families belonging to their sister faiths was to acknowledge the philosophical consensus that was gradually transforming them from a parochial subgroup to part of a broad, inclusive mainstream. But while they had such a wealth of printed material to choose from, it also diminished the importance they had traditionally placed on the Heidelberg Catechism as the household's main teaching tool.

The Heidelberg Catechism, since its publication in 1563, had had a secure place as the primary instrument of instruction for Reformed Dutch families. It had always been regarded as a sufficient instrument for supplying parents with guidance regarding the right of their children to be baptized, to be brought up in the faith, and "to be prepared by catechetical discipline for the other great sacrament, the Lord's Supper." The catechism's question-and-answer format was ideally suited to the memorization of correct responses to doctrinal points, while its "passional, personal, practical" tone was intended to appeal directly to the heart and soul of the young confirmand. Its comforting tone did not detract, however, from one of its most important underlying messages: that one's obedience to God was to be reflected in one's strict obedience to one's earthly parents. The importance of obedience in the religious culture of the evangelical era cannot be overstated. Obedience was central, the logic being that the child who did not obey its parents would not obey God. And the child who did not obey God was surely destined to spend eternity in hell.[2] (See figure 13.)

In the nineteenth century, as ministers increasingly turned their attention to the ills of society, so increasingly sermonic literature and tracts outlining the duties of parents and the duties of children added their weight to the catechism in addressing family life and child-rearing issues—and in the emphasis on obedience. Reformed ministers and the General Synod of the denomination, taking advantage of new printing and circulation means, published innumerable sermons on these subjects.

Like the catechism, both sermons and tracts emphasized parents' responsibility for having their children baptized, and thereafter for regarding them as church members and training them to perform all the Christian duties appropriate to their age. This could be accomplished only if parents established their authority early, maintained it uniformly, and saw to it that it was as pervasive as the light of heaven itself, as the prominent Reformed minister John Knox told his Middle Dutch Church congregation in New

THE

# HEIDELBERG

# CATECHISM.

Mother I know my Catechism, will you hear me?

NEW YORK:

FOR THE SABBATH SCHOOL UNION,
BY THE
BOARD OF PUBLICATION OF THE REF. PROTESTANT
DUTCH CHURCH.

SYNOD'S ROOMS.

FIGURE 13. For four hundred years, the main teaching tool of the Reformed Dutch Church was the Heidelberg Catechism, published in countless editions since 1563. It has fallen into disuse. *Courtesy Archives, Reformed Church in America.*

York City in 1834. If they did not, their children would be disobedient and "vile," and they would be to blame. Vile children displayed temper, indulged "unholy gratifications," associated with wicked children, and neglected the Sabbath. Severe punishment was in order for offspring of this sort.[3]

Attention to the child's salvation must be relentless. Parents must speak to their children about their salvation "in the house and by the way, rising up and lying down," Knox insisted. "Especially let Christian *mothers* devote themselves to this work," a Reformed Dutch Church tract stressed. "Lead them daily to the cross. Teach them to pray. Take them with you and pray for them. Let them hear your earnest intercessions for them. . . . Teach your little ones to sing the songs of Zion, and labor to make your dwelling a pure and peaceful abode, a school of Christian courtesy, the home of every social and spiritual grace."[4]

Reformed sermons emphasized that both parents played an important part in child rearing. To the father, the head of the household (at least nominally, as we shall see), belonged the delicate and arduous work of training up those whom God had confided to his care, as Reformed minister Gilbert Livingston put it in 1825, "so that they may become useful members of society and may walk in the path of virtue and the 'way everlasting.'" A conscientious evangelical father knew that his children were "destined to an eternity of unspeakable woe, or of indescribable blessedness," so it behooved him to do everything in his power to assist them on the path to eternal bliss, wrote Livingston.[5]

It was the father's responsibility to form his children's habits, give a tone to their morals, direct their pursuits, and instill in their minds virtuous principles. Just as every individual ought to pray for himself, Livingston wrote, "every head of family should pray with and for his family." And just as every family has wants to be supplied and sins to be confessed, so every family receives blessings from God that "demand their united gratitude . . . as a family, and therefore require them as a family to address the throne of grace."

Livingston spelled out the benefits of family worship: it rewards the father, because it lights the fire of divine love in his breast and excites him to more zeal in the cause of the Redeemer. It gives him an "influence and an authority over his children . . . that they cannot but reverence." And it serves as a "useful restraint" upon his actions, for the "eyes of all those around him . . . watching his movements . . . will do more to close [his] imprudent lips and arrest [his] wandering steps than anything else besides." To his children, family worship sets a good example, for if a father "prays in secret, his children are ignorant of it, and they presume . . . he does not pray at all." It has a direct effect on family members in dissuading them from vicious habits. And it promotes family concord and unity as hearts are bound together in fraternal affection.

Family worship on a daily basis and with a specific order and tone—a Reformed Dutch order and tone—was essential. Not only the family's spiritual fate depended upon it, but the denomination's future. "Remember, the children are the hope of the church," one Reformed tract warned; and "In the family . . . ," the Reformed preacher James Romeyn told the General Synod in 1842, "the church will prosper or decline." But also understood was a general belief that all parents, no matter their denomination, must teach religion at home not by "short, hurried, meagre general prayers," Romeyn declared, "but in such a manner as to be acceptable to the Holy Ghost." There should be, "by the father of the household, the summons to the family service, a ready order, a solemnity, a psalm," and then the "patriarchal grace with which the family Bible is opened" as the whole family kneels to hear the prayer of "saint, husband, and father."[6]

Reformed minister Isaac Ferris, who likened the Christian father to "both King and Priest at home," described his duties. Besides leading daily family worship, he should devote time on the Sabbath evening to the examination of divine truth with his assembled family. In addition, he should make a point of taking each child aside for "closet prayer." Wayward children's hearts were often melted when fathers took them to the prayer closet, and one pious widower, who every evening "poured out his heart" over his son in prayer, was rewarded when his son as an adult became a "useful minister of Christ"—Ferris himself.[7]

Even in pious church-adhering families, however, family worship was often neglected. Parents found time for "zeal for the heathen," the temperance movement, and revivals and public worship services, one minister complained, but their own children were "growing up as unrestrained and lawless as wild asses' colts."[8] The charge that parents neglected family worship was a frequent one. Fathers protested a lack of time, but they had time for visiting and entertaining and engaging in worldly amusements and indulging in carnal appetites, one minister alleged. Or they complained they were too tired from working, although there was no "record of a man becoming impoverished because he allowed himself time to worship God in his family." The Reverend Livingston admitted no excuses. Men who claimed they lacked confidence or ability could read printed prayers, and to those who complained they had neglected family worship for so long that to commence it now would expose them to ridicule, Livingston had a ready answer: "Isn't it better to brave the sneers and derision of a 'fellow worm' than to offend God?"[9]

Even where fathers were not deficient, ministers turned ever more to mothers in the task of saving children's souls. "A father's influence is un-doubtedly very important," the Reverend Talbot W. Chambers wrote in 1870, "but it is vastly exceeded by the mother's [in childhood] . . . when the seeds of the future are planted. . . . Let every mother . . . remember she is daily reproducing her own character in that of her children. . . . If her life be worldly, also [doomed are] the immortal souls given her to train."[10]

In pious middle- and upper-middle-class households, girls were ac-quainted from their earliest years with the awesome responsibilities they would one day bear for the harmony and godliness of their future families. Their training for this role began as soon as they could talk, and it was a training that was remarkably similar in all evangelical families in the nine-teenth century, as daughters across denominational lines were exposed to efforts by their own families and by church and society to form them into pious wives and mothers. For those of Dutch background, this universality or commonality of values ultimately had the effect of loosening ethnic ties. Yet it did not overrule the reality that, especially in rural areas, for women in Reformed Dutch communities, geographical imperatives—the ongoing manifestations of ancient settlement patterns—continued for generations to dictate blueprints for their lives. In the countryside of New York and New Jersey, a push-pull dialectic was always at work, erasing ethnic barriers on some levels while reinforcing them on others.

From a practical standpoint, mothers were considered to be more im-portant than fathers in the process of getting children saved simply because mothers spent more time with their offspring. The changing employment patterns of an industrializing America now required many men to leave home every day and go into the workplace, whereas in earlier times their livelihood had been practiced at home. But this was not the only basis for the mother's role. A work highly recommended by the Reformed clergy articulated the theological footing: because Eve, a woman, had been the first transgressor, "the world's redeeming influence . . . must come from a mother's lips. She who was first in the transgression must be yet the prin-cipal earthly instrument in the restoration . . . the great agent in bringing back our guilty race to duty and happiness. . . . O mothers!," the author of this popular guide wrote, "reflect upon the power your Maker has placed in your hands. . . . God has constituted you the guardians and the control-lers of the human family."[11]

Other scriptural foundation was found for a mother's role in the reli-gious education of her family: "By woman came the apostasy of Adam, and by woman the recovery through Jesus. It was a woman that imbued the mind and formed the character of Moses. . . . It was woman that led the choir . . . which went forth to celebrate . . . the overthrow of Pharaoh. . . .

[On the other hand], it was not woman who slept during the agonies of Gethsemane, . . . denied her Lord at the palace of Caiaphas, . . . deserted His cross on the hill of Calvary." And now as then, it was her office to stay the fainting head and wipe away the tear of anguish.[12]

Fathers had their role to play, but the "sphere occupied by a mother is one of transcendent importance," declared the Parents and Children column of the *Intelligencer*. Her sphere "extends beyond time—it reaches, in its blessed or baleful effects—through eternity. . . . To qualify her for . . . her high duty, she needs intelligence, virtue, and religion." And she needed to exercise a special concern for her female children, for mothers who cared more about their daughters' dress and social accomplishments than their moral attributes "will produce daughters who will raise up an intellectually feeble and effeminate race, and thus prove a curse . . . to the world."[13]

Mothers were charged by the church with teaching their children the first step toward salvation: obedience. In prescriptive literature published specifically for them, they were instructed that no act of disobedience was too small for concern. It was not a little thing to disobey a mother's command. After all, "The eating of an apple banished our first parents from paradise."[14] And mothers were told to expect more than a "languid and dilatory yielding to repeated threats. . . . [It is not enough] that a child should yield to your arguments and persuasions. It is essential that he should submit to your authority" promptly and cheerfully.[15]

Conscientious mothers were expected to use guilt, fear, and anxiety as everyday weapons in the war of getting children saved. Children, mothers were told, should be made to feel that they have been bought with a price and that they must live as becomes the children of God: "Train them to the habit of secret prayer, to attendance on prayer meetings, to regularity at public worship, to reverence for the name of God and for his holy day. Train them to [have] respect for the aged, for ministers, elders, teachers, and all who are in office. Train them to a sacred regard for their own word; to punctuality and integrity . . . to habits of politeness and kindness . . . and to regular and systematic benevolence." And "observe that you are to *train* [them] thus, . . . not simply teach or advise them, but authoritatively to require them to form these habits." This will indeed demand pains, patience, and prayer on your part, this tract acknowledged. "But will you . . . neglect it? Dare you? Can you?"[16]

Ministers reflected tenderly on their training by their own mothers. Sabbath evenings with his brothers and sisters around their mother's knee, reciting the catechism, reading Scripture, reporting on their reading and the public worship services of the day Isaac Ferris recalled as the happiest evenings of his youth. To Ferris, there was "not a more interesting sight than that of a family . . . gathered around a beloved parent, and hearing from his or her lips the words of eternal life." Often, a glistening tear, a heaving breast will be evident as children apprehend the evil of sin and "personal unworthiness," he wrote. "Such a circle how truly a nursery for Heaven!"[17] Home was sacred, and mother was its high priestess. In fact, the tenth commandment (Thou shalt not covet . . . ) was viewed as God's "homestead law," in which he recognizes home "as a sacred spot . . . and source of every good affection."[18]

Evangelicals of all denominations learned from one another contemporary techniques for bringing children into harmony with their heavenly father. Anonymously, a Baptist clergyman—subsequently identified as the Reverend Francis Wayland, president of Brown University from 1827–1855—described in a letter to the editor of the *American Baptist Magazine* (October 1831) how he had successfully secured his fifteen-month-old son's obedience by withholding food and drink from the infant for thirty-six hours. Two years later, in *The Mother at Home*, a guide published by the American Tract Society, Congregational minister John S. C. Abbott related the history of a disobedient boy whose father was obliged to punish him harshly for a minor infraction—a history that echoed Francis Wayland's in every detail and demonstrates that a formula for child rearing had evolved and was circulating among evangelicals.

First, as Wayland's father had, Abbott's father inflicted physical punishment as severely as he dared. The little boy, however, "with his whole frame in agitation, refused to yield." Then Father, though knowing he had "already punished his child with a severity he feared to exceed," removed him from the room for additional reparations. (Meanwhile, Mother, though suffering most acutely, was "perfectly satisfied" that the child must be subdued and that she must not interfere.) To everyone's relief, little John at last obeyed his father and "learnt a lesson he never forgot . . . that [obedience] was the safest and happiest course to follow." Far from being cruel, Abbott stressed, this father was showing mercy and love to his child. Indeed, it would have been cruel had he "shrunk from his painful duty," for it is probable that the "character and happiness of that child for life and even for eternity" were decided at that moment.[19]

Although Abbott was a Congregational clergyman, it was the policy of the American Tract Society to publish only works approved by all members of its board, and on its board always sat a Reformed Dutch clergyman or lay leader. Thus it can be assumed that the advice *The Mother at Home* dispensed echoed from Reformed pulpits and in Reformed households throughout this period. Indeed, *The Mother at Home* is representative of the kind of "suitable mental aliment" read and recommended by all evangelical denominations for the mothers in their congregations.[20]

*The Mother at Home* was nothing if not specific in its advice. Mothers were encouraged not to supply children a reason for their every command. Rather, to "bring your child under perfect subjection . . . sometimes give him your reasons; [sometimes] withhold them. But let him perfectly understand that he is to do as he is bid," for without absolute, immediate, and cheerful obedience, "your family will present one continued scene of noise and confusion . . . [and] your heart will be broken by [your children's] future licentiousness or ingratitude." Mothers should never give commands they do not intend shall be obeyed, lest the child become used to discount them. Tell the child once and only once what you want her to do, and then punish her if she disobeys. The first rule of family government is to enforce obedience to every command in order to establish the principle that a mother's word is never to be disregarded.[21]

God had given mothers the power to obtain their children's prompt obedience, but mothers must start to do so when the children were very young. Even a fifteen-month-old child could be taught "by the serious tone of her mother's voice, and the sad expression of her countenance." If her helpless babe disobeyed her, the mother was advised "to cut off its sources of enjoyment, or inflict bodily pain, so steadily and so invariably that disobedience and suffering shall be indissolubly connected" in the child's mind. The too-tender mother who cannot summon herself to deprive her baby of pleasure and to inflict pain when it is necessary must prepare for a broken heart and an old age of sorrow—when her dissolute sons and ungrateful daughters will remind her that in their infancy she might have checked their disobedient propensities. "And when at Judgment Day you meet your children and they say to you 'It was through your neglect of duty that we are banished from heaven and consigned to endless wo[e],' you must feel what no tongue can tell."[22]

To maintain their authority, mothers were cautioned against being overly severe. A mother had to rule her children by striking a careful balance between making them fear her and making them love her. "Fear is a useful and a necessary principle in family government. God makes use of it in governing his creatures." But mothers who attempted to control children exclusively by this method would find that home would become an "irksome prison" instead of a happy retreat of peace and joy. In recommending another such guide, *The Duty of Mothers* (1840) by E. N. Kirk, the *Intelligencer* printed an extract: "Would that mothers knew the virtue and power of a frown and a kiss, for with those instruments of terror and love, a child may be governed almost entirely before it can speak." Smiles were an important weapon in her arsenal: "Do you smile [at your children] swectly, heavenly, joyfully—with Jesus in your soul? Well, smile on, keep smiling, day in, day out . . . [until your] little one smile[s] in return. . . . Mothers beloved, . . . who knows but those smiling sermons were the secret of secrets" of the mothers of Moses, Samuel, and Timothy? Mothers should be affectionate and mild. They should "sympathise with [their children] in their little sports" and gain their confidence by indulging their wants. Greet them with smiles, reward them with caresses, address them in tones of mildness and affection, govern by kindness, but when kindness fails "punish as severely as necessary."[23]

If mothers must punish their children, they should do it in sorrow, not in anger. The "judicious" mother should first remove her disobedient or unruly child from the scene and tell him kindly but sorrowfully that she and God are most displeased with his conduct. Then she should put him to bed, kneel by his side, and ask God to forgive him. In the morning, when he agrees that he is sorry for his misdeeds, she should suggest that he ask for forgiveness, both from her and from God. "Thus, by judicious management, the desired object [obedience] is . . . perfectly attained, while the contest is avoided."[24] Mothers had to be manipulative, almost Machiavellian, in the challenge of getting their children saved.

As for mothers themselves, they must at all times control their passions and never fly into a rage and beat a child. They must construct limits to their own power and never punish their children by exciting imaginary fears about ghosts and monsters, or by locking them up in cellars or dark closets, apparently a favorite chastisement of the day. And they must keep a careful eye on their domestic help. One three-year-old shut up by a maid for a few minutes in a dark closet went into a fit and remained for life an idiot; "thousands upon thousands of human beings have been deprived of their senses" by such means, Abbott assured his readers.[25] The underlying message to mothers in all of this literature was that, in a well-governed Christian home, *they*, not their household help, not their children, not their husbands or relatives, *they* must be in control of their families at all times. The model was Elizabeth, "walking in all the commandments and ordinances of the Lord blameless"—and it was a hard act to follow.

The faults and errors of the evangelical mother included talking about her children in their presence, praising them, deceiving them, and continually finding fault with them. But her most egregious defect was not to be religious herself. "It is vain to hope you can fix your children's affections upon another world, while yours are fixed upon this," Abbott wrote. If a mother has not given her heart to God, she could be sure that she and her children would end in hell. In "A Thought for Prayerless Mothers," a dying young man exclaims, "You are the cause of it, [mother]! I am just going into eternity . . . [and] black despair, and you are the cause of it," because she had allowed him to fish and hunt on the Sabbath. If a mother did not seek God for herself and her child, then through all eternity she must gaze upon the wreck of its immortal spirit "when both [mother and child] might have been reposing in heaven."[26]

Mothers were advised to take advantage of every occasion when their children might be particularly susceptible to religious discussions. If a little girl in the neighborhood died, for instance, a mother might take her own daughter to the funeral: "As she looks upon the lifeless corpse of her companion . . . speak to her of the eternal world to which her friend has gone—of the judgment-seat . . . of the new scenes of joy or wo[e] she has entered . . . [and] tell her that she too soon must die; leave all her friends; [and] appear before Christ to be judged. . . . There are few children who can resist such appeals." The "raging storm, the hour of sickness, the funeral procession, the tolling bell" all presented opportunities for pious mothers to lead their children's thoughts to God.[27]

Heaven should be presented in as attractive a manner as possible, and it was a mother's privilege and duty to describe heaven to her children in such a way as to inspire them to want to go there. If your son has a thirst for knowledge, tell him that in heaven he shall understand all the wonders of God's works and comprehend all the machinery of nature. If your daughter loves music, "carry her thoughts away to companies of happy angels, with celestial harps and divine voices rolling their notes of joy through heaven's wide concave." Mothers must "present heaven to [their] children as . . . crowded with images of delight . . . till their hearts are warmed . . . [and they] listen with interest to how salvation is to be obtained." Dwell particularly on the Savior and his suffering. This will "awaken contrition and melt the heart. . . . Your child will listen with tearful eye; . . . [and to] his tender mind will be conveyed an idea of God's kindness as nothing else can produce." It was common in this era for even very young children to have significant conversion experiences, and if their own children did not show early evidence of piety, mothers were told that much of the blame was theirs.[28]

Reformed clergymen were amply represented among the authors of the prescriptive literature and religious juvenilia in which society was awash, and the works of the Reformed medical missionary to India, John Scudder, were among those most widely read. Theoretically, the evangelical mother's dearest dream was that her son enter the ministry, but in reality it seemed that not enough mothers encouraged their sons to do so. Scudder, in his *Appeal to Mothers* published in 1844, excoriated parents for failing to dedicate their children to the promotion of the gospel. As a result, young men were shunning the ministry as a career. They "profess" the cross, but do not bear it, Scudder scolded. They pray "Thy kingdom come," but they refuse to make it come. "The sapling has grown into a tree, and every effort to bend it [now] is useless." And nothing will change, he prophesied, until the church is blessed with a "different race of mothers"—a race of mothers who will impress upon their sons, starting in infancy, their obligations to enter the ministry.[29] (See figure 14.)

Early training was imperative. The different race of mothers that Scudder envisioned must begin to teach the coming generation while still in the cradle to turn away from earthly chains. He believed and preached that because Christian mothers were powerful instrumentalities for the conversion of the entire world they must infuse the missionary spirit in the heart of the rising generation at the earliest opportunity. Referring to the Lockean idea that a child learns more by the time it is four years old than during all the rest of its life, Scudder informed mothers that their children's hearts "are like melted wax, and readily run into the moulds you make for them." Depending on his mother, a child can have a "martial or a peaceful character, a money-grasping or a generous one, a suspicious or a frank one." And he could enter the ministry or reject it. It was up to mother, and she ignored her charge to her everlasting peril. "Mothers who profess to be Christians but who are unwilling to have their sons enter the ministry . . . may expect to weep over ungodly sons, and break their hearts over graves on whose tombstones there shall be no record of hope," he warned.[30]

In addressing the Female Sabbath School of the Collegiate Dutch Church in New York at its nineteenth anniversary celebration in 1835, the Reverend Thomas De Witt told the gathered women that they should teach their children, "as soon as they can lisp, their dependence on divine grace." A generation later, Reformed clergymen were still echoing this advice. In fact, the editors of the *Intelligencer* now believed that the lisping stage was too late. Mother's influence commenced even before the child's birth: "No one can tell how powerful are the impulses which her spirit communicates to it [in the womb]. She may be . . . forming a Jeremiah or John the Baptist."[31]

By impressing upon her son's mind in infancy that he was meant for the Lord's work, "he will grow up with but one thought and one design . . . to live and labor for a dying world." Mothers were to furnish their sons with simple nursery books and periodical papers that drew their attention to the heathen and to choose books for them that "in simple historical portraitures, display[ed] the grand reasons of the world's wretchedness." Eschew such frivolous and dangerous books as "Jack the Giant Killer," Scudder advised. Give children facts, not airy fancies.[32]

" When you are grown, will you not become a Missionary and come to India ?"

Page 306.

FIGURE 14. John Scudder's *A Voice from the East to the Young* was addressed to the children of the Reformed Dutch Church, but it was a best-seller among all evangelicals. *Courtesy Gardner A. Sage Library, New Brunswick Theological Seminary.*

"O Christian mothers," he concluded, "Bestir yourselves. . . . The church looks to you with deep solicitude. The church of the coming generation has its germs in your families. You are the guardians over Christ's nursery. Shall they be plants standing like green olive-trees in the house of God, or shall they be like the present dwarfish race of Christians[?]"[33]

*A*lthough classic Calvinist doctrine was undermined in the evangelical era by Arminian ideas—by what Philip Schaff called the "elastic tenets" of Methodism—it was never the case that pious Christian parents were persuaded that salvation was theirs and their loved ones' simply for the asking.[34]

Rather, many struggled mightily with the burdens placed on them for their family's spiritual condition. Clergy as well as the laity, men as well as women, agonized over the spiritual state of their children's souls—and their grandchildren's. The Reformed minister Samuel B. How wrote to his daughter-in-law Mary:

> I hope Blanche and Johnny are well and are good children. . . . I trust my dear Mary that both you and Henry are endeavouring to bring them up for God and Heaven. How great and fearful is the responsibility of parents for the right education of their children. I trust you do not forget your own soul and it would afford me high pleasure to have seen you at the sacramental table devoting yourself to Christ and a sincere and humble follower of his. Oh! my Dear Mary . . . Give your heart . . . to God and bring up your children in his fear and for his glory and the blessing of God will then rest on you and them.[35]

Women's anxieties for their children's spiritual welfare dominated their attention. In 1870, at the tenth anniversary of the Mothers' Concert of Prayer in a Reformed church in Brooklyn Heights, "three great questions" were discussed: How can the conversion of our children be secured while they are in childhood? How can they be shielded from the evil that surrounds them? And how can they become so strong in Christianity as to be fitted for a life of self-sacrifice? In her address to the group, Mrs. Rufus W. Clark of Albany, wife of the minister of the North Dutch Church there, spoke of God as having given to women "the highest gift, that of influence: it is a royal prerogative, more precious than a diadem." Another speaker "dwelt upon self-government on the part of the mother as the essential requisite in the training of children and of consecration of [her own] heart as the only preparation for any Christian work." Mrs. Pruyn, also of the Albany Reformed Church, revealed to her colleagues that the death of her own son had moved her to become a mother to those that had none, and "now to consecrate the remainder of her life to the destitute children of Japan," which she did.[36]

The burden of responsibility for their children's welfare not only in this life but in the life hereafter sorely taxed pious parents, especially mothers, with their greater obligations, and especially when the children showed signs of disobedience or of disaffection from the church. Some mothers had to face the painful reality that their children were not susceptible to their redemptive powers and thus were not to inherit the Kingdom. "My beloved but wayward son," Mary Ann Gansevoort wrote to Stanwyx, age twenty-two, "Before your eyes ever saw the light of the sun, the most fervent prayers were put up at the Throne of Grace for you. [Your drunken behavior] grieves me when I think of the many ten thousand mercies I have done you." She begs him to leave his evil friends and to ask God's forgiveness.[37]

A series of nine deaths in five months in the family of Margaret Schenck Nevius in New Jersey aroused in her terrible fears for the spiritual condition of her son, away at school: "While you are trying to store your mind with useful knowledge," she wrote to him, "may you get that Wisdom which cometh from above[.] Choose Jesus as your friend then you will be happy[,] put it not off for 'Now is the accepted time' . . . you know not that another day is yours. . . . Oh my dear son how would I feel if I should get . . . word of you[r death]. Give your heart to the *Saviour now*," she beseeched him.[38]

Maria Ferdon, a Bergen County spinster, had no children of her own, but she agonized time and again over the spiritual deficiencies of her brother and his wife and blamed their carefree, fun-loving ways for the wicked and even "Satanic" behavior of their children (her niece became pregnant out of wedlock). And Phebe Davis, a member of the First Reformed Church in Somerville, shared with her cousin Margaret the feeling that "it is a consolation to parents to see their children follow . . . Christ. . . . [I]f we could persuade the young to think, and examine their thoughts," she wrote, "they would soon be convinced their affections were not set on God[,] their kind and bountyfull benefactor, and as they must give an account to him of their thoughts and ways, they would know they must have one [intermediator] to stand between them and an offended God."[39]

Although some unfortunate mothers had to acknowledge the failure of their redemptive powers, it was a great day when a mother knew her children were safe in the knowledge of Christ's redeeming love—and a great day for the community. The Reverend Thomas De Witt Talmage, one of the giants of the Reformed Church in the nineteenth century, reported how his grandmother in Somerville prayed that her children might be saved, and they were saved, and the "news spread . . . and there was a great turning unto God; and over two hundred souls, in one day, stood up in the village church to profess faith in Christ."[40]

Because the mother's role in the spiritual life of the family was, ultimately, more important than the father's, praises for those who succeeded in bringing their children to the Lord rang loud. Jacob Chamberlain, a student at New Brunswick Theological Seminary, wrote to his mother that he had just returned from the riverbanks, where "concealed by clumps of cedar shrubs" he had spent the twilight hour on his knees commending his dear ones to God. "I am thankfull My dear Mother that you trained us from infancy to consider that hour sacred to that purpose, for however widely scattered we are we know that while we have a mother living her prayers are then ascending for us." And another student, of Rutgers' class of '66, wrote that "Nothing will sooner move the sensibilities of the hardest heart than the memory of a sainted mother." Mother is the child's first instructor, he declared, and the domestic fireside a seminary of infinite importance, "the great institution of Providence for the education of man." How vast is a mother's power, "how limitless her dominion!"[41]

In the end, the pious mother's real power issued not from her ability to assert her authority over her children, or to inflict pain and guilt on them, but in the loving and selfless "ten thousand mercies" she showered upon them. Theodore Frelinghuysen credited the loving ways of his grandmother, Dina van den Bergh Frelinghuysen Hardenbergh, for leading him to the Savior. "Though deservedly eminent for her piety, she was far from being austere, but, on the contrary, gracious and winning," his biographer wrote of Dina Hardenbergh.[42] And "Be kind to thy mother," cautioned *Our Sabbath School Messenger* in one of hundreds of similar verses of the era, "for lo! on her brow, / May traces of sorrow be seen! / Oh, well may'st thou cherish and comfort her now, / For loving and kind she has been."

*I*t was a universal characteristic of evangelical churches in the nineteenth century to use fear, guilt, dread, and anxiety to generate in their adherents a desire for salvation, to terrify its members, young and old, with the possibility of sudden death and the prospect of spending eternity in the lake of never-ending fire. But as it embraced the characteristic means and methods of the evolving religious culture of the day, the Reformed Church was inevitably hastening its own drift away from Dort and Dutchness toward a more secularized religion and Americanness.

Its approval of the "delightful juvenile books" published by the American Sunday School Union and the American Tract Society characterized this drift. Reformed clergymen cheerfully recommended to their flocks, for instance, and the editors of the *Intelligencer* frequently reprinted excerpts from the Reverend John Todd's *Lectures to Children*. Todd's *Lectures* embody the religious climate of the era as it applied to children. The pastor of a Congregational church in Andover, Massachusetts, Todd acknowledged that children are a very important class in every congregation, but he also admitted that they are a difficult part of the flock to feed. To talk to them as they ought to be talked to, he wrote, requires a "vigorous imagination" and "extensive knowledge . . . to call in illustration from the four corners of the earth."[43] (See figure 15.)

Todd had a vigorous imagination, and he used it unsparingly to frighten his little readers into being good—even if he stretched the limits of Calvinist theology in doing so. To praise his works, as Reformed ministers did in recommending them, was often in effect to shun the careful Bible-oriented theology of Dort for the lurid inventions of the evangelical mind—and to credit the fears of the Ultras who saw all too clearly the deficiencies of such literature. One page of the Bible perishes forever every time a child sins, Todd assured his innocent readers. And how would you like it if God said one of your bones must be broken for every sin you commit? Or if the person nearest you dropped down dead every time you sinned?

Todd's *Lectures* are full of gruesome, macabre tales of physical mutilation, of parents suddenly sickening and dying, their children scattered to the winds; tales of being lost at sea in a terrible storm, of poor ragged children frozen with cold, no home, no food, no friends were his specialty. Losing an eye, fatal illnesses, drowning, being bitten by fiery serpents, breaking a limb so dreadfully it must be cut off or you will die, having to live in a tent in a strange land forever, trapped in a flooded mine, parents dying of grief because of their children's wickedness were the stuff of every lecture. Even if Reformed parents did not purchase Todd's "delightful" stories in book form, they entered every Reformed Dutch household that subscribed to the *Christian Intelligencer* every week of the year. Designed to inspire children to be as perfect as possible (for did not the Bible say "be thou perfect"?), to aspire with all their might and main to live for eternity with God and his angels, the *Lectures* stayed in print for decades.

In order to get to heaven, many rules had to be followed. Children should think of God all day long every day, Todd cautioned, and pray that God will keep them from sinning, repent their sins, and obey their parents. They must always speak the truth, love God as much as they love their earthly parent, and keep the Sabbath. Be careful what you say, he wrote, as if he were speaking to them face to face. Tell one lie and you might be ruined for life. Be careful what company you keep. One half-hour spent in wicked company can ruin you. Everyone has sinned, and if you do not re-

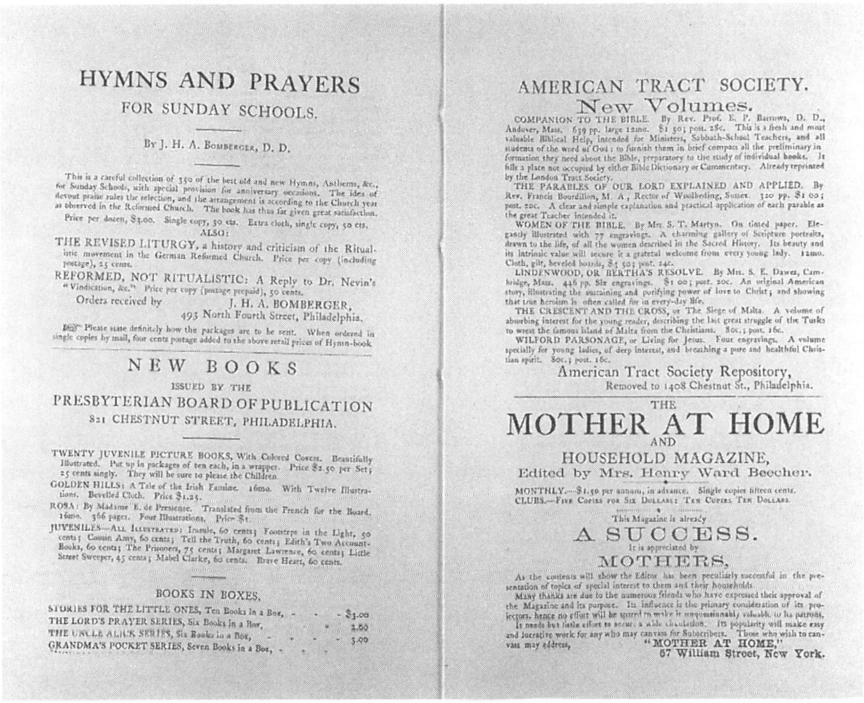

HYMNS AND PRAYERS

FOR SUNDAY SCHOOLS.

By J. H. A. Bomberger, D. D.

This is a careful collection of 350 of the best old and new Hymns, Anthems, &c., for Sunday Schools, with special provision for anniversary occasions. The idea of devout praise rules the selection, and the arrangement is according to the Church year as observed in the Reformed Church. The book has thus far given great satisfaction.

Price per dozen, $3.00. Single copy, 30 cts. Extra cloth, single copy, 50 cts.

ALSO:

THE REVISED LITURGY, a history and criticism of the Ritualistic movement in the German Reformed Church. Price per copy (including postage), 25 cents.

REFORMED, NOT RITUALISTIC: A Reply to Dr. Nevin's "Vindication, &c." Price per copy (postage prepaid), 50 cents.

Orders received by J. H. A. BOMBERGER,
493 North Fourth Street, Philadelphia.

Please state definitely how the packages are to be sent. When ordered in single copies by mail, four cents postage added to the above retail prices of Hymn-book

NEW BOOKS

ISSUED BY THE

PRESBYTERIAN BOARD OF PUBLICATION

821 CHESTNUT STREET, PHILADELPHIA.

TWENTY JUVENILE PICTURE BOOKS, With Colored Covers. Beautifully Illustrated. Put up in packages of ten each, in a wrapper. Price $2.50 per Set; 25 cents singly. They will be sure to please the Children.

GOLDEN HILLS: A Tale of the Irish Famine. 16mo. With Twelve Illustrations. Bevelled Cloth. Price $1.25.

ROSA: By Madame E. de Presense. Translated from the French for the Board. 16mo. 366 pages. Four Illustrations. Price $1.

JUVENILES—All Illustrated: Irasule, 60 cents; Footsteps in the Light, 50 cents; Cousin Amy, 60 cents; Tell the Truth, 60 cents; Edith's Two Account-Books, 60 cents; The Prisoners, 75 cents; Margaret Lawrence, 60 cents; Little Street Sweeper, 45 cents; Mabel Clarke, 60 cents. Brave Heart, 60 cents.

BOOKS IN BOXES.

STORIES FOR THE LITTLE ONES, Ten Books in a Box, - - - $3.00
THE LORD'S PRAYER SERIES, Six Books in a Box, - 2.00
THE UNCLE ALICK SERIES, Six Books in a Box, - - - - 3.00
GRANDMA'S POCKET SERIES, Seven Books in a Box, - - -

AMERICAN TRACT SOCIETY.

New Volumes.

COMPANION TO THE BIBLE. By Rev. Prof. E. P. Barrows, D. D., Andover, Mass. 639 pp. large 12mo. $1 50; post. 28c. This is a fresh and most valuable Biblical Help, intended for Ministers, Sabbath-School Teachers, and all students of the word of God: to furnish them in brief compass all the preliminary information they need about the Bible, preparatory to the study of individual books. It fills a place not occupied by either Bible Dictionary or Commentary. Already reprinted by the London Tract Society.

THE PARABLES OF OUR LORD EXPLAINED AND APPLIED. By Rev. Francis Bourdillon, M. A., Rector of Woolbeding, Sussex. 320 pp. $1 00; post. 20c. A clear and simple explanation and practical application of each parable as the great Teacher intended it.

WOMEN OF THE BIBLE. By Mrs. S. T. Martyn. On tinted paper. Elegantly illustrated with 77 engravings. A charming gallery of Scripture portraits, drawn to the life, of all the women described in the Sacred History. Its beauty and its intrinsic value will secure it a grateful welcome from every young lady. 12mo. Cloth, gilt, beveled boards, $3 50; post. 24c.

LINDENWOOD, OR BERTHA'S RESOLVE. By Mrs. S. E. Dawes, Cambridge, Mass. 446 pp. Six engravings. $1 00; post. 20c. An original American story, illustrating the sustaining and purifying power of love to Christ; and showing that true heroism is often called for in every-day life.

THE CRESCENT AND THE CROSS, or The Siege of Malta. A volume of absorbing interest for the young reader, describing the last great struggle of the Turks to wrest the famous island of Malta from the Christians. 80c.; post. 16c.

WILFORD PARSONAGE, or Living for Jesus. Four engravings. A volume specially for young ladies, of deep interest, and breathing a pure and healthful Christian spirit. 80c.; post. 16c.

American Tract Society Repository,
Removed to 1408 Chestnut St., Philadelphia.

THE

MOTHER AT HOME

AND

HOUSEHOLD MAGAZINE,

Edited by Mrs. Henry Ward Beecher.

MONTHLY.—$1.50 per annum, in advance. Single copies fifteen cents.
CLUBS.—Five Copies for Six Dollars: Ten Copies Ten Dollars.

This Magazine is already

A SUCCESS.

It is appreciated by

MOTHERS,

As the contents will show the Editor has been peculiarly successful in the presentation of topics of special interest to them and their households.

Many thanks are due to the numerous friends who have expressed their approval of the Magazine and its purpose. Its influence is the primary consideration of its projectors, hence no effort will be spared to make it unquestionably valuable to its patrons.

It needs but little effort to secure a wide circulation. Its popularity will make easy and lucrative work for any who may canvass for Subscribers. Those who wish to canvass may address, "MOTHER AT HOME,"
57 William Street, New York.

FIGURE 15. *The Reformed Church Monthly* for June 1869 advertised the latest works of interest to evangelicals. *Courtesy Gardner A. Sage Library, New Brunswick Theological Seminary*

pent, you will grow up sinners, live sinners, die sinners, and be sinners, accursed by God forever and ever.

In contrast, when anyone repents, the angels are happy, because they know he will go to heaven—and have a pleasant home for eternity. Hell is worse than losing an eye or an arm or even one's reason, Todd wrote. Hell is to be put into the fire, and kept burning all day and all night, for ten thousand years. Hell is to lose one's soul and be covered with shame and everlasting contempt, and to be bitten by fiery and brazen serpents every day for the rest of time. Todd's imagination knew no bounds, but his main message to children was that they could not go to heaven without repenting. You will all be very wicked if you do not repent immediately, he scolded his little readers.

Dr. John Scudder outdid even Todd in trying to capture children's attention with the exotic wickedness of the 130 million wretched "Hindoos" and their 330 million bloodthirsty gods and goddesses. The Reformed Church's foreign missionary efforts in the nineteenth century were second in intensity only to its efforts to save its own children from perdition, and

missionaries like Scudder used their experiences among the far-away heathens to exhort little ones at home in America.

In the misguided and heathen land of India, Yogis and Fakeers tortured themselves in the vain hope of getting to heaven, Dr. Scudder told
his readers, and the people committed every sin mentioned by Paul and
others so terrible they were omitted from the Bible, lest we be unable to
open it. Scudder warmed to his task in regaling his audience with tales of
infanticide, especially of female infants, and cannibalism, self-immolation,
children thrown to crocodiles in the River Ganges by their own mothers.
"Had you been born in India, my dear children," he wrote, "some of
you . . . might now be in training to become such [murderers]. How thank-
ful ought you to be to your heavenly Father that you were . . . born . . . in a
Christian land!" God naturally expected some return for his goodness in
causing one to be born in a Christian land. If you don't repent your sins and
give your hearts to Christ, Scudder warned, "you are ungrateful and wicked
children, and if you die in your present state, you will be in a worse condition than those poor heathen children who never heard of a Saviour. . . .
They will be beaten with fewer stripes, because they did not know their
Master's will. . . . You will be beaten with many stripes, because . . . you
know his will" but do not submit to it.[44]

As the decades passed, this approach to getting children saved, which
the English social historian E. P. Thompson has aptly described as religious
terrorism, did not abate, but rather heated up. By the 1840s professional
evangelists, pastors, and parents all over America were placing ever increasing pressure upon children to save their souls, and the effort continued, with
some stylistic modifications, throughout the 1850s, '60s, and '70s.

How did children react to these pressures? Some, like little Emilie
Griswold, became exceedingly pious. Emilie was so spiritually precocious
that at age two and a half she was familiar with many difficult Bible stories, and at three she "readily comprehended all the important points of
that wonderful mystery" of Christ's coming to suffer and die for sinners.
Little Emilie was fond of drawing pictures of graveyards and discoursing
with her mother on missionary activities. Her aim at three and a half was
to buy Bibles for the heathen, and when she fell ill, from the time of her
sickness until her untimely death, she never ceased talking of God and
heaven.[45]

The *Intelligencer*'s bottomless pit of pious-child accounts, which appeared relentlessly week in and week out for decades, was rivaled only by
its ample fund of wicked-child stories. Some children, perhaps respond-
ing to the pressure to be good, persisted in being bad. In one Sunday school,
children, with tears in their eyes, confessed their faults while the minister

wrote them on the blackboard for all to read—a procedure recommended in the prescriptive literature. The besetting sins of children, as they themselves described them, were lying, swearing, telling false tales, Sabbath breaking, playing truant, disobeying, stealing, and deceiving.[46] Swearing (that is, saying I vow! By golly! I declare! or Gracious!) was much frowned upon, for just as one little sin led to another, such loose expressions inevitably led to obscenity, profanity, blasphemy, and hell. Even young ladies, "beautiful specimens of God's workmanship," indulged in this verbal vice, which is as repulsive to the ear as a jewel of gold in a swine's snout is to the eye, scolded the monthly magazine of the Second Reformed Church Sabbath School in Philadelphia.[47]

Just as evangelicals viewed the end of our journey on earth to be either heaven or hell, just as they viewed children as either saved or doomed, so they brooked no gray area where behavior was concerned, only Manicheaean black and white. There were good children, and there were bad children, repentant children and unrepentant, heaven-bound children and hell-bound. The behavior of disobedient and wicked children inflicted unbearable distress on pious parents, for they knew beyond a doubt that these children were doomed to spend eternity in hell.

The literature is replete with reports of boys and girls gone bad, and parents dying of broken hearts as a result. Only the child's repentance could save him from the fires of hell and his parents from blackest despair. Jacob Van Benschooten, the wayward son of the Reverend William Brownlee's fictional character Hans Van Benschooten, "is thought of only as one dead—or worse than dead." Jacob's misfortune was to have been "allured into the ways of sin" by his friend Richard Van Winkle, who enticed him first to a fair, then to a tavern, the racecourse, and finally "to that Hell in which the ruin of our youth is consummated—the theatre—then to the table of the gambler—and the company of the wanton!" This particular story has a "happy" ending, for on his deathbed, Jacob asks for forgiveness and finds redemption, to the unutterable relief of his aged parents and young widow. But such stories often as not ended with the sinner dying without repenting, doomed for eternity.[48]

It is impossible to know how many of these accounts were true or even partly true, and how many of them ministers invented out of whole cloth. Whether true or fabricated, they were meant to serve the purpose of striking sufficient fear in the hearts of pious parents and their children that they would seek salvation.

Death heightened the urgency of this goal. Death always lurked around the corner in nineteenth-century America, and children were made certain of this grim fact in floods of literature directed specifically at them. In an age ignorant of germs, much less antibiotics, healthy children perished in a night, and the evangelical clergy never missed an opportunity to remind boys and girls of the omnipresent grim reaper. The Reverend William C. Brownlee, also known as the "Children's Friend" in his weekly column in the *Intelligencer*, supplies a typical example: "How little can your parents do for you, children, when death approaches! They can wipe away the cold sweat of death, but they cannot prevent the *shiver of horror* in that hour from passing over your frame. . . . [Only] Jesus can go with you into the cold, dark grave. . . . Are you willing . . . to go into the cold dark grave [without him]?"[49]

Even the most pious of children were snatched away from their parents, even the children of famous Reformed Church ministers like the Reverend Thomas De Witt who lost his first-born child in infancy, then a son of two, then a daughter of eleven, then another son of two. Of the four children left to the De Witts, a daughter died in the "early dawn of womanhood," and six months later, in May 1862, their beloved nineteen-year-old son died suddenly, "without any apparent illness, of conjestion [*sic*] of the brain." Two De Witt children of eight survived to marry.[50]

Young readers of Brownlee's column were apprised of the fate of little Elsie Ann De Witt, the seeds of whose death had been laid in her delicate constitution from her earliest years. "My dear children . . . , You must die too," Brownlee wrote, taking advantage of the opportunity offered by the death of his colleague's child to heighten his readers' anxieties about the condition of their souls. Brownlee's descriptions of Elsie Ann's decline, her palpitations, her gradual enfeeblement, and finally her extreme difficulty in breathing were meant to frighten children and parents alike, saved or unsaved. Little Elsie Ann, of course, was fortunate in that she was saved. When her father told her that death was near, Brownlee reported, the brave child received "this painful intimation without any visible agitation," and assured her parents that she knew the Lord. After pouring our her heart in humble confession, the "poor dying lamb of the flock [was] . . . solemnly surrendered into the bosom of the good Shepherd of Israel."[51]

The emphasis on death in sermons, in children's literature, and in the *Intelligencer* was relentless. "If you are [six], you ought to be very good," the Parents and Children column informed its young readers. "You have lived six years, but do you know whether you will live six more? . . . [Do] you ever think how very, very soon you may die? John was not two . . . when he died; Mary [was five] . . . Eliza [less than six]. . . . Now, can you say whether the nightgown that is laid in your drawer will not soon be your shroud? Are you, Francis, fit to die? O! little children, go and kneel down, and pray to God to prepare you for death! for there are but two worlds hereafter, and to one or the other you must go."[52]

"A little Sermon for Little Folks" warned children that they would not always be young, nor would they necessarily arrive at adulthood. "Death does not select his victims alone from the adult and aged. . . . Your parents cannot save you. . . . [Only God can.] Remember now thy Creator in the days of your youth."[53]

"Parents, are your children ready to die?" the Parents and Children column demanded in another issue. For to be sure, "Death is waiting for them— . . . his shaft is even now poised; and soon perhaps will quiver in their vitals. . . . [You] cannot save them from the destroyer, or . . . purchase for them one hour's exemption from the dread decree." The only resort of frightened parents was to bring their "little ones to the good Shepherd and convert the king of terrors into a smiling friend."[54] Clergymen sympathized with parents' anxieties for their children's welfare. They were parents themselves. "Not even crime in a child can extinguish the affection of a parent," the Reverend John Knox acknowledged, and "intelligent Christian parents suffer agony, bleeding heart, and bitterness of spirit" when their children spurn the Lord. Even so, the fault must in the end lie with the parents themselves: "If your children are . . . careless and disobedient, it becomes you, however painful and humbling the exercise, to examine whether you have not been remiss in the discharge of your duties to them, and whether God is not, through them, punishing you for your delinquencies."[55]

Or as the Reverend Douw Van Olinda told an audience in 1835, "The evil propensities of our natures we bring with us into this world and long before the understanding can be enlightened with Gospel precepts . . . a heart prone to evil will urge us on . . . to ruin . . . [and] to the very gates of Eternal death. God has appointed [parents] to communicate to [their] children and urge upon their attention these rules of life . . . to restrain their vicious and promote their industrious habits. No other persons My Dear Friends can supply your place in this respect."[56]

Not even, indeed, the Sabbath school teacher, a figure in nineteenth-century evangelical culture who came to exercise almost as much influence over children as their parents. The *Sunday School Teacher's Companion*, a compilation of advice articles reprinted from various publications, appeared in 1834 and provided young men and women from all the evangelical faiths with a common bible of Sunday school philosophy and Sunday school mores and methods. In its instructive purposes, it was akin to advice books such as Abbott's *The Mother at Home* and *The Child at Home* that modeled the behavior of the ideal evangelical family.

Exactly like parents, teachers were charged not only with the interests of the nation, the purity of the Church, and the salvation of the souls

118   RULES OF BEHAVIOUR.

14. I must go away from the church as soon as I go out.

RULES OF GOOD BEHAVIOUR FOR THE CHILDREN OF THE SUNDAY-SCHOOL.

1. I must be obedient to my parents and teachers and love them for their kindness to me.

2. I must be affectionate to my brothers and sisters, and especially to such as are younger than myself.

3. I must respect old people, and be civil to everybody.

4. I must never mock lame or deformed persons.

5. I must be kind to dumb animals.

6. I must never use bad words, or call ill names.

7. I must avoid bad habits, such as foolish jesting, smoking or chewing tobacco, or using strong drink.

8. I must avoid quarrelling and contention.

9. I must be temperate in what I eat or drink.

10. I must be clean, neat and industrious.

11. I must pray to God and praise him, every morning and evening.

12. I must keep the Sabbath-day holy by reading God's word, attending on his worship, and avoiding all work and amusements.

There are some particular points in discipline, to which special attention seems necessary. Among them the first perhaps is *punctuality*. To secure this, various expedients are employed. Sometimes each scholar has been furnished with a card containing the following matter in large type.

What time does school begin?

It commences in the *morning* at NINE o'clock · in the *afternoon*, at half past ONE o'clock.

PUNCTUAL ATTENDANCE.   119

At these times, every scholar and teacher should be in his seat. ☞ THE DOOR IS THEN CLOSED. Every one must therefore leave home in sufficient season to be punctual; for it is only

To *Punctuality*, then we say, ☞ WELCOME, COME IN.

To *Tardiness*, it is—NO ADMITTANCE.

\*\* *The parents, and all who wish to visit the school, are not excluded by this regulation; but admitted at any time with great pleasure.*

We have seen another card, of which the following is a copy.

**WHAT TIME DOES SCHOOL BEGIN?**

*In the MORNING at*          *In the AFTERNOON at*

ALL THE YEAR ROUND

☞ *Always try to be in ten minutes before the time.*

In some schools a large card is placed directly in view of every scholar and teacher as the door is opened. Until the hour of beginning, the card displays the words, "I AM EARLY." As soon as the time arrives it is turned, and shows, "I AM LATE." This contrivance for silent rebuke has often been very successful in producing punctuality.

The importance of strict conformity to this prin-

FIGURE 16. Rules of behavior for Sunday school children emphasized obedience, the importance of kindness, and punctuality. *Courtesy Gardner A. Sage Library, New Brunswick Theological Seminary.*

committed to them, they were to do all in their power "to plant some ruling principle in [children's] minds. . . . [T]heir moral culture is in your care," they were told, "and momentous interests depend upon their early training. The heart of the coming generation is . . . [in] your charge while it is soft and tender, like melted wax; and you are placing your stamp upon it, and leaving impressions which time cannot efface. . . . You are hewing out the foundation stones . . . for that spiritual edifice which is soon to be the American church. You are shaping the moral character of those who are to stand up in your places, and live and act for the conversion of the world, when you are in the grave."[57] (See figure 16.)

Teachers, like parents, were expected to achieve not just some general improvement of character in their students, "but an entire renovation" of their hearts, not just to form good moral habits, but to "train them up in the way of sincere and undefiled religion" and to do everything in their power to save the immortal souls of their little charges.[58] To bring about these awesome goals, they were cautioned to be mild, gentle, amiable, con-

ciliating, and affectionate, and even tempered, patient, persevering, industrious, and of ardent piety themselves. They must make a right impression
at the earliest moment and never show vicious or selfish propensities or
peevish, violent tempers. But while governing their tempers, they must learn
to unite firmness and stability with mildness and kindness. It was acknowledged that teachers, being human, were likely to be moved to vehemence,
peevishness, and ill-humor by wayward children, but they must learn by
guarding their tone, manner, and feeling to counteract childish insubordi-
nation, disobedience, selfishness, unkindness, and even violence.[59]

Every detail of a teacher's being was considered in the prescriptive
literature. Gravity of deportment was indispensable: teachers should evidence neither a melancholy moroseness nor a trifling levity. A sedate manner was necessary to maintain their authority, and they should dress
modestly, as wearing gay clothes only engendered in their pupils envy and
discontent. "An assuming [proud] habit in a Sunday School teacher is not
only very disgusting to lookers-on, but fearfully calculated to mar the whole
undertaking."[60]

Above all, they must maintain their dignity. While showing affection
to their students was important, and they must thus stoop from their eminence to give it, they must never descend from that eminence to the
children's level. "As in a family, authority is the parent of the social virtues," so in a Sunday school, "if authority is well established, all will prosper." The line between maintaining authority and taking a stern, tyrannical
manner was a narrow one, but teachers of religion, and a religion that has
so much to do with love, must recognize that it was inconsistent and contradictory to act in a harsh and surly manner.[61]

Immersion in the Bible, punctuality, and regular attendance were imperative, as were pedagogical techniques such as brevity (children have short
attentions and will grow to dislike religion if you weary them with it), plain
language, and the frequent use of simple images, appropriate anecdotes and
narratives, and pointed and striking questions. Discipline should be established and administered on fixed principles, not on sudden rages or impulses. Commands, threats, and blows should be avoided for other methods
of eliciting good behavior, such as example, reward, praise, and the development of conscience. "Grinding teeth, flashing eyes, quivering lips and
angry words are not likely to bring a child to penitence."[62]

Teachers were repeatedly advised to spare the rod. "Brute force is the
worst species of correction; it irritates and hardens, but seldom subdues."
It was considered that "the severe application of the rod to chastise rest-
lessness or ill-behaviour [in children] during divine worship" was a fla-
grant outrage of propriety and decorum. "[The] whole congregation [is]

disturbed by such blows as an incensed teacher has thought to inflict, [especially at the very moment] when the preacher is just inculcating the gospel of peace, or recommending the wisdom of meekness." Rather than beating him, the offending child should be expelled.[63]

The teacher's work, like a mother's, was never done. Every Sunday, after the service, each teacher should call on two families and read the Scriptures, a sermon, or a tract to them, for "without regular and constant visiting to look after absentees, to assist the ignorant, to encourage the timid, to rebuke the vicious, the better half of the object of the Sunday School is lost."[64] Guides like the *Companion* readily acknowledged the teacher's problems: uncooperative parents, the "constitutional dullness" of the students, their "heedless attention . . . wilful neglect . . . insolent disobedience . . . innumerable and unceasing vexations and irritations, and the untutored minds and habits of the children of the poor." Teachers, it was agreed, were forced into contact with the "most disagreeable persons, collision with the most unruly tempers, exposure to the most uncomfortable circumstances." Worst of all, their best efforts to save their little charges' souls were all too often resisted by parents so indifferent to religion that they did not attend church and thus could not observe, much less control their children's deportment in the pews.[65]

William Bogert, a Sunday school teacher in the Second Reformed Church in New Brunswick, found this to be all too true, lamenting that "it is trying sometimes to see the levity and inattention of those we make sacrifices to benefit." Bogert often felt despair, thinking his prayers and efforts on behalf of his students all in vain. "I have laboured a score of years and yet I know not that I have even been instrumental in bringing one of [my] many scholars to Christ," he wrote.[66] Teachers complained that it was difficult to achieve the goals of the schools, especially when in many cases they first had to spend weeks or months teaching their little flocks to read, and then deal with students deficient not only in their lessons but in their behavior. "The patience of the teacher is often tried by the inattention and perverseness of the scholars," a teacher in Somerville, New Jersey, wrote in his diary. "But for the hope that we are sowing seed which will in after times produce good fruit," he added, "we would be utterly discouraged."[67]

Women teachers seemed to be more effective than men. H.E.B., in her column in the *Intelligencer*, voiced a common belief when she wrote that the Sunday school teacher should be a woman (even though women often quit teaching upon marrying), because women were more intuitive, sympathetic, loving, and tactful, and had more patience, energy, and geniality for this vital work. "It is safer for our sons, as well as our daughters, to be entrusted in their earliest years, to the care of woman," she wrote.

The agent of the Massachusetts Sabbath School Union put it more succinctly: "God had Sunday Schools in mind when he created woman."[68]

As the numbers of Sunday schools grew in number, one of their chief problems was obtaining teachers. This is hardly surprising, considering the responsibilities teachers were expected to bear and the conditions they had to face, which discouraged many from taking up the cause, many to abandon it, and many to gravitate toward schools that served a homogeneous and already churched clientele.

To follow the latter path was to defeat one of the goals of the schools, for bringing children of all backgrounds into a common culture of childhood that would efface social differences among them was an ideal of the ASSU, although it was not always the reality, especially in cities. "Our Sabbath schools are often filled with the children of the rich, the enlightened and the pious, while the poor, the ignorant and the vicious are cast out," reported the Committee on the Condition of Sabbath Schools in New York City in 1840. This committee, which was appointed by the General Association of Sabbath-School Teachers, estimated that of the 65,000 children in the city between the ages of four and sixteen, 34,000 were "cut off from the sacred influence [of the schools] . . . because 'no man careth for their souls.'" A severe lack of teachers in 1839 had caused five schools to give up, and a hundred classes in other schools were disbanded for a lack of teachers. It is the duty of all "professors" of religion, the report advised, to go into the vineyard so that the multitudes of unchurched urchins who desecrated the Sabbath with their "plays and broils, cursing and blaspheming" might be controlled.[69]

The problem of social class was endemic to Sunday schools, whether sectarian or ecumenical, and whether it was the teachers or the students who were affected or affecting. Some young people refused to teach, or left their posts "because there were none in the school of equal standing with themselves in life." If teachers "of very different standing in life" should find themselves in the same school, the richer and better-educated teachers should avoid "pride of station," they were instructed. Although they should act affably in the school with those beneath them, they did not have to associate with them out of school. Those in the humbler stations "will do well to guard against an obtrusive and forward disposition, and without being servile, they should always be respectful. All they ought to expect from their superiors is a kind co-operation in the duties of the school, without the familiarity of friends and companions in general." This advice conflicted with the ideal of the schools as "a holy family; a beautiful fraternity, associated by the bond of affection." Ideally, the school was to form a little community whose integrity it was a sort of high treason to violate. All were to "act together . . . and not form little separate associations" and backbiting cliques.[70]

The clergy attempted to address these problems year in and year out. In 1850, the Reformed minister George W. Bethune asked in a sermon, "Who goes to Sunday school?" When "some supposed better sort of children" attend, he wrote, the "less wealthy begin to leave, not being able to bear the taunts and jeers." But the church must educate all children. It had no right to do otherwise. "The Sunday School teacher, gathering the children . . . in his arms, is the very image of Jesus Christ" and must be the model for the teacher. Yet, a quarter-century later, the Reverend Thomas De Witt Talmage wrote, "God hasten the time when our Sabbath-Schools, instead of being flower-pots for a few choice children, shall gather up the perishing rabble outside." There was not much chance in fashionable Sunday schools, he went on, for a boy out at the elbows, especially if he were of another race. "Many of our schools pride themselves on being gilt-edged; and when we go out to fulfill the Saviour's command, 'Feed my lambs,' we look out chiefly for white fleeces."[71]

Increasingly, economics and social class, consumerism and materialism, civic religion and patriotism were coming to characterize the culture of the schools that had originally been imbued only with the zeal to teach reading in order to save souls. To illustrate, one need only observe the elegant decor of one of the most successful of the schools—and the ever increasing panoply with which it and others like it celebrated their success as the decades passed.

Although it had had its humble origins in May 1853 in an obscure cottage in the rural neighborhood of Hewes Street and Bedford Avenue, the Lee Avenue Reformed Dutch Church Sabbath School in Brooklyn was in the 1860s and 1870s the largest Sabbath school in the United States. The original school comprised eight children and three teachers. But under the direction of an able and talented leader, this little flock quickly grew. Within two years the Lee Avenue Sabbath School could boast 700 students and 80 teachers and by January 1, 1857, it had 1,000 enrollees and 115 teachers.[72]

In 1860, the Lee Avenue Sabbath school was so successful that it was able to erect a fabulous new building. Lit by 200 jets of gas and heated by furnaces in the cellar and hot-air registers in the rooms, it was proclaimed the largest and finest Sunday school hall in the world. The building, which seated 1,500 students and infant scholars, received such heavy use that within ten years extensive improvements to it were necessary. The elaborate and elegant redecoration of the building illuminates the materialism of even pre–Gilded Age America, and the curious intermixture of secular and religious iconography in the decoration suggests the civic and the sacred impulses that together informed the Sunday school as a cultural institution. The auditorium, the scene of many an elaborate program over the decades, was redecorated in Tuscan style, with ornate and exquisite frescoes, a gilded ceiling, Tuscan moldings around the windows, and sidewalls "marked off harmoniously in three different tints." The black walnut woodwork was repolished and new carpeting laid. On the parlor ceiling, which was spanned by "Saracenic" arches, a "tracery of foliage and frondage, Etruscan in character," was finely frescoed in sepia on a greenish gray ground. The "School-room," the largest in the United States, contained lifesized portraits of the twelve Apostles in the niches, and the Lecture Room was splendidly decorated with a painting of Evergreen Cemetery and figures illustrating the parable of the Good Samaritan. Entablatures contained the Lord's Prayer and the Ten Commandments.[73]

This fine setting was a far cry not only from this school's own small beginnings, but from the austere ideals with which Sabbath schools in general had been inspired a half-century before, as were the elaborate activities they planned and produced to celebrate their success. In 1865, for example, the school of the Second Reformed Dutch Church in Philadelphia celebrated its thirteenth anniversary.[74] At 3 P.M., the sanctuary, including galleries, vestibule, and aisles, was densely packed with spectators. Many more, unable to gain admittance, milled about outside. An array of ministers, officers of the school, and "ladies and gentlemen sufficient in numbers to organize several smaller Sunday schools" were seated in the pulpit area. The festivities began with hymns and the reading of the Annual Report of the school, followed by an address by the Reverend W. C. Van Meter of the Howard Mission in New York, who urged the gathered children "to make an offering of their hearts to the Saviour." Soon to follow this spiritual offering was a lavish display of worldly offerings, gifts by the students to school officials and to their teachers.

On the rollbook of this school were 470 scholars (210 boys, 260 girls) and 52 teachers (19 male, 33 female). The boys were organized into bands, the girls into circles, the names of the bands and circles revealing the gender-determined behavior expected of Victorian children. The boys' bands had action names: Carrier Dove, Good Samaritan, King of Zion, Rising Star, Robert Raikes (the founder of the Sunday school in Britain), the Superintendent's Body Guard, the Union Band, the Ulysses S. Grant Band. Girls were grouped in circles with passive names: the Blossom of Hope Circle, the Bow of Promise, the Bud of Promise, the Cheerful Helpers, the Feeble Helpers, the Forget-Me-Nots, the Gleaners, the Happy Circle, the Little by Little Circle, and so on.

The children's offerings to their teachers also reveal gender expectations as well as evidence of the linkage in the evangelical mind between the material and secular and the spiritual. Boys' gifts were often patriotic and action oriented: an American flag and a testament bound to a miniature piece of artillery. Or they were spiritual and action oriented: the Good Samaritan Band presented the superintendent with a silver cup of cold water and a verse: "Our offering today is the cup of cold water. / While we hope that we never from duty will falter, / But ever be ready, with true noble heart, / To cheerfully act the Samaritan's part." Girls' gifts were more likely bouquets of flowers, hanging baskets, vases of wax flowers, flowers fashioned into stars and crosses, and ferns.

Striking in both their obvious monetary value and their patriotic symbolism were the gifts bestowed on this occasion upon the minister and his wife, the Reverend Thomas De Witt Talmage and Mrs. Talmage: for him, a California gold piece, five volumes of the *American Encyclopedia*, and a handsome Bible entwined with imported olive branches; for Mrs. Talmage a $50 savings bond. The cup presented to the superintendent was made of silver, and he also received an American flag (but from the girls' circles, bouquets, baskets of flowers, and a vase of ferns).

These gifts and offerings were followed by another address, by the Reverend John H. Suydam of the First Reformed Church. "Although the little ones were somewhat wearied by the length of the exercises, yet such was the enlivening strain of [Mr. Suydam's] . . . remarks that he secured their attention throughout." The whole service lasted for two hours and fifteen minutes and included the singing of a "thrilling" multiverse piece written for the occasion, "Sabbath School Bells, Chime On." ("To leave the world of care, / To greet one day in seven, / To join in praise and prayer, / And learn the way to heaven; / The Sabbath bells invite us all, / Faint emblem of God's holy call.") "The wave of song as it rolled up from the sea of youthful faces, blended with the swelling sounds of the organ, and seemed almost to rock the church with its volume of harmony," according to a reporter. Five years later, the anniversary platform where the children of this same Sabbath school sat at its eighteenth anniversary was decorated with an "exuberance of foliage and flowers, intermingled with jets of gas, a fountain, and the warbling of birds . . . [and] had all the appearance of a garden or some fairy land." In terms of numbers, with now 500 scholars and 70 teachers, this Reformed Sunday school had become one of the largest and most successful in the nation.[75] In terms of advancing Christian values such as brotherhood and social justice, it had turned away from the original ideals of the schools.

At the beginning of the age of revivals, clergymen like Bethune and

Talmage and the lay leaders in their congregations had placed their faith in Sunday schools, public education, and in the moral reform and benevolent efforts of a thousand agencies to change the world. But change was slow in coming. In 1865, the Reformed minister Thomas De Witt, president of the New-York City Mission at 10 Bible House, described the evils that continued to foster pauperism and crime in the city: crowding (15,000 tenements housed 486,000 persons); priorities (one grog shop for every 100 persons, but only one church for every 3,000; $700 million spent annually on public amusements, but only $200,000 per year on police salaries); and unregulated immigration.[76]

Ten years later, the city's ragamuffins were viewed as a threat to the very security of the nation, indeed of Christendom itself. All over America, the Reverend Thomas De Witt Talmage wrote in 1876, are multitudes of homeless and godless children. "Could you gather them all together, what a scene of rags, and filth, and hunger, and desolation! . . . little feet on the broad way to death . . . words of cursing blistering those lips that ought to be [praising God] . . . hearts become the sewers of iniquity [and] . . . disgusting depravity." Talmage blamed the churches for not taking greater responsibility for the souls of these children. "The Spartans who threw their sickly children to the wild beasts were merciful compared with [us] . . . who with stolid indifference give up the destitute youth of our country to destruction," he wrote. "We must act upon them, or they will act upon us. We must Christianize them, or they will heathenize us."[77]

If in his fears, he spoke one word for the poor and two for the Church, his priorities were shared by many evangelicals, who feared that the ragamuffins would become in maturity a great army "gathering recruits from every grog-shop and den of infamy in the country to take the ballot-box." Talmage's plea was that parents, Sabbath schools, tract and Bible societies, and the religious press work harder than ever to gather in these children so that families might become truly nurseries of godliness and children truly adults "of right and God in future years."[78]

CHAPTER 8

# The World

## "LIVING ONLY TO BE USEFUL"

*God has made our land the teacher of nations. We are literally a city set upon a hill, whose light*
*cannot be hid. . . . American institutions and ideas are today sending their beneficent and*
*ameliorizing influences to the extremities of human society.*
—*Acts and Proceedings of the General Synod*, 1872

*E*vangelical concepts of family life and child rearing, through their dissemination in the religious press and their ready acceptance by pious parents, hastened the decline of Dutch cultural distinctions in New York and New Jersey. Reformed households came to recognize the private, domestic goals and challenges they had in common with their fellow Protestants.

Three public areas—the rise of the public school system, the burgeoning moral reform, benevolent, and missionary movements, and the crisis building to the Civil War—also generated commonalities of feeling that led to the further breakdown of the Dutch sense of themselves as somehow "apart." As Reformed clergy and their congregations joined with their fellow evangelicals in attempting to educate the masses, erase vice and crime, ease poverty, legislate good behavior and civic order, spread the gospel around the world, and deal with the problem of slavery, they came to develop a sense of themselves not as foreign and different, but simply as generic Americans stumbling along with everyone else into the mainstream culture, for better or for worse.

*U*nregulated immigration was believed to be at the root of the social problems that plagued the nation. In 1850 foreigners entered New York at the rate of 17,000 every month, and while some evangelicals might hope that prayer and Sunday school would erase the immigrants' illiteracy and poverty, most had realized, even as early as the 1830s, that church and state must work together to create a system of public education to inculcate American civic values. Before there could be effective moral control, there

*160*

had to be a system of state-supported schools open to all. Only then, it was reasoned, could the Republic possibly survive the onslaught of so many diverse peoples commonly ignorant not only of the English language but of American political ideology, American religious, moral, and ethical values, and American history, traditions, and customs.[1]

Indeed, as it evolved, education in nineteenth-century America came to mean education in Protestant moral values, with emphasis on building good character, inculcating virtuous behavior, and forming useful and solid citizens. The proliferation of the Sunday school in the 1820s and the creation of the American Sunday School Union, the American Tract Society, and the American Bible Society, with their vast publishing programs, were attempts not only to spread literacy and then the gospel but to spread America's civil religion of law and order, cleanliness, sobriety, and industry. By the 1830s, the leaders of America, the vast majority of whom were churchgoing, do-gooding, evangelical humanitarians, were committed to the task of socializing and civilizing, then proselytizing and Americanizing the illiterate, innumerate, intemperate, unwashed, and unsaved human beings in their midst, whether native born, foreign born, willing or not. Education was the means, and church and state, in the form of free common schools and Sabbath schools, joined forces in the battle.

One Reformed layman expressed these sentiments in 1837, speaking to the alumni of Rutgers College:

> Unless we fortify our cities, and villages, and country towns with libraries of useful and moral books . . . unless we see to our common and higher schools—to the character and competency of our instructors, and increase their numbers—unless we furnish our own destitute places with those who shall proclaim the truths of the gospel . . . unless we encourage, and aid, and multiply our Sabbath schools, and guard the instruction of our children and youth, and give free course to the word of life; in one word, unless religion is more widely diffused . . . through our land, our very liberties will prove "savors of death unto death," and in letters of blood, the page of history shall record . . . that *the American revolution was a curse instead of a blessing to mankind.*[2]

But just as education was intended to be the means by which the waves of immigrants pouring into the Atlantic ports were assimilated into American society, it was also one of the means—though undoubtedly unintended by some and unwelcome by others—by which the assimilation of the New York and New Jersey Dutch, especially women, was accomplished.

In the goal of saving the Republic, women were regarded as important expediters, and it was generally held by the enlightened that an educated woman was a more effective instrument in this goal than an uneducated one. The Reformed Church's philosophy regarding the secular education of women was often enunciated in the pages of the *Christian Intelligencer.* In 1835, an item called simply "Woman" even advocated educating women over men, if a choice had to be made between the two:

> Woman is the most important sex, and if but one half of our race can be educated, let it be the woman instead of man. Woman forms our character, she watches by us in sickness, soothes us in distress, and cheers us in the melancholy of old age. Her rank determines that of the race. If she be high minded and virtuous, with a soul thirsting for that which is lofty, true, and disinterested, so it is with the race. If she be light and vain, with her heart set only on trifles, fond only of pleasure—alas! for the community where she is so, it is ruined.[3]

Because of woman's presumed molding, modifying influence upon society, the *Intelligencer* argued, her nature should not only be properly understood, but her education duly estimated. . . . No people can advance far, while woman . . . is treated as inferior to man."[4] Reformed laymen of the same mind wrote to the editors: "We found no more conclusive mark of progress than the attention given to female education," one correspondent wrote. "[It used to be that] a young lady who could show a 'mourning piece' [a sentimental embroidered graveyard scene] . . . was regarded as a literary prodigy, whether or not she could read, write, or cipher. . . . [But today] the idea of excluding one half of the race from the higher walks of literature and science is happily exploded, and our daughters . . . share with [our sons] . . . successful competition in mental, moral, and physical science."[5]

An educated womanhood, however, raised an awkward question: in nineteenth-century evangelical families, as we have seen, both parents were important attendants in their nurseries of religion and godliness, but it was understood that mother had the chief role, and her first work and her most important work was at home. Her primary sphere of influence was the household, the arena where she ruled supreme in the moral training and spiritual growth of her children, where she formed them to take their rightful places in the world and in the Kingdom of Christ, where hers was the hand that rocked the cradle that would one day rule the nation. If women were meant by God to stay at home and see to the order and harmony of their households and to the religious and moral training of their families, what purpose was served by giving them an education that—as schools proliferated and slowly improved under conscientious administrators and curriculum builders—was coming to be in many cases equal to men's?

The ideal of the pious woman contentedly managing her sphere—her home, her husband, and her children—was, doubtless, put into practice by many evangelical families of all denominations. But the clergymen who fostered the ideal, and the authors and publishers of the scores of nineteenth-century guides to female behavior that made the ideal widely known even among nonchurchgoers, embraced the notion that the divine plantation was mother's proper and her *only* sphere of influence more enthusiastically than did many women themselves. For sphere theory ran into direct conflict with the idea of women's education—and its purposes. One Reformed woman wrote, almost wailed, *"What are daughters for?"* She was not alone in suspecting that girls' education in that era intended them not for a wider sphere of profession or career but rather for the circle of the family from which they had come. But had God intended that woman was to be useful only within her own four walls?

The tension between the idea of women's place as only in the home and the development of educational opportunities that gave women a taste for life outside the home created a sense of sisterhood among women of all religious backgrounds. For Reformed women, it had the additional effect of helping to diminish their sense of separateness and difference. In going out into the world, they took their traditional Dutch values and attitudes of independence with them as models for others. But at the same time, they also acquired new American values and attitudes in the inevitable and inexorable process of acculturation and assimilation in which they were gradually losing their proclivities for insularity and their sense of ethnic specialness.

By midcentury in New York and New Jersey, public and private schools were so ubiquitous that young women of every religious affiliation, every level of ability, and every pocketbook were finding it increasingly possible to obtain an education.[6] Private boarding and day schools hopeful of attracting the children of Reformed Dutch families advertised as a matter of course in the *Intelligencer*, and schools fortunate enough to come recommended by prominent Reformed clergyman were quick to mention this in their advertisements. Clerical encomiums were taken seriously by pious Reformed lay people and clergy, with their penchant for face-to-face interaction with others of a similar background, and schools where their children could be among their own kind were sought after. Retaining their Dutchness was still valued enough that, even as late as 1870, Reformed Dutch parents continued to be wary of sending their children to schools where "sectarianism and proselytism" might have too much influence over unformed minds and perhaps prejudice them against the Reformed Church. As one letter writer to the *Intelligencer* warned that year, "some of the children of our own Church [have been] lost to it in this way, and won over to some other church to the great grief of [their] parents."[7] Education was a two-edged sword. It opened and broadened young minds, but it also opened and broadened opportunities for leaving Dutchness in the dust, as is clear in the views of H.E.B.

In the 1850s, H.E.B. began to write a regular column for the *Christian Intelligencer*. She was not otherwise identified, but she was probably the wife of a Reformed clergyman known to the editors, who considered her articles important enough to place them regularly on page one. On the subject of women's education, H.E.B. was consistently thoughtful and often provocative. "What shall our children study?" she asked. This was easy to answer regarding boys, for the boy's abilities, his parents' finances, and his chosen vocation determined what he would need to learn to earn his living and to support a family. "But far different is the case with our girls. *What are daughters for?*" H.E.B. demanded. "*What is their use in society?—what [is] the post they are designed to fill?*"[8]

H.E.B. answered her own queries: women, even those fortunate enough to receive the kind of quality education provided by schools such as the Rutgers Female Institute and another popular Reformed Dutch school, Claverack Academy, in Columbia County, New York, "are not to be our future statesmen and philosophers . . . religious teachers, editors, physicians, classical professors. True, there are some vigorous [women who] . . . may press upward into these honorable positions, and the world may grudgingly and reluctantly accord its permission. . . . But generally, these stations . . . are not for them. They are reserved for . . . *men*. . . . [O]ur daughters [are] designed . . . to be the waiters and tenders upon the selfish caprices of man; to be household drudges; slaves to the appetites and whims of the other half of creation."

H.E.B.'s indignation, even rage, at the true condition of women spilled down the columns of the *Intelligencer*: "*To be married!* This . . . is the acknowledged end and aim of a girl's existence. . . . [But once married] she is lost to view, swallowed up in the inexorable maelstrom of the family, and none, save the circumscribed group of fireside friends, will ever know that she exists. No more parental anxiety, no more hopes or fears, doubts or difficulties are experienced in her behalf. She is *fixed* . . . put on the *chemin-de-fer* of life, and moves on and on to its terminus in its continuous, unvarying track. Of course she does not need much education [only enough] to put her through the circles of society, as she whirls along in search of a partner"—that special "somebody" who would take care of her for life, as a Reformed minister described him.[9]

When and if she did marry, she should not allow her marriage to become a sinkhole of docile anonymity, H.E.B. declared, but rather a foundation from which to "be useful," to make society better. "Oh why," she went on, "debase the holy ordinance of marriage by reducing [woman's] life to so low a level? Marriage is not a Sebastopol into which a woman can retire with all her resources of talent, wit, beauty, and grace. . . . It should rather be a besieging garrison, supplied with every engine of power and influence for the aggressive and glorious conflict of this probationary state [on earth]. . . . Our daughters must be taught that they are to become *women*, strong *women*, effective *women*."[10]

A woman's education was a far cry from a passport to everywhere, as Isaac Ferris had optimistically pronounced it. But it was also clear that H.E.B.'s own education had put her into the mainstream of feminist thinking of the day, as it did and would for generations of Reformed women gradually moving out of their isolated Dutch enclaves in the river valleys of New York and New Jersey into a world where they were entreated to "look beyond. . . . Ask why you were put into this world." They had not come into the world by chance, but by design, wrote H.E.B., good Calvinist that she was, and their object in life should be to educate themselves, so that all the powers of their being should be brought to bear upon the chief object of life—"to glorify and enjoy God, to please him and to benefit his creatures." Deeply steeped in the tenets of Reformed theology, H.E.B. recommended that young women read, write, and think with a double purpose—that they might profit themselves and be *useful* to those around them.[11]

That the *Intelligencer* printed H.E.B.'s views, especially so prominently, suggests that the clergymen editors were supportive of the changes taking place in their Reformed Zion. But their support had its limits. The notion of women's sphere as being solely in the home was gradually widened to include, beyond volunteerism, teaching and missionary work in the field. But that was as far as many thought things should go. "We do not . . . plead for the widening of the sphere [women occupy] . . . or its extension," the *Intelligencer*'s clergymen editors wrote in 1870 in a series of articles on women's role. "It is wide enough now to satisfy the largest laudable ambition." There was no need for women to covet public honor or high places, for by her very nature she was already a "ruler in the highest, noblest sense," appointed by God "queen in a realm universally acknowledged all her own." Her subjects were only too glad to recognize the benefits of her rule, and the world and the church do as well, they added. Women did not need to ask how they ruled. They were assured on every hand that they ruled in that they formed the future rulers of the land. Theirs was the power behind the throne. So, "why need woman care herself to hold the reins of government, if she can do so much to shape the character . . . of the future rulers, or [why should she care to vote] . . . if she can educate the minds and hearts of the voters?"[12]

After the Civil War, when women in greater numbers began to enter customary male occupations, Reformed clergymen like the Reverend T. L. Cuyler joined their colleagues in other denominations in urging them to refrain from "rush[ing] into the already over-crowded trades and professions" that were normally the preserve of men, for men needed these jobs to support their families. A woman was entitled to compensation for services rendered equal to men's, but she must remember the law of demand and supply. "Women who desire to be both independent and useful should seek those fields not oversupplied." They were advised, if they must extend their sphere into the world, to take up teaching, horticulture, benevolent work, missionary work, the "art and science of diet," and, as always, of course, the proper control of their households.[13]

Overly ambitious women were perceived as tampering with the way society worked—even of undermining civilization—and the Reverend Dr. Cuyler was only one of many clergymen of all denominations who urged their female parishioners to forgo working outside of the home, and not to clamor for the vote either. Many women, among them the wives of ministers, took this as sound advice. In the tart words of the wife of Reformed minister James Van Campen Romeyn of Hackensack, "Let ministers mind their congregations, and let their wives take charge of their families."[14]

Clergymen were amenable to the expansion of a woman's sphere, in other words, but only for its expansion in a way that might overlap, but not impede upon a man's role. A woman should use her education to make her influence felt, they declared, through the church and those organized institutions and associations, boards and societies that worked to ameliorate the evil condition of unchurched women. The mission field was ideal. Go to India, Reformed clergymen advised, where the Reformed Church sponsored the Arcot Mission, made famous by Dr. John Scudder and his family, and influence for good the greatly degraded position of women there. They extolled such women as Mrs. Sarah Ann Chamberlain, wife of the Reformed minister Dr. Joseph Scudder, who possessed such superior talents and judgment and acquired such a command of the Tamil language in India that she was able to superintend the schools under her husband's charge, but they would have blanched at the idea that she might have schools in her own charge.[15]

Women not sufficiently educated to engage directly in mission work, as Sarah Chamberlain was, could, by marrying a missionary, at least teach by example in the mission household the comforts and blessings of a Christian home to those amid the "darkness, sorrow and oppression of domestic life in homes without the gospel." Even if her stay "be brief in the land of the Pagan," she will have left an impression on the pagan mind, "for they will have seen both in what purity a Christian can live and in what peace [she] can die."[16]

Under the influence of this line of thought, the missionary movement became an important outlet for Reformed women to feel that they were leading useful Christian lives. David Abeel, one of the first American Protestant missionaries to the Far East, early on encouraged women to go to foreign lands for the purpose of evangelizing women, alleviating their suffering, and educating their children. Instrumental in establishing in England the Society for Promoting Female Education in the East, his zeal affected many in the American Reformed Church as well.[17]

By 1875, the Woman's Board of the Reformed Church supported a girls' seminary in Arcot, India; sponsored an American teacher, Miss Martha J. Mandeville, who superintended three girls' schools; employed twelve Christian native school-mistresses teaching classes of twenty to thirty Indian children each; and supported a class of nurses in the hospital at Arcot. Meanwhile, at the Reformed mission in Amoy, China, two women of the denomination taught a girls' school of twenty to thirty students and also assisted Mrs. Talmage and Mrs. Kip, missionary wives, in instructing three classes of adult women in reading, Bible study, needlework, and proper family care. And in Japan, two Reformed women supervised the Girls' School at Yokohama.

*W*hen on her deathbed in 1850, Sarah Garretson, age seventeen, daughter of Reformed minister John Garretson, wrote to her brothers and sister in New Brunswick that "they should all be sure to meet her in heaven, and live only to be useful," the term *useful* was new as she used it. What Sarah meant was essentially the same concept of personal holiness or godly living that had been brought to the New World by the seventeenth- and eighteenth-century Dutch Pietists.[18]

Also called sanctification, the idea of usefulness gripped the evangelical mind in the nineteenth century and led untold thousands of Christians to attack the social problems of the day. In New York, the problem that attracted evangelicals' closest attention was the condition of children. At the midpoint of the century, January 1850, the editors of the *Christian Intelligencer* called attention to a recent report of the chief of New York Police regarding the crowds of rowdy and vicious children "infesting" the streets, docks, and hotels of Manhattan. The offspring of what the editors described as careless, intemperate, immoral, and dishonest parents, these children did not attend school but were left to roam day and night wherever they pleased, to pilfer, beg, maraud, and even to sell their bodies. Little girls as young as eight years were "addicted to immoralities of the most loathsome description." Reports from captains in every police district in the city reported 2,955 children in the penitentiary and state prison, two-thirds of them females between eight and sixteen years of age.[19]

An estimated 770 "embryo courtesans and felons" were in the habit of congregating around the piers, where they daily pilfered immense quantities of merchandise being landed or shipped. A hundred child beggars spent their earnings at night in the loathsome quarter known as Five Points, "in the lowest dens of drunkenness and disease, engaging in disgusting scenes of precocious dissipation and debauchery." Hundreds of girls of tender years entered rooms and offices ostensibly to sell nuts, fruits, socks, and toothpicks, but for a few shillings submitted to the "most degrading familiarities"—and gave their earnings to their lazy, drunken parents, who sent them out again the next day on the same errand.

Homeless boys, "baggage smashers," congregated in depots and on the piers, where they offered to carry the parcels and valises of innocent travelers and then ran off with them. Nearly 2,000 boys had homes, and even respectable parents, but the parents allowed them to loiter on the Sabbath and on weekday evenings, wrangling and fighting, swearing and blaspheming, often stealing, staying out for weeks on end, and consorting with the vilest of both sexes. And finally, an estimated 2,383 children were truants. (See figure 17.)

The remedies recommended in 1850 were compulsory school attendance, apprenticeships, and Sunday school. To encourage attendance in the last, twenty-one of the city's churches joined together for a simultaneous prayer meeting in November 1850. Motivated by the ominous police statistics, and by what they referred to as a deep solicitude for the moral culture and spiritual welfare of the estimated 70,000 children in the city who did not attend Sabbath school, the churches set aside this specific time for Sabbath school superintendents, teachers, scholars, and parents to meet and pray together that the Holy Spirit would work upon the hearts of the unchurched.

Prayer and Sunday school were in order, no doubt, but to address such urgent societal ills, action was required on every front, and the General Synod of the Reformed Church encouraged its members, both men and women, to become active in Sabbatarian and temperance societies and in an ever proliferating host of reform and benevolent organizations. Pious women, especially educated ones, answered the call, emerging from their

FIGURE 17. Evangelicals feared that in the tenements, hovels, and beer cellars of the infamous Five Points, near Chatham Square in lower Manhattan, pauperism, filth, vice, and crime threatened the very security of the nation. "We must Christianize them, or they will heathenize us," declared one Reformed minister. *Courtesy Picture Collection, Newark Public Library, Newark, N.J.*

households to play extraordinarily effective roles in improving society. Men represented the first wave of the reformers, but women soon followed. And far from being the shrinking violets and pale, pious nincompoops that evangelical females have sometimes been portrayed as, they organized and joined reform and benevolent societies with a clarity of purpose and even a militancy of spirit that expressed their empowering confidence that they were meant to do the Lord's work and would do it. If they were motivated on one level by a desire to demonstrate the efficacy of their own conversion, society was not the loser.

Although the officers of the prominent national associations were exclusively men, women participated in their activities, held office in their "female branches," or auxiliaries, and organized moral reform and benevolent societies of their own with the goal of converting all America and perfecting every corner of it. Woman, evangelicals generally agreed, could never achieve the "full extent of her capacity [for moral benevolence] until all her power is put forth in the God-like work of saving immortal natures from crime and sorrow, until she finds her highest happiness where lies her true glory, in doing good."[20]

In New York and New Jersey, Reformed women bent on useful lives could choose among literally scores, perhaps hundreds of societies, many of which were directed at their own sex and were governed and managed by it: the Female Education Society, the Female Missionary Society, the New York Magdalen Society, the New York Female Moral Reform Society (whose goals were to convert prostitutes to religion and to close down New York brothels), the New York Female Benevolent Association, the Female Bible and Tract Association, the Female City Tract Association, the Association for the Relief of Respectable, Aged, and Indigent Females, the Female Society for the Support of Schools in Africa, the New York Society for the Relief of the Poor, the Ladies' Effort for Foreign Tract Distribution, and the New York Female Assistance Society for the Relief of the Sick Poor are just a few of those whose meetings and affairs were reported regularly in the *Christian Intelligencer* starting in the 1830s. One young divinity student at New Brunswick Seminary wrote, in a great understatement, "The present is emphatically a benevolent age. Societies are formed for almost every charitable purpose."[21]

In what one historian has described as the "vigorous, near-volcanic growth of women's societies" in the nineteenth century, women in Reformed communities easily took to putting their desire for usefulness or sanctification to work in building the Kingdom.[22] Not only in the high-profile national ecumenical societies, but in every congregation, from the most prominent in Manhattan to tiny parishes in obscure towns like Chittenango in upstate New York, women formed sewing societies, or "fragment societies," and made articles for sale at church fairs. The proceeds went to support seminarians and missionaries, to liquidate a church debt, to furnish a Sunday school classroom, or to complete an unfinished church building or project. Reformed women donated untold amounts of time and raised uncountable sums of money, confident in the faith that they were doing what the Bible told them to do: love their neighbors, clothe the naked, feed the hungry, visit prisoners, and preach the gospel to every living creature.

In their enthusiasm to be useful, women in Reformed congregations and communities everywhere early on—by 1810 at least—approached their clergymen to allow them to convene Dorcas societies. The response to the formation of a Dorcas Society in New Brunswick in 1813 was eager, with 184 women subscribing. The all-woman board chose five managers (married ladies, one for each of the five wards of the city), and "visitors" (usually unmarried young ladies, two working under each manager with each visitor assigned responsibility for a particular district within a ward), to carry out its work. The group met every other Monday at 3:30 P.M. in members' homes. Rules stated that every lady come furnished with work-bag, thread case, and other implements for sewing. Once she was seated, she was presented with some article of clothing to make. At precisely four o'clock, a chapter in the Bible was read by one of the directresses, along with an approved commentary. The business of the meeting came next, the main business being to consider the needy cases presented, one by one.[23]

Beyond savoring the positive bonds of sisterhood and the good they were doing in society, as they organized themselves into effective action units, women were developing rudimentary executive skills and learning to work together within an organizational structure toward a common goal, to administer, to cooperate, and to give direction and to take it. For Reformed women, acquiring these modern skills reinforced their bonds with other American do-gooding women and allowed them to think of themselves as part of a wide and rising class, rather than as a narrow, old-fashioned, and foreign subgroup.

In the course of their work, they relied on the intuition and judgment that served them well at home to determine which of the supplicant women they interviewed were truly worthy of help. It was a rule of the New Brunswick Dorcas Society that no family be granted any relief until the manager had made a home visit to verify the family members' characters and circumstances. Nor were any applicants for aid, except in special cases, to be assisted if they refused to put their older children out to service or trades, or their young ones in school. The quality of mercy offered was strained by the society's need to husband its own resources and by its stated desire to avoid the "professional pauperism" that experience had taught was the result of indiscriminate charity.

As women tasted the joys of autonomy, they were reluctant to give them up. In 1845, the *Intelligencer* reported that the New York Female Assistance Society for the Sick Poor had broken off from a brief alliance with the male-dominated New York Society for the Relief of the Poor to pursue its original, independent path. Women, the female members believed, could give a kind and degree of attention and relief to the sick and poor of their own sex "more delicately and usefully than any other organization yet devised." Because women were often the victims of desertion and abandonment by men, they noted, and often under circumstances "peculiar to wives and mothers," their particular needs could be appreciated only when revealed to female visitors.[24]

Most of the female societies were ecumenical. The Newark Orphan Asylum Association, for example, was organized by women of the Reformed Dutch, Baptist, Protestant Episcopal, Methodist Episcopal, and Presbyterian churches of the city—a typical coalition in which a Reformed Dutch woman more often than not typically held the chair. The first and long-time chair of this particular organization, Mrs. Elizabeth Ricord, eldest daughter of the well-known Reformed minister Peter Stryker of Belleville, New Jersey, presided over a thirty-member all-woman board and five standing committees. Mrs. Ricord, who "move[d] about among her sex in queenly dignity," was a lady of "refined manners, scientific attainments, and eminent piety." All bowed in admiration of her "superior excellence," and the sophistication of the corporate structure of the organization she led reflected what women had learned in a few short decades about working together to realize a common goal.[25]

Mrs. Ricord's board divided the city into twelve districts, and charged the finance committee with raising funds by visiting each district to obtain donations and subscriptions. This committee superintended the pecuniary affairs of the association. The admissions committee reviewed applications, admitted those orphans who met the criteria, oversaw their eventual binding out, or adoption, and kept the orphans' records. The education committee engaged teachers, supplied books, stationery, and apparatus for instruction, examined the students, and superintended the school, reporting to the board those children who qualified for indenture. The domestic affairs committee oversaw the order, neatness, and economy of the plant and its premises, furnished supplies, and superintended the wardrobe of the children. Finally, the visiting committee's members rotated on weekly visits to the asylum to see that everything was in good order.

Concern for the orphaned children was evident in the association's policies: matrons had to be of good moral character and a member of some evangelical Protestant church. Blessings were asked and thanks returned at every meal. Children were instructed in private prayer, kneeling at their bedside, morning and evening, and all were required to attend worship, not only on Sunday, but as a group every morning and evening. Bread and milk, or mush and molasses, was daily fare for breakfast and supper. Dinner at midday consisted in turn of beef, soup, mutton or veal stew, pork and beans, and corned beef. Both boys and girls were taught to knit and sew.

Evangelical women were indefatigable in trying to make their world a better place, and they were nothing if not thorough. When the Newark Orphan Asylum Association decided to build a new school and dormitory in 1857, the women formed a ladies' building committee and held nearly a hundred meetings before they launched their plans, visiting orphan asylums on Staten Island and Long Island and in New York, Pennsylvania, Maryland, Washington, D.C., and as far west as Ohio and Indiana to consult superintendents, managers, and patrons. A gentlemen's building committee oversaw the actual construction.[26]

Newark had eight Reformed Dutch churches, organized between 1833 and 1871. These were known as First, Second, Third, North, West, South, East, and Belleville Avenue. Thanks to Cornelia R. Abeel, who set out in 1871 to canvas the women's societies in all the churches in the city, a great deal is known about the benevolent activities of the Reformed Dutch women in these congregations.[27]

Cornelia Abeel's records indicate that a Dorcas Society was organized in a Reformed church in Newark as early as 1810. A clothing society was organized in 1834. Five tract distributors, all ladies, visited from house to house every month, "carrying the word of life to over 250 families." In two sewing schools within Reformed congregations, women taught sixty children at a time how to sew, the goal to "make them useful in their homes," while teaching them a Bible verse each week for the good of their souls. (The garments they made they were allowed to keep.)

They established a home for "destitute worthy" women of Newark. Incorporated as the Society for the Relief of Respectable Aged Women, it was supervised by a board of managers of forty-five ladies, and an advisory board of fourteen men, representing various denominations. The board purchased a building capable of accommodating thirteen aged women. When the need for a larger building soon became apparent, the board purchased a lot and built a thirty-seven-room brick building, supplied with all the modern improvements, to house sixty women. The board received no aid from either city or state, but depended entirely on annual subscriptions, admission fees, and the fund-raising efforts of its managers.

*B*ecause evangelical women were given the dominant part in raising Christian families, and a major part in making the world a better place, the pressures this put on them deserve particular attention. Not all the good works in the world could convince some women that they were useful, worthy, or indeed heaven bound. Personal letters, as well as diaries and spiritual narratives, funeral discourses, and obituaries reveal that many Reformed women, like their sisters in other denominations, suffered various named and unnamed maladies, bouts of mental anguish, severe nervous apprehension, depression, and recurrent sick headaches so debilitating as to oblige them to withdraw periodically from the "maelstrom" of the family, as one put it. Women often refer to these symptoms in the context of their anxieties regarding their own and their families' spiritual condition. It is fair to speculate that the physical symptoms and the spiritual unease were pathologically connected, and that they served to unite pious women, whatever their ethnic or faith backgrounds, in a sympathetic and universal bond.

Mothers, aunts, and grandmothers, ministers' wives and farmers' wives, maiden ladies and girls at school all suffered disquietude and doubt about their own spiritual deficiencies. The saintly Joanna Bethune, mother of the Reformed minister Dr. George Bethune, suffered concern for her "impenitent" grandchildren and anguished that she had failed to bring them to the Lord. Anna Lansing Monteath, wife of a Reformed minister, wrote to her sister in 1828: "Tell [my nieces] from me the thread of life is brittle. A moment & we are in eternity. . . . Oh I find as I travel along in this world that I have much to learn & very little time to learn it in—I wish very much to be a consistent useful humble Domine's wife, but oh how much is wanted for this."[28]

Not every pious woman whose letters and diaries survive recorded her moments of religious unbelief, but Maria Ferdon, for one, was consumed with hers. Am I saved? she asked herself over and again, sure that a "secret besetting sin somewhere," the "winter in her soul," and her "hard & unbelieving heart" disqualified her from ever attaining salvation. Maria recorded in 1876 that she had "twice seen the Lord in four weeks," yet the same day her unbelief caused her to abstain from communion. Though others around her could welcome the idea that "all go to heaven there is no hell," she could not. She had been too thoroughly instilled with Calvinist images of sinners in the hands of an angry God.[29]

Spiritual anxiety did not decline in old age. The elderly Catherine Hardenbergh of New Brunswick received a letter from a friend: "Now for [the] spiritual—tell me dear C—— how is your heart revived? . . . tell me all about it for I am anxious to know why my heart cannot be warmed. I dont doubt my having grace any more than I would doubt yours," she went on, "but you have more faith by your fruits." Although the friend believed she was saved (had grace), then, why, she appears to have wondered, wasn't she a better person (more "useful"), more eager to multiply her good works? A Christian truly saved would want to be doing good all the day long. Another aged friend wrote to Catherine with the same problem: "I continually find a mar in my spirit, and . . . the good I would do—I do not, and so my wicked heart is continually in a ferment."[30]

Maria Frelinghuysen, wife of the Reformed Domine John Cornell, and highly admired for her piety, was inclined throughout her life, according to her brother's biographer, "to seasons of religious darkness, when a deep sense of unworthiness clouded every prospect." Indeed, Maria's own letters tell the story. At age fifty she wrote to her daughter: "Sometimes, Dear Anna, I can exercise a comfortable hope in that God, from whom I have received so many, so great, and so undeserved favors. Then again darkness and depondence [*sic*] seize my soul, and hold it in agonizing dread." And to her daughter Catharine, she wrote "I slept little last night, owing in some measure to a disturbed mind. We are frail creatures, My Dear Child, although God has given us exceeding great and precious promises, yet our unbelieving hearts prevent the application of them at all times." Two years before her death at age fifty-four she wrote to her son Frederick: "[May you never] have cause for those self-reproaches which so often torture the peace of your mother. When I review my past-life, oh what bitter reflections! How much neglected duty! How much committed evil! What abused privileges! What forgotten or disregarded Providences! . . . It seems to me I must still be classed among those who are in the gall of bitterness & the bonds of iniquity."[31]

Despite the inroads Arminianism and revivalism had made in the evangelical age, among the orthodox, Calvinist thought as formulated in the Canons of Dort still ruled in many a heart and mind. Mrs. Jane Kirkpatrick of New Brunswick, a devout Christian, was engulfed with spiritual apprehensions, to the point where, at times, "with agony indescribable, she would place herself among the 'fearful,' at the last day, and in horror dwelt on the thought of a final dismissal from the favor of God."[32] For some evangelicals, such unending cycles of doubt and recurrent self-beratings take on a ritualistic quality that recalls the medieval, monkish practices of self-castigation and flagellation.

Each week the *Christian Intelligencer* reported in its obituary columns specific deaths, replete with detailed biographical information, lengthy descriptions of the deceased's spiritual condition at death, as well as his or her particular conversion experience, and details of the deceased's good works. Mrs. Charity Heermans of Saugerties, New York, loved the "doctrines of the Reformed Dutch Church exceedingly," but despite her accomplishments in the faith, she saw "failure, imperfection, and corruption in all she had ever done" and hesitated to claim perfect assurance in her salvation, believing herself to be unworthy. For some pious evangelicals, such agonizing ups and downs in their spiritual journeys may have served a purpose—may perhaps have been a way of actually controlling their anxiety. Mrs. Heermans, for instance, believed that to claim assurance of her salvation "might interfere with her humility, minister to her pride, or thwart the work of self-examination," thereby angering her Maker. She thus preferred the feelings that "attended deep humiliation and penitence to those . . . implied in the lofty raptures of infallible assurance." On the other hand, she frequently "experienced paroxisms [*sic*] of distress, in which she supposed . . . she had begun her march through the 'dark vale.' But, on being revived, she expressed great disappointment in finding herself still on earth in this world of sin. Then . . . she would lament her impatience and express great fear that by excessive solicitude to depart, she might have offended her Heavenly Master."[33] "Be thou perfect," the Bible commanded, but the emphasis the age put upon achieving moral perfection took a cruel personal toll on pious Christians by thrusting them onto a perpetual rollercoaster of alarms and dreads.

The classic question "What must I do to be saved?", echoing down the ages from the days of the Apostle Paul, led in Calvinist circles from the colonial period into the evangelical age to an even more poignant question: how can I be sure of my salvation? But the question as asked even in the supposedly post-Calvinist nineteenth century is still squarely in the tradition of the meditations and sermons of the Puritan ministers and minister/poets of New England, who for all their faith and learning could not be absolutely, positively certain that a wrathful God would not slam the pearly gates in their faces at the very last instant. Mrs. Mary Ann Browning, a member in full communion of the Reformed Dutch Church at Bergen (Jersey City), had such a sense of her own depravity and wretchedness as a sinner that, for some years after professing her faith, "it was difficult for her to accredit the genuineness" of it. It seemed impossible to her that she should be the recipient of grace, yet she felt compelled to pray. But what she called the "'sinfulness of her prayers' only increased [her sense of] the displesure [*sic*] of the Lord toward her."[34]

Although she had dedicated herself to the Lord, the spiritual condition of Sarah Elizabeth Upson, of a Reformed congregation in Orange County, New York, "was often the occasion of absorbing anxiety and gloomy apprehensions, arising from her deep sense of the purity of God's holy law . . . contrasted with her own short-comings; and from a constitutional timidity that kept her in constant dread of self-deception in a matter of such momentous interest." When she looked to herself, she told a friend, "I feel a loathing which I cannot express, but when I look to Christ I think I know what it is to lean on Him." On her seesaw of hope and doubt, she finally found peace. A "fearful malady" spread its ravages through her body, causing suffering as "few have been called to bear," but she never complained and died calmly in the Lord.[35]

More Reformed Dutch women than not whose deaths are recorded in the obituary columns of the *Intelligencer* did die sure in the Lord. But this may be a reflection of the fact that the obituary served an important religious purpose. It was not only a way of broadcasting the news of a death. Its larger function was to record a "happy" death as a testimony to the hope all should have concerning the resurrection of the dead, as the editors of the *Intelligencer* succinctly put it.[36] Like Mrs. Eve Egberts, age ninety, of Cohoes, New York, who "ever felt a sense of her own unworthiness," most obituaries were able to report that, in the end, despite all her spiritual struggles, the dying one had found her hope in Jesus. And the obituary often commemorated this happy ending with an appropriate verse: "In age and feebleness extreme, / Who shall a helpless worm redeem? / Jesus, my only hope thou art, / Strength of my failing flesh and heart."[37]

Just as it served as an inspiration to believers, the obituary also functioned as a warning to nonbelievers, for it was generally accepted in the religious community that "a sober, discriminating, honest obituary notice does more than perpetuate the memory of the just—it does good. . . . Thousands of people have been comforted, guided, and strengthened by [them] . . . and there are instances in which they have been the means of awakening and conversion."[38]

Like funeral discourses, obituary notices were often written to intimidate, if not terrorize, the reader into seeking his or her salvation. When death came to a young woman member of a Reformed church in Columbia County, New York, her minister described the fierce and dark disease "clad in unusual horrors" that had suddenly made its visitation, "disturbing a happy home, and exciting a panic and alarm in the minds of many; yet there is another malady here," he wrote, "far more awful in its nature, more destructive in its effects." This was, of course, the "foul disease of sin . . . hastening many away to the darkness and desolation of the second death."[39]

In the same vein, the obituary notice of Anna Maria Varick, age sixty, described the mysterious disease that with little warning snatched her life away. But although her flesh and spirit became, suddenly, "a wreck together," her attention could be roused to no subject "except the name and character of the Saviour." She could and did speak totally coherently on this subject and this alone, for she knew she was dying happy in the Lord.[40] The obituary's emphasis on the suddenness with which death can come was meant to suggest to the dilatory, of course, that the hour was at hand for them, too, to make their decision for Christ.

Women who died happy deaths were described in a thousand different ways, all intended to have a salutary effect on the living: They succumbed to death with a patient acquiescence to the will of Divine Providence. They received death as a glorious deliverance and fell asleep in Jesus. They submitted with Christian fortitude and humble resignation. They looked upon their departure with complacency. They died in the triumphant consolation that they were going to their Savior. Their clergymen, who were usually the authors of their obituaries, praised women for their entire resignation to the Divine Will, their peace of mind, their calmness at the hour of death, the meekness with which they endured their protracted sufferings, their calm but triumphant exulting in the prospect of eternal life. Their dying words were offered by the clergymen editors of the *Intelligencer* as examples of commendable sentiments upon leaving the world: "O, those rays of Glory!" "My God, I come flying to Thee!" "O, the greatness of the glory revealed to me." "Welcome, Joy!" "O, sweet, sweet dying." "If this be dying, it is the pleasantest thing imaginable."[41]

The obituary served a secular purpose as well, for in it the good works of the deceased in making the world a better place was intended to induce others to follow her example: the deceased was known for "going about and doing good" as a Sabbath school teacher, a tract distributor, and a member of the Bible class. The deceased walked four miles to church services, often with too little regard to the state of the weather. In her the poor found a helper. She was a useful member and an ornament of society. She was a sincere and consistent disciple of Christ. From childhood she had known the Scriptures and read the Bible through four times each year. She descended from a lineage honoring and honored of God, whose descendants had done more to strengthen and adorn the church than any lineage recalled.

Finally, obituaries offered pious Reformed women weekly consolation that they were not alone in their struggles to lead godly lives, that all around them their sisters in other faiths were enduring not only the same doubts and anxieties, but were also receiving from the Comforter the support promised to them in the Scriptures. As the next chapter will make clear, in the rich and complex evangelical way of death, this confidence in the mutuality of their experience was one of the ways in which Reformed people's attachment to Dutchness finally gave up its hold.

𝓕rom the arcane to the mundane, all the religious matters and social controversies of the nation engaged the close attention of evangelicals. The propriety of marrying an in-law, infant baptism, divorce, crime, the relationship between church and state, Sabbath legislation, the conversion of the Jews, animal rights, funding for parochial schools, African colonization, alcoholism, abolition, immigration, the Pope's suspected plan to take over the Mississippi Valley, Darwin's theories of evolution: all called forth from the busy pens of clergymen and laymen uncountable sermons, discourses, and essays. In every form of print from letters to the editor to learned tomes, evangelicals aired and argued their views in public.

But high-minded, informed, principled, and conscientious as they were, on the most problematic matter of the century, slavery, neither the clergy nor lay church leaders, with some exceptions, exercised meaningful moral leadership. Cultural assumptions—that Africans were inferior to whites and that Christianity was the only true religion—in general guided the Western outlook on race. That Christianity and slavery were philosophically incompatible, a truth obvious today, did not influence mainstream Christian thought to any significant degree in the first half of the nineteenth century.

In this Reformed ministers and laity were no different from those in other denominations, from the average nineteenth-century American—Universalists, Quakers, and Abolitionists aside—or indeed from the generations reaching back into antiquity for whom slavery, albeit not always linked to race, was considered a norm. Indeed, their common attitude toward slavery was a bond linking them. In the modern era, as the historian Gerald F. De Jong has written of prerevolutionary America, churches all along the religious spectrum "were apathetic toward slavery as an evil institution." Apathy continued to be characteristic of the nineteenth-century church until the 1850s.[42]

In their apathy, Reformed clergy and laity revealed an imperfect understanding of Article 59 of the Reformed Constitution of 1793, which begins, "In the Church there is no difference between bond and free, but all are one in Christ." This article goes on to state that whenever slaves or blacks shall be baptized they shall be extended equal privileges with all other members, and their children shall be entitled to baptism and in every respect treated the same as children of white parents in the church.[43]

A conundrum was inherent in this promise, however, for it was usually the case that neither slaves nor their children were educated to the extent necessary to exercise these privileges. As De Jong has pointed out of the Reformed Church—especially after the English takeover, when the Dutch minister Henry Selyns was the chief spokesman for denominational policy—"children of non-Christian Negroes could not be baptized until their parents were baptized; but the parents could not be baptized until they were ready to become full communicant members." This entailed memorizing and understanding the Heidelberg Catechism and various hymns, psalms, and set prayers—a difficult undertaking for the literate and for the illiterate or semiliterate virtually impossible.[44]

The same held true of the nineteenth century: "The religious welfare of the negroes was not cared for as it should have been in that region in those days [Bergen County before 1850]," according to the Reformed minister David D. Demarest in 1896. "The Constitution of the Dutch Church provided that Masters ought to have slave children baptized and religiously educated. But all this was sadly neglected. The idea of brotherhood was unknown. Rarely did colored persons attend church. Very few were among the communicants."[45]

Public school authorities were as insensitive as church authorities to the welfare of the former slaves. An examination of Board of Education records for Flatbush, New York, an area heavily Dutch, reveals that, although schools had been established for the former slaves in 1828 (the year after emancipation in New York), two decades later these schools remained vastly inferior to the schools for whites, as statistics from just one year indicate: in 1849, 1,008 books were added to the libraries in the thirteen white schools in Flatbush, which had a total of 15,483 books. The black schools had no libraries. The superintendent of schools visited the white schools 228 times in 1849, the two black schools 14 times. The district committee visited the white schools 660 times in 1849, the black schools a mere 4 times.[46]

Uncertainty over whether Christianity and slavery were mutually exclusive continued to muddy the waters. Domine Godefridus Udemans, a Dutch pastor, had reasoned in 1638 that if slaves desired to "submit themselves to the lovely yoke of our Lord Jesus Christ, Christian love requires that they be discharged from the yoke of human slavery." But a century later another Dutchman—this one an ordained black domine, Jacobus Elisa Joannes Capitein (1717–1747)—argued from a Bible text, II Corinthians 3:17, that slavery was not contrary to Christianity: "Now the Lord is the Spirit; and where the spirit of the Lord is, there is liberty." This meant, according to this writer, that what mattered was spiritual freedom from sin, not physical freedom from slavery, an argument made earlier by certain writers of ancient Greece and Rome. Such thinking was just what slaveowners wanted to hear, apparently, for the author's treatise became a bestseller and went through four editions (in Dutch) in the first year of publication.[47]

In colonial New York and New Jersey, where the Reformed Church was strong, farming had become reliant on slaves, and slaves constituted a major part of farmers' wealth. It was no light matter to speak of separating the farmer from his property, and most ministers did not speak of it, for fear of finding their pews, and the church coffers, empty. Rather, most let themselves be content with arguments eked out of Scripture to condone the practice, or with specious hopes that in all good time it would disappear as "people learned to love one another."

By the end of the eighteenth century, the Declaration of Independence and the U.S. Constitution, with their assertions of equal rights and liberty and justice for all, had begun to throw the obvious inequality and unfreedom and injustice of American society into harsh relief. Antislavery sentiment grew, the Abolitionist movement gained force, churches and the press took up the cry, slave auctions became reprehensible, and resort was made to legal redress. In 1799, New York State passed an Act for the Gradual Abolition of Slavery, freeing children of slaves born after July 5, 1799, when they became 28 years old. New Jersey passed a similar law. In 1817, New York State enacted a law freeing every slave born before July 4, 1799, on July 4, 1827. Children of slaves born between July 5, 1799, and before March 31, 1817, were freed, but were bound for service until age twenty-eight for males and twenty-five for females. In gradual steps, the last vestiges of legal slavery were finally fully abolished in New York in 1841 and in New Jersey in 1844. New Jersey's approaching date of final abolishment, however, did not prevent churchgoing Somerville citizens in 1842 from deciding in the negative on the question "Ought free colored freeholders be allowed to vote?"[48] (See figure 18.)

In fact, the antislavery laws themselves were flouted. S.L.B. Baldwin, the editor of the Somerville newspaper, noted in his diary on July 19, 1842: "We advertised the time of a colored girl for sale yesterday, and there have been three applications already." There is a reference in 1853 in the Van Derveer Papers to the sale of a slave boy. And slave running, though illegal, continued up to the time of the Civil War off the coast of Long Island.[49]

Other "solutions" than emancipation were also tried. In 1817 the American Colonization Society offered an approach to the problem with the novel idea of encouraging America's black people to settle in Africa. The General Synod of the Reformed Dutch Church endorsed the society's plan in 1820 and commended it to the churches as a benevolent goal that, if "judiciously executed [was] . . . calculated to be useful here and in Africa, and to the cause of humanity."[50]

Most Protestant denominations were in favor of the colonization enterprise, which they regarded as an important way not only of solving

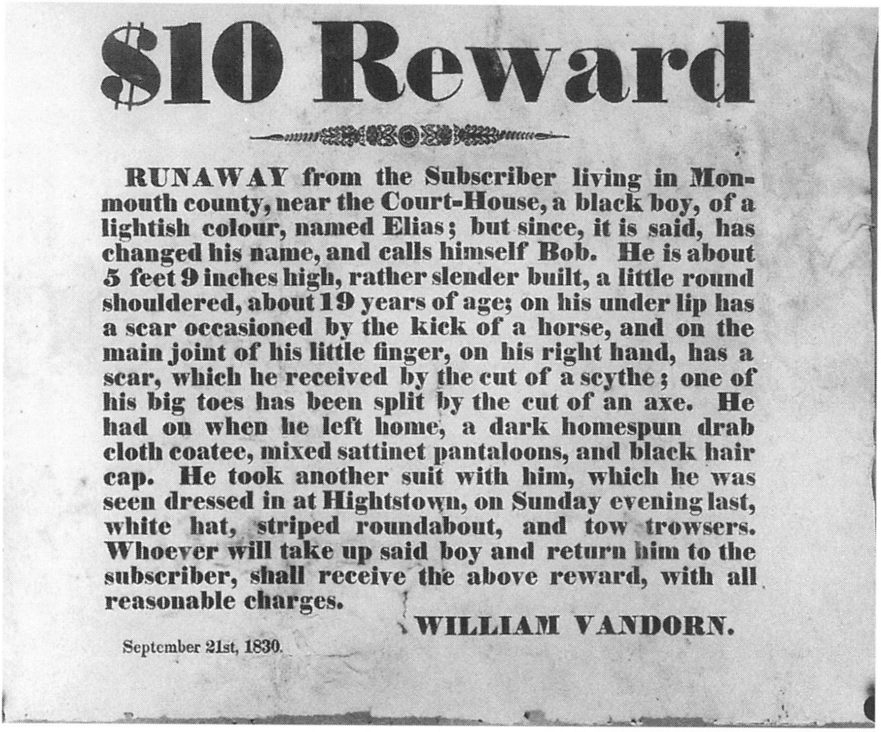

# $10 Reward

RUNAWAY from the Subscriber living in Monmouth county, near the Court-House, a black boy, of a lightish colour, named Elias; but since, it is said, has changed his name, and calls himself Bob. He is about 5 feet 9 inches high, rather slender built, a little round shouldered, about 19 years of age; on his under lip has a scar occasioned by the kick of a horse, and on the main joint of his little finger, on his right hand, has a scar, which he received by the cut of a scythe; one of his big toes has been split by the cut of an axe. He had on when he left home, a dark homespun drab cloth coatee, mixed sattinet pantaloons, and black hair cap. He took another suit with him, which he was seen dressed in at Hightstown, on Sunday evening last, white hat, striped roundabout, and tow trowsers. Whoever will take up said boy and return him to the subscriber, shall receive the above reward, with all reasonable charges.

**WILLIAM VANDORN.**

September 21st, 1830.

FIGURE 18. In changing his name from old-fashioned Elias to modern Bob, this runaway slave was indicating his intention not only to secure his freedom, but to take on a whole new identity. Slavery was not fully abolished in New Jersey until 1844. *Courtesy Special Collections and University Archives, Rutgers University Libraries.*

America's most intractable social problem, but also of Christianizing the African continent. The Reformed minister John A. Todd, an outspoken opponent of slavery, and one of the first members of the society, considered Liberia to be a "most important center of missionary effort, from which . . . our missionaries may scatter the good seed of the word through the whole of southwestern Africa, and from ocean to ocean." And as another minister put it, "The only way that Africa is to be civilized and christianized is to reach them by the enlightened of their own color." The "injury done the colored race can never be repaired," he added, "by giving them their freedom in this country." In Liberia, which was rich in natural resources (indigo, sugar cane, cane wood, cotton), they would find not only political freedom but economic freedom in trade goods as well.[51]

For decades, progress on the plan to colonize Africa with America's blacks was enthusiastically covered by the *Christian Intelligencer*, along with full reports of the annual meetings of the society, accounts of the slave trade carried on by smugglers despite laws against it, ads for chartered ships sailing to Liberia, requests for donations from the churches and laity in money and in supplies of every description, letters to the editors both pro and con the plan, and addresses promoting it. But it was not the answer to America's tragic involvement with slavery, for the people who were meant to take advantage of it showed little relish for settling themselves in Africa, and even the advocates of the plan may have wished it to succeed not as in the best interests of black people, but as the most likely way of dealing with an unyielding problem.

The seemingly incorrigible ability of Americans, even clergymen, to ignore the calamitous gap in American life between preaching and practice, Christian doctrine and daily behavior, the idealism of the great national documents and the reality of blacks' everyday experience is captured in a nutshell in an incident that the ever observant S.L.B. Baldwin recorded in his diary in 1842. The Reverend Talbot Chambers of the Somerville, New Jersey, Reformed Church lectured, Baldwin wrote, to a large audience on the subject "Love your brother, fear God, honor the King." Baldwin added that the Reverend Mr. Chambers "incidentally considered the subject of slavery, and insisted that the institution in a proper form was sanctioned by Scripture."[52]

The telling phrase is "in a proper form," which implies that slavery was acceptable as long as the slaveowner treated his human property with a certain degree of human decency. The city set upon a hill, the Reformed Zion, the home of the free and the brave, and liberty and justice for all were empty phrases to those who toiled their lives away on other men's land and who, while no doubt brave, were not much more free than tethered animals. But among their white fellow Americans, even pious Christians, there were few who cared, as long as "proper form" was observed.

Yet although clergymen and pious laymen of all denominations may have combed Scripture for arguments in defense of slavery, and although the Reverend David Demarest may have lamented that the idea of brotherhood toward blacks was unknown in Bergen County, private recollections, including Demarest's own, tell another story. Whether they acted out of guilt, humanity, conscience, or Christian charity cannot be said, but the diaries and letters of ordinary nineteenth-century Reformed clergy and laity record many acts of human kindness toward black people, slave and former slave. A few examples are offered here, not to whitewash slaveholders, or to suggest that the pulpit managed to convey to the pew, or that the pew managed to understand, a correlation between the teachings of the New Testament and the relations between blacks and whites. It is forever to be regretted that nineteenth-century evangelicals so diligently worked and prayed to make the world a better place, but had blinders on when it came to ensuring former slaves their equal rights under the law, or the education to equip them to compete for equal opportunities. The following accounts are offered here simply to add another dimension to this description of the religious culture of New York and New Jersey in the evangelical era—and to underscore another area where the Dutch stream encountered and blended into the mainstream.

In Bergen County, David Demarest's mother dressed Tom's running, loathsome leg sores daily, "cared for him as if he had been her father, until his death released her from this service." Jackie begged Demarest's grand-father to buy him when his old master died before some stranger bought him, and he did, for "he could not bear to think of the old darkey's days of infirmity made heavy by neglect or cruelty." Jackie received tender care in the old homestead until his death. In the family, Demarest recalled, "the darkies were our playmates, there was no such thing known as young master or young missus. They never waited on us or did anything for us, more than one of us would do for the other. Never was the flogging of an adult slave known and the youngsters received their whippings when deserved just the same as the white children and they were usually administered by their own mother." (The fathers generally lived on other farms and saw their families only when they visited on Sundays.)[53]

Adriance Van Brunt, on his Brooklyn farm, got up at two o'clock in the morning to see to Nancy, a twelve-year-old black girl who had worked for him for only two days, and who died that night in the garret over his kitchen. "I sent Michael and William with the little waggon to fetch her mother, she came immediately," he wrote. "Also sent for Isabelle and Mrs. Schoonmaker's Peggy. They did all that was to be done. Wee went to bed again." The next morning, "Frank brought up a coffin. . . . Stephen and Michael attended to digging the grave inviting the people etc. Michael took some [people] down to Brooklyn and fetched Nancy's mother back again with our Horses and waggon."[54]

Catherine Hardenbergh, age eighteen, of New Brunswick made a wedding veil for Phoebe, "one of the colored women," and took it to her and put it on her on the day of her wedding. Two weeks later Catherine learned that one of the "Southern colored people" was very sick. "Went down there this evening and took her some wine and a pillow, and did all that we could for her. I think she has consumption."[55]

New York law required that owners provide medical care and support for slaves in old age. After emancipation, when such law no longer applied, white families continued to serve an important function in caring for former slaves who could not fend for themselves. In 1869 John Lefferts and his sister Gertrude, looking back at the period around manumission in the 1820s, described aged freed slaves having to live in those years in the guard house at the edge of the Flatbush Dutch Reformed Church cemetery, until an almshouse was built for them in about 1830.

Both before and after Emancipation, aged slaves made themselves as useful around the house and farm as they could, but decades of overwork had often ruined their health and made them a financial burden to their masters. Wealthy farmers like John Vanderbilt of Flatbush, Gertrude Lefferts's future father-in-law, could afford dental and medical care for his slaves when they needed it, but many men could not. And when this was the case, and always in the cases of indigent freed slaves, the Flatbush Board of Health paid the medical bills.

In 1832, the Board paid the physician John Zabriskie for one visit to Francis, a black man; four visits to a black man at Thomas Williams's; three visits to Joe Hallida, one by night; three visits to Hanna, one by night; four visits to May; four visits to a black man at Cornelius Stryker's; seven days' attendance upon Molly, and when Molly did not improve, another twelve days' attendance upon her "with use of leeches."[56]

This model for master–slave relations carried over from the colonial experience. In 1777, during Peter Lefferts's day, an aging and valued slave like Ben, who may have been "given" to Peter as a child and who had been his trusted friend through life and the overseer of the Lefferts farm itself for many decades, was paid at death the honor and respect of a major Dutch-style funeral. At Ben's funeral on September 22, 1777, his body was wrapped in a linen sheet and laid in a coffin on a bier, perhaps even in the Leffertses' parlor. In the old Dutch manner, the assembled mourners consumed $5^1/_2$ quarts of rum and quantities of funeral breads and sugar and smoked four dozen pipes and five papers of tobacco paid for by the Lefferts. Thomas, another slave in the family, perhaps Ben's eldest son, was paid for "tending" at the funeral and for escorting the body to its burial place—whether in a section of the Flatbush Dutch Reformed Church cemetery reserved for slaves, or to a slave burial ground on the farm itself is not known.[57]

Fifty years later, with slavery outlawed in New York, the funerals of free blacks with no family or friends to bury them became the responsibility of the Flatbush Board of Health. In 1832, the Board paid William Allgeo of Flatbush $21.37$^1/_2$ for "making nine pine coffins for coloured people," and the Board records are replete during the 1830s with references to anonymous black men who died while at work in Flatbush. In one month alone, William Brown of Flatbush, was paid $6.00 for "digging grave and burying a black man at work at Mr. Charbone's & who died at Tom's, for digging a grave and burying a black man who died at John C. Bergen's, and for digging a grave and burying Henry a black man who died at the hospital."[58]

The slavery issue came to a head for the Reformed Dutch Church in 1855, when the Classis of North Carolina of the German Reformed Church, unhappy with alleged Romanizing tendencies in its own body (the Mercersberg Theology), expressed a desire to effect an ecclesiastical relation with the Reformed Dutch Church. But in the General Synod debate that year over the proposed union, the Reverend Isaac G. Duryee of Schenectady, a longtime Abolitionist, dropped a bombshell when he argued eloquently against the admission of the German classis on the grounds that three of the eight German ministers in it owned slaves.[59]

In the ensuing discussions, the Reverend Samuel B. How of New Brunswick pointed out that slaves were still held in New Jersey at that time "in the old Dutch families" (which was illegal in 1855), and argued that slaveholding was not sinful, because it was not specifically condemned in the Bible. Still, the General Synod, always walking on eggs, always chary of alienating any elements within the church, voted against union, although the vote was close. The vote, plus How's subsequent publication of a notorious sermon, "Slaveholding Not Sinful," opened the subject for wide debate that grew as events moved toward war.[60]

Hundreds of sermons, addresses, and editorials originating from the pens of Reformed clergy and laymen and printed in the *Intelligencer* and in secular papers "on the War, its causes, Divine Providence therein, and its results" illuminate the issues debated—and Christianity's long blindness to the loathsome system of slavery. This body of material, or what survives of it, documents the intelligence that at least some enlightened Reformed ministers brought to the discussion in the antebellum period.[61]

This material also illustrates the process the discussion served in bringing the Dutch stream of thought into the mainstream—and in illustrating to the Dutch themselves, once again, that they were not a homogeneously monolithic community, somehow separate and apart from their fellow Americans, but a heterogeneously divided community, just like the rest of the country. The crabbed Maria Ferdon of Bergen County might confide in her diary that Abraham Lincoln's assassination served him right. But a first-year student was summarily expelled from New Brunswick Seminary in 1865 for voicing a similar sentiment. On this most divisive of American issues, the Dutch, consulting their consciences as well as their wallets, had in the end, individual by individual, to place themselves somewhere on this spectrum of opinion along with every one of their fellow Americans.

# CHAPTER 9

# The Evangelical
# Way of Death

*In the fellowship of sorrow, sects are unknown, and the consolations of the gospel,
come through whatsoever channel they may, are always welcome to bleeding hearts.*
—Rev. William Sprague, 1847

*O*f all the various factors that acted in
the nineteenth century to erase the sense of a distinctive peoplehood among
Dutch Americans, none may have been more instrumental than the powerful culture that grew up around death and dying. Characterized by intricate
mourning etiquette and dress, and widely disseminated in the ubiquitous
literature of consolation, the Romantic sentiments surrounding death and
dying in the nineteenth century formed cultural bonds between and among
Christians of all persuasions. Both in adopting the styles in which death
and dying were accoutered and in imparting certain of their own ancient
mortuary customs to the larger culture, the Dutch erased the last customary ties that bound them to the Old World; they became American in a final sense. Death was, in this manner, the Great Leveler. We will look at a
number of areas surrounding the culture of death in the Age of Revivals
where Dutch Reformed clergy and laity found common ground with their
fellow Christians—specifically, contemporary conceptions of heaven and
hell, deathbed scenes, funerals, and the rural cemetery movement. First,
however, some background is in order.

*I*n a seventeenth-century treatise first published in English in 1793 and
popular in Reformed circles throughout the nineteenth century, the Dutch
theologian Abraham Hellenbroek delineated three kinds of death: corporal
death, the separation of the body from the soul; spiritual death, estrangement from God; and eternal death, or hell. On January 2, 1842, when the
Reverend Cornelius S. Van Santvoord preached a New Year's sermon in
the Reformed Dutch Church in Saugerties, New York, titled "The Possibility of Dying This Year," there was no need for him to refer to these

distinctions by name, for his listeners would have been completely conversant with them. Corporal death was a constant reality. On spiritual death they had listened to sermons and read pious texts by the thousands. And eternal death, hell, was as feared a fate as heaven, eternal life, was hoped for.[1]

Nineteenth-century evangelicals of all faiths were deeply preoccupied with the subject of death, and in a time before antibiotics or even a knowledge of germs, sermons like Van Santvoord's were meant to impress upon members of a vulnerable population that their opportunities to save their souls from hell were harrowingly limited. He bluntly pointed out, "Not one of us can positively say at what precise time it may please the Sovereign Disposer to stop the pulsations of our hearts," and thus it behooved all to make their peace with God at the earliest possible moment.

As the minister developed his case that New Year's Sunday, he illustrated it with irrefutable evidence that sudden death was not only a possibility but a good probability, for during the past year, he reminded his congregation, thousands had left this world who only a year before had "had as little expectation of dying as any of you can have at the present moment. . . . No one can scarce avoid the aim of the 'Insatiate Archer'— Death!" But who shall those persons be, he went on, "whose bodies shall during this present year go forth from the land of the living?" And "how solemn the thought that this year will perhaps be the last for some members of this communion!" he exclaimed. The King of Terrors, whom the minister characterized also as an "appalling visitant," a destroying angel, and a "grim and repulsive tyrant, clad in unimaginable horrors," waited to wield his sword. He may in fact have already received his commission, the minister added ominously.

Evangelicals' preoccupation with corporal death sprang from its presence among them. In 1822 alone, 1,600 New Yorkers succumbed to an epidemic of yellow fever. Death was omnipresent, on a scale both large and small. On December 27, 1823, Sarah Mynderse Campbell received a letter from her brother informing her of the death of his son. Shortly thereafter, Sarah herself was "taken with a strange disorder upon a sudden . . . so that I could not breathe clear but had to pant for breath. . . . I remained so as much as an hour my family were all alarmed they did not know what to do[.] O how uncertain is Life in the midst of Life we are in death nothing is certain in this side of Eternity." It was a common refrain. In the midst of life, ministers repeatedly informed their congregations, they were "dying creatures, and must ere long be unknown and unnumbered among the living. A blissful or dreadful eternity will soon become your unchanging destiny."[2]

Death was a matter of intense public interest, and books and other printed matter acquainted evangelicals with all its facets from the physical to the metaphysical. Long articles described the precise symptoms of dying, as if to know them was to demystify them. The immediate symptom, one author told his readers, was a feeling that death is near. Then, the half-closed eyes turn upward and sink in their sockets; eyeballs take on a faded, filmy appearance. Temples and cheeks hollow out, the nose becomes sharp, the lips depend, the face is either pale because circulation is failing, or livid from the blood settling in the veins. Coldness of the extremities starts to spread. The breath is chill, the skin is clammy, the voice falters, the pulse is feeble. The death rattle is next. Some gasp for breath and expire. Some when they are sinking toss the clothes from their chests. They slip downward in bed. Their muscles are flabby like silk. Some pick the sheets, or work them through their fingers. Some hear themselves called.[3]

Newspapers both secular and religious fed the interest in the acts and facts of dying. Each week, the *Christian Intelligencer* printed a report of deaths as compiled with grim exactitude by the New York City Health Inspector. As an example, in the week ending August 14, 1830, there were 166 deaths in the city: 34 men, 21 women, 59 boys, and 52 girls. Of these 64 were of or under the age of one year, 25 were between one and two years of age, 15 between two and five, 4 between five and ten, 3 between ten and twenty, 14 between twenty and thirty, 12 between thirty and forty, 13 between forty and fifty, 4 between fifty and sixty, 3 between sixty and seventy, 2 between seventy and eighty, and 2 between eighty and ninety. Causes of death were given as asthma (1), child bed (2), cholera morbus (1), cholic (2), consumption (22), convulsions (19), contusion (1), diarrhoea (4), dropsy (3), dropsy in the chest (2), dropsy in the head (9), and so on through the alphabet.[4]

As these figures indicate, infant mortality was high. The Reverend Aaron Lloyd, a Reformed minister in Jersey City, kept a record of the deaths of children in his congregation between July 1851 and April 1855. In this 45-month period, 21 children died, or about 1 every 2 months. In one case, he noted that a certain family was "greatly afflicted—Mother has lost 3 brothers, 1 sister, her mother and [this] child in 19 months."[5]

Families that lost little children were legion, but families also lost adult children, and children lost parents with alarming regularity. During one eleven-month period while he kept a diary between June 1828 and March 1830, Adriance Van Brunt noted the day's deaths in his Brooklyn community of Flatbush at the top of each page. In those eleven months, he recorded 35 deaths—an average of 3.2 per month—among his family and fellow churchgoers. Both his brother Cornelius and his mother were among them. And Adriance did not write in the diary every day. A genealogy of his family indicates that, among his siblings, Elizabeth died young; a second Elizabeth died at age 31; Theodore died in childhood; Jane died at age 41; Cornelius died at age 33; John and Stephen died when Adriance was 29 and 36; and Sarah Maria died at age 35.[6]

Impelled by the lurking presence of corporal death and the prospect of eternal death for the unrepentant, ministers emphasized in works directed to parents that the sooner they got their children saved the better. "Many children, when they go to bed at night, say the prayer, 'Now I lay me down to sleep' [with its infamous couplet: 'If I die before I wake / I pray the Lord my soul to take'], . . . and Almost every night some children go to bed well, and before morning are dead. It is, therefore, very dangerous to delay repentance. Love the Savior immediately, and prepare to die," recommended one such guide often quoted and advertised in the *Intelligencer*.[7]

The notion of a "happy death" was popular. "The pious child," one author wrote, "can be happy even when dying. . . . [One boy near death, hearing his playmates outside] said, 'Oh, how much more happy am I now than I used to be when well and out at play, not thinking of God or Heaven! There is not a boy in the street so happy as I.'"[8] Parents were assured that when the Christian child dies, "how happy must he be! He rises above the clouds, and the blue sky, and the twinkling stars, till he enters the home of God and the angels. There he becomes an angel himself [with] . . . a body of perfect beauty and . . . wings with which he can fly from world to world." Such "enrapturing thoughts" were virtually daily fare for evangelicals, and parents were inundated with advice not to let their children put off becoming Christians for another moment, for "the fact is, you are never certain of the dangers to which [they] are continually exposed."

> The rising morning can't assure,
> That we shall spend the day;
> For death stands ready at the door,
> To snatch our lives away.[9]

The fact is, it was true.

Distinguished clergymen published literature intended to console bereaved parents. The Reformed minister T. L. Cuyler was one of the most popular. His account of his son's death, *The Empty Crib: The Memorial of Little Georgie* (1868), touched thousands of fellow mourners. Another immensely popular author in this genre was the Reformed minister George W. Bethune, who contributed chapters to *The Smitten Household; or, Thoughts for the Afflicted*, a work containing "elegant and appropriate treatises, messages of comfort and peace, and sweet consolations" to suit every eventuality: the loss of a child, a wife, a husband, a parent, and a friend. In 1846, Bethune produced a classic of this genre, *Early Lost; Early Saved.*[10]

Bethune's attempts at consolation led him so far as to suggest to parents that early death had its advantages: The little one escapes from pain ("How many, whose beginning is of healthful promise, develop, as they grow, the seeds of constitutional suffering . . . ? Some dwindle into helpless idiotcy [*sic*], some grow blind, or deaf, or dumb; etc. It is better to die young"). Another benefit of early death is that the little one is then forever free from sin ("safe from the pollutions of the flesh, the temptations of the world, the malice of Satan"). And a final advantage, the deceased child is now in the perfect knowledge of God ("God is now his best Teacher, and the angels are his companions and fellow students"). Parents evidently found this line of reasoning consoling, for the book went through a number of editions.[11]

Ministers endlessly pondered the mysteries of death aloud and in print. We often ask, the Reformed minister Thomas Vermilye mused at the funeral of a "happy mother of nine," why Christians should have to endure the shock of death. But then, why shouldn't they?, he reasoned. For "What distracting griefs would the obvious separation between the righteous and the wicked cause if only sinners died?" Besides, he went on, the death of the body is necessary so that saints might be purified from all the sinful infirmities that cleave to their flesh in this world. "And thus, oh! wonderful result! sin, by which came death, through death shall die."[12]

It is desirable to die the death of the righteous, another Reformed minister told his congregation, not because there is less of physical suffering in it, for the righteous as well as the unrighteous experience agonizing death throes. And in both, the "strugglings of the spirit to escape from its house of clay" are distressing and painful to the highest degree. Yet both righteous and nonrighteous can depart as gently and peacefully as the fading away of a summer evening cloud. Nor is the separation from friends and family less painful to the righteous than to others, nor is it because the righteous one has professed Christ. ("A *mere profession* of religion does not prove anyone a righteous person. . . . Judas was a professor of religion!") Nor is it because he is willing to die. Multitudes of the nonrighteous have been willing to die. Rather, it is because the righteous man is at peace with God, repentant and reconciled. And it is because—even though he does not feel guiltless ("far from it")—he is truly prepared to die, certain that Jesus will be present in his passage through the dark valley to death. "Are all of you ready and prepared to die?" was the inevitable conclusion to such sermons.[13]

In an age when death was such a frequent visitor to households, consolation was ever called for, and friends and relations were practiced in forms of condolence. From Claverack, New York, a woman friend of Catherine L. Hardenbergh of New Brunswick wrote to her on the loss of her brother: "My dearest Friend, I know by bitter experience what must be the poignancy of your sorrow. The Lord has done it & who are we that dare reply against our maker? or say unto Him what doest thou? tho his ways appear to us mysterious the God of all the earth cannot do but what is right."[14]

When Catherine was not comforted by these thoughts, as, theoretically, she should have been, her correspondent reproved her in language heavily laced with biblical allusions: "I regret my incapacity to console your desponding spirit—but is there not a balm in Gilead? Is there not a Physician there? No trial however poignant no sorrow however agonizing—he can alleviate [it]—He alone can bind up the broken hearted give the oil of joy for mourning and the garment of praise for the spirit of heaviness; rejoice then that you have such a friend [Jesus] to whom you can repair in every affliction . . . & I will lend a listening ear to your cries. . . . remember that 'this nether world hath no charms'—there is dear Catherine a world where sorrows, & passing of friends are not known. . . . Let us then be resigned to his dealings with us—"

"What havoc [death] makes of all our earthly endearments," the Reverend Samuel B. How wrote to a former parishioner of his congregation in New Brunswick, who in quick succession had lost her father, her sister, and three of her sister's children. In the course of a typical year, clergymen spent a significant portion of their time visiting the sick and dying, consoling survivors, explaining the enigma of death to their congregations, urging them to resign themselves to the will of the Almighty, rationalizing pain and grief, and conducting funerals, which were public occasions of enormous scale, often attracting as many as a thousand mourners and in special cases even more.[15]

Finally, when death occurred, neighbors knew exactly what to do. "Mrs. Seaman lost her Babe I have to make her shroud and cap," Sarah Mynderse Campbell wrote in her diary. In April 1829, Adriance Van Brunt was sent for by Mr. Beekman, a Flatbush neighbor whose father-in-law had just expired. "Mr. Polhemus and R. Baizley (carpenter) laid him out. Mr. A. Cortelyou and myself set up with the corpse," Adriance wrote.[16] It was Garretson Hageman's charge to invite "some of the relations" to the funeral of John V. L. Van Doren of Middlebush. As it had been for his ancestors in New Netherland and before that in the Netherlands, his mission was a social occasion in itself, as he went first locally to invite mourners, and then to Raritan, to Millstone, to Lamington, and to Vleet's Mills. Along the way he enjoyed dinner and supper with the various families, and spent the night at Benjamin Van Doren's in New Germantown.[17]

On another occasion, Garretson was summoned by Amos, a black man, to go to Mrs. John P. Smith and tell her that her husband had been thrown off his wagon and killed. Garretson not only undertook this responsibility but also organized others to bring the body home. The men commenced to dress the body, while Garretson searched the clothing of the deceased and gave his pocketbook to the widow. He shaved the corpse "without cutting him once." Then he spent the night sitting up beside the body ("and the Rats did hold a noisy meeting"), he added.

The next day, Garretson handled John Smith's funeral arrangements. In the old Dutch manner, he made his lists and went out into the town to inform and to invite. He stayed again all night with the body. The next day, he went about again inviting people and finding pallbearers. Then, "making three nights without seeing a bed," he stayed a third night all alone with the body. "There was a great many present [at the funeral] and everything passed off nicely," he wrote, "except that when [the eight pallbearers] went to carry the corps[e] out in the hall one handle broke."[18]

One important area of common ground that tended to blur ethnic and ideological distinctions among evangelicals, and to reinforce their awareness of their collective fate, was their shared understanding of the doctrines of heaven and hell. Bible derived and reinforced in the creeds and confessions of all faiths, this body of theological thought had a unifying and ecumenical effect on believers. Heaven and hell, they were universally taught, were not mere metaphorical concepts. They were real places, territories whose geographical vividness was drawn for both children and adults in the sermons, Sunday school curriculum material, and juvenilia of all the denominations. The mind, wrote the Reformed minister Thomas Vermilye, "cannot fully comprehend [heaven's] adorable perfections yet we know from the Scriptures that it is a place, not a condition." Just as eternal death, hell, was the stick that ministers used to prod their congregations toward repentance and salvation, so eternal life was the carrot of hope where the Christian dead "escape[d] the exhaustion of sickness [and stepped] . . . into the health of Heaven."[19]

Curiosity abounded among evangelicals as to every detail and facet of heaven. "What Is Heaven?" an article in the *Intelligencer* asked in 1835. It was a question of unending fascination, and uncountable sermons, discourses, essays, and books tried to answer it. For Christian ministers, Revelations was their chief source of information—or according to their precepts and training, should have been. But in the age of Shelley, Byron, and Keats—much less Mrs. Lydia Sigourney, a hugely popular poet and writer who dwelt on death—Romantic poetry seems to have been another, as the Reformed minister John C. Cruickshank's descriptions of heaven suggest: it was, he wrote, in 1838, a place of "delightful feasts, charming music, enchanting scenes, shining garments, abiding riches, extensive powers, and glorious thrones," a place where men of all nations, kindreds, and tongues stand before the throne of the Lamb and, "clothed in white robes and palms in their hands," unite with the angels in their everlasting song of praise. In heaven, Christians will serve God day and night, "And O! how sweet and ravishing to the heart . . . to anticipate the near approach of that day when [we] shall be permitted to join that holy, praising, shouting throng, and freely share in all their celestial blessedness."[20] Just as heaven's ecumenicity and underlying democracy reflected the earthly ideals of the Era of the Common Man, so they encouraged the Reformed Dutch to believe that, as in heaven they would be at one with all, so even in their Reformed Zion they were increasingly less "apart" than they had historically seen themselves.

"When we think of it, either as a state or a place, many questions spring up in our minds," one author wrote in a book excerpted in the *Intelligencer* in 1845. For instance, "How do spirits communicate their ideas to each other?— . . . [how] can those who knew each other only in the body, recognise each other when disembodied? What kind of interchange . . . takes place between human and angelic spirits in the mansions of glory?— and . . . what kind and degree of fellowship with God is permitted?"[21]

This intense interest in the afterlife formed bonds among and between evangelicals of all backgrounds as they concerned themselves with the kind of intimacy they would be allowed in heaven with their families, the relation they would have to the "original inhabitants" of the place, and the facilities that would be afforded to them for acquainting themselves with the past history of heaven. Some wondered if they would recognize one another there. Readers wrote to the *Intelligencer* to suggest answers to such conundrums. One concluded with evangelical logic and confidence that believers will recognize one another in heaven, because they will retain their memory. And this is certain, he declared, because if our memory were destroyed, this would mean that we would have minds less like God's than we had on earth, clearly an improbability. "The power of recalling past events is one in which our mind resembles God's."[22]

The Reformed minister Thomas Vermilye described the "exquisite order" of heaven. "Yonder stars roll on in their prescribed orbits with such accuracy of time," he wrote, "that for centuries their places can be calculated even to a moment; and with such harmony of motion that . . . poets speak of the music of the spheres. . . . There is no jarring note in the melody of Heaven; no discord in the music of its holy choir; no separate interests are known . . . nor private ends sought." He extolled, among heaven's "adorable perfections," its tripartite geography: the atmosphere, encompassing our globe, the visible firmament "enbosoming suns and stars and adamantine spheres," and the highest heavens, which lie off in regions beyond the rest, and far exceed them in amplitude and splendor. As John had written in Revelations, all the luster of diamonds, fire of rubies, brightness of pearls, and preciousness of gold are valueless in comparison with the splendor of heaven, this minister assured the gathered mourners at a funeral. He went on for fifteen pages to describe in detail the many mansions in heaven, designed to last when the lower heavens and the earth had passed away, and the innumerable company of angels dwelling there, and the accommodations prepared for the numbers upon numbers to be gathered there at the end, all of whom would spend eternity investigating heaven's riches.[23]

New metaphors for heaven and new insights into its mysteries were always welcome in the *Intelligencer*, which in 1870 reprinted in full the Reverend Elon Foster's article in the *New Cyclopaedia of Illustrations* detailing heaven's "ten meanings." Heaven is likened to a banquet, where our souls shall be satisfied forevermore; to a paradise—a garden of fruits and flowers, on which our spiritual natures will be regaled through one ever-verdant spring and golden summer; to an inheritance incorruptible and undefiled. Heaven is a kingdom splendid and vast; a country we shall traverse discovering fresh harvests of intelligence; and a city of golden walls whose inhabitants neither hunger nor thirst, sicken nor weep. It is a palace, where dwells the Lord; a building with immortality for its walls and eternity for its day; a sanctuary for the adoration of Immanence; and a temple bright with divine glory.[24]

Another disquisition on heaven's characteristics described it as a "scene in which the Christian finds himself at home." Home was a frequent analogy used to describe heaven. When the Reverend Samuel B. How was away from New Brunswick attending General Synod in Albany, he wrote to his wife of their "irksome separation." Yet, he added, "there is nothing My dear Wife really worth living for in this world but the cultivation of true piety. . . . If we are real Christians *Heaven is our Home*—The place of our abode for eternity—what a tremendous overwhelming calamity must it be to miss Heaven. How appalling is the thought."[25]

Heaven, like one's earthly home, was viewed as a place of peace and rest where one could retire after the rigors of life, or a hard day's work. "I'm Going Home," a poem inspired by an aged woman's cry on her deathbed, typifies a genre familiar to the age:

Earth has its cares; for threescore years and ten
My lot has been 'midst thorny paths to roam;
I would not track those desert scenes again—
'Tis past!—I'm going home![26]

Children in evangelical households were introduced to the idea of heaven at an early age—and hell as its alternative for those not saved—in terms of its domestic attributes: "This world is not your home. You are to remain here but a few years, and then go to that home of joy or wo[e], which you never, never will leave." In *Paradise*, published in 1838 by the American Sunday School Union, children were told that heaven was a place of rest, one long, everlasting holiday for all good children after their hard lessons, hard work, and hard sufferings on earth. Unlike this world, it was also a healthful home. There, "children were never heard crying for pain, nor seen pining away by disease. There is no burning fever, no wasting consumption, no racking agony. . . . [Rather] children flourish in immortal youth . . . like unto angels in undecaying vigor and unfading bliss."[27]

No chilling winds or poisonous breath
Can reach that healthful shore;
Sickness and sorrow, pain and death
Are felt and feared no more.

And how could children be sure of getting to that "happy, happy place"? *Paradise* spelled out six ways familiar to all pious households: by attending Sunday school; reading the Bible every day; praying morning and evening; not telling lies or cursing, swearing, cheating, and stealing; obeying God and their elders; and bravely enduring all one's troubles, for "this world is a desert land, a valley of tears, through which all God's pilgrims must pass on their way to Heaven."[28]

Hell had perhaps even more emotive power than heaven, and legions of clergymen took advantage of this in their descriptions of it. The Reformed minister William C. Brownlee was one of the most eloquent. Hell, he assured his readers in one of countless depictions, was an immense and barren plain containing no speck of vegetation. Scathed by fire, it was inhabited by black-clothed multitudes with horror-stricken countenances, who under their black cloaks were a mass of blazing flames from their heads to the soles of their feet. Hell was often summed up as a place of eternal woe, while heaven was one of eternal happiness.[29]

Like heaven, hell was also of acute interest to pious laymen, and clergymen labored mightily not only to describe its fearsome terrors, but to

convince their flocks that it was the one and only alternative to heaven. To
lay to rest the wishful notion held by some that other places mentioned in
the Bible—Hades, Sheol, and Gehenna—were lesser evils where the unsaved might do penance until Judgment Day offered them a second chance
at heaven, the Reformed minister John C. Cruickshank turned to philol-
ogy. Hades, in the Greek, he wrote, was the place of departed spirits; Sheol,
in Hebrew, was the place of everlasting punishment; and Gehenna meant
lake or valley of fire. If hell is a lake of fire, he reasoned, so is Hades, for
when the idea of punishment (Sheol) is connected with the idea of departure (Hades), both places have all the force of a lake of fire. There, in that
burning, smoking, charred, and hideously hot region, excluded forever from
all the hopes and enjoyments of heaven, the unrepentant sinner is "utter
prey to the anguish of eternal despair" and "must feel eternally the gnaw-
ings of the worm that never dies, and the burnings of the fire never
quenched."[30]

Evangelicals had little trouble agreeing that Purgatory and Limbo,
which are not mentioned in the Bible, were Roman Catholic inventions.
There was only one happy place after death, and it was especially important that children understood this. "[T]here is no middle state between
Heaven and Hell," the author of *Paradise* assured them. "If you are not on
the way to the one, you must be on the way to the other. My dear young
friend, where are *you* going? on which of the two roads are *you* walking?
where will *you* be forever? If you were to die this night (and who knows
but you may?) would your soul awaken in Heaven or in Hell?"[31]

"Hell," wrote a prominent Reformed minister, "is the banishment from
God, and from Life, and friends, and joy, and hope forever and ever! Hell
is the place where the acutest pains are inflicted on soul, and on body. These
pains [are] . . . shadowed forth under the similes of fire,—of fire and brimstone; of fire blown into fierceness by the breath of a just Judge; as fire
burning ever intensely . . . for ever and ever."[32]

Dr. John Scudder, the Reformed medical missionary to India, took a
special interest in acquainting children back home with the horrors of hell.
In his *Voice from the East*, he speaks of a young woman he attended as she
died. Miss Matthews did not know God, for she had put off repenting until
it was too late and thus passed away without hope of salvation. "Now very
dear children, you would not like to die as she died. . . . And if you would
die differently, you must live differently . . . you must live for Christ. . . .
And are you Christ's? or are you yet gay and thoughtless. . . . If so . . . your
season of sorrow will certainly come, and it may come when you expect it
not." As an insect dazzled by a candle's brightness feels nothing but pleasure
until it is swallowed up in the flame, so the flames of hell could swallow

up an unsuspecting child in a moment. "Oh! that the death-bed scenes of Miss Matthews might have their becoming effect upon you! . . . She calls upon you from the tomb . . . to delay your repentance no longer. Will you . . . be so mad as to turn a deaf ear . . . ? Will you ever take another sip from the cup of unhallowed pleasure? . . . Oh! you must not, you must not! It will not do for you to be lost! Who, oh! who can lie down in everlasting burnings? . . . Can you, my dear children? No, no; you can not—you can not; and yet you must . . . unless you . . . give yourselves to Christ."[33]

With such frightening rhetoric a feature of everyday life, it may be wondered why the fear of hell was not incapacitating to evangelicals. The *Intelligencer* addressed this question in 1875: to paraphrase, the believer is not afraid of hell to the point of panic, because his dread of everlasting banishment from God is too profound to throw him into a mere fright, as it does the skeptic, who on the thought of sudden death often becomes consternated that he may be immortal after all and thus in danger of eternal damnation. Rather, the Christian is calm and obeys the command to trust that Christ came to save him from hell. As a believer, he both fears hell and rejoices that he himself will not be going there.

*T*his answer is theologically correct, but personal diaries, letters, and accounts of deathbed scenes indicate that evangelicals, as they lay dying, were not always so certain that they were, indeed, heaven bound. Many on their deathbeds were tortured with doubt as to the condition of their souls. (See the Appendix for a particularly detailed but very typical deathbed scene, that of Maria Vredenburgh of Somerville, New Jersey, in 1829.)

Just as piety was demonstrated publicly in the evangelical era, so was death a public event. The long-drawn-out deathbed scene was ubiquitous, and it was a public scene, for the dying one was surrounded at every moment of his or her last ordeal by numerous members of the family and the community. Subsequently, an account of the ordeal was often published in the newspaper.

The deathbed scene was an important ritual that functioned for evangelicals in several ways. On one level, it put death in its place. Death truly did lose at least some of its sting, when the expiring figure was witnessed by family and friends to be passing before their eyes almost bodily into heaven, so stirring were his or her expressions of joy, both ineffable and verbal, at the moment of departure.

On another level, the deathbed scene reinforced and paid homage to the centrality in evangelical culture of family and community. Of his mother's death, Henry Hoagland wrote: "Her hours are numbered . . . and she must gather her feet up into the bed and yield up the ghost. . . . But suddenly [as the sun scts], a wonderful strength is given to her . . . and she takes each of her children by the hand and commends each to the care of God." The sorrow of her husband, children, and friends is mitigated by the joyful hope of resurrection: "She is not dead but sleepeth."[34]

Death was an event that afforded the dying person's loved ones an opportunity to recount their own religious experiences and beliefs to one another and to indulge in what was surely one of the sweetest pleasures of evangelical society: unfettered and unembarrassed religious conversation. Some evangelicals, those who perhaps were more comfortable with the written word than with the spoken, kept spiritual histories of their families, expressing their beliefs regarding death and eternity. When Henry Hoagland's father died, after a long and tedious illness, there was joy for his eternal life. But when Henry's oldest brother goes to his account, unconverted, the family can simply "bow in submission. God will be his judge." Among his surviving brothers, Henry records that three children of one brother and two children of another are known to be "enrolled among them that call upon the name of the Lord," as well as his wife's sister and her daughter.

Perhaps most important, the deathbed scene was an unparalleled opportunity to bring unsaved members of the household into the fold, for the vivid testimony and detailed visions of the dying one as she or he made the passage from life to death were a powerful affirmation of the Christian belief in an afterlife. Those who had not yet chosen the Lord were reminded once more that the only possible alternative was to choose the devil.

Alice Schenck White's memoir of her brother Ferdinand S. Schenck, Jr., who died in 1856 at age twenty-one, illustrates all of the ways in which dying and the deathbed functioned. Ferdinand had been a sickly child, and his health worsened in his teenage years until he eventually was unable to attend his college lectures. By Christmas Day of 1854, it was clear to his sister, the wife of a minister, that the "family constellation would soon be obscured by the loss of one of its brightest stars." Ferdinand, knowing he was to die, at first feared for his eternal safety. His brothers and sisters wrote to him, urging him "to persevere at the throne of grace." On New Year's Eve, according to Alice, his prayers were answered while in the sanctuary where he had gone to pray, in great weakness and oppressed with many anxious doubts.[35]

After this experience, when his "inward man was renewed," Ferdinand made rapid advances in spiritual things, and his conversation became now always of heaven, his sister reported. He began to fear for the spiritual condition of his family, urging two of his brothers known to have not yet accepted the Lord to refuse Christ no longer. "Brothers, oh stop and think,— . . . will you accept [God's love, mercy, and pardon]?—My heart yearns over you."

Ferdinand's dying was drawn out through the year 1855, during which his greatest anxiety was the spiritual and eternal welfare of his family. He especially hoped to "see his father come out more decidedly upon the Lord's side, and his [eldest] brother John . . . become a sincere Christian."

Ferdinand took his dying well. In fact, he tells Alice that his dying year is the happiest of his life. Death has its advantages, for "had health been spared, there is no telling how I might have wandered." In November he writes to his brother John again, urging him to remove the difficulty that stands in the way of his conversion.

Ferdinand's concerns for his family's spiritual state extended to the children of another sister. "Bring them up for Christ, teach them the Catechism," he writes to this sister. As death nears, his anxiety deepens for all of his family and friends, including his cousins and Harriet, a "faithful domestic" who feels she is a sinner. Now the bedside visitors multiply, and Alice faithfully records the tears, hymns, prayers, advice, Bible readings, farewells, kisses goodbye, and final instructions to each. Besides Alice and his parents, Ferdinand's regular visitors include two other sisters, three brothers, a cousin, two women servants, a judge, a minister, the minister's wife and daughter, a neighbor, his brother-in-law, and the men servants.

Far from being in any respect remarkable, Ferdinand's final days, as recorded by his pious sister, duplicated the typical evangelical experience of crossing the bar. Death was a public event in which the most private feelings were expressed aloud. The poignancy of the situation permitted all in attendance freely to verbalize their own religious feelings, their doubts, their convictions, their experiences in approaching the Lord—and presumably gave rise to much interesting conversation among the grievers afterward.

Death was especially poignant when it deprived young children of a parent. S.L.B. Baldwin was beside himself with despair when his wife and the mother of their five children sickened. "What dreadful days! The Lord sustain me!" he wrote on April 2, 1847, four days after she became ill. "My mind is so occupied by her illness and the prospect of her departure, that I am unfitted for everything. I feel depressed and dejected; already a sense of utter desolation has fallen upon me, and all nature has a serious aspect."[36]

Nine days later Mrs. Baldwin was dead. In the two-week period between her falling ill and her death, which Baldwin recorded daily in his diary, the congregation of the Somerville Reformed Church, and indeed the whole community, acted the role of family for the harried father and his children, four of whom also were ill with various ailments. On the first day, Mrs. John Van Doren came to assist, but her own child was restless in a strange house, and this added to the general confusion. Baldwin sent for a black servant woman and "secured one for a few days." Besides this woman, Mrs. Baldwin's sister Charlotte was in attendance, as were Mrs. Cook, Mrs. Hedges, and Polly. The doctor came in twice and bled the patient. Three women attended Mrs. Baldwin, and P. Willett held the sick baby of five months the whole night. "Our situation is pitiful," the distracted father wrote.

On March 31, in addition to Charlotte, four women friends came to help, the minister (Talbot Chambers) prayed "in his own impressive and appropriate manner," and the doctor cupped Mrs. Baldwin again, as he did on April 1 as well. This day, Mrs. Van Derveer came to help. Mrs. Williamson called. Miss Baraclow came to help in the evening and, with Aunt Charlotte, sat up all night with the patient.

On April 2, the young doctor sent for old Dr. Van Derveer, but both physicians "appeared convinced that it was a most unpromising case. They applied a new blister and left a new medicine." Miss Susan Van Derveer came to help. The Reverend Mr. Chambers came in the evening. Mrs. Cook rendered valuable assistance with the family, Mrs. Joseph Van Derveer came to spend the night, and Mrs. Kennedy came to take care of the baby. Mary Willets and Charlotte stayed up all night with Mrs. Baldwin. Both doctors called in the evening, and the young doctor came again later.

Dwight, age four, broke out in hives and nearly suffocated on April 3. Mrs. Kennedy nursed him, and she and Miss Baraclow attended on Mrs. Baldwin all day. Mary Van Derveer rendered some assistance in the afternoon. Mrs. Cook came in the evening and took Eliza, one of the five Baldwin children, home with her for the night. Three women friends spent the night. The baby came down with the mumps, and little Dwight lay in his cradle and piteously begged to be rocked.

On Sunday, April 4, Baldwin, a devout churchgoer, could not leave his wife, but via his eldest son, Bloomie, age eight, sent a request to the minister to be remembered in the prayers of the morning. Bloomie reported that the minister announced that "a member of this church whose wife, also a member, is dangerously ill, desires to be remembered in your prayers, that she may be restored to health if consistent with the Divine will, and that the family may be prepared for any event of Providence." That day, a Mrs. Gore tendered her services to the family, and several women friends called, as well as Major Talmage and Mr. Sanborn. "Mrs. Gore joined the watchers to-night; she has seen sickness and trouble and knows how to administer to the suffering." Miss Van Derveer attended to Dwight, Mrs. Gore to Mrs. Baldwin, and Charlotte to the baby. Both doctors called, and Mrs. Tunison and Mrs. Kennedy came to pass the night.

On the fifth, Mr. Baldwin's sister arrived. His wife was able to converse a little. "She says her trust is in the Lord. She appeared to be wholly resigned to the Divine will, and has an unwavering faith in the all-sufficiency of her blessed Redeemer; but still she is anxious to live for the sake of her little children. On her own account it would be much more desirable to depart and be with Christ, which is far better than to suffer the tribulations of this cheerless world," her husband wrote.

By the seventh, the doctors had given up all hope. Over the next trying last days of Mrs. Baldwin's life, she was nursed and her household was served by fifteen different women, not all of whom are listed in the church rolls, suggesting that when death came it was an occasion for the whole community to pitch in. Mr. Baldwin's brother-in-law appeared, and his brother's wife arrived from another quarter. Joseph, age two, suffered a cold, Eliza had an ear ache, and the baby and Dwight continued very ill. Doctors and various ministers came and went. "Verily, the hand of the Lord is heavy upon me," Baldwin wrote on the eleventh. "I am almost overwhelmed with my sorrows, but I trust in the grace and goodness of the Lord. My hope is in His mercy." A few hours later, the "dear companion of [his] heart was released from her cares and entered upon the joys of her Lord."

As her death had been a community event, so was her funeral, which took place the following day.

*I*n the Netherlands, the Reformed Church from its first appearance in the sixteenth century had insisted that burial be an extremely simple ceremony, devoid of pomp. A complete break was made with the old Roman Catholic and ancient Germanic burial rituals of "ringing bells, raising crosses, lighting candles, laying crosses of straw on the doorsteps of the deceased, [and] braiding floral wreaths." These were now deemed superstitious, Papist, heathenish, and idolatrous. "Even funeral orations were maintained only under pressure."[37]

Some of these older practices gradually crept back into Dutch funerary customs, in the Netherlands as in America. The Synod of Dort had ordained in 1619 that where funeral discourses, for instance, were not in use, they must not be introduced, and where they were in use, efforts should be made to abolish them. But in 1793, recognizing that "it is often found to answer a good purpose to speak a word of exhortation at the time of funerals," the American Reformed Dutch Church in its first Constitution left the matter of the funeral discourse to the discretion of the individual minister. It was hardly lost on practical church leaders at the dawn of the Second Great Awakening that the funeral offered a golden opportunity for the minister to extol the virtues of a pious life and to preach the Christian message of repentance and resurrection on an occasion when it would be likely to have the greatest effect.

By the nineteenth century, funerals of evangelicals had become community events of major importance at which the living congregated, sometimes by the thousands and always in an ecumenical spirit, to hear the deceased eulogized, to accompany the body to its final resting place, and to console and comfort the survivors. As the Reverend William B. Sprague, a Presbyterian, put it, "if there is any occasion on which we must feel that we are all one in Christ, it is when we have in the midst of us the remains of a beloved disciple, who has just gone up to join the community of the ransomed, and to mingle in their harmonious and ecstatic songs."[38]

The death of a young person enhanced the poignancy of the occasion and the urgency of the message of redemption and resurrection. In June 1831, a thousand mourners attended a memorial service for three students of the New Brunswick Theological Seminary who had died within three weeks of each other, all of consumption, all at age twenty-three. In 1850, when Mr. A. T. Story, twenty-seven, of Catskill, New York, died, the "demise of this excellent and much respected young man was *suitably improved* for the benefit of survivors" in a funeral discourse at the Reformed Dutch Church in his community. This discourse was considered so important, and so capable of "improving" those who needed improvement, that it was published on the front page of the *Christian Intelligencer*. Intended as a warning and a caution to all youth to attend to the spiritual before the material, it related how Mr. Story had gone to California to find gold and died instead. Based on Lamentations 4:1, "How the gold has grown dim, how the pure gold is changed!," the sermon made the point clear that "We now behold [gold] in the gloom of sickness, exile, and death."[39]

The largest funeral ever seen in Paterson, New Jersey, was that in 1855 of James J. Wiggins, the only child of the Reverend Ebenezer Wiggins of the Totowa First Reformed Dutch Church. James, a graduate of Rutgers, was planning to enter medical school and also entertained serious thoughts of the ministry. A pious young man of twenty, he died suddenly of a "ruptured blood vessel in his head." Perhaps because his father was a clergyman, perhaps because he was an only child, perhaps because a promising young life had been snatched so suddenly away, six thousand people were moved to attend the funeral, among whom were forty physicians as well as all the local clergy. The Methodist minister offered prayer at the Wigginses' house, the Baptist minister at the church. The minister of the Second Reformed Church of Totowa preached the sermon ("Are not the days of my life few?" from Job 10:20). A Presbyterian minister made a special appeal "to the youth, to the unprepared, to the aspirant after professional

and literary distinction, and to parents," and another Presbyterian clergymen ended with "one of the most deeply touching and appropriate prayers
we ever heard," according to the *Intelligencer*. Most of the six thousand
proceeded to the cemetery, where an Episcopalian minister officiated.[40]

In 1861 Clarence D. McKenzie, a little drummer boy from New York,
was accidentally shot and killed on board a troop ship bound for the southern battlefields. The death of saintly little Clarence—a model Christian child
who loved to pray and read his Bible, who was always obedient and kind
and respectful, especially to his superiors, and who had found in Christ a
precious Savior—presented an opportunity for the Board of Publication of
the Reformed Dutch Church to publish a 144-page description of his death
and funeral, and his character and spiritual life, even though the child was
neither of Reformed nor of Dutch background. The Board had one purpose: to persuade readers that "no little child need read long in the Scriptures without finding Christ. . . . If you feel that you are poor, lost, undone,
miserable, perishing sinners, as you really are, it is not hard for you to find
salvation in Christ. Believe on him, as a Saviour, with all your heart, and
you are saved."[41] Clearly the evangelical agenda was more urgent than the
ethnic one, and the theology had become Arminian.

Clarence's funeral was so thronged that thousands could not gain admittance. The streets about the church were packed with spectators. What
brought out this teeming mass? "It was more than the mere fact that he
was a child of a regiment, and had met his death by such a mysterious
providence. . . . It was that mystical bond which binds the hearts of all God's
children in one great brotherhood." Clarence's funeral reminded Reformed
witnesses to it that a narrow parochialism was neither pleasing to God nor
edifying to man. They were to be Christians first, Dutch second.

Funerals in the evangelical age were public rituals that served to console, edify, and improve. Pious folk loved to gather together where they
could hear religious ideas, renew their own religious convictions, and indulge their thirst for religious conversation—and what better place for this
than a funeral? But they were also a form of recreation or entertainment.
In rural communities in the Dutch culture areas, it was traditional for rum,
brandy, gin, pipes, and tobacco to be handed around before the funeral
began, and "it was not an unusual thing to see the farmers congregate in
warm weather under the shade of trees . . . smoking their long pipes and
drinking . . . and laughing and talking for two or three hours before the funeral" got under way. In Zion on the Hudson, a typical Dutch funeral could
be a major expense. In the eighteenth century, the Dutch were said to spend
a small fortune on a funeral. The tradition continued into the nineteenth
century. Gifts of linen or silk scarves and gloves were presented to clergy-

men and prominent mourners, and after the funeral a large meal, a buffet of turkeys, hams, roast beef, and all the accompaniments and side dishes and desserts, and most prominently, alcohol, was usually served at the house of the deceased.[42]

Funerals of clergymen, especially prominent ones such as the Reverend Dr. Jacob Brodhead in 1855, were elaborately staged ceremonies, lengthy, solemn, and imposing. It was considered symbolically significant that the illustrious Dr. Brodhead, age seventy-three, had died at the very moment when the General Synod was convening in New Brunswick, and to his funeral in New York came a deputation of twelve clergy and elders directly from the synod meeting.

The funeral, which lasted for two and a half hours, was held in the Collegiate Reformed Dutch Church at Fulton and William streets—the venerable North Church. The large congregation included clergy of all denominations. The coffin, according to the report in the *Intelligencer*, was carried from the vestry room by six pallbearers and placed in front of the pulpit. The pulpit and altar piece were hung with "massive black silk drapery," enhancing the solemnity of the occasion and reminding all of a tradition going back in time to the Netherlands. In the pulpit were the famous Reformed ministers De Witt, Vermilye, Bethune, and Knox, and the Methodist Reverend Dr. Bangs. The service consisted of a requiem by the choir, Bible readings, impressive prayers, a resolution of respect from the General Synod, and an "extended and solemn exordium" delivered by Dr. De Witt, after which the body of the deceased was conveyed to a vault under the pulpit, again an ancient Dutch custom.[43]

Prominent laymen received funerals as ornate and solemn as the most distinguished of clergymen. When General Solomon Van Rensselaer of Albany died in 1852, the "obsequies paid to the remains of this distinguished soldier . . . were of an impressive and fitting character." The funeral took place at his residence, Cherry Hill, and was attended by a multitude of family, friends, neighbors, and official mourners. Three eminent Reformed clergymen conducted the services, after which the hearse and cortege moved in procession to the solemn strains of funeral music to the cemetery. The procession was led by the colonel and staff of the 25th Regiment, followed by the Albany Emmett Guards, the Albany Burgesses Corps, the Washington Rifle Corps, the Albany Republican Artillery, the Albany City Cavalry, two brass bands, and the hearse. The general's horse, caparisoned and led by two grooms, followed the hearse. The mourners and clergy, the governor, the members of the state and city governments, and citizens in carriages followed. Military honors accompanied the depositing of the remains in the family vault in the North Dutch Church cemetery. The similarities between this funeral and noble funerals in seventeenth-century Holland are striking and a testament to the survival of Dutch customs in America for hundreds of years after the original settlers brought them to the New World.[44]

One did not have to be a famous clergyman or a rich and celebrated hero like General Van Rensselaer to receive an impressive funeral. At the service for the humble but pious milliner Miss Harriet Toms of Somerville, New Jersey, the Reverend Mr. Whitehead of the First Reformed Church gave a solemn and deeply interesting discourse, and the Reverend Mr. Abraham Messler made the concluding prayer. Both ministers and the physician headed the procession "with scarfs," and a large and attentive congregation appeared to be affected by the solemn scene. Another "mother in Israel," Mrs. Ann Demarest of Newburgh, was, at her own request, "attended to that narrow house appointed for all the living, by her Consistory." These men, again arrayed in "scarfs," and bearing her pall, were followed to the graveside by her immediate relations and a numerous train of respectable citizens.[45] When Mrs. J. Howard Suydam, wife of the minister of the Park Reformed Church in Jersey City, died in 1876, "long before the hour" of her funeral a vast audience filled every inch of the large sanctuary. Some forty clergymen were present, representing every denomination in the city several times over, and floral decorations were profuse. From the consistory came a large medallion of exquisite white flowers in which were wrought with purple blossoms the words "Asleep in Jesus"; from the Sunday school came a floral harp; friends vied to give the choicest flowers; and family members sent elaborate arrangements with "Auntie," "Sister," and so on spelled out in blossoms.[46] In 1876, no one any longer remembered the association of floral decorations, or cared about it, with Roman Catholic or pagan traditions. It was the new American traditions that mattered.

The casket was carried from the house to the church by eight clergymen acting as pallbearers. The choir sang "Lord, Let Me Know My End." In the chancel were nine ministers. The Reverend Dr. Romeyn of the Bergen Neck Reformed Church read the burial service. The choir sang "Beyond the Smiling and the Weeping." The Reverend Dr. Van Cleef of the Second Reformed Church of Jersey City prayed. The choir sang "Safe in the Arms of Jesus," the last hymn Mrs. Suydam herself had sung in life, it was noted. Another minister gave the sermon, words of hope and consolation, and the congregation sang "I Know That My Redeemer Liveth." One minister reminisced about the deceased, the choir sang "Asleep in Jesus," and yet another minister gave the benediction. The remains were accompanied by a large delegation from the church and by many friends to the First Reformed Church cemetery in New Brunswick.

The distribution of scarves and gloves is frequently mentioned in descriptions of nineteenth-century funerals. The scarves tradition had origins in the Middle Ages in the medieval mourning hood, worn "slung over the left shoulder and wound around the neck by long narrow tippets, with the point of the tippet falling down the left front of the gown." In her will, dated March 3, 1788, Maria Farmer of New York specified that her funeral be conducted "according to the ancient Dutch Custom and mode" and that those officiating and attending should be given "Scarfs and Gloves . . . exactly conformable to the old Dutch Custom."[47]

Scarves were given to the chief mourners, the pallbearers, the clergymen, and the physicians, as were gloves of either black silk or black kid. According to one report, the scarves distributed at a funeral were of white linen sufficient in quantity to make a shirt and were worn across the shoulder. If the deceased was old, or married, the scarf was tied with a black ribbon, and the gloves were white. Another account describes the ministers and pallbearers as clad in "long pleated scarfs of white linen, fastened with black rosettes." They wore black gloves.[48]

The custom of distributing funeral scarves was not confined in Europe to the Dutch, nor was it confined in America to the Dutch. In western New Jersey, in a Presbyterian community, the "custom was to prepare scarfs and present them to the minister, and sometimes to the physician also. . . . The scarfs were made of cambric muslin looped in the middle with a bow of black ribbon that was placed on the right shoulder, then it crossed under the left arm where it was tied with a black ribbon."[49]

The custom of funeral scarves is thought to have started in 1270–71 when Philippe III conveyed his father's body back to France from the Crusades. Royal burials in France gradually developed into the "highly elaborate and lavish rituals which laid the foundations of mourning etiquette" throughout Europe. The riderless horse, the funeral cortege with its strict order, the expensive mourning dress, cloaks, palls, and draperies supplied to the mourners by the bereaved, and the elaborate funeral feast in every country where they are found thus have a common source. For centuries, strict supervision of funeral rites by courts of heralds kept the lower ranks in society from adopting them, but over time the customs inevitably filtered down from royalty to the nobility, aristocracy, and at last to the merchant, middling, and lower classes.[50]

When the European middle classes were finally allowed their versions of the grand royal funeral, gifts such as scarves of rich material for the minister, kid gloves and silk hatbands for the chief mourners, and rented cloaks and hoods and scarves for the other mourners, porters, and coachmen became standard, with the royal and richer regalia and paraphernalia (such as the pall of cloth of gold) gradually disappearing.

Traced to its roots, the custom of funeral gifts illuminates the way in which folk practices filtered across Europe, down from the upper classes to the lower, and finally made their way over the Atlantic, where they took root, hybridized, and thrived, revealing themselves centuries later in survivals of almost impenetrable genesis. The survival of the funeral scarf is an example of the cultural cross-fertilization and social change by which Netherlandish religious, social, and folk customs of all sorts passed to America. As they underwent alteration here under the influence of nineteenth-century evangelical culture, Dutch Americans adopted the evolving customs—in the process becoming less and less aware of their (and their own) foreign connections.

*P*erhaps no other single example of the way in which the Reformed Dutch gave up their traditional customs for American ways exists than in their embrace of the nineteenth-century rural cemetery movement. In the Netherlands, both pre- and post-Reformation, the church (or churchyard, more specifically), was the general burial place for all in the community, regardless of religious affiliation or lack thereof. And this was so in seventeenth- and eighteenth-century America as well. The remains of ministers and the most prominent elders and deacons were buried in vaults or laid in coffins on shelves beneath the floor of the church; the rest of the congregation and even those not members of it were buried in and near the shadows of its walls. Some chose to be buried in small family cemeteries in a corner of the farm, but for the most part the last resting place of Reformed churchgoers in New York and New Jersey was a grave in a churchyard.

This practice became less feasible as the population grew and congregations expanded. Especially in cities, by the postrevolutionary period overfull churchyards had become noxious sources of disease, menaces to public health. In addition, the inexorable expansion of urban neighborhoods played havoc with burial grounds, with the dead often unceremoniously ejected from their resting places to make room for municipal extension and improvement. Changes were sudden and sometimes ruthless, and no one could be sure how long one's loved ones might be allowed to occupy their graves, or how soon required to give them up to progress. As the residents of Albany, New York, pointed out in the 1840s, when they decided to acquire land for a cemetery outside the city limits, "in modern times, especially in large cities and towns, insufficient and slovenly provision has been made for interments—often leading to unfeeling and unseemly practices."[51] In New York City, the yellow fever epidemic in 1822, which resulted in 1,600 corpses that had to be dealt with, gave the coup de grace to church-yard burial within the city limits.

The rural cemetery movement in the Northeast began to gather steam after the success of the New Burial Ground in New Haven (1796), which served as inspiration for Mount Auburn Cemetery near Boston (1831). These garden cemeteries popularized the establishment of spacious and beautifully landscaped burial areas on the outskirts of cities, where families could permanently own their plots, where gravestones and monuments "invited contemplation and education with their display of architecture and sculpture," and where Nature could serve as moral teacher. Among the first rural cemeteries in New York were Greenwood in Brooklyn (1838), followed a decade later by Calvary and Oakwood in Brooklyn (both 1848), and the Rural Albany Cemetery (1841). Trinity Church's rural cemetery in upper Manhattan and rural, or in some cases expanded churchyard cemeteries in Sparkill, Tappan, Poughkeepsie, Kingston, Amsterdam, Schenectady, the Bronx, Yonkers, and Staten Island soon followed.[52]

Just as death was conceptualized as the Great Leveler, the place of burial in the evangelical era came to be thought of as a place of ecumenicity, where "all shall meet on terms of common fellowship and brotherhood." There were to be no distinctions based on religion or national origin. The new Albany cemetery was to be public and open to all, a democratic place with room for those of every class and every faith. There was to be plenty of space, and no crowding of grave upon grave, or heaping of bodies one upon another. "Here all will take their places in amiable proximity, peaceful harmonies, undisturbed and undisturbing, the same shadows deepening on them, the same sunlight over them . . . waiting for the same resurrection."[53] And in the spirit of Christian brotherhood, there were to be no petty feuds, no disturbing jealousies, party animosities, or sectarian dissensions in the institution's administration.

To prepare "pleasant habitations for the dead, apart from the bustle and throng . . . in grounds selected for the beauty of their position and outline, and susceptible of every kind of sylvan embellishment," the subscribers to the Albany Rural Cemetery—among whom were many of the surnames of old New Netherland—procured 120 acres on the road to Troy.[54]

Evangelical idealism and optimism imbued these new-style cemeteries with the power to accomplish "high moral purposes beneficial to the living" by their location on grounds where "nature will put on all her loveliness to tempt the mourner forth to frequent communion with her, with the spirits of the departed, and with God, Author of all." In such a setting, it was hoped, visitors will find a "great moral Teacher; and many valuable lessons . . . of humility, moderation, charity, contentment, mercy, and peace. . . . We think there is wisdom in it above the wisdom of men and . . . unspeakable profit, both for the life that now is, and for that which is to come."[55]

At the opening ceremonies of the Albany Rural Cemetery on October 7, 1844, a choir of several hundred sang specially written hymns, bands played "solemn funereal strains," ministers prayed impressive prayers and delivered stirring addresses, original poems were recited, and crowds of "citizens and ladies," military companies, firemen, and civic associations heeded the ceremonies with reverent and profound attention. It was a magnificent and exciting occasion, a public occasion blending the sacred, the civic, and the bucolic. "What pleasant hills and knolls—what gentle slopes—what abrupt declivities—what bushy dells," the Honorable D. D. Barnard effused. And "what expressive silence, religious repose! Think of all this natural beauty at once fully brought out and softened by the hand of art—at once heightened, yet subdued by the civilizing and humanizing processes to which it may be subjected—and then think of it inhabited only by the dead. . . . What scene in nature could be more beautiful, more attractive, more impressive, more improving!"[56]

The rules and regulations of the Albany cemetery were strict. Tickets of admission were necessary, and no carriages or other conveyances were allowed on Sundays or holidays. Proprietors on foot could be admitted on the Sabbath by applying to the lodge keeper. No vehicle was to exceed the speed of three miles per hour, there was to be no picnicking, no smoking, no picking of flowers, no unfastened horses wandering about, and no defacing of any monument, fence, or structure, on pain of a fine of one thousand dollars. To the rules was appended a list of shade-loving trees, shrubs, vines, and creepers, as well as detailed remarks on the best rose bushes and herbaceous plants for sunny areas.[57]

Not every Reformed Dutch community was prepared to abandon the ancient tradition of churchyard burial, nor did every one need to. In some cases, land for expansion of the burial yard was available in the immediate vicinity of the church, as was the case, for example, in Tappan, New York, and in English Neighborhood (Englewood), New Jersey. A notice in the *Intelligencer* in 1854 advised that the Reformed Dutch Church in the latter community had purchased an elegant piece of land "immediately adjoining the church and old burying ground" and laid it out in lots. "It may not be improper to inform those who do not know the locality," the notice read, "that it cannot be surpassed for beauty, retirement, and security, and that [it is] only 7 miles from Hoboken by a new plank road to the very gates of the cemetery . . . which will always be opened for those who desire the service of their own pastors."[58] This congregation, in the most conservative area in all of old New Netherland, Bergen County, wanted it both ways: they would keep up the old Dutch custom of burial in the sight of the church, while adopting the evangelical ethic of ecumenicity, opening their gates for all who desired to enter.

# CHAPTER 10

# "A New American Thing," 1850–1876

*They are generally considered . . . the stiffest and most immovable of all the most respectable Protestant churches in America, and would fain be regarded as the very Gibraltar of old-fashioned Protestantism, in the happy dream that the venerable Synod of Dort settled all the theological questions in 1618.*
—Philip Schaff, 1877

*I*n his memoirs, Dr. Alexander Coventry of Columbia County, New York, presented accounts of his frequent trips around New York and New Jersey in the decades after the Revolution and into the nineteenth century. A Scotsman with an eye for detail, Dr. Coventry often commented upon the customs and manners of the Dutch he encountered on his travels. In 1825, just at the time when the Reformed Dutch leadership was making up its mind to Americanize the denomination, Coventry was describing New Brunswick as having an "old appearance; Dutch like," and Staten Island as having "some ancient looking Dutch houses." Near Schenectady, in 1828, Dr. Coventry "stopt . . . at Degroat's, . . . an old Dutchman's. . . . The Dutch, I think, are more polite and more friendly than formerly," he wrote. He described Schenectady as containing "many old Dutch houses. . . . The population about 12,000, most low Dutch." In Colonie, near Albany, the houses, he noticed, were "of the old Dutch peaked [roof] style." In July 1829 Dr. Coventry visited New York City, where he called on Nicholas Stuyvesant "in a pleasant Mansion near the East River." Although Mr. Stuyvesant was not at home, Dr. Coventry was not invited in to wait for him. "What I call Dutch politeness," he grumbled.[1]

Coventry's observations are not simply isolated examples provided by an individual of peculiar sensitivity. Allusions to the survival of Dutch manners and Dutch culture throughout the nineteenth century appear in the testimonies of a large and varied group of Dutch and their observers. In 1833, Washington Irving and Martin Van Buren toured the Hudson Valley from

Albany to Jersey City. The farmers lived in what Irving described as "very neat Dutch stone houses." Their wagons were "Dutch" wagons, they spoke Dutch, and the women wore Dutch sunbonnets.[2]

S.L.B. Baldwin, the Somerset County newspaper editor, observed in 1836 that the "Methodist Church does not appear to grow here. It is difficult to turn the Dutch population from their old established ways." Two years later Baldwin noted that the "Rev. Mr. Knox preached morning and evening. He wore a gown, etc., in imitation of the Dutch Divines of Holland." And in 1842, he observed of a local cobbler, who refused to hand over a pair of resoled boots without first being paid, "He is too Dutch by half."[3]

The Rutgers College Grammar School in New Brunswick offered instruction in the Dutch language in 1845, and that same year, a letter from an Ulster County correspondent to the *Christian Intelligencer* noted that English was now used for preaching in that rural area. But opposition to the change from Dutch preaching had been strong, he added, especially among the old people, "who regarded it almost a profanation to worship God in any other language than the good old Duch [*sic*] of their Fatherland."[4]

New Year's Day, with its custom of visiting, was cherished for the opportunities it offered for "keeping alive and fostering those genial sentiments which endear to each other the members of a given community." This was a shorthand way of saying that the day was well suited for reinforcing Dutch ethnic bonds, a feat accomplished among the nineteenth-century Dutch through visiting on a scale unimaginable today. Men made calls. Women stayed at home to receive them. In 1866 Catherine Gansevoort of Albany recorded receiving 140 calls, a typical number.[5]

In Albany, even in the late 1860s, Dutch traditions were recollected yearningly when New Year's Day rolled around, especially if they were commemorated with bygone foodways, St. Nicholas cookies perhaps, or oelykoeks (spelled many ways). "Many thanks my dear Mrs. Gansevoort for the delicious olekoks," wrote one friend of her gift of the forerunner of the modern doughnut, which Susan Lansing Gansevoort distributed annually on New Year's to her friends and relations. "Accept our united thanks for this annual remembrance of former times," Maria Melville wrote to Catherine Gansevoort Lansing. "A world of reminiscences rush to my mind when I behold those cakes."[6]

The torrent of such references suggests that observers saw the descendants of the ancient Dutch settlers as set apart by their manner, their manners, their customs, their dress, their language, their religion, their architecture, their food, and even by other people's childhood memories of them. An American visitor to Amsterdam in 1855 was reminded of Albany, where he had lived as a child, and of the "old Dutch ladies, in high caps, who [had told him] that Amsterdam was the terrestrial paradise." Amsterdam reminded him, too, of the step-gabled Dutch houses in Albany and of the baker there who used to sell him "oely-coeks." "I went to school in one of those Dutch houses," he remembered, "and a Dutch dame . . . taught me to read."[7]

Observations of persistent Dutchness continue nearly unabated into the third and fourth quarters of the nineteenth century. In 1873 two young men, touring northern New Jersey, arrived at the village of Ponds and noted the Reformed Dutch Church, which they described as a "quaint old stone edifice in a mouldy graveyard, the outpost of the Dutch country." They then began to keep a lookout "for the first old Dutch farmhouse" and noted that "some of the descendants of the early settlers in the neighborhood speak a hideous jargon called Jersey Dutch."[8] And a local historian has written that, in Dutch-settled areas of New Jersey, Dutch seems to have been used in the Sunday afternoon church services well down into the 1860s and 1870s, a comment corroborated by another observer, who reported in 1878 that the Dutch language was still heard in the "decayed village of Tappan . . . and probably more there than anywhere else in the country." Leiby quotes a visitor to the area who wrote in 1899 that "hundreds who speak the tongue still live within a five-mile radius" of the Schraalenburgh Reformed Church (Dumont today).[9]

*T*his work has suggested that the persistence of Dutchness in New York and New Jersey throughout the nineteenth century was intimately related to the ethnicizing influence of the Reformed Dutch Church. But it has also suggested that powerful de-ethnicizing, modernizing forces that conveyed the Dutch and their church into the mainstream of American life ultimately prevailed.

Striking evidence of this occurred in 1846. When a group of strict Dutch Calvinists who had seceded from the national Reformed Church in the Netherlands over theological differences arrived in New York that year, they were shocked to find their American brethren "*heel anders*": entirely different from themselves.[10] Although they were met at the dock by American Reformed Dutch clergymen who spoke Dutch as if it were their native language, the newcomers soon noticed that these ministers and their flocks conversed, and worshiped, in English. More unsettling, the newcomers observed, the Americans no longer read the "*oude schrijvers*" (the ancient writers in the Dutch Pietist tradition) as their forefathers had in the Reformation and throughout the eighteenth century in America, and as they themselves still did.[11]

Although in 1846 the American Reformed people believed themselves to be entirely devoted to their Dutch ecclesiastical traditions, they had, it appeared to the new Dutch emigrants, lost much of their "Reformedness," and the emigrants were right.[12] The American Reformed now sang hymns (man-made) rather than solely Psalms (God-given) and, worse, the hymns had in most cases been composed by non-Reformed persons and were found in the hymnals of all evangelical denominations. Further, the American Reformed neglected the Heidelberg Catechism not only in the preaching cycle but in the training of their young. Elders did not visit every family in their districts as diligently as they should to instruct, comfort, and exhort (and to report their needs, progress, and shortcomings to the consistory). Rather, elders in America seemed to maintain a low profile, suggesting standards that deviated from Dort by deemphasizing strict church discipline. In the sanctuary, elders and deacons sat with their families, no longer in official pews at the front of the congregation.

Standards of personal worthiness to receive communion may not officially have been relaxed, but American Reformed Church members appeared to feel freer to approach the table than did their newly arrived counterparts from the Old World—and they permitted persons of all Protestant denominations to join them. Worst of all, in the view of the Dutch Calvinists, the American churches recognized other Protestant churches as equals, whereas they themselves regarded Christ's pure bride, the Reformed Church, "as a barred garden, a spring shut up, and a fountain sealed."[13] In the area of social religion, funerals and weddings in Reformed circles in New York and New Jersey were strangely elaborate and expensive; Christmas was celebrated amid blasts of consumerism that seemed utterly foreign to the bewildered emigrants; and the Sunday school picnic and the Fourth of July recalled a Dutch peasant *kermiss* or raucous harvest festival more than a sober quarter of the Lord's vineyard.

Even Jesus had changed. The Redeemer worshiped by Reformed people in America was now a new and modern "feeling" savior. What touches us touches him, "Old Dominie Scattergood" assured his listeners. What annoys us annoys him. "He is the great nerve-centre to which thrill all sensations which touch us who are his members." His temperament is "finely strung," like ours, and he is as sympathetic with our rheumatism, neuralgia, dyspepsia, inflamed muscles, and pangs of indigestion as a dearest friend. He never laughs at our whims and notions. Because "by his own hand he fashioned our every bone, strung every nerve, grew every eyelash, set every tooth in its sockets," he responds to our every physical disorder with sympathy. He is nothing but touched by the imperfections of our prayers and kindly overlooks our lack of concentration while praying, yet "he will pick out the one earnest petition from the rubbish and answer it." Yes, he understands our imperfections of temper, too, and overlooks our "explosive temperament" and all our bunglings, as long as our intentions are good.[14]

The "good old way," it was clear, was increasingly being replaced by a new way and new customs: the fashions of the religious culture of evangelical America. In embracing revivals, Sunday schools, fund-raising ladies' fairs, choirs and professional singers, the flamboyant Anniversaries, the ecumenical benevolent associations, the custom of closing the church in the summer, to name a few, Reformed churchgoers, interacting with and relating to the world around them, had seamlessly merged into the mainstream of American Protestantism and become almost unrecognizable as fellow Reformed to the strict and stern Seceders from the Netherlands. The ethnicizing forces of Dort and doctrine, national history and national pride, seminary and college, and daily face-to-face socializing had proved to be less potent in the long run than the de-ethnicizing, modernizing forces of the larger culture.[15]

The Reformed Church's adjustment to revivalism illustrates the evolution. In the 1820s, as chapter 2 made clear, the Reformed Church considered "man-made" revivals and New Measures to be heretical. But just a generation later, in 1857—the year the Dutch emigrants separated from the Reformed Church in America to form their own austere denomination, the Christian Reformed Church—the Fulton Street Noon Day Prayer Meeting in the North Dutch Church in Manhattan was sparking a religious revival that spread not only around the city, but across the nation and around the world.[16]

The Reformed Church never officially embraced New Measures. It left their use to the discretion of individual ministers and congregations, most of whom found a middle way to be comfortable, even in the conservative "Collegiate" Reformed Protestant Dutch churches in Manhattan of which the North Dutch Church was one.[17] But even in this bastion of conservatism, so many had come to believe in the efficacy of human ability in saving souls that, on the third anniversary of the meeting, in September 1860, the Reverend Dr. Thomas Vermilye, one of the foremost ministers in the Collegiate churches, spoke before a dense crowd of men and women, including ministers of all the evangelical denominations, and confessed himself to be "almost unmanned to think that in the . . . bustling city of New-York, at mid-day of a week-day, such a congregation as this . . . have assembled here . . . for the purpose of commemorating a prayer-meeting."[18]

Six other ministers as well as several laymen also addressed the crowd that day, according to the *Intelligencer*, which devoted five and a half columns to its coverage of the event, and the Fulton Street Noon Day Prayer Meeting was pronounced then and there to be the Lord's work. "It is not of man; it is God's work; it is the Spirit Almighty that has . . . been to thousands as a . . . guide toward heaven." It was felt that God was about to revive his work afresh in the hearts of the people on a very large scale, and was "using the meeting to bring greater blessing to the city, country, and world, than it has hitherto [enjoyed]."[19]

The Fulton Street Noon Day Prayer Meeting grew out of changing circumstances in the city. As Talbot W. Chambers, a Collegiate minister, wrote, the old "staid and settled families of fixed principles and ordinary habits" who had once filled the churches in lower Manhattan to capacity had moved uptown. The area was being taken over by business enterprises, and the streets were filled with a "mixed multitude" of unchurched immigrants from every part of Europe and "heathens" from remote parts of Asia. The immigrant people were clearly in need of religious instruction, in the view of the consistory, which met in a building adjacent to the church at the corner of William and Fulton streets and which that year hired a lay missionary, one Jeremiah C. Lanphier, to visit the immigrant families, invite them to worship, and induce them to enroll their children in the North Dutch Church's Sabbath school.[20] (See figure 19.)

Before long, Lanphier had the idea of holding a prayer meeting for the businessmen in the neighborhood, each day at noon, also in the consistory building. "Businessmen" was in fact a misnomer. The meeting was open to people of all classes, clerks, apprentices, porters, day-laborers, young, old, male, and, before long, female. Not only democratic, it was also determinedly nondenominational. It vowed to start promptly at noon, and to end in one hour, so that workers could get back to their jobs, and it was an immediate hit. The noon meeting went on for decades and was extensively covered by the *Christian Intelligencer*, which considered it so important that for years it placed its report every week, almost without fail, on page one of the paper.

By 1860, the meeting was so popular that it was "crowded every day, rain or shine, to the greatest excess," the *Intelligencer* reported. "All wonder that it is confined in such narrow quarters. All inquire, Why are not these meetings held where seven or eight hundred can be accommodated, instead of a little meeting of not more than two hundred, and many of these most uncomfortably seated on camp-stools, choking up all the passages?" Scheduled for the same time, same place, every weekday year in and year out, with rules and regulations that were strictly followed, the meeting was nevertheless considered to be a revival produced not by any "human

FIGURE 19. The Fulton Street Noon Day Prayer Meeting in the North Dutch Reformed Church was a prominent feature of religious life in New York City for years. *Picture Collection, The Branch Libraries, The New York Public Library.*

contrivances or instrumentalities." This was truly a "genuine" revival, "because, and simply because, the Holy Spirit takes care of it and guides and directs its movements, and inspires it."[21]

People walked in off the street and prayed for a "great variety of objects—scattered . . . from Maine to California, and from Canada to the Gulf of Mexico." Parents came to pray for wayward children, children came to pray for unsaved parents, the sick and despairing prayed for themselves. "The anxiety of the awakened to be made the subjects of prayer, and the rejoicing spirit of the hopefully converted" were manifested every day. Salvation was a constant subject. "Scarcely a day passes in which there is not some one . . . who arise[s] in the meeting . . . and request[s] that prayer be offered in his behalf." The young man was typical who rose to say that he was anxious to become a Christian, but did not know what steps to take, that he knew he was a sinner, but did not know how and could not comprehend how to exercise faith in Christ.[22]

It was a people's meeting. Ministers attended, but stayed in the background, letting the people express what was in their hearts. Each day a different person, sometimes a clergyman, but more often a layman, acted as leader, and each day it was customary for the leader to record his comments in a daily journal. The daily journals are in the archives of the Collegiate Reformed Protestant Dutch Church in Manhattan. A random selection of the comments reveals that what was prized about the prayer meeting was that the "spirit of our God was pre-eminently present." "It was indeed a season of refreshing." "The Lord continued to meet his people here." "The meeting was full and spirited." "Here heart meets heart." "A deep religious feeling prevails." "The divine Spirit was present." "A very precious meeting—no wasted moments." "Jesus was here."

Not everyone was of this mind. Conservatives looked upon the Fulton Street Noon Day Prayer Meeting "with distrust and disfavor and think it of doubtful utility," the *Intelligencer* reported. And others were bitterly hostile to it and regarded it as the "result of clap-trap and human device." Some Reformed ministers among the Ultras still regretted that revivals in general had come to be so large a part of church life. In his sermon at the 1870 meeting of the General Synod, the Reverend C. H. Stitt of the Second Reformed Church in Kingston, New York, described nineteenth-century church life as "unstable as water." Now, he said, the church "merges into the world, almost ignores the gospel, and loses herself in secular civilization, and then, to regain her lost ground, she organizes and prays herself into a revival, and when . . . she has begun to fulfil her destiny, she again relaxes her hold and sinks away into another spasm of spiritual paralysis, and thus her life, instead of an even-toned, healthful progress, is a fever or a sleep."[23]

This was the voice of the Ultras, those who still yearned for the good old way and rejected any innovations that might weaken the significance of Dort. But twenty years after its inception, the Reverend Dr. Talmage hinted that perhaps the Noon Day Prayer Meeting had done just that: "One of the grandest results," he wrote, is that the meeting had revolutionized devotional services throughout the country. Although it had its down side (it had spawned a tradition of "religious bores" and "ecclesiastical vagabonds," who wandered around pestering the churches, trying to speak, and spoiling the devotional tone of the meetings), its attention to the clock had led to shorter prayers and exhortations in general, and it had led to the growth of weeknight prayer meetings throughout the country that allowed "church membership utterance." By attending these meetings, a clergyman could discover how his congregation wanted him to preach, and discover the religious state of the people ("feel the pulse before giving the medicine").[24]

The success of the Fulton Street Noon Day Prayer Meeting was an important factor in demonstrating to all but the most conservative of its clergy and laity that the Reformed Church must learn to accommodate the people's desire for periodic spiritual refreshment—even though arranged and "managed" by mere men—and their wish to believe in a loving and merciful God, not a vengeful, capricious one. By 1875, when the evangelical preacher Dwight L. Moody and the gospel hymn writer Ira D. Sankey came to town, the progressives had won the day.

The 1875 Moody revival began on October 24 of that year in a skating rink on Claremont Avenue, converted to seat six thousand, and went on for almost six months. By 8:00 A.M. on opening day, the Brooklyn Rink was filled to capacity for the morning service. At the 3:00 P.M. service, up to twenty-five thousand waited in line to get in. The women's meeting was considered "remarkable." The rink was filled two hours prior to the start of the meeting, sixty-five hundred were present, and three hundred stood desiring to be prayed for and afterward went to an inquiry meeting with Mr. Moody "characterized by great tenderness and devotion." Many climbed up into the windows, which fit three persons each, in order to hear the preaching and singing, and many distinguished Reformed Dutch clergymen, including the Reverends Duryea, Talmage, Cuyler, and Inglis, shared the platform at both morning and afternoon services with Moody and Sankey. The Reverend Dr. Talmage offered prayer that day, and Moody preached on "The Need and Opportunities for Religious Revival."[25] (See figure 20.)

The meetings were "eminently decorous, with no extravagances, claptrap, or sensational methods," according to the *Intelligencer*. Week after week, the morning, afternoon, and evening services were attended by between six thousand and seven thousand persons. Two-thirds were females. Moody's preaching was "simple, tender, and profoundly earnest"; he made no attempt to excite the feelings. Yet hundreds wept at the close of the services, and hundreds were saved. Preparatory prayer meetings were held in the nearby Brooklyn Tabernacle, where the Reverend Thomas De Witt Talmage was minister, "branch" meetings were crammed with those "seriously inclined" to talk with Moody about the state of their souls after the main meetings, and religious interest extended into "distant localities." Hardly a congregation within thirty miles of New York was said to be unaffected.

In February 1876, the revival moved to the Hippodrome in Manhattan, a huge building that took up the whole block from Madison to Fourth Avenue and from 26th to 27th Street and that had once housed P. T. Barnum's menagerie and circus. In preparation for the move to Manhattan,

FIGURE 20. Sixty-five hundred jammed into the Brooklyn Rink to hear the revivalists Moody and Sankey in 1875, while twenty-five thousand clamored outside to get in. *Picture Collection, The Branch Libraries, The New York Public Library.*

a Committee on Arrangements met daily; $30,000 was budgeted to make alterations in the building and in an adjacent hall to contain the overflow, and a series of fifteen lectures was announced at the Marble Collegiate Reformed Church nearby at Fifth Avenue and 29th Street to train the large numbers of volunteers needed to assist during the services. Three classes of volunteers had to be trained: a number to give religious instruction and counsel in the inquiry rooms after the meetings; five hundred men and women to form a choir to be conducted by Sankey; and five hundred men to act as ushers. All volunteers except the ushers had to be communicants. At the same time, a preparatory daily prayer meeting was announced for the St. Nicholas Collegiate Reformed Church at Fifth Avenue and 48th Street that was attended each day by anywhere from three hundred to eight hundred persons.[26]

In Manhattan, five meetings a day were held at the Hippodrome, with twenty thousand in attendance every day, yet there was no trace of "emotional excitement." Rather, "intense earnestness and solicitude" were exhibited. As many as three thousand attended the daily noon prayer meetings, and the ladies' meetings and young men's meetings were filled to capacity. After each meeting, two hundred to three hundred remained in the inquiry rooms, people of all ages, ranks, and classes "seeking their souls' salvation, anxiously asking, 'What shall I do to be saved?'" On Sunday, February 13, twenty-seven thousand attended the meetings. The revival had such an impact on the pious that a year after Helen Verbryck Clark made the trip from Rockland County to attend a meeting, she reverently recorded the anniversary of it in her diary.[27]

Yet, as to be expected, the Ultras objected to Moody and Sankey, particularly on the grounds that neither was an ordained minister. How, then, could they have authority to preach the gospel? Their movement diminished confidence in the Christian ministry, conservatives charged, for many took their success as a sign that the regular ordained ministry had been a failure and that laymen could do the job more effectively. Even some of the ministry thought so: "they surrender the solemn work of the services" to Moody as leader and consent to serve simply as his helpers, "thus reversing the divine order" and sinking the holiest of all offices into disrepute.[28]

It is a measure of how flexible the Reformed laity, and even the editors of the *Intelligencer*, had become by 1876 that they had ready answers to such charges. "Let us be careful how we hinder their work," wrote "A Lady" from Passaic, New Jersey. "Are they not working in Christ's name?" Another correspondent signing himself "A Layman" wrote: "Whenever God's word reaches the heart with true, convincing, converting power, . . . it is indisputable proof that God has set the seal of His approval on such an agency." And in an editorial in the same edition of the paper, it was pointed out that every Christian has a right to preach the gospel. "Mr. Moody is a lay preacher. A man who says 'Come!'—an exhorter—a lay evangelist." We class him, the editors wrote, with those messengers whom God occasionally raises up to do a great work. And besides, they added, no proof exists that John Calvin himself was ever ordained. "And who licensed or ordained John Bunyan?"[29]

The age of revivals, which through its ecumenical boards and benevolent societies and cooperative missionary efforts had served to unite evangelicals of all backgrounds into a more or less generic Protestantism, eventually came to its inevitable twilight. The high evangelical ardor could not be sustained indefinitely; the rhetoric lost its power to sway; new concerns and new styles of worship evolved. The inclination of denominations to stress their particular origins had caused them to develop their own independent boards and missions, and to accent their own traditions and usages, so that denominationalism ended by succeeding beyond conservatives' dreams for it. By 1876 the older theological issues—including the principles of Christian brotherhood and the organic unity of the Church Universal dear to the ecumenically minded and once discussed so earnestly in the religious press—were hushed, according to one editor of the *Intelligencer*, "by the sweeter strains of a tolerant charity."[30]

With theological controversy seemingly passé, evangelical fervor directed itself at seemly appearances. In August 1875, more outrage was expressed over the running on the Sabbath of an excursion train from New York to Philadelphia, where the Centennial buildings were under construction, than had been expressed over slavery only a few years before. "The Christian Sabbath Threatened!" the *Intelligencer* blared, fearing the train was a "method of feeling the pulse of our people" as to the running of regular Sunday excursion trains during the actual Centennial to come.[31]

These fears were well founded; by September 1875 the excursion trains were an established fact with a large patronage, and the *Intelligencer*, in addition to printing its own pointed views, reprinted articles from seven fellow religious papers expressing deepest concern that the Centennial buildings and grounds would be open on the Sabbath in 1876. Pernicious, if so, a sin against good morals, an impious outrage, screeched the press, imagining trains rushing through the villages and towns of New Jersey every Sunday morning and evening, laden with "debauched men and women and thoughtless youths of both sexes." What right had the Pennsylvania Railroad to commit this outrage? What excuse did it have to violate the laws of God and man? The Sunday trains were an "inexcusable insult to the moral sense of the peaceful Christian community." "No more demoralizing act has been perpetrated within our memory." A "sacreligious [*sic*] invasion of the rights of the Christian public," the trains were "unnecessary and a most injurious desecration." Tirades against the "unlawful and depraving" traffic went on for a year, until in July 1876, with the Centennial well under way, the Sabbatarians finally triumphed, at which point the religious press turned its attention to revoking licenses to sell beer and wine on Centennial grounds.[32]

One senses behind these unmistakable echoes of the nineteenth-century contretemps with multiculturalism the shrill protests of an evangelical community beleaguered by social change, overwhelmed by secular trends, conscious of its dwindling authority in the face of postbellum America's new and vocal constituencies and values. Even the staid old *Intelligencer*, wondering in print whether there was "too much preaching" going on for Reformed congregants' own good, recommended replacing the Sunday evening worship service in the sanctuary with a "social meeting for prayer and praise" in the lecture room.[33] Better to join the new *Zeitgeist* on one's own terms than to be divided by it was the attitude, although many of the strictest newcomer Dutch Calvinists, now settled in the Midwest and officially separated from the main body, would never agree.

The conflict of the Reformed Dutch Church in the nineteenth century as it attempted to maintain its fabled purity in the American melting pot culminated in a decades-long discussion, conducted in pulpit and press, over dropping the word *Dutch* from the official name of the denomination.[34] It was agreed by many that the "name has had an unhappy influence," as the Reverend Isaac Ferris wrote in 1848. "It is foreign—it begets a prejudice on its mention. . . . The great majority of families . . . [come] into our body from love to our 'principles and institutions and conservative character.' These are the glory of the Church, and these therefore are to be perpetuated," not the name.[35]

This was one view, and it ultimately prevailed. But another was expressed in the heat of the battle, in January 1854, by fifty-four laymen (twenty-nine from New York and Brooklyn, fourteen from the Hudson Valley, and eleven from New Jersey) in a pamphlet addressed to the ministers, elders, deacons, and members of the Reformed Protestant Dutch Church in North America. After declaring that the proposed name change would strike at the very existence of the church as an effective body of Christians, the signatories gave their reasons for wishing to retain the traditional and legal name. Chief among them was that the reputation of the

Dutch Church in America had "been earned by two centuries of undeviating adherence to the principles of the Reformation" and to the doctrines and actions of the Synod of Dort.[36]

It is highly ironic that these fifty-four laymen, among whom were some of the most prominent old New Netherland names in New York and New Jersey, were under the impression that the Reformed Church was the same unchanged and unchanging body that had established itself in the horse-mill near the fort on the Battery in 1628. Apparently oblivious of the changes the denomination had undergone in America, they continued to believe in the happy dream, as the historian of religion Philip Schaff would call it, that the venerable Synod of Dort had settled all the theological questions forever.

Yet the Constitution of the denomination, in its Preface and in its Explanatory Articles, had already in 1793 expressly differentiated the American body from its Dutch parent, and revisions of the Constitution in 1833 and 1874 further refined the differences.[37] Even more significantly, when the Canons of Dort were published in English for the first time within the body of the 1793 Constitution, neither the Arminian arguments against them nor the salient biblical proofs cited by the Calvinists to back up their refutations of the Arminian positions (called the "Rejection of Errors") were included in the text.

It is not clear why the constitutional committee, headed by the Reverend John H. Livingston, omitted this crucial material. But it seems likely that the purpose may have been either to make the Reformed Dutch Church seem more palatable to outsiders by quietly excluding the powerful biblical case for the doctrines of total depravity, unconditional election, limited atonement, the irresistibility of grace, and the perseverance of the saints. Or their exclusion may have represented a tactful attempt to inhibit internal controversy over them. Or it may even be, though they are silent on the matter, that Livingston and his committee of clergymen may have felt that the Synod of Dort had overemphasized this material, or even misinterpreted it. What is clear is that omitting this important material effectively diminished the full original force of the doctrines of Dort.[38]

Equally ironic is the recent discovery by Daniel J. Meeter that the liturgy of the church, as first published in English in New York in 1767, and later incorporated into the Constitution of 1793, was not the liturgy decided upon at Dort in 1619. Rather, large parts of it were based on versions of the Psalms, Ten Commandments, creeds, Lord's Prayer, Heidelberg Catechism, and Confession of Faith as published in New York in 1767 that were themselves based on versions used in the provinces of Holland and Zeeland in the sixteenth century by English Puritan worshipers. Meeter's finding heightens the irony that the Reformed Church and its people, who for so long had devotedly claimed the "purity of Dort" as their unwavering standard, had been unaware how in fact they been separated from Dort in this way, as in many ways, large and small, for many generations.[39]

Seen from this perspective, to drop the word *Dutch* from the name of the denomination was hardly to offend the principles of the Reformation or the faith of the Fathers. Instead, it was to accept the fact, at long last, that the Constitution had, as early as 1793, represented even then a new stage in the history of the denomination, a new American stage. Inspired not only by sacred precedents but obviously by a secular one as well—the U.S. Constitution and its articles and amendments, just recently adopted—the Constitution's American metamorphosis is most vividly expressed in its preface, which allowed for freedom of conscience on the part of every individual, and for a church subject neither to the "emoluments" nor the "penalties" of the state—a certain echo of the First Amendment's disestablishment clause.

On its two hundredth anniversary in 1993, several Reformed scholars took another look at this compilation of doctrine, rules, and liturgical elements called the Constitution and at the Reverend John H. Livingston, who had headed the committee that translated and edited them for American consumption. The preface to the document, Reformed theologian Eugene Heideman concluded, had "placed the Reformed Church fully in the American milieu" in 1793 by acknowledging that, even then, it no longer saw itself as a Dutch national church serving the whole baptized population, as was the case in the Netherlands and in New Netherland before the English takeover. Rather, it now viewed itself as a "voluntary-membership denomination."[40]

The Constitution had made the break between state and church official in 1793, no doubt, but the American insistence on religion's voluntary nature had permeated Reformed thinking even well before then—as had the notions of freedom of conscience, the rights of man, and John Locke's views on toleration, according to historian John W. Coakley. At the height of the American Revolution and fifteen years before he headed the committee to produce the church's Constitution, John H. Livingston wrote to his cousin Robert Livingston to say that Locke's *Letter on Toleration* had "enlarged" his views on the subject of the rights of mankind and liberty of conscience. All people have a natural right, he wrote, to "believe for themselves and worship God according to the dictates of their conscience without depending upon fellow subjects, sister churches, or even the civil magistrates in religion."[41]

In other words, the denomination's own Constitution had been intended to be a force for change within the church, an intention that has not been adequately recognized until recently. In this light, the Constitution may be seen, however belatedly, as having a double, "almost contradictory" purpose: to preserve the tradition represented by the Synod of Dort, and to unfetter the church from the "shackles" imposed on it by that tradition.[42] In the service of the latter goal, the Constitution welcomed the denomination's status as the voluntary institution, not a state-linked one, that the U.S. Constitution had stipulated for all religions; and it recognized just as cheerfully the equal validity of all religions to coexist within the same body politic—a far cry from Dort, which had insisted that the Reformed Church was the official church of the Dutch nation.

Further, this unique document democratically gave more power to congregations, consistories, and classes (that is, to the laity) than they had been given by the Synod of Dort. It included a full-fledged liturgy (unique among Calvinist churches), yet it did not insist that every part of the liturgy be obligatory, as Dort had. Finally, it conceived of the Great Consistory, an innovation that strengthened the power of the laity by permitting those laymen who had ever been ordained as deacon or elder to continue beyond the terms of their office to play a role in calling ministers, forming new churches, and settling matters related to the peace and prosperity of the denomination.

*S*till, the fifty-four laymen who objected to the name change in 1854 were hardly alone in their conviction that the Reformed Church had not deviated in America from its Reformation roots. It was a common perception. A few months after the publication of their pamphlet, when the matter of the name change was scheduled to be brought to a vote at the General Synod in June, only one classis in sixteen in advance of the synod meeting voted for the change—and that classis by only a single vote. Believing the matter settled at last by this overwhelmingly conservative reaction, the synod expressed a fond hope that "any further agitation on this subject may be discontinued."[43] It was discontinued for a while, but in 1867, after decades of battle royal, a vote of the General Synod finally changed the name of the denomination to the Reformed Church in America, which it remains today.

Dutchness died hard, however—very hard. The change so long in the making was not accepted on an emotional level by many in the denomination for years to come. A decade after the change, at the celebration ceremonies of the 250th anniversary of the Reformed Church's existence in America, Reformed minister Dr. Thomas Vermilye displayed a gold-headed cane made of a piece of the wood used in the old North Church, recently demolished. Within the gold top of the cane, he told his listeners, was a "thimbleful of the soil of the Netherlands mingled with a little earth taken from the spot where the first Dutch Church on this continent was planted." It was almost as if the denomination itself had forgotten the long-fought battle to drop the word *Dutch* from its name, for its Board of Publications issued the proceedings of this celebration under the title *The Quarter-Millennial Anniversary of the Protestant Reformed Dutch Church*.[44]

For others, things Dutch were best forgotten. Henry S. Gansevoort, in an 1866 letter to his sister Kate in which he referred to the change in the name of the church, stated, "The Americanization idea . . . should govern in the Church as well as in the State." He perhaps said it best when he added, "We are an original people, no more like our Dutch progenitors than a steam-engine is like a windmill."[45] This was true in 1866, but some would not accept it for another generation or even two, so powerful and so profound was the desire to identify with a traditional past, even one with its spurious aspects.

The last word must be that, as the Reformed Dutch Church tried to maintain unity amid proliferating diversity, to keep faith with those who had gone before while making itself appealing to those who would come after, by turns it shaped itself to new circumstances, and by turns it was itself shaped by forces over which it had little control. The same can be said of the people who made up the church. The history of both is one of cultural adaptation, as together, borrowing and modifying, giving and taking, resisting and relenting, and always debating and declaiming in the pages of the *Christian Intelligencer*, pulpit and pew grappled toward their American destiny, with the theology of Dort, the history of the Dutch nation, and the Dutch language their bumpy wrestling ground. In the process, they created a culture, a "web of significance" that many interpreted as Dutch, but that was in truth a hybrid—a "new American thing," as William Carlos Williams had called the larger culture.

The quintessential American experience is said to be the process by which individuals of diverse ethnic, religious, and racial backgrounds achieve a new national identity in the melting pot of American culture. But it may also be that the obverse is just as quintessential: the process by which individuals of diverse national origins and cultural backgrounds resist the melting pot in an attempt to retain the distinctive identities of their personal pasts. If, as the historian Gordon S. Wood has conjectured, American history turns out to be "one long story" of different peoples struggling to identify themselves with their racial, ethnic, or national origins, that will be a sublime irony in the land that has long prided itself on its melting-pot model of assimilation. Irony it may be, but it is a story that well describes the Dutch experience in America.[46]

# APPENDIX: THE DEATHBED SCENE
## OF MARIA VREDENBURGH

*Mrs. Esther Finley recorded the last hours of her niece Maria Vredenburgh in Somerville, New Jersey, in the year 1829. Maria was the daughter of the Reverend John Shureman Vredenburgh, minister of the Reformed Dutch Church of Somerville. Mrs. Finley and Mrs. Vredenburgh (Sarah) were sisters. Esther's husband was the Reverend Dr. Robert Finley of Basking Ridge.*

For several months Maria had experienced a severe conflict of spirit as to the reality of her faith in Christ—& it seemed as if no ordinary attainments of grace would give her the full assurance of hope. She said to a friend early in the winter that many had thought her disease had been of a mild character, till that period it had been so. But she said, what I have been spared in bodily suffering, I have had double in mental agony, no one knows what I have endured. This darkness continued with very few glimmerings of light or joy through all the extremity of her disease, yet her patience & calm endurance was most exemplary, she even acknowledged that the ways of providence were righteous altogether & that her trials were all needfull. Two days previous to her death, her mental night began to be dispelled by some rays of the approaching morn, on Tuesday morning she repeated the hymn, There is a land of pure delight, & said it had been recurring to her all the night & all the day before, & expressed the confidence it had given her. Early in the afternoon previous to her death she took up the Dutch Hymn book that lay on her bed & opened to the 22$^d$ hymn, Amazing grace how sweet the sound, said that hymn was very precious to her & enquired of me if I did not believe it was the spirit that had applied it to her soul. I answered I believed it was (the spirit that had applied it to her soul) shortly after this she had one of her sinking times & we began to think that her last conflict was at hand, though she still conversed with her usual calmness

& fortitude with those around her. To question her often as to her hopes in her extreme weak state, I did not think judicious, but endeavoured as often as possible to lead her into a religious conversation or talk with others in her presence, which always greatly interested her & in this way she was led insensibly to express her doubts & fears & sometimes her ground of hope. She would sometimes say I cannot, I dare not say, that I have not an interest in Christ, no doubt that his faithfulness will yet be manifested to me in the hour of Death. At others she would say, Oh the awfull fear that it may be an everlasting darkness. My great anxiety to know what were her views, as she appeared to be sinking in death, made me repeat the question whether she could not now rest on her Saviour, she answered her fears were not yet gone (this was in the afternoon) I then endeavoured to cheer her mind, by observing that this might not be her death, as we had frequently seen her before as we thought dying, yet revive, & it might be so now & that when death really come I had no doubt she would have that manifestation of her Saviour's Love, that would make her rejoice. These thoughts seemed to sustain her feeble spirit. She became more composed & recovered from this extreme lowness, Mrs. Kirkpatrick called early in the evening & seeing the change that had taken place, proposed staying with her all night, which seemed to please her, we endeavoured to cheer her mind, by conversing on the animating truths of the Gospel, & the comforts derived from the word of God, in seasons of afflictions, to this she listened with much interest though not able to bear a part in the conversation, a fear was expressed that so much talking might injure her. No said she not at all I love to hear you. I had to leave the room for a while, but Mrs. Kirkpatrick continued sitting by her. After an interval of silence, she all at once exclaimed in the language of [doubting] Thomas, My Lord & My God, she paused & then said with faith may I not say it is well, the reply was it is enough you may rejoice. She had frequently alluded to the incredibility of Thomas, & said a few days before to her sister Mrs. V. P. [Margaret], I am like Thomas, cannot I beleive [*sic*] untill I have the same evidence he asked for in this conviction her use of his words, when his heart was filled with perfect faith & every doubt was banished by a full conviction of his senses, brings a forcible proof of his entire persuasion & full satisfaction with the great salvation of the Gospel. This was the first evidence she had given of an established confidence, but as it was not heard by me—nor the rest of the family we were not apprised of brightened hopes, & still felt our anxiety about the state of her mind. About 12 oclock I thought I saw a perceptible change her weakness & difficulty of breathing was so great, that we ceased all attempts to converse with her & she appeared entirely regardless of every thing around her, seeing her thus sinking in death, without giving us one kind assuring word that her fears were gone & her heaven commencing, my grief was great. It had been the frequent subject of Prayer that her great High Preist [*sic*] would pass before her & divide the river of death, that she might pass this dry shod. It was an exercise I thought of[,] faith which I had long cherished & I had used every argument to inspire her mind with the same hope, & now when the end seemed approaching & I saw no gleam to cheer the gloom [and] for a few moments, my own soul felt something like the bitterness of despair, I strove however to compose myself & with all the resolution I could commend went to her bed-side & took her hand. She discerned my agitation & said with a clearer voice than we ever expected to hear again & with a sweet smile, My Dear Aunt why are you so agitated do be composed, her manner did compose & tranquilize me, I then began to question her as to her hopes, the form of which I do not distinctly remember owing to the state of my feelings but the answers were such as to induce me to beleive [*sic*] her fears had vanished & that the everlasting arms of a compassionate Saviour was underneath her & she might now with triumph say, Death where is thy sting. Her Sister said, Maria you are almost home, Yes she answered with a sort of joyful alacrity, at Your Father's house. Yes she spoke it with an emphasis not to be described. We all listened with intense interest to catch every word. After a long pause, she said distinctly I am walking through Jordan dry shod, the waters break dried up, I am almost through, she now appeared so much exhausted that we scarcely expected to hear her accents again, when one of those sudden changes took place like the kindling up of an expiring candle & she with difficulty panting for breath at first scarcely audible to exclaim Glory, Glory, Glory, her voice becoming stronger at every repetition of the word & her countenance beaming with heavenly joy, Heaven has begun, Jesus is here, Oh sweet Jesus, free grace, Glory, Glory. It seemed as if the whole Gospel was revealed in her soul, all doubt all fear fled away. After a short interval Mrs. K asked her have you Dear Maria still any terrors of Death[?] all gone she said with a sweet voice & animated smile that might be almost triumphant, we all exclaimed with one accord, Thank God, the Lord be praised, she rejoiced Oh yes all praise him as long as you live, do praise him she repeated with an almost animating countenance, Anna [Kirkpatrick] sent a message of love thinking she was just gone, Tell her good bye I shall soon follow her, soon meet her. In reply to which she [Maria] said blessed hope & pressing the hands of Mrs. K between both of hers with great tenderness said to her I shall meet your daughters this shows how perfectly she had her recollection [that Mrs. Kirkpatrick's daughters were deceased] & how vivid were her sympathies, she sent her love to Mary K[irkpatrick] with an assurance of her affection & a half uttered prayer which she had not power to express. Between 3 & 4 oclock all the family were called & collected around her bed, spoke to each of her sisters urging those that had not professed faith in Christ to come to the Saviour without delay she pressed the younger to read their Bible, to be daily in the exercise of prayer, to be dutiful & affectionate to their sisters, to have ever a strict regard to truth, this she endeavoured to press on their consciences. To [the] Colored Girl who attend[ed] her in her illness she expressed herself with earnestness urging her to come to Christ, in whom was neither bond nor free, said that God was no respecter of persons that in his Father's house were many mansions, that there was a mansion for her if [she] would come to the Saviour, She seemed as if [she] did not know how to give up talking, to poor Black Cate, Oh do love Jesus, do come to Christ, pausing at ever few words from weakness. After taking leave of her family she spoke most affectionately of those friends who were with her, of their kindness, of the affection & gratitude she felt towards them, to one friend she said, calling her by name, I love you. You love Jesus, we have often had communion together you have been a christian friend to me, she sent messages to her absent friends to her little Brother repeating for him what she had said to the rest, give my love to dear uncle Doctor [Peter Vredenburgh, physician at Somerville] tell him from me to come to Christ, tell him what he has done for my soul, that there is a reality in religion. My love to Peter [her cousin?] give him my testament ask him to read it for my sake, tell him to seek an interest in Christ, before he gets engaged in the world, Oh tell him from me to seek Jesus, then sent her love to her Aunt & each of the children mentioning them by name, Tell the Davis's that I love them & thank them for all their kindness, I want you all to love them, tell Aunty Davis we shall soon meet, & tell Uncle to seek Jesus & not to grovel here below, tell him from me, he must seek Jesus, Dear Mr. Frelinghuysen I love him, & the Lord will reward him for his kindness to the Orphan, he has been a dear & precious friend & Mrs. F. too. I thank her for all her kindness. My love to Gertrude, tell her not [to] set her heart on this world, My love to dear Elizabeth tell her to seek Jesus, my love to all the dear children. She sent her love to Madame McKay, tell her I love her because she loves Jesus, to her sister Hannah she sent her special love with many expressions of affection & regard, she begged her sister Harriet to go & live with her & be a comfort to her, she repeat[ed]ly mentioned Sally, saying dear Sally. A short time before she expired when Nature seemed almost exhausted, & her feeble pulse like a fine thread, her eyes were closed & we thought her gone, Mrs. V. P. [her sister Margaret] lying by her said to her do you know me Maria. Oh yes she said you are dear sister Margaret. She after this noticed the approach of day, & said in her low broken voice, Morning, Morning. She said it with such an effort that it gave rise to the thought whether she did not allude to the dawn of the celestial day that was then breaking in on her soul. After this looked up to me & with a sweet smile said, Through, Through. This it is beleived [*sic*] was the last word she articulated, her breathing became shorter & shorter, till it ceased without a sign, & as the sun arose her happy spirit was realized [released] from the fetters of mortality. She fell asleep in Jesus. She has finished her course & is gone to receive her reward, like gold seven times tried & purified from its dross, she has passed through the furnace of affliction, to shine with a brighter lustre in the temple of her God, Tribulation has worked patience & patience experience & experience hope, her example teaches us that it is not a vain thing to seek the Lord that his promises are sure, that none who trust in him are forsaken. Though for a moment he may hide his face from his people, yet with everlasting kindness will he have mercy on them, with truth may it be said—Lo this is our God, we have waited for him (not in vain) we will be glad & rejoice in his salvation. Blessed are the dead who die in the Lord, they rest from all their sorrows—their example shall confirm the faith of many and their works shall follow them.

*[Transcribed with occasional additions of punctuation for clarity. From the Collections of the New Jersey Historical Society, Newark, New Jersey. Manuscript Group 25.]*

# NOTES

## Introduction

1. For a useful overview of the First Great Awakening, see Michael J. Crawford, "Revivalism and the Great Awakening," *Encyclopedia of the North American Colonies,* ed. Jacob Ernest Cooke, 3 vols. (New York, 1993), 3:665–684. A classic of the Second Great Awakening is Whitney R. Cross, *The Burned-over District: The Social and Intellectual History of Enthusiastic Religion in Western New York, 1800–1850* (Ithaca, N.Y., 1950), a study of the revivals that swept upper New York State. These revivals attracted many unchurched as well as an assortment of extremists and perfectionists and were light on doctrine, heavy on New Measures and other innovations. In the formal old-line denominations long established in lower New York State and in New Jersey, such as the Reformed Dutch Church, doctrine was paramount, revivalism's assaults on it were vigorously repelled, and enthusiasm and New Measures were suspect. See also James D. Folts, "The Fanatic and the Prophetess: Religious Perfectionism in Western New York, 1835–1839," *New York History* 72 (October 1991):357–387.

2. References to the vast literature on the relationship between religion and ethnicity can be found in Harold J. Abramson, "Religion," in *Harvard Encyclopedia of American Ethnic Groups,* ed. Stephen Thernstrom (Cambridge, Mass., 1980), 869–875; and Laura L. Becker, "Ethnicity and Religion," in *Encyclopedia of the American Religious Experience: Studies of Traditions and Movements,* 3 vols., ed. Charles H. Lippy and Peter W. Williams (New York, 1988), 3:1477–1491.

   Regarding the dynamics and repercussions of ethnicity on American Protestantism, surprisingly little has been written, despite strong indications that studying this topic has been fruitful for Catholicism, Judaism, and various sects and new religions. As early as 1975, Harry S. Stout advised that the history of American churches could not be described solely in terms of the frontier, urbanization, or the rise of denominations, "but must recognize the centrality of ethnicity in American religious life." Stout, "Ethnicity: The Vital Center of Religion in America," *Ethnicity* 2 (1975):220. See also Martin E. Marty, "Ethnicity: The Skeleton of Religion in America," *Church History* 41 (1972):521; the seminal article by Timothy L. Smith, "Religion and Ethnicity in America," *American Historical Review* 83 (December 1978):1155–1185; and John Higham, "Integrating America: The Problem of Assimilation in the Nineteenth Century," *Journal of American Ethnic History* (Fall 1981):7–25. See also John

Higham, "Ethnicity and American Protestants: Collective Identity in the Mainstream," in *New Directions in American Religious History,* ed. Harry S. Stout and D. G. Hart (New York, 1997), 239–259. Higham says that the "making and unmaking of a specifically ethnic consciousness within the so-called 'mainstream' of American Protestantism" is the "truly neglected dimension in the abundant ethnic studies of the last thirty years," p. 242.

3. The insistence on the "purity of the doctrines as determined at Dort" is a constant refrain in Reformed literature throughout the nineteenth century. Its meaning is discussed in chapter 2.

4. Leonard I. Sweet, ed., *The Evangelical Tradition in America* (Macon, Ga., 1984), 45.

5. John Lankford, "An End and a Beginning: Reflections on Sydney Ahlstrom's 'Religious History of the American People' and the Future of Sociologically Informed Inquiry into Religion in American Life," *Anglican Theological Review* 56 (1974):479.

6. See Randall H. Balmer, *A Perfect Babel of Confusion: Dutch Religion and English Culture in the Middle Colonies* (New York, 1989). Joyce D. Goodfriend, *Before the Melting Pot: Society and Culture in Colonial New York City, 1664–1730* (Princeton, N.J., 1992), takes a more moderate position, arguing that ethnic identity became "less salient" for the Dutch "only as supraethnic loyalties were generated by the wave of evangelical religion of the 1740s and the republicanism of the revolutionary era," p. 220.

   Eric Nooter, "Between Heaven and Earth: Church and Society in Pre-Revolutionary Flatbush, Long Island" (diss., Free University of Amsterdam, 1994), establishes, however, that in that Brooklyn community, as no doubt in many others, the "Americanization of the Dutch Reformed Church . . . did not start much before the nineteenth century," pp. 170–171. He concludes that the Reformed Dutch Church in Flatbush was very much a "Dutch" institution throughout the eighteenth century and that the majority of Flatbush's inhabitants were officially affiliated with it, pp. 167–171.

   Finally, David Steven Cohen, in *The Dutch-American Farm* (New York, 1992), has demonstrated through a study of material culture, particularly house forms, how a distinctive Dutch American regional subculture thrived throughout the nineteenth century in New York and New Jersey.

7. S.L.B. Baldwin, Diary, January 14, 1838. The diary has been lost. It is reprinted in the *Unionist Gazette* (Somerville, N.J., 1897), available in the Special Collections, Alexander Library, Rutgers University. *Christian Intelligencer,* August 28, 1845; and D. Buddingh, Voorede (Foreword), "De School, in de Vereenigde Staten van Noord-Amerika," *De Kerk, School en Wetenschap in de Vereenigde Staten van Noord-Amerika,* 2 vols. (Utrecht, 1852), 2:xi.

8. On Finney, see Charles E. Hambrick-Stowe, *Charles G. Finney and the Spirit of American Evangelicalism* (Grand Rapids, Mich., 1996).

9. It may be observed that the Dutch still identify themselves today as a separate ethnic group. But today, in the Eastern states at least, this identification is made through historical, genealogical, patriotic, and cultural societies, not through a connection with Reformed Dutch doctrine. Annette Stott, in *Holland Mania: The Unknown Dutch Period in American Art and Culture* (Woodstock, N.Y., 1998) has recently identified a fascinating and little-known forty-year period in U.S. history, from 1880 to 1920, when a significant portion of the U.S. population rediscovered and celebrated Dutchness by collecting Dutch art, emulating the Old Dutch Masters, and romanticizing Dutch folk customs. But again, there was in this phenomenon nothing of the older ecclesiastical connection associated with Dutchness as it will be discussed here.

CHAPTER 1 *Being Dutch and Being the Reformed Dutch Church*

1. Oliver Rink, "The People of New Netherland: Notes on Non-English Immigration to New York in the Seventeenth Century," *New York History* 62 (January 1981):5–42; David Steven Cohen, "How Dutch Were the Dutch of New Netherland?" *New York History* 62 (January 1981):43–60; and David William Voorhees, "New Amsterdam as a Multicultural Community," talk given at the Museum of the City of New York, August 4, 1997. Many scholars believe that the population figures for New Netherland are too low and that a demographic study is sorely needed.

2. Jan Lucassen, "Labour and Early Modern Economic Development," in *A Miracle Mirrored: The Dutch Republic in European Perspective*, ed. Karel Davids and Jan Lucassen (Cambridge, 1995), 368–369.

3. As late as 1689, a full quarter-century after the change in administrations from Dutch to English, jurisprudence in New York continued to refer to Dutch legal practices. Jacob Leisler based his program in 1689 on the Dutch laws of New York Province and the laws and customs of England, choosing the best of both worlds, twenty-five years after the supposed "conquest" had extinguished Dutch influence. He did so even in his private life. See Firth Haring Fabend, "'According to Holland Custome': Jacob Leisler and the Loockermans Estate Feud," *de Halve Maen* 67 (Spring 1994):1–8. On the merits of Dutch testamentary law, see David E. Narrett, *Inheritance and Family Life in Colonial New York City* (Ithaca, N.Y., 1992).

4. [Reformed Dutch Church], *Quarter-Millennial Anniversary of the Protestant Reformed Dutch Church of the City of New York* [November 21, 1878] (New York, 1878), 95; and Isaac Ferris, D.D., "A Discourse in Commemoration of the Life and Character of the Late George W. Bethune, D.D., Delivered in the Church on the Heights, Brooklyn, on Sunday Morning, June 8th, 1862" (in *Writings,* bound sermons of Ferris, Sage Library, New Brunswick Theological Seminary, 26–27). One other stumbling block in attempting to identify who was Dutch and who was not has been pointed out by Oliver Rink. In discussing immigrants from the Netherlands to New Netherland whose names appear on ship lists, Rink observes that the tendency of Dutch notaries "to Hollandize all names makes any attempt at ethnic classification by name not only pointless, but rather misleading." Rink, "The People of New Netherland," table 4, note 4. The fact that Dutch notaries "Hollandized" names does not mean, of course, that immigrants used those names in New Netherland, but rather only that they might have used them.

5. Werner Sollors, ed., *The Invention of Ethnicity* (New York, 1989), has suggested that ethnicity may be invented and reinvented with each generation. "Introduction," passim.

6. E. T. Corwin, *A Digest of Constitutional and Synodical Legislation of the Reformed Church in America* (New York, 1906), passim; John Pershing Luidens, "The Americanization of the Dutch Reformed Church" (diss., University of Oklahoma, 1969), 24–25; Russell Gasero, archivist of the denomination, personal conversation with the author, May 12, 1994; Daniel J. Meeter, "The 'North American Liturgy': A Critical Edition of the Liturgy of the Reformed Dutch Church in North America, 1793" (diss., Drew University, 1989); and George S. Bishop, "Ten Years' Review: The Place, History and Responsibility of the Reformed Church," sermon delivered in the First Reformed Church of Orange, N.J., April 19, 1885.

7. John M. Murrin, "English Rights as Ethnic Aggression: The English Conquest, the Charter of Liberties of 1683, and Leisler's Rebellion in New York," in *Authority and Resistance in Early New York*, ed. William Pencak and Conrad Edick Wright (New

York, 1988), 58. Taking this a step further, Joyce Goodfriend has suggested that the institutionalization of ethnic pluralism in New York had positive consequences, acting ultimately to foster stability in the diverse society, even as it enabled and encouraged the continuance of Dutch cultural patterns, particularly religious patterns, for generations. Goodfriend, *Before the Melting Pot: Society and Culture in Colonial New York City, 1664–1730* (Princeton, N.J., 1992). For further corroboration, see David E. Narrett, *Inheritance and Family Life in Colonial New York City* (Ithaca, N.Y., 1992), and for evidence of the persistence of Dutchness in rural areas, see Firth Haring Fabend, *A Dutch Family in the Middle Colonies, 1660–1800* (New Brunswick, N.J., 1991). On Batavianization, see also David William Voorhees, "The Editor's Corner," *de Halve Maen* 69 (Summer 1996): "As the already diverse ethnic composition of the [New York and New Jersey] region became less Dutch in the eighteenth century, there was a countervailing tendency toward increasing 'Batavianization' that has been little explored."

8. Tacitus, *The Histories,* trans. Kenneth Wellesley, book 4 (Baltimore, 1964), 211ff. The quoted phrase is from Eric Hobsbawm and Terence Ranger, eds., *The Invention of Tradition* (Cambridge, 1983).

9. Simon Schama, *The Embarrassment of Riches: An Interpretation of Dutch Culture in the Golden Age* (New York, 1987), 53–54, 68, 122, 72–90.

10. Ibid., 53–54. Jonathan Israel has pointed out that the notion that the ancient Batavians, "heroic, virtuous, and freedomloving," had successfully revolted against the Romans was a potent factor in building the Netherlands' sense of itself as a political, moral, and cultural entity, "as patria [fatherland] and 'nation.'" When the Dutch Patriots rose against the Orangists in 1795, the power of this ancient legend was such that the victorious Patriots called their revolutionary government the Batavian Republic, in romantic allusion to their supposed ancestors in freedom. Jonathan I. Israel, *The Dutch Republic: Its Rise, Greatness, and Fall, 1477–1806* (New York, 1995), 57–58. See also Jan Willem Schulte Nordholt, *The Dutch Republic and American Independence*, trans. Herbert H. Rowen (Chapel Hill, N.C., 1979), 284–290.

11. On the persistence of Dutch dialects into the nineteenth century, see H. L. Mencken, *The American Language* (New York, 1919); Van Cleaf Bachman, Alice P. Kenney, and Lawrence G. Van Loon, "'Het Poelmeisie': An Introduction to the Hudson Valley Dutch Dialect," *New York History* (April 1980):161–171; J. Dyneley Prince, "A Text in Jersey Dutch," *Tijdschrift voor Nederlandsche Taal—en Letterkunde* 32 (1913):306–312; Lawrence G. Van Loon, *Crumbs from an Old Dutch Closet: The Dutch Dialect of New York* (The Hague, 1938); and Charles T. Gehring, "The Survival of the Dutch Language in New York and New Jersey," *de Halve Maen* 58 (October 1984):7–9, 24. For material culture, see Roderic H. Blackburn and Ruth Piwonka, *Remembrance of Patria: Dutch Arts and Culture in Colonial America, 1609–1776* (Albany, N.Y., 1988).

12. In 1856, the appearance of John L. Motley's *The Rise of the Dutch Republic* fed directly into Dutchophiliac fancies. An instant best-seller, this work went through many editions in every price range over decades. It was eventually shown to be deficient as history (by Pieter Geyl and other historians). But it was an important factor in the nineteenth century in "creating and magnifying" the virtues of the Dutch in the minds of American readers who did not discriminate between Motley's facts and his polemic. "Motley's sweeping colors and rhetorical invective, superlatives and expletives, easily rode their way into the welcome of audiences wallowing in the North Atlantic highflown romanticism of the 1840's and 1850's. . . . Carlyle had taught [the public] to seek for heroes; Motley obliged with William the Silent." The quoted passages are

from D. D. Edwards, "John Lothrop Motley and the Netherlands," in *A Bilateral Bi-centennial: A History of Dutch-American Relations, 1782–1982*, ed. J. W. Schulte Nordholt and Robert P. Swierenga (New York and Amsterdam, 1982), 171–198.

Long before Motley, the Reformed Church in America had embraced William the Silent. His coat of arms decorated the first issue of the *Magazine of the Reformed Dutch Church* in 1826 (the forerunner of the *Christian Intelligencer*), and in 1839 the *Intelligencer* adopted this coat of arms as its logo. As Corwin noted in the *Digest of Synodical Legislation*, "This Emblem associates the Reformed Church in America with the Reformed Church in the Netherlands, whose Union of States and unprecedented freedom of religion became the model of the United States," 253. (Whether they were the model or not and to what extent is a matter of dispute among historians.)

13. Indispensable works published by the denomination include *Acts and Proceedings of the General Synod of the Reformed Protestant Dutch Church of North America* (New York, annually); C. E. Corwin, *A Manual of the Reformed Church in America, 1628–1922,* 5th ed. (New York, 1922); E. T. Corwin, *Digest of Constitutional and Synodical Legislation of the Reformed Church in America*; David D. Demarest, *The Reformed Church in America: Its Origin, Development, and Characteristics,* 4th ed., rev. and enlgd. (New York, 1889); *Centennial Discourses: A Series of Sermons Delivered in the Year 1876, by the Order of the General Synod of the Reformed (Dutch) Church in America* (New York, 1877); *Tercentenary Studies 1928, Reformed Church in America, A Record of Beginnings* (New York, 1928). Also useful are Howard G. Hageman, *Lily among the Thorns* (New York, 1975); M. Eugene Osterhaven, "The Founding of a Church," *Reformed Review* 34 (Spring 1981):186–192; and Luidens, "The Americanization of the Dutch Reformed Church." The correspondence between the Classis of Amsterdam in the Netherlands and the American churches up to 1800 is found in E. T. Corwin, comp. and ed., *Ecclesiastical Records of the State of New York,* 7 vols. (Albany, 1901–1916).

14. Important secondary studies published by the denomination are found in The Historical Series of the Reformed Church in America. These include Gerald F. De Jong, *The Dutch Reformed Church in the American Colonies* (Grand Rapids, Mich., 1978); Herman Harmelink III, *Ecumenism and the Reformed Church* (Grand Rapids, Mich., 1968); Elton J. Bruins, *The Americanization of a Congregation,* rev. ed. (Grand Rapids, Mich., 1995); James W. Van Hoeven, ed., *Piety and Patriotism: Bicentennial Studies of the Reformed Church in America, 1776–1976* (Grand Rapids, Mich., 1976); James W. Van Hoeven, ed., *Word and World: Reformed Theology in America* (Grand Rapids, Mich., 1986); John W. Beardslee III, ed., *Vision from the Hill* (Grand Rapids, Mich., 1984); Howard G. Hageman, *Two Centuries Plus: The Story of New Brunswick Seminary* (Grand Rapids, Mich., 1984); Daniel J. Meeter, *Meeting Each Other in Doctrine, Liturgy, and Government: The Bicentennial of the Celebration of the Constitution of the Reformed Church in America* (Grand Rapids, Mich., 1993); and *Patterns and Portraits: Women in the History of the Reformed Church in America,* ed. Renée S. House and John W. Coakley (Grand Rapids, Mich., 1999). See also M. Eugene Osterhaven, *The Faith of the Church: A Reformed Perspective on Its Historical Development* (Grand Rapids, Mich., 1982). Linda P. Doezema's *Dutch Americans: A Guide to Information Sources,* Ethnic Studies Information Guide Series, vol. 3 (Detroit, 1979), is an annotated bibliography of general works, including those on religious topics.

15. See Willem Frijhoff, "The West India Company and the Reformed Church: Neglect or Concern?" *de Halve Maen* 70 (Fall 1997):59–68.

16. See John W. Beardslee III, "Orthodoxy and Piety: Two Styles of Faith in the Colonial Period," in *Word and World*, ed. Van Hoeven, 1–14. Beardslee makes clear that the distinction between the orthodox and the Pietists lay in their worship styles and modes of expression, not in doctrinal differences. In doctrinal matters, the Pietists' orthodoxy was not a question.

17. For a full discussion, see James W. Van Hoeven, "Dort and Albany: Reformed Theology Engages a New Culture," in *Word and World*, ed. Van Hoeven, 15–30.

18. James R. Tanis, *Dutch Calvinistic Pietism in the Middle Colonies: A Study of the Life and Theology of Theodorus J. Frelinghuysen* (The Hague, 1967), 7. Personal holiness found new expression in the nineteenth century in the pervasive concept among evangelicals of "personal sanctification," or usefulness, as it was often termed. This is discussed in chapter 8 of the present work. To be certain of living a "useful" life was a matter of great anxiety, for if one were not useful, or convinced of one's usefulness, one could infer that one's conversion to the Lord had not been authentic, a prostrating notion to an evangelical.

19. Beardslee, "Orthodoxy and Piety," 8.

20. Tanis, *Dutch Calvinistic Pietism*, 2, 53. The Frisian Catechism, Tanis makes clear, did not stray from orthodox Reformed doctrine. Frelinghuysen and his supporters were always to insist on his orthodoxy, and Frelinghuysen himself, although he held Pietist beliefs, rejected the appellation, associating it with Jean de Labadie and his separatist tendencies. See also J. J. Mol, *The Breaking of Traditions: Theological Convictions in Colonial America* (Berkeley, 1968), 17, who writes that, in his sermons, Frelinghuysen "quoted with approval from Wilhelmus a Brakel's *Logika Latreia* (1700) in which we find a fervent emphasis on regeneration combined with acceptance of traditional Calvinistic doctrines."

21. Herman Harmelink III, "Another Look at Frelinghuysen and His 'Awakening,'" *Church History* (1968):423–438.

22. Herman Harmelink III, William W. Coventry, and Sharon Thoms Scholten, *The Reformed Church in New Jersey* (n.p., Synod of New Jersey, 1969), 19.

23. See, for instance, the essays in *Continental Pietism and Early American Christianity*, ed. Ernest Stoeffler (Grand Rapids, Mich., 1976); and M. Eugene Osterhaven, "The Experiential Theology of Early Dutch Calvinism," *Reformed Review* 27 (Spring, 1974):186–192.

24. For Bogardus, see Willem Frijhoff, "The Healing of a Lay Saint: Evert Willemsz. Bogardus's Conversion between Personal Achievement and Social Legitimation," *de Halve Maen* 68 (Spring 1995): 1–12. Primary source materials on Bertholf (also spelled Bartholf) are the *Ecclesiastical Records of the State of New York*, 7 vols., ed. E. T. Corwin (Albany, N.Y., 1901–1914). (See Volume 7, index, for page references.)

Articles about Bertholf include Howard G. Hageman, "William Bertholf: Pioneer Domine of New Jersey," *Reformed Review* 29 (Winter 1976):73–80; Howard G. Hageman, "Colonial New Jersey's First Domine: I and II," *de Halve Maen* 44 (October 1969, January 1970); Randall H. Balmer, "From Rebellion to Revivalism: The Fortunes of the Dutch Reformed Church in Colonial New York, 1689–1715," *de Halve Maen* 56 (Fall 1981), and 57 (Winter 1982).

Adrian C. Leiby, in *The United Churches of Hackensack and Schraalenburgh, New Jersey, 1686–1822* (River Edge, N.J., 1976), devotes a chapter to Bertholf. See also

Tanis, *Dutch Calvinistic Pietism*, passim; and Tanis, "Reformed Pietism in Colonial America," in *Continental Pietism and Early American Christianity*, ed. Stoeffler. David Cole, *History of the Reformed Church of Tappan, New York* (New York, 1894), and Firth Haring Fabend, *A Dutch Family in the Middle Colonies, 1660–1800* (New Brunswick, N.J., 1991), explore his pastorate in a church he organized in 1694 and served on a supply basis for three decades.

See also Joseph Anthony Loux, trans. and ed., *Boel's "Complaint" against Frelinghuysen* (Rensselaer, N.Y., 1979).

25. Coetus rhymes with *meet us*. On the role of the clergy in the Revolution, see John W. Beardslee III, "The Reformed Church and the American Revolution," in *Piety and Patriotism, Bicentennial Studies of the Reformed Church in America, 1776–1976,* ed. James W. Van Hoeven (Grand Rapids, Mich., 1976); Luidens, "The Americanization of the Dutch Reformed Church," chap. 4; Dennis N. Voskuil, "Piety and Patriotism: Reformed Theology and Civil Religion," in *Word and World*, ed. Van Hoeven; James R. Tanis, "The Dutch Reformed Clergy and the American Revolution," in *Wegen en Gestalten in het Gereformeerd Protestantisme*, Festschrift for Professor Dr. S. van der Linde (Amsterdam, 1976), 235–256; and Tanis, "The American Dutch, Their Church, and the Revolution," in *A Bilateral Bicentennial*, ed. Nordholt and Swierenga, 115–126.

26. See Gerald F. De Jong, *The Dutch Reformed Church in the American Colonies* (Grand Rapids, Mich., 1978), for a detailed discussion.

CHAPTER 2    *"So Like Heaven": The Synod of Dort*

1. For the web metaphor, see Clifford Geertz, "Religion as a Cultural System," in *Anthropological Approaches to the Study of Religion,* ed. M. Banton (London, 1966). Reprinted in *The Interpretation of Cultures: Selected Essays by Clifford Geertz* (New York, 1973), 87–125.
2. James W. Van Hoeven, "Introduction," in *Word and World: Reformed Theology in America,* ed. James W. Van Hoeven (Grand Rapids, Mich., 1986); M. Eugene Osterhaven, *The Faith of the Church: A Reformed Perspective on Its Historical Development* (Grand Rapids, Mich., 1982); Eugene Heideman, "Theology," in *Piety and Patriotism: Bicentennial Studies of the Reformed Church in America, 1776–1976,* ed. James W. Van Hoeven (Grand Rapids, Mich., 1976); Philip Schaff, *The Creeds of Christendom, with a History and Critical Notes*, 3 vols. (New York, 1884), 1:438. The Arminians did not remonstrate or take a position on a fifth doctrine, the perseverance of the saints (the belief that it was impossible for the elect ever to fall from grace).
3. Schaff, *Creeds,* 1:509.
4. The full text of the Canons of Dort, along with the "Rejections" of the Arminian errors, and Bible proofs for them as cited by the Calvinists, can be found in a recent translation, *Ecumenical Creeds and Reformed Confessions* (Grand Rapids, Mich., 1987), as well as in the Psalter Hymnal of the Christian Reformed Church, both copyright 1987 by CRC Publications, 2850 Kalamazoo SE, Grand Rapids, Michigan 49560. See also Schaff, *Creeds*, 1: chap. 7, sections 65–67; Thomas Scott, D.D., trans., *The Articles of the Synod of Dort, Translated from the Latin, with Notes, . . . with an Introductory Essay, by the Rev. Samuel Miller, D.D.* (Philadelphia, 1856); Maurice G. Hansen, *The Reformed Church in the Netherlands* (New York, 1884), especially "Defensive Period"; and David D. Demarest, *The Reformed Church in America: Its*

*Origin, Development and Characteristics*, 4th ed., rev. and enlgd. (New York, 1889), 29–43.

See also Carl Bangs, *Arminius: A Study in the Dutch Reformation* (Nashville, 1971); Jonathan I. Israel, *The Dutch Republic: Its Rise, Greatness, and Fall, 1477–1806* (New York, 1995), chap. 16.; and Peter Y. De Jong, ed., *Crisis in the Reformed Churches: Essays in Commemoration of the Great Synod of Dort, 1618–1619* (Grand Rapids, Mich., 1968).

5. Because the other Reformed churches that gathered at Dort did not in the long run put the same emphasis on the primary necessity for recognizing the sovereignty of God and glorifying him for it as the Dutch Church did, but rather after Dort gradually adopted other confessions, with slightly different emphases, standards, and forms, the Reformed Church claimed a unique "purity" in its loyalty to all matters agreed upon at the synod. The quoted phrase in the text from Schaff is in *Creeds,* 1:514. The second quoted phrase is John W. Nevin's in *History and Genius of the Heidelberg Catechism* (Chambersburg, Pa., 1847), 122.

    For Schaff on the "defects" of the Westminster Confession, as they regard the doctrine of predestination, see *Creeds,* 1:790–796. See Schaff, *Creeds,* 1: chaps. 5, 6, and 7, for the distinctions and differences among the creeds and confessions of the various Protestant churches. For a recent examination of Reformed religion as it developed and diversified in America, see David F. Wells, ed., *Reformed Theology in America: A History of Its Modern Development* (Grand Rapids, Mich., 1997), particularly the Introduction by George M. Marsden, "The Princeton Theology" by Mark A. Noll, and "The Dutch Schools" by James D. Bratt. See also Firth Haring Fabend, "The Synod of Dort and the Persistence of Dutchness in Nineteenth-Century New York and New Jersey," *New York History* 77 (July 1996):273–300.

6. For modern-day views on the Canons of Dort and the doctrine of limited atonement, in particular, see a series of three articles by Howard Dekker in the *Reformed Journal* (January, March, and June, 1964); and James Daane, "What Doctrine of Limited Atonement?" *Reformed Journal* (December 1964):13–15.

7. George W. Bethune, "Reasons for Preferring a Union with the Reformed Dutch Church of North America" (Philadelphia, 1836), 8, 10, 11. Bethune here gives his reasons for leaving the Presbyterian Church for the Reformed Dutch Church, the main one being the "purity of its doctrine."

8. The most significant of the doctrinal grounds worked out at Dort that distinguished the Reformed churches in Europe from other Protestant churches, particularly the Lutheran, was the Calvinist view of God's role in man's eternal fate. The Reformed churches insisted upon the sovereignty of God in the work of salvation, whereas from its beginnings the Lutheran Church emphasized "justification," or salvation by faith in Jesus Christ.

    Martin Luther's idea of justification by faith was, in the words of a Reformed theologian, "almost the cardinal discovery of the Reformation, the keystone in the arch of its thought," and Reformed Christians were wholeheartedly in accord with the importance of faith to salvation. But Calvinists feared that justification by faith connoted that men are saved by something they do (repenting and believing), rather than by something God does out of his love, goodness, and grace, and at Dort they affirmed this. The chief purpose in life for the Reformed Dutch, according to this theologian, "is not to save our own souls, to do good, to develop our characters. . . . Our chief purpose in life, the end for which we were created, is to glorify God" for his goodness in offering his love and grace to mankind. Howard G. Hageman, *Lily among the Thorns* (New York, 1975), 101–102.

9. William J. R. Taylor, "Influence of the Theological Seminary on the Denominational Life of the Church," *Centennial of the Theological Seminary of the Reformed Church in America, 1784–1884* (New York, 1885), 165.

10. See Schaff, *Creeds*, 6th ed. (1931), vols. 1 and 2.

11. "Divine Election and Reprobation," Article 16 of the First Head of Doctrine in the Canons of Dort.

12. William G. McLoughlin, ed., *The American Evangelicals, 1800–1900: An Anthology* (New York, 1968), 1. McLoughlin goes on to say that "both as motivation and as rationale, evangelical religion lay behind . . . rugged individualism in business enterprise, laissez faire in economic theory, constitutional democracy in political thought, the Protestant ethic in morality, and the millennial hope in the manifest destiny of white Anglo-Saxon, Protestant America to lead the world to its latter-day Glory." The literature on the evangelical era is immense. For an introduction to it, see Leonard I. Sweet, "Nineteenth-Century Evangelicalism," in *Encyclopedia of the American Religious Experience: Studies of Traditions and Movements*, 3 vols., ed. Charles H. Lippy and Peter W. Williams (New York, 1988), 2:875–899, including the bibliography and cross-references, 898–899. Since 1988, references may be found in the quarterly *Evangelical Studies Bulletin*, Institute for the Study of American Evangelicals, Wheaton, Ill. For what he calls a "corrective" to the model, see James D. Bratt, "The Reorientation of American Protestantism, 1835–1845," *Church History: Studies in Christianity and Culture* 67 (March 1998):52–82.

13. George M. Marsden, *Religion and American Culture* (New York, 1990), 50.

14. These figures may be found in Herman Harmelink III, William W. Coventry, and Sharon Thoms Scholten, *The Reformed Church in New Jersey* (n.p., Synod of New Jersey, 1969), 35; and "Classical Reports," *Acts and Proceedings of the General Synod of the Reformed Protestant Dutch Church of North America* (New York, 1826), 37–43. The percentages are my own.

15. See *Centennial of the Theological Seminary of the Reformed Church in America, 1784–1884* (New York, 1885). The secession was led by the Reverend Solomon Froeligh of the First Reformed churches in Hackensack and Schraalenburgh. Froeligh's account of some of the events leading up to it, "God's Marvelous Thunder," and a sympathetic account of it by his friend and fellow minister, Cornelius T. Demarest, were published as *A Lamentation over the Reverend Solomon Froeligh* (New York, 1827). For an unsympathetic account written fifty years after the secession, see Jacob Brinkerhoff, *The History of the True Reformed Dutch Church in the U.S.A.* (New York, 1873). These are in the Special Collections, Alexander Library, Rutgers University.

Also at Rutgers are John V. S. Lansing, "Address to the Friends of Sound Doctrine, Experimental Piety, and Ministerial Faithfulness in the True Reformed Dutch Church" (New York, 1828); Christian Z. Paulison, "A Development of Facts and Circumstances Justifying a Union with the True Reformed Church" (New York, 1831); Paulison, "An Address to the Friends of True Godliness Yet in Connection with the True Reformed Dutch Church" (New York, 1832); and Bradley Randall, "Zion Triumphant Over All Opposition" (New York, 1826).

At the New Jersey Historical Society are Solomon Froeligh, "A Real Dutchman" (New York, 1823); and Peter Haring, " 'Hopkinsianism Unmasked'; or, A Brief Review of a Pamphlet Lately Published, under the Signature of 'A Dutchman Not Double

Hearted'" (Paterson, N.J., 1825). Another pamphlet by a Peter Haring (there were several men of this name), "Brief Exposition of the Errors and Corruptions in the True Reformed Church; or, The Deviation from That Body from Her Standards Both of Faith and Practice" (n.p., 1835), could not be found. This work is missing at the New York State Library in Albany, which has a record of an actual holding. Another rare pamphlet, apparently not listed in any bibliographic record, is "The Little Horn; or, Letters of Correspondence between John Haring . . . and [the Reverend] Mr. Wilhelmus Eltinge" (Paterson, N.J., 1822). In the author's possession, this is a series of letters written between 1800 and 1802 that, because they had a bearing on the 1822 secession, were published twenty years after they were written.

The 1822 secession resounded into the twentieth century. See Edward T. Corwin, *A Manual of the Reformed Church in America, 1628–1902* (New York, 1902), 480, for nineteenth-century accounts of it. The facts as seen by William O. Van Eyck were published in his *Landmarks of the Reformed Fathers* (Grand Rapids, Mich., 1922), one hundred years after the secession. The remnant of the secession joined the Christian Reformed Church, itself a secession from the Reformed Church in America, in 1890. See M. Eugene Osterhaven, "Saints and Sinners: Secession and the Christian Reformed Church," in *Word and World: Reformed Theology in America*, ed. James W. Van Hoeven (Grand Rapids, Mich., 1986).

CHAPTER 3   *The 1820s: Arraying for a New Century*

1. See Charles E. Corwin, *A Manual of the Reformed Church in America, 1628–1922*, 5th ed., rev. (New York, 1922), for a biographical sketch and primary and secondary sources, and Alexander Gunn, *Memoirs of the Rev. John H. Livingston* (New York, 1829). See also Elton Bruins, "John Henry Livingston: His Life and Work" (S.T.M. thesis, Union Theological Seminary, 1957); James R. Tanis, "Reformed Pietism and Protestant Missions," *Harvard Theological Review* 67 (1974), 65–73; John W. Beardslee III, "John Henry Livingston and the Rise of American Mission Theology," *Reformed Review* 19 (Winter 1976), 101–108; Beardslee, "John Henry Livingston and the Rise of the American Mission Movement," *Historical Highlights* 8 (October 1989); and John W. Coakley, "John Henry Livinston and the Liberty of the Conscience," *Reformed Review* 46 (Winter 1992):119–135.
2. The seminary is the oldest graduate school of theology in the United States. For background, see Howard G. Hageman, *Two Centuries Plus: The Story of New Brunswick Seminary* (Grand Rapids, Mich., 1984), 13–14; and Norman Kansfield, "Education," in *Piety and Patriotism: Bicentennial Studies of the Reformed Church in America, 1776–1976*, ed. James W. Van Hoeven (Grand Rapids, Mich., 1976), 130–148. Richard P. McCormick, *Rutgers: A Bicentennial History* (New Brunswick, N.J., 1966), is the standard source on the college.
3. *The Christian Intelligencer,* September 16, 1860; hereafter *CI.*
4. *CI,* August 15, 1851; William H. Campbell, "The Relation of the Theological Seminary and Rutgers College to Each Other," *Centennial of the Theological Seminary of the Reformed Church in America* (New York, 1885), 155; T. C. Easton, "Address of Welcome," *Centennial of the Theological Seminary,* 7, 6.
5. Easton, "Address of Welcome," 7, 6, 8; Campbell, "Relation of Seminary and College," 155–157.
6. *CI,* August 1, 1850.

7. *CI,* September 11, 1845.
8. Campbell, "Relation of Seminary and College," 156.
9. Philetus T. Pockman, quoting Isaac Ferris, in "Centennial of the First Reformed Dutch Sunday School at New Brunswick, N.J., May 21st, 1899," 57. New Brunswick History Club Files, Special Collections, Alexander Library, Rutgers University; hereafter Sp. Cols., RUL.
10. *CI,* September 13, 20, 1855.
11. *CI,* September 13, September 20, 1855; Pockman, "Centennial," 12, 13, 21, 22, 39, 55, 57; Edwin Wilbur Rice, *The Sunday-School Movement and the American Sunday-School Union,* 2d ed. (Philadelphia, 1917), 146. For an excellent recent study of Sunday schools, see Anne Boylan, *Sunday School: The Formation of an American Institution, 1790–1880* (New Haven, 1988).
12. A. Th. Van Deursen, *Plain Lives in a Golden Age: Popular Culture, Religion and Society in Seventeenth-Century Holland,* trans. Maarten Ultee (New York, 1991), chap. 8. The quotation is on pp. 115–116. The separation of church and state in America augured against the inclusion in the Constitution of the Reformed Church (1793) of such a clause as Dort's Article 21, which had stipulated in 1619 that the consistories in every congregation "shall be careful to provide good Schoolmasters, who are able, not only to instruct children in reading, writing, grammar, and the liberal sciences; but also to teach them the catechism, and the first principles of religion." But the Constitution attempted in Explanatory Article 56 to have a say in the matter anyway, by decreeing that parents "endeavor to prevail upon [public] School-masters to make the children belonging to the Dutch Church, commit to memory, *and publicly repeat in school,* one section of the Heidelberg Catechism, at least once every week." (Emphasis added.) If parents were successful in forcing such a weekly recitation, this would have the effect, of course, of exposing all schoolchildren to Reformed doctrine. See also Kansfield, "Education," 131–138.
13. Quoted in Jonathan Israel, *The Dutch Republic: Its Rise, Greatness, and Fall, 1477–1806* (New York, 1995), 686. On the importance of literacy and numeracy in the early Netherlands, see particularly Margaret Spufford, "Literacy, Trade and Religion in the Commercial Centres of Europe," in *A Miracle Mirrored: The Dutch Republic in European Perspective,* ed. Karel Davids and Jan Lucassen (Cambridge, 1995), chap. 8, esp. 248ff.
14. Isaac Ferris, "Farewell Address on Resigning the Presidency of the Rutgers Female Institute, New York, July 2, 1856," 13, Mss. Room, New York Public Library. See also Isaac Ferris, Personal Miscellany, Mss. Room, New York Public Library.
15. Isaac Ferris, "Address Delivered 27th April, 1839, at the Opening of the Rutgers Female Institute, New York"; and *CI,* July 17, 1851. The high esteem in which the institute was held by the Reformed Dutch community is testified to by the publication of an extraordinary "extra" edition of the *Intelligencer* in 1851 that printed not only the public commencement exercises of the school but in their entirety the prize-winning compositions of the students. Although typically Victorian in their subject matter and sentiments ("Flowers in Life's Pathway," "How Strange Is Life"), these compositions reveal a superior command of the written language. In mathematics, too, students manifested a high degree of proficiency. They were examined in algebra, plane and solid geometry, and plane and spherical trigonometry by an outside committee, and the examination was of four days' duration. See *CI,* July 17, 1851.
16. *CI,* September 13, September 20, 1855. The families included Amerman, Backus,

Barstow, Berry, Brower, Concklin, De Forest, De Jonge, Duryea, Duykinck, Edsall, Ferris, Freeman, Gantz, Hagadorn, Hardenbrook, Haughwout, Hoagland, Napier, Nostrand, Polhemus, Schenck, Stuyvesant, Ten Eyck, Tiebout, Van Boskerck, Vanderpool, Vandewater, Van Ness, Vermeule, Voorhees, and Winfield.

17. A full run of the *Christian Intelligencer* is preserved, bound, at New Brunswick Theological Seminary's Gardner A. Sage Library in New Brunswick, New Jersey. It was published continuously into the twentieth century and survives today as the *Church Herald*.

18. In 1826, according to Frank Luther Mott, *A History of American Magazines, 1741–1850,* 5 vols. (Cambridge, Mass., 1930), there were 30 religious monthlies and 75 or 80 religious newspapers in the country. In 1848, there were 52 religious periodicals in New York City alone, and the census of 1850 counted 191 in the United States, about half of which were newspapers. See also Martin E. Marty, *Religious Press in America* (New York, 1963); Charles H. Lippy, ed., *Religious Periodicals of the United States: Academic and Scholarly Journals* (Westport, Conn., 1986); and P. Mark Fackler and Charles H. Lippy, eds., *Popular Religious Magazines of the United States* (Westport, Conn., 1995).

19. *CI,* July 23, 1842; Elbert S. Porter, "The Literature of the Church during the Last Hundred Years," in *Centennial Discourses. A Series of Sermons Delivered in the Year 1876. By the Order of the General Synod of the Reformed (Dutch) Church in America,* 2d ed. (New York, 1877), 10–11.

20. The paper was a "terror to evildoers," one observer wrote of it in 1850, and it showed a "tremendous opposition to liberalism" in doctrine. William O. Van Eyck, *The Union of 1850: A Collection of Papers . . . on the Union of the Classis of Holland [Michigan], with the Reformed Church in America, in June, 1850,* selected and edited by the Permanent Committee on History and Research of the General Synod of the Reformed Church in America (Grand Rapids, Mich., 1950), 23. See also *Hudson Star,* testimonial in *CI,* February 15, 1855.

21. *CI,* August 7, 1830, July 23, 1842, January 4, 1855.

22. For a discussion, see Leonard I. Sweet, "Nineteenth-Century Evangelicalism," in *Encyclopedia of the American Religious Experience: Studies of Traditions and Movements*, 3 vols., ed. Charles H. Lippy and Peter W. Williams (New York, 1988). See also Genevieve McCoy, "The Women of the ABCFM Oregon Mission and the Conflicted Language of Calvinism," *Church History* 64, no. 1 (March 1995):62–82, for a discussion of the continuing tensions in nineteenth-century theological discourse regarding the ability of the unregenerate to have an effect on their own spiritual condition. Even that seemingly steadfast Arminian Charles G. Finney, McCoy points out, frequently told his hearers that "because humans were disinclined to obey God, they required the Spirit's irresistible convincing light" and could not be the "authors of their own rebirths," p. 67.

23. Charles I. Foster, *An Errand of Mercy: The Evangelical United Front, 1790–1837* (Chapel Hill, N.C., 1960), 275–279. See also Paul Boyer, *Urban Masses and Moral Order in America, 1820–1920* (Cambridge, Mass., 1978), esp. parts 1–2.

24. Minutes, Dorcas and Day Nursery Society Records, Ac. 208, Book I, 1813–1838, Sp. Cols., RUL.

CHAPTER 4    *"Our Reformed Zion," 1830–1860*

1. John Gray, Imprint A837.G779, Box 95, Special Collections, Alexander Library, Rutgers University, 14; hereafter Sp. Cols., RUL.
2. *The Christian Intelligencer,* June 10, 1837; hereafter *CI.*
3. John A. Todd, *Memoir of the Rev. Peter Labagh, D.D. with Notices of the History of the Reformed Protestant Dutch Church in North America* (New York, 1860), 152–164.
4. S.L.B. Baldwin, Diary, May 30, 1837. The original of the diary, which Baldwin kept from June 19, 1835, to March 11, 1848, is lost, but extracts from it were printed weekly from February 19, 1885, to July 21, 1887, in the *Unionist Gazette* (Somerville, N.J.), which is available at Sp. Cols., RUL.
5. David D. Demarest, "Life Recollections," written in 1896 and read before the New Brunswick History Club, October 20, 1927. The manuscript, which in another copy is called "Some Memories Informally Written, 1896," is in Sp. Cols., RUL.
6. Richard Steele, D.D., *Historical Discourse Delivered at the Celebration of the One Hundred and Fiftieth Anniversary of the First Reformed Dutch Church, New-Brunswick, N.J., October 1, 1867* (New Brunswick, N.J., 1867), 127–129.
7. *CI,* February 24, 1876.
8. How to Mrs. Eliza Anderson, September 11, 1847, Samuel B. How Papers, Sp. Cols., RUL.
9. James Spencer Cannon, *Lectures on Pastoral Theology* (New York, 1853), 582, 584.
10. David D. Demarest, *History and Characteristics of the Reformed Protestant Dutch Church*, 2d ed. (New York, 1856), 142–143.
11. Demarest, "Recollections."
12. *CI,* October 16, 1845.
13. *CI,* September 25, 1845.
14. E. T. Corwin, D.D., *A Digest of Constitutional and Synodical Legislation of the Reformed Church in America, Prepared by Order of General Synod* (New York, 1906), 621; hereafter *Digest.*
15. *Magazine of the Reformed Dutch Church* 3 (July 1828):4. Samuel Hopkins was a student of Jonathan Edwards, from whose theological precepts he had slightly diverged, inflaming all of Calvinist Protestantism in the process. See Joseph A. Conforti, *Samuel Hopkins and the New Divinity Movement: Calvinism, the Congregational Ministry, and Reform in New England between the Great Awakenings* (Grand Rapids., Mich., 1981).
16. Edwin Wilbur Rice, *The Sunday-School Movement and the American Sunday-School Union,* 2d ed. (Philadelphia, 1917), 146, 149. A more recent study of Sunday schools is Anne Boylan, *Sunday School: The Formation of an American Institution, 1790–1880* (New Haven, Conn., 1988).
17. Rice, *Sunday-School Movement*, 146; Isaac Ferris, "Domestic Christian Education: A Sermon" (Albany, N.Y., 1835), 23, Imp. A835.F394, Sp. Cols., RUL.
18. Abraham Messler, *CI,* July 4, 1840.
19. Nicholas I. Marselus, "The Good Old Way: A Sermon Preached in the Middle Dutch Church . . . in Behalf of the Sabbath School Union of the Reformed Dutch Church" (New York, 1830), iii and iv, Imprints, Box 85, Sp. Cols., RUL. The "good old way" referred to a golden age of piety described by the prophet Jeremiah that was often evoked by both Reformed clergy and laity in the nineteenth century to mean something distinctively Reformed and Dutch. In this golden age, never precisely located in time, right-thinking folk looked for the ancient path, where the good way was, and found rest for their Reformed souls in obeying God's law.

20. Corwin, *Digest,* 662. The Synod's board was active until 1869 when, in the interests of efficiency, it divided its responsibilities between the Board of Publication, now authorized to publish a "suitable literature for the Sabbath Schools of the Church," and the Board of Domestic Missions, charged with establishing and maintaining the schools. The controversy can be followed in the minutes of the General Synod for these years. The summary here is extracted from the *Digest,* 659–664. The Dutch were not alone in wanting control over their own doctrines. As the denominations became stronger and more self-confident, Methodists, Baptists, Episcopalians and others set up their own various supervisory boards and formed their own publishing programs. The ecumenical united front began to fall apart as early as 1837, according to Charles I. Foster, *An Errand of Mercy: The Evangelical United Front, 1790–1837* (Chapel Hill, N.C., 1960), chap. 12.

21. Ferris, "Ecclesiastical Characteristics of the Reformed Dutch Church," 1848, 5, in *Writings* (bound sermons, addresses, and discourses), Sage Library, New Brunswick Theological Seminary; hereafter Sage, NBTS.

22. Romeyn, in *CI,* July 11, 1840.

23. Corwin, *Digest,* 662.

24. *The Sunday School Teacher's Companion* (New York, 1834), 172–173. This is a compilation of advice articles reprinted from various publications.

25. *CI,* September 13, 1860.

26. *CI,* January 25, 1840. See also Corwin, *Digest,* 785–786.

27. *CI,* October 31, 1835.

28. James D. Bratt, *Dutch Calvinism in Modern America: A History of a Conservative Subculture* (Grand Rapids, Mich., 1984).

29. Foster, *An Errand of Mercy,* 148.

30. *CI,* May 24, 1860. Andrew Reed and James Matheson, *A Narrative of the Visit to the American Churches by the Deputation from the Congregational Union of England and Wales* (New York, 1835), letter 4, 596–598, reprinted in *The Christian Library* (New York, 1846), vol. 1.

31. Paul Van Cleef, Diary, Sage, NBTS; *CI,* May 1, 1845.

32. *CI,* May 24, 1860.

33. *CI,* May 2, May 16, May 23, May 30, June 6, June 13, 1850.

34. Charles D. Deshler, Manuscripts, typed version, "Choirs," Book Twelve, 2, Sp. Cols., RUL.

35. Ibid., 3.

36. Ibid., 4; *CI,* August, 7, 1830.

37. Deshler, Manuscripts, typed version, "Choirs," Book Twelve, 4. Deshler was speaking of the 1820s and 1830s.

38. Van Cleef, Diary, November 29, 1839; Baldwin, Diary, May 3, 1840.

39. *CI,* November 8, 1855.

40. *CI,* May 26, 1870; T. De Witt Talmage, *Around the Tea-table* (Philadelphia, 1875), 140, 141.

41. *CI,* December 1, 1870; W.H.S. Demarest, "Some Incidents in New Brunswick Church History," *New Brunswick Seminary Bulletin* 6 (June 1931), 35.

42. Deshler, Manuscripts, typed version, "Choirs," Book Twelve, 4.

43. D. Buddingh, Voorede (Foreword), "De School, in de Vereenigde Staten van Noord-Amerika," *De Kerk, School en Wetenschap in de Vereenigde Staten van Noord-Amerika,* 2 vols. (Utrecht, 1852), 2: xi. *Forty Years' Familiar Letters of James W. Alexander, D.D.,* 2 vols. (New York, 1860), 2:334, 336.

44. Among these were *The History of America, Abridged for the Use of Children of All Denominations* (1795); Charles A. Goodrich, *History of the United States of America* (1823); and Emma Willard, *History of the United States or Republic of America: Exhibited in Connexion with Its Chronology & Progressive Geography: By Means of a Series of Maps* (1828).

45. Oliver Rink, "The People of New Netherland: Notes on Non-English Immigration to New York in the Seventeenth Century," *New York History*, 62 (January 1981): 41; Adrian C. Leiby, *The Revolutionary War in the Hackensack Valley: The Jersey Dutch and the Neutral Ground, 1775–1783* (New Brunswick, N.J., 1962), viii; John Pershing Luidens, "The Americanization of the Dutch Reformed Church" (diss., University of Oklahoma, 1969), chap. 4; *CI,* January 10, 1856.

46. Washington Irving, "The Author's Apology," *The Works of Washington Irving,* vol. 1, *Knickerbocker's New York,* rev. ed. (New York, 1864), 11–14; Teunis Bergen, Netherlands Society of Philadelphia, Annual Banquet, January 23, 1896, in W. E. Griffis, *Holland and America Pamphlets,* III, 15, bound, Sp. Cols., RUL. The *Oxford English Dictionary* identifies a butter-box as a contemptuous reference to a Dutchman.

47. For this and the following paragraph, see *CI,* November 4, 1875.

48. For background on the impact of Dutch political ideas (as expressed in the Union of Utrecht of 1579) on the Albany Plan of Union, the Continental Congresses, and the Articles of Confederation, and Benjamin Franklin's role in transmitting them, see James R. Tanis, "The Dutch-American Connection: The Impact of the Dutch Example on American Constitutional Beginnings," in *New York and the Union: Contributions to the American Constitutional Experience,* ed. Stephen L. Schechter and Richard B. Bernstein (Albany, N.Y., 1990), 22–28; and James R. Tanis, "The American Dutch, Their Church, and the Revolution," in *A Bilateral Bicentennial: A History of Dutch-American Relations, 1782–1982,* ed. J. W. Schulte Nordholt and Robert P. Swierenga (New York and Amsterdam, 1982), 115–126.

    Even less noticed is the Dutch Act of Abjuration of July 26, 1581, as a model for the Declaration of Independence. See Stephen E. Lucas, "The *Plakkaat van Verlatinge*: A Neglected Model for the American Declaration of Independence," in *Connecting Cultures: The Netherlands in Five Centuries of Transatlantic Exchange,* ed. Rosemarijn Hoefte and Johanna C. Kardux (Amsterdam, 1994), 187–207.

49. *Magazine,* 1 (April 1826):1, 29–32.

50. William Craig Brownlee, *Lights and Shadows of Christian Life: Designed for the Instruction of the Young* (New York, 1837), 26.

51. *CI,* July 22, 1845.

52. Brownlee, *Lights and Shadows,* 28.


CHAPTER 5    *Pulpit and Pew: A Portrait*

1. Computed from Edward T. Corwin, *A Manual of the Reformed Church in America, 1628–1902,* 4th ed. (New York, 1902).

2. The Rev. Walter Monteath to his parents, Gansevoort-Lansing Collection, New York Public Library, Box 185, Folder 11, November 20, 1826.

3. The charge was to the Reverend Henry Heermance, when he became pastor of the Blawenburgh Reformed Church in 1832. See John A. Todd, *Memoir of the Rev. Peter Labagh, D.D., with Notices of the History of the Reformed Protestant Dutch Church in North America* (New York, 1860), 170–177. The minister's qualifications, graces, gifts, and duties as interpreted by the Reformed Church are most fully set out by James

Spencer Cannon, *Lectures in Pastoral Theology* (New York, 1853). There are 36 lectures in all, covering everything from the minister's call to his various trials.

4. Nicholas J. Marselus, "The Gospel Ministry and Its Results: A Sermon Delivered in the Reformed Dutch Church, Corner of Bleeker and Amos Streets, in the City of New-York, on the 3d of April, 1842" (New York, 1843), 25, 31, Imprint A842.M364, Box 108, Special Collections, Alexander Library, Rutgers University; hereafter Sp. Cols., RUL.

5. Benjamin C. Taylor, "A Journal of Public Religious Services Performed by B. C. Taylor," 4 vols. (1838, 1846, 1861, 1879), Sage Library, New Brunswick Theological Seminary, hereafter Sage, NBTS; Gabriel Ludlow, "Fifty Years of Pastoral Work: A Sermon Preached in the Reformed Church, Neshanic, N.J., September 5, 1871, on the Fiftieth Anniversary of His Ordination" (New Brunswick, N.J., 1871), 43, 27.

6. "A Minister's Multifarious Duties," *CI,* January 20, 1870; *CI,* June 14, 1855.

7. *CI,* March 22, 1860.

8. *CI,* March 21, 1835; *CI,* January 26, 1865; T. S. Doolittle, Scrapbook, Sage, NBTS; Schenck Family Papers, Sp. Cols., RUL.

9. See Barbara Welter, "The Feminization of Religion in Nineteenth-Century America," in *Dimity Convictions: The American Woman in the Nineteenth Century* (Athens, Ohio, 1976); Nancy F. Cott, *The Bonds of Womanhood: Woman's Sphere in New England, 1780–1835* (New Haven, Conn., 1976); Ann Douglas, *The Feminization of American Culture* (New York, 1977); and David S. Reynolds, "The Feminization Controversy: Sexual Stereotypes and the Paradoxes of Piety in Nineteenth-Century America," *New England Quarterly* 53 (March 1980):96–106, for various views on this topic. Reynolds's is the most appealing. Discussion of nineteenth-century American religion, he says, is "distorted when based on a single sexual stereotype. In its endorsement of reform, perfectibility, and soldierly endeavor, religion of the period tended to be 'masculine' or 'feminist.' In its advocacy of benevolence and emotion it tended to be 'feminine.'" Reynolds, "Feminization," 101.

10. Corwin, *Manual,* 291–934.

11. S.L.B. Baldwin, Diary, January 27, 1836, Sp. Cols., RUL. He was referring to the Reverend Charles Whitehead. The original manuscript of Baldwin's Diary has been lost, but was reprinted in the *Unionist Gazette* (Somerville, N.J., 1897).

12. Todd, *Memoir of the Rev. Peter Labagh,* 107.

13. W. B. Van Benschoten, "A Historical Discourse on the Churches of Ponds and Wyckoff, Delivered Dec. 25, 1868," in *Bergen County Democrat* (Hackensack, N.J.), March 12, 1869, 1, 4.

14. For a full account, see James W. Van Hoeven, "Dort and Albany: Reformed Theology Engages a New Culture," in *Word and World: Reformed Theology in America*, ed. James Van Hoeven (Grand Rapids, Mich., 1986). The quoted passage is from David G. Hackett, *The Rude Hand of Innovation: Religion and Social Order in Albany, New York, 1652–1836* (New York, 1991), 78. See also Whitney R. Cross, *The Burned-Over District: The Social and Intellectual History of Enthusiastic Religion in Western New York, 1800–1850* (Ithaca, N.Y., 1950); and James D. Folts, "The Fanatic and the Prophetess: Religious Perfectionism in Western New York, 1835–1839," *New York History* 72 (October 1991):357–387.

15. Van Hoeven, "Dort and Albany," 21.

16. See Adrian C. Leiby, *The Revolutionary War in the Hackensack Valley: The Jersey Dutch and the Neutral Ground, 1775–1783* (New Brunswick, N.J., 1962), and

Frederick W. Bogert, *The Revolutionary Years, 1776–1783*, vol. 3 in *Bergen County, New Jersey, History and Heritage*, 7 vols. (n.p., 1983).

17. Constitution of 1833, Article III, Chapter II, "Of Ecclesiastical Assemblies," in Edward T. Corwin, ed., *A Digest of the Constitutional and Synodical Legislation of the Reformed Church in America* (New York, 1906). The classis reports referred to in this chapter may be found in the particular year's volume in *Acts and Proceedings of the General Synod of the Reformed Church in America* (New York, annually).

18. See Allan J. Janssen, *Gathered at Albany* (Grand Rapids, Mich., 1995), for the history of a particular classis.

19. Constitution of 1833, Article III, section 73, Corwin, *Digest*, lv.

20. Again, excluding the classes outside of New York and New Jersey—those in Illinois, Michigan, Wisconsin, and Arcot in India.

21. Daniel J. Meeter, *Meeting Each Other in Doctrine, Liturgy, and Government: The Bicentennial of the Celebration of the Constitution of the Reformed Church in America* (Grand Rapids, Mich., 1993), 83. See also Daniel J. Meeter, "The 'North American Liturgy': A Critical Edition of the Liturgy of the Reformed Dutch Church in North America, 1793" (diss., Drew University, 1989).

22. Constitution of 1793, Article 32, in Corwin, *Digest*, xxxviii. See also Howard G. Hageman, *Pulpit and Table: Some Chapters in the History of Worship in the Reformed Churches* (Richmond, Va., 1962).

23. Today, the liturgy in use in the denomination removes this language, the explanation being that the part of the form that encourages self-examination can be read at a service of preparation: "The Supper is not the place for an exposition of the whole Christian faith. . . . We can assume that because of [their] Reformed catechetical training, those who come to the Lord's Supper will be well grounded in Christian doctrine. [That is, will know that they are obliged to have examined their sins beforehand and to have asked forgiveness.] At this time and place the didactic ought not to dominate the devotional." Howard G. Hageman, "The Order for the Sacrament of the Lord's Supper," in *A Companion to the Liturgy: A Guide to Worship in the Reformed Church in America*, ed. Garrett C. Roorda (New York, 1971), 37.

24. Corwin, *Digest*, 369–378.

25. *CI,* July 16, 1831.

26. T. De Witt Talmage, *Around the Tea-table* (Philadelphia, 1875), 198, 426, 428.

27. Talmage, *Tea-table*, 198, 416, 428.

28. Baldwin, Diary, June 16, 1844.

29. Mary Van Dyke, Diary, December 23, 1849, and March 17, 1850, Sp. Cols., RUL.

30. Paul Van Cleef, Diary, July 26, 1840, Sage, NBTS; Garrett Schenck, Diary, November 12, 1850, and January 26, 1851, Schenck Family Papers, Sp. Cols., RUL.

31. July 19, 1841, Folder 4, Hardenbergh Family Papers, Sp. Cols., RUL.

32. Maria Ferdon, Diaries, 5 vols., Bergen County Historical Society, passim.

33. James Romeyn, "The Crisis, and Its Claims upon the Church of God" (New York, 1842), 43, Imprint A842.R764, Box 108, Sp. Cols., RUL.

34. Ibid., 44, 45.

35. Ibid., 9, 12, 14, 15.

36. *CI,* July 4, 1840.

37. *CI,* August 15, 1835.

38. [Thomas De Witt], *Memorials of Rev. Thomas De Witt, D.D.* (New York, 1875), 110; *CI,* November 16, 1865.

39. [Sabbath Schools of the Second Reformed Dutch Church, Philadelphia], *Our Sabbath School Messenger*, ed. George H. Hartman and William E. Griffis, vol. 1, no. 1 (January 1865):41. Griffis Collection, Sp. Cols., RUL. After one year, this monthly publication ceased.

40. Talmage, *Tea-table,* 152–157 passim.

41. Ibid., 240.

42. John W. Beardslee III, "Orthodoxy and Piety: Two Styles of Faith in the Colonial Period," in *Word and World,* ed. Van Hoeven, 6.

43. E. T. Corwin et al., *A History of the Reformed Church, Dutch, the Reformed Church, German, and the Moravian Church in the United States* (New York, 1895), 136.

44. Baldwin, Diary, October [n.d.], 1836, and April 25, 1837; and Baldwin, Diary, October 16, 1841.

45. *CI,* December 11, 1845.

46. Talmage, *Tea-table,* 73–74.

47. Baldwin, Diary, August 30, 1842 (he was referring to Talbot Chambers); and *CI,* September 29, 1870.

48. William B. Sprague, "An Address Delivered in the Middle Dutch Church, Albany, at the Funeral of Mrs. Jane Wyckoff, Wife of the Reverend I. N. Wyckoff, D.D., Monday, January 31, 1847" (Albany, N.Y., 1848), 6, Imprint A848.S766, Box 126, Sp. Cols., RUL; I. N. Wyckoff, Pruyn Family Papers, DO584, Folder 3, Albany Institute of History and Art; and the Reverend Peter Stryker, *CI,* April 12, 1855.

CHAPTER 6    *A Good Year in Zion*

1. See Firth Haring Fabend, *A Dutch Family in the Middle Colonies* (New Brunswick, N.J., 1991), chap. 2.

2. Cornelius C. Vermeule, AC no. 1879, Special Collections, Alexander Library, Rutgers University; hereafter Sp. Cols., RUL.

3. Adriance Van Brunt, Diary and Journal Kept on His Farm near Brooklyn, N.Y., 1828 June 8–1830 March 20, Mss. Room, New York Public Library; and Teunis G. Bergen, *Genealogy of the Van Brunt Family* (Albany, N.Y., 1867). For background on the origins of recreational pastimes in the Netherlands, see P. M. Hough, *Dutch Life in Town and Country* (New York, 1902); D. S. Meldrum, *Home Life in Holland* (New York, 1911); Paul Zumthor, *Daily Life in Rembrandt's Holland* (New York, 1963); Simon Schama, *The Embarrassment of Riches: An Interpretation of Dutch Culture in the Golden Age* (New York, 1987); and A. Th. Van Deursen, *Private Lives in a Golden Age: Popular Culture, Religion, and Society in Seventeenth-Century Holland,* trans. Maarten Ultee (Cambridge, 1991).

4. Margaret Schenck, Diary, uncatalogued Nevius-Schenck Papers, Sp. Cols., RUL.

5. John S. Nevius, Jr., Diary, 1869, Schenck Family Papers, Sp. Cols., RUL; Benjamin Smith to John S. Nevius, Jr., November 18, 1862, Box 7, Folder 109, Schenck Family Papers, Sp. Cols., RUL.

6. T. L. Cuyler, *The Christian Intelligencer*, July 19, 1855; hereafter *CI.*

7. *CI,* December 25, 1830.

8. *CI,* December 25, 1856.

9. S.L.B. Baldwin, Diary, reprinted in the *Unionist Gazette* (Somerville, N.J., 1897), December 25, 1842, Sp. Cols., RUL.

10. Baldwin, Diary, December 25, 1844.

11. Gansevoort-Lansing Collection, Box 183, Folder 1, January 17, 1851, Mss. Room, New York Public Library; hereafter G-L Coll.
12. *CI,* January 10, 1856.
13. *CI,* January 3, 1861.
14. Catherine Low Hardenbergh, Diary, December 25, 1869, Sp. Cols., RUL.
15. *CI,* January 7, 1875.
16. *CI,* December 23, 1875; *CI,* December 21, 1876.
17. Charles W. Jones, *St. Nicholas of Myra, Bari, and Manhattan: Biography of a Legend* (Chicago, 1978), 327, 333. A few references to him have surfaced, including listings in colonial almanacs and references to St. Nicholas cakes. David Steven Cohen, *The Dutch-American Farm* (New York, 1992), 163, and Field Horne, "Winter Holidays," Sleepy Hollow Restorations Research Report no. 23, November 12, 1976, n.p. There appears to have been a St. Nicholas society in New York in the 1760s (not connected to the present society of the same name).
18. Jones, *St. Nicholas of Myra,* 340–341, 63, 344–345; Stephen Nissenbaum, *The Battle for Christmas* (New York, 1997).
19. Paul Van Cleef, Diary, Gardner Sage Library, New Brunswick Theological Seminary, May 14, 1841; hereafter Sage, NBTS.
20. *CI,* July 4, 1840.
21. *CI,* July 19, 1860.
22. *CI,* July 3, 1845.
23. Margaret S. Nevius, Diary, July 4, 1844, uncatalogued Nevius-Schenck Papers, Sp. Cols., RUL.
24. *CI,* June 7, 1855.
25. *CI,* September 30, 1875.
26. T. De Witt Talmage, *Around the Tea-table* (Philadelphia, 1875), 286.
27. *CI,* July 31, 1845.
28. *CI,* August 16, August 23, 1855.
29. *CI,* July 7, 1870.
30. *CI,* June 2, 1870 (advertisement). Summer holidays were not without peril. The Reverend John A. Todd and Mrs. Todd of the Reformed Dutch Church in Tarrytown, New York, and a party stopping at the Occan House, Cape May, hired a vehicle for a pleasure ride in the summer of 1865. While crossing a stream about 40 feet wide, the wooden bridge collapsed, precipitating horses, carriage, and party into the oozy mud below.
31. Effie Matilda Blauvelt, Diary, August 11, 1888, Historical Society of Rockland County. See also the Diary of Julia Ann Schureman, Sp. Cols., RUL, who on her travels by steamboat in the summer of 1828 renewed the bonds of friendship with the Bleecker, Boice, Condict, Dey, Fonda, Gansevoort, Hendricks, Ludlow, Van Orden, Van Rensselear, Van Veeten, Van Vranken, Vermilyea, Wyckoff, and Yates families—most or all of New Netherland origin.
32. *CI,* August 31, 1865; Henry Gansevoort to Susan Lansing Gansevoort, August 15, 1853, G-L Coll., Box 154, Folder 1; *CI,* September 20, 1855; Elbert Herring to Dr. Peter E. Elmendorf, August 23, 1865, Cherry Hill Papers, Series 4, Subseries .1, Box 37, Folder 3, New York State Library, Albany, N.Y..
33. Firth Haring Fabend, "Life On and Off the Farm: Diaries of Helen Verbryck Clark, 1876 and 1877," *South of the Mountains* (Historical Society of Rockland County), 36 (October–December, 1992):11.

34. John T. Cunningham, *Railroading in New Jersey* (Associated Railroads of New Jersey, n.d.), passim.
35. John Scott, "Excerpts from the Diaries of Effie Matilda Blauvelt," *South of the Mountains* (Historical Society of Rockland County), 28 (July–September 1984):10; Fabend, "Life On and Off the Farm"; and Maria Ferdon, Diaries, 5 vols., Bergen County Historical Society, passim.
36. Margaret Schenck Nevius, Diary, 1866, uncatalogued Nevius-Schenck Papers, Sp. Cols., RUL.
37. All references to and quotations from the diary are from Volume 1 (of 18), Sp. Cols., RUL, Ac. no. 2703. For courting in general in this era, see Ellen K. Rothman, *Hands and Hearts: A History of Courtship in America* (New York, 1984).
38. Van Deursen, *Plain Lives,* 90–92.
39. James Demarest, June 30, 1855, "Letters . . . While at NBTS," Archives, Sage, NBTS.
40. Adriance Van Brunt, Diary, October 2, and October 23, 1828.
41. "The Awful Use," *CI,* May 26, 1870, reprinted from the *Christian Secretary.*
42. *CI,* January 10, 1850.
43. Diary, Garret C. Schenck, January 2, 1851, Schenck Papers, Sp. Cols., RUL.
44. Diary, Garretson Hageman, January 1, 1870, Sp. Cols., RUL.
45. Anna Lansing to brother Abraham Lansing, October 25, 1853, Box 183, Folder 1, G-L Coll.
46. Cherry Hill Papers, Series 4, Subseries .1, Box 39, Folder 16, New York State Library, Albany, N.Y.
47. Alice Nevius to brother John, November 23, 1863, Box 8, Schenck Family Papers, Sp. Cols., RUL.
48. Hageman, Diary, 1870, Sp. Cols., RUL.
49. Baldwin, Diary, October 23, 1844; May 2, 1845; Schenck Family Papers, December 18, 1863, Box 8, Sp. Cols., RUL.
50. *The Oxford English Dictionary* documents the etymological connection.
51. Cherry Hill Papers, Series e, subseries .1, Box 41, Folder 3. Bergen, Cuyler, Gansevoort, Herring, Kipp, Lansing, Pruyn, Sanders, Schemerhorn, Schuyler, Ten Broeck, Ten Eyck, Vanderbergh, Vanderpoel, Van Santvoort, Van Vechten, and Vroom are some of the names.
52. *CI,* January 13, 1870.
53. *CI,* June 2, 1870. *Juffrow* is the Dutch term for wife.
54. *The Democratic Republican Weekly New Era*, November 18, 1839.
55. Baldwin, Diary, August 30–September 2, 1842.
56. *CI,* November 21, 1850.
57. *CI,* May 2, 1850.
58. *CI,* September 20, 1855.
59. *CI,* February 15, 1855; May 31, 1860.
60. Van Deursen, *Plain Lives,* p. 87.
61. *CI,* June 21, 1855.
62. B. C. Taylor, Diary, 1841, Archives, Sage, NBTS.

CHAPTER 7    *The Family: A Nursery of Godliness*

1. "The Young Singer's Friend; or the Lee Avenue Collection of Hymns and Songs, Sacred and Secular, Suitable for Sabbath-Schools, Social Circles, Children's Meetings,

Concerts, Anniversaries, etc., Compiled by the Superintendent of the Lee Avenue Reformed Dutch Church, Brooklyn, N.Y." (New York, 1858).

2. John W. Nevins's *History and Genius of the Heidelberg Catechism* (Chambersburg, Pa., 1847) provides a succinct appreciation of the catechism. The quoted passages are found on pp. 157 and 160 in a discussion of the rights of children to a Christian education.

3. John Knox, "Parental Responsibility and Parental Solicitude; Two Discourses, Delivered in the Middle Dutch Church" (New York, 1834), 16, 8–17.

4. Knox, "Parental Responsibility," 16; and Reformed Protestant Dutch Church, *Tracts*, 2 vols. (New York, 1858), vol. 1, no. 12, 4.

5. Quoted material in this and the following paragraphs are from Gilbert R. Livingston, "Family Worship, a Sermon," *Columbia and Greene County Preacher, Comprising Sermons on Various Important Subjects, by Different Ministers of the Gospel* (Hudson, N.Y., 1825), 263–265.

6. Reformed Protestant Dutch Church, *Tracts,* vol. 1, no. 12, 1–4; James Romeyn, "The Crisis and Its Claims upon the Church of God" (New York, 1842), 39–40.

7. Isaac Ferris, "Domestic Christian Education: A Sermon" (Albany, N.Y., 1835), Imprint A835.F394, Box 91, Sp. Cols., RUL, 21, 25. Ferris founded the Rutgers Female Institute in New York City and later became the first chancellor of the University of the City of New York (New York University today).

8. Romeyn, "Crisis," 40.

9. Livingston, "Family Worship," 272, 275.

10. Chambers, *The Christian Intelligencer,* March 31, 1870; hereafter *CI.*

11. John S. C. Abbott, *The Mother at Home; or, The Principles of Maternal Duty Familiarly Illustrated* (New York, 1833), 160–161.

12. *CI,* July 11, 1850.

13. *CI,* April 3, 1845.

14. Abbott, *Mother at Home,* 38.

15. Ibid., 25

16. Reformed Protestant Dutch Church, *Tracts*, vol. 1, no. 12, 2–3.

17. Ferris, "Domestic Christian Education," 26–28.

18. *CI,* October 5, 1865.

19. William G. McLoughlin, "Evangelical Child-Rearing in the Age of Jackson: Francis Wayland's View of When and How to Subdue the Willfulness of Children," *Journal of Social History* 9 (1975):21–43; Abbott, *Mother at Home,* 43–44. It is also probable that some children were damaged forever by such treatment. See Philip Greven, *The Protestant Temperament: Patterns of Child-Rearing, Religious Experience, and the Self in Early America* (Ithaca, N.Y., 1977), and Greven, "The Self Shaped and Misshaped: *The Protestant Temperament* Reconsidered," in *Through a Glass Darkly: Reflections on Personal Identity in Early America,* ed. Ronald Hoffman, Mechal Sobel, and Fredrika J. Teute (Chapel Hill, N.C., 1997), 348–369.

20. The same is true of the American Sunday School Union, whose board of directors included members of all the evangelical denominations. Even one dissenting voice would halt the publication of any work considered. Edwin W. Rice, *The Sunday-School Movement and the American Sunday-School Union,* 2d ed. (Philadelphia, 1917), 143.

21. Abbott, *Mother at Home,* 28, 37.

22. Ibid., 38–40, 57.

23. Ibid., 61–62; *CI,* November 28, 1840, and March 31, 1870.

24. Abbott, *Mother at Home,* 61, 47–48.
25. Ibid., 109.
26. Ibid., 113–116; *CI,* Parents and Children column, May 8, 1845.
27. Abbott, *Mother at Home,* 123–125.
28. Ibid., 125–138.
29. John Scudder, *An Appeal to Christian Mothers, in Behalf of the Heathen* (New York, 1844), 6–8.
30. Ibid., 14, 63.
31. *CI,* May 2, 1835; August 11, 1870.
32. Scudder, *Appeal,* 52–54. The idea that spiritual growth should start in the nursery is basic to Reformed doctrine and theology. Scudder's own *Letters to Sabbath-school Children on the Condition of the Heathen, Voice from the East,* and *Grand Papa's Talk with His Little Mary* perfectly fit these descriptions of preferred reading and were all best-sellers.
33. Scudder, *Appeal,* 64.
34. "Calvinism traces salvation to the eternal purpose of God, and confines it to the elect; Methodism makes it dependent on man's free acceptance of that grace which is offered alike to all and on the same terms. Calvinism emphasizes the divine side, Methodism the human. Herein Methodism entirely agrees with Arminianism, and is even more emphatically opposed to the doctrines of absolute predestination, limited atonement, and the perseverance of saints than Arminius was, who left the last point undecided." Philip Schaff, *The Creeds of Christendom, with a History and Critical Notes,* 3 vols. (New York, 1884), 1:895.
35. Samuel B. How Papers, Box 6, August 4, 1861, Special Collections, Alexander Library, Rutgers University; hereafter Sp. Cols., RUL.
36. *CI,* November 3, 1870.
37. Gansevoort-Lansing Collection, Box 177, Folder 10, March 12, 1844, Mss. Room, New York Public Library.
38. Schenck Family Papers, May 30, 1864, Sp. Cols., RUL.
39. Maria Ferdon, Diaries, 5 vols., Bergen County Historical Society, passim; Cornelius C. Vermeule Papers, Box 4, correspondence folder, Sp. Cols., RUL.
40. T. De Witt Talmage, *Around the Tea-table* (Philadelphia, 1875), 440–441.
41. Chamberlain Family Papers, MG 1228, March 22, 1857, New Jersey Historical Society. Jacob became a Reformed Dutch missionary. The Rutgers student wrote "Mother's Influence," an article in *Our Sabbath School Messenger,* a monthly publication of the Second Reformed Dutch Church in Philadelphia, ed. George H. Hartman and William E. Griffis, vol. 1, no. 1 (1865):98. Griffis Collection, Sp. Cols., RUL. Though the article is signed only with the initials JGVS, the editor, William E. Griffis, identified the author as J. G. Van Slyke in his copy.
42. Talbot W. Chambers, *Memoir of the Life and Character of the Late Hon. Theodore Frelinghuysen, LLD.* (New York, 1862), 129. For a biographical treatment of Mrs. Hardenbergh, see Johan H. van de Bank, *De leiding van des Heeren liefde met Dina van den Bergh* (Den Hertog B.V.-Houten, 1994).
43. John Todd, *Lectures to Children, Familiarly Illustrating Important Truth . . . ,* 2d ed. (Northampton, Mass., 1834), preface, 5. Todd is not to be confused with his contemporary, the Reformed minister John A. Todd.
44. John Scudder, *Letters to Sabbath-School Children on the Condition of the Heathen* (Philadelphia, 1843), 31, 12, 32. This publication was commissioned by the American Sunday School Union.

45. *CI,* May 21, 1842.
46. Henry Clay Trumbull, *Children in the Temple; a Hand-book for the Sunday School Concert* (Springfield, Mass., 1869), 332.
47. [Sabbath Schools of the Second Reformed Dutch Church, Philadelphia], *Our Sabbath School Messenger,* ed. George H. Hartman and William E. Griffis, vol. 1, no. 1 (January 1865):40. Griffis Collection, Sp. Cols., RUL. After one year, this monthly publication ceased.
48. William C. Brownlee, *Lights and Shadows of Christian Life: Designed for the Instruction of the Young* (New York, 1837), 321. The happy-death theme was the basis for a genre of literature well known in England and elsewhere in Europe in the eighteenth and nineteenth centuries.
49. *CI,* January 15, 1842, 104.
50. [Thomas De Witt], *Memorials of Rev. Thomas De Witt, D.D.* (New York, 1875), 14–15.
51. *CI,* February 12, 1842.
52. *CI,* April 9, 1842.
53. *CI,* April 30, 1842.
54. *CI,* February 19, 1942.
55. Knox, "Parental Solicitude," 28, 33.
56. Douw Van Olinda, "Lecture," December 6, 1835, Douw Van Olinda Papers, CC 8814, Box 1, New York State Library, Albany, N.Y.
57. *The Sunday School Teacher's Companion* (New York, 1834), 10–22; Scudder, *Letters,* 51–52.
58. *Teacher's Companion,* 27–28.
59. Ibid., 33.
60. Ibid., 41, 42–43, 52.
61. Ibid., 52, 53, 57.
62. Ibid., 86–87, 114, 120.
63. Ibid., 126, 127, 128.
64. Ibid., 132.
65. Ibid., 50, 19, 20.
66. William Bogert, Diary, September 1861, Sp. Cols., RUL.
67. S.L.B. Baldwin, Diary, October 30, 1842, Sp. Cols., RUL.
68. *CI,* April 19, 1855; September 27, 1855.
69. *CI,* January 25, 1840.
70. *Teacher's Companion,* 146, 155–156, 147–150.
71. Bethune, *CI,* January 10, 1850; Talmage, *Around the Tea-table,* 340–341.
72. *Brief History of the Lee Avenue Reformed Dutch Church and Sabbath-School, Brooklyn* (New York, 1858), 425–426.
73. *CI,* October 20, 1870.
74. What follows is found in *Our Sabbath School Messenger,* 25–32.
75. *CI,* March 31, 1870.
76. *CI,* October 5, 1865. It was the object of the mission at 10 Bible House, De Witt wrote, by systematic visitation, mission stations, Sabbath schools, and tenant-house prayer-meetings "to bring the whole population under the influence of divine truth."
77. Thomas De Witt Talmage, "Ragamuffins," in *Around the Tea-table,* 495–496.
78. Edward T. Corwin, *A Manual of the Reformed Church in America, 1628 1902,* 4th ed. (New York, 1902), 771–772; Talmage, "Ragamuffins," 499–500.

CHAPTER 8    **The World: "Living Only to Be Useful"**

1. For background, see Diane Ravitch, *The Great School Wars, New York City, 1805–1873: A History of the Public Schools as a Battlefield of Social Change* (New York, 1974).
2. Cornelius C. Vanarsdalen, "The Christian Patriot: An Oration before the Alumni of Rutger's [*sic*] College; Pronounced in the College Chapel, at New Brunswick, N.J., . . . July 18, 1837" (Hartford, 1837), 30.
3. *The Christian Intelligencer,* February 28, 1835; hereafter, *CI.*
4. *CI,* March 29, 1855.
5. *CI,* August 16, 1855.
6. Among girls' schools advertising in the *Intelligencer* in just the summer of 1860, for instance, were the Misses Havens' Boarding and Day School and the Misses Bucknalls' Boarding and Day School in Manhattan, Miss A. Van Wagenen's Boarding and Day School on West 33rd Street, the Misses Taylors' School for Young Ladies at 102 Waverly Place, Miss Forbes's School at 22 North Moore Street, Professor Metcalfe's Ladies' Seminary in Brooklyn, Greenleaf Female Institute in Brooklyn Heights, Miss Clark's Boarding and Day School for Young Ladies in Brooklyn, Madame Burkhardt's English and French Boarding and Day School, Miss Hoyt's Boarding and Day School in New Brunswick, Maple Hall Boarding School for Young Ladies in Jamaica, the Poughkeepsie Female Academy, and the Poughkeepsie Female Collegiate Institute. Five years later, in August and September 1865, many of these schools survived, and many new ones had appeared: Miss Haven's French and English Boarding and Day School for Young Ladies and Mlle. de Janon's English and French Boarding and Day School for Young Ladies and Children in New York City, the Cottage Hill Seminary for Young Ladies and Vassar Female College in Poughkeepsie, Elmira Female College in Elmira, New York, and the Somerset Young Ladies Academy in Somerville, New Jersey.
7. *CI,* August 18, 1870.
8. For this and the following paragraph, see *CI,* February 8, 1855.
9. "The curse of our American society is that our young women are taught that the first . . . [and last] thing in their life is to get somebody to take care of them. Instead of that, the first lesson should be, how, under God, they may take care of themselves." Thomas De Witt Talmage, *Abominations of Modern Society* (New York, 1872), 96.
10. In September 1855, during the Crimean War, the fortress city of Sebastopol was abandoned by the Russians to the British, French, and Turks, who had besieged it for eleven months. When H.E.B. wrote this in February of that year the city was still being defended.
11. *CI,* April 26, 1855.
12. *CI,* November 24, December 1, December 8, 1870. The historiography of the Reformed Church in America has had little to say about the role of women in this denomination, until the publication in 1999, in the denomination's Historical Series, of Renée S. House and John W. Coakley, eds., *Patterns and Portraits: Women in the History of the Reformed Church in America* (Grand Rapids, Mich., 1999).
13. *CI,* March 3, 1870; June 23, 1870.
14. See Barbara Welter, "The Cult of True Womanhood," in *Dimity Convictions: The American Woman in the Nineteenth Century* (Athens, Ohio, 1976); Theodore B. Romeyn, *Historical Discourse Delivered on the Occasion of the Re-Opening and Dedication of the First Reformed (Dutch) Church at Hackensack, N.J., May 2, 1869* (New York, 1870), 98.

15. *CI*, March 24, 1870. Even though Sarah Chamberlain had not herself been raised in the Reformed culture, she kept her own name after her marriage to a man who had been, as it was the ancient custom of Dutch women to do.

16. *CI*, December 1, 1870.

17. George R. Williamson, *Memoir of the Rev. David Abeel, D.D., Late Missionary to China* (New York, 1848). The usual practice was for missionaries to learn the native languages, and teach in them, while also attempting to teach the English language to the natives. Besides fields in China and India, the Reformed Church established a third important foreign mission in Arabia in 1889. See Lewis R. Scudder III, *The Arabian Mission's Story: In Search of Abraham's Other Son* (Grand Rapids, Mich., 1998). For China, see Gerald F. De Jong, *The Reformed Church in China, 1842–1951* (Grand Rapids, Mich., 1992).

18. *CI*, February 14, 1850.

19. *CI*, January 24, 1850.

20. *CI*, January 24, 1835.

21. Paul Van Cleef, Diary, May 13, 1841, Archives, Gardner A. Sage Library, New Brunswick Theological Seminary, New Brunswick, N.J.; hereafter Sage, NBTS.

22. See Leonard I. Sweet, *The Minister's Wife: Her Role in Nineteenth-Century American Evangelicalism* (Philadelphia, 1983). The quoted phrase is on pp. 148–149.

23. Minutes, Dorcas and Day Nursery Society Records, Ac. 208, Book I, 1813–1838, Special Collections, Alexander Library, Rutgers University; hereafter Sp. Col., RUL.

24. *CI*, December 18, 1845.

25. Mrs. Ricord earlier in her career had served as the principal of the Geneva, N.Y., Female Seminary, written an "able work," *Mental Philosophy*, and abounded in general charities, according to her obituary. *CI*, November 2, 1865.

26. Minute Book, Newark Orphan Asylum Association, Ms. Group 1087, New Jersey Historical Society.

27. Cornelia R. Abeel, Ms. Group 1008, New Jersey Historical Society.

28. Mrs. Joanna Bethune, *Memoirs* (New York, 1863), 243; and Gansevoort-Lansing Collection, Box 285, Folder 11, February 28, 1828, Mss. Division, New York Public Library.

29. Maria Ferdon, Diaries, 5 vols., Bergen County Historical Society.

30. Hardenbergh Family Papers, Folder 4, April 17, 1831, and Folder 4, February 27, 1832, Sp. Cols., RUL.

31. Talbot W. Chambers, *Memoir of the Life and Character of the Late Honorable Theodore Frelinghuysen, LLD* (New York, 1862), 280; memoir of Maria Frelinghuysen Cornell, 1828, typescript, Sage, NBTS.

32. From Introduction to *The Light of Other Days, Selections from the Writings of the Late Mrs. Jane Kirkpatrick* (New Brunswick, N.J., 1856), n.p.

33. *CI*, March 7, 1840.

34. *CI*, April 4, 1840.

35. *CI*, January 3, 1850.

36. *CI*, July 19, 1855.

37. *CI*, July 26, 1860.

38. *CI*, July 19, 1860. Item reprinted from the *Nashville Christian Advocate*.

39. The Reverend Elbert S. Porter, "The Language of Affliction: A Sermon . . . [on the] Death of Adeline Rider . . . " (Albany, N.Y., 1846), 23, Imprint A846.P844, Box 123, Sp. Cols., RUL.

40. *CI,* September 13, 1855.
41. *CI,* February 18, 1875.
42. De Jong, "The Dutch Reformed Church and Negro Slavery in Colonial America," *Church History* 40 (1971):434. But see Christine Leigh Heyrman, *Southern Cross: The Beginnings of the Bible Belt* (New York, 1997), for a different view: that in the Southern states early Baptist and Methodist ministers challenged slaveholders to free their human labor, until it became clear that they were not winning any converts among white males with this message, but rather were turning them away, at which point they toned down their rhetoric and abandoned this path.
43. The Constitution of 1793 ("Articles Explanatory") appears in Edward T. Corwin, *A Digest of Constitutional and Synodical Legislation of the Reformed Church in America* (New York, 1906), v–lxxxvii, along with the Rules of Church Government of Dort (1619), and the revised Constitutions of 1833 and 1874.
44. De Jong, "The Dutch Reformed Church and Negro Slavery," p. 432. See also John W. Beardslee III, "The Reformed Church in America and the African American Community," *Reformed Review* 46 (Winter 1992):101–118; John A. De Jong, "Social Concerns," in *Piety and Patriotism: Bicentennial Studies of the Reformed Church in America, 1776–1976,* ed. James W. Van Hoeven (Grand Rapids, Mich., 1976), 111–129; and Noel Leo Erskine, *Black People and the Reformed Church in America* (n.p., Reformed Church Press, 1978). Church records indicate, however, that, in New Netherland, black participation in Reformed Church life was fuller than it was to become after the English takeover.
45. David D. Demarest, "Life Recollections . . . written in 1896 at the age of 77 two years before his death," 4–5, typescript, Sp. Cols., RUL.
46. Firth Haring Fabend, Exhibition Script, "Black Roots on a Brooklyn Farm, Lefferts Homestead, 1790–1840," 1988. The original school records can be found in the Brooklyn Historical Society, Brooklyn Heights, New York. The Exhibition Script, along with other material relating to this exhibit, is in the archives of Lefferts Homestead, a historic house owned by the City of New York in Prospect Park, Brooklyn.
47. Quoted in De Jong, "The Dutch Reformed Church and Negro Slavery," 430, 424–425.
48. S.L.B. Baldwin, Diary, November 1, 8, 1842, reprinted in the *Unionist Gazette* (Somerville, N.J.), 1897. (The diary itself has been lost.) Sp. Cols., RUL.
49. Baldwin, ibid.; Van Derveer Papers, May 7, 1853, Ms. Group 481, New Jersey Historical Society.
50. Corwin, *Digest,* 20.
51. John A. Todd, *Memoir of the Rev. Peter Labagh, D.D., with Notices of the History of the Reformed Protestant Dutch Church in North America* (New York, 1860), 137–138; and quoted in Baldwin, Diary, July 4, 1839.
52. Baldwin, Diary, May 14, 1842.
53. Demarest, "Life Recollections," 4, 5.
54. Adriance Van Brunt, Diary, October 1, 1828, Mss. Room, New York Public Library.
55. Catherine Hardenbergh, Diary, May 3, May 16, 1870, Sp. Cols., RUL.
56. Minutes, Board of Health, 1832–1887, Flatbush Town Records, Bundle 4, Roll 17, Municipal Archives, 31 Chambers St., New York, N.Y.
57. Fabend, "Black Roots on a Brooklyn Farm," 20, 21.
58. Minutes, Board of Health, Flatbush, N.Y., 1832.
59. Minutes, *Acts and Proceedings of the General Synod of the Reformed Protestant Dutch*

*Church of North America* (New York, 1855). In 1862, at age fifty-two, Duryee, this "great friend of the colored race" (Corwin, *Manual,* 445), enlisted in the Union Army as a chaplain, served at Hilton Head, South Carolina, and died of his exertions in 1866.

60. Samuel Blanchard How, "Slaveholding Not Sinful. Slavery, the Punishment of Man's Sin, Its Remedy, the Gospel of Christ" (New York, 1856). See also Forrest G. Wood, *The Arrogance of Faith: Christianity and Race in America from the Colonial Era to the Twentieth Century* (New York, 1990), esp. chaps. 1–3.

61. "Calendar," archives of the Collegiate Reformed Protestant Dutch Church, 45 John St., New York, N.Y., typescript, entry 1861–65.

CHAPTER 9    *The Evangelical Way of Death*

1. Abraham Hellenbroek, "A Specimen of Divine Truths for the Instruction of Youth . . ." (New York, 1793; reprt. 1831); Cornelius S. Van Santvoord, "'The Possibility of Dying This Year.' A Discourse Delivered in the Reformed Dutch Church at Saugerties [N.Y.], on Sabbath January 2, 1842" (Kingston, N.Y., 1842).

2. Sarah Mynderse Campbell, Diary, January 8, 1824, New York State Library, Albany, N.Y.; Nicholas J. Marselus, "The Gospel Ministry and Its Results: A Sermon Delivered in the Reformed Dutch Church, Corner of Bleeker and Amos-Streets, in the City of New-York, on the 3d of April, 1842" (New York, 1842), 11, Box 108, Special Collections, Alexander Library, Rutgers University; hereafter Sp. Cols., RUL.

3. *The Christian Intelligencer*, April 18, 1850; hereafter *CI.*

4. *CI,* August 21, 1830.

5. Rev. Aaron Lloyd, Records, 1851–1856, Ms. Group 1045, New Jersey Historical Society.

6. Adriance Van Brunt, Diary and Journal Kept on His Farm near Brooklyn, N.Y., 1828 June 8–1830 March 20, Mss. Room, New York Public Library; Teunis G. Bergen, *Genealogy of the Van Brunt Family* (Albany, N.Y., 1867).

7. John S. C. Abbott, *The Child at Home; or, The Principles of Filial Duty Familiarly Illustrated* (New York, 1833), 146.

8. Ibid., 142. See also David E. Stannard, "Death and the Puritan Child," in *Death in America*, ed., David E. Stannard (Philadelphia, 1975), for attitudes toward children and happy or joyful dying in the seventeenth and eighteenth centuries; and Ann Douglas, "Heaven Our Home: Consolation Literature in the Northern U.S., 1830–1880," in the same volume.

9. Abbott, *Child at Home*, 143–144.

10. Theodore L. Cuyler, *The Empty Crib: A Memorial of Little Georgie, with Words of Consolation for Bereaved Parents* (New York, 1868); *CI,* December 13, 1855.

11. George W. Bethune, *Early Lost; Early Saved: An Argument for the Salvation of Infants* (Philadelphia, 1846), 101–109.

12. Thomas E. Vermilye, "A Funeral Discourse Occasioned by the Death of Mrs. Cornelia Van Rensselaer . . . Delivered in the North Dutch Church, Albany, on Sabbath, the 1st September, 1844" (New York, 1844), 22, Box 117, Imprints, Sp. Cols., RUL.

13. L. H. Van Dyke, "The Death of the Righteous Desirable: A Sermon Preached at the Funeral of Mrs. Clarissa Paige, May 16, 1846, in the Reformed Dutch Church, Gilboa, N.Y." (n.p., 1846), 4–6.

14. For this and the next paragraph, see Hardenbergh Family Papers, Folder 4, n.d., Sp. Cols., RUL.

15. Samuel B. How to Mrs. Eliza Anderson, How Papers, September 11, 1847, Sp. Cols., RUL.

16. Sarah M. Campbell, Diary, September 11, 1824; Adriance Van Brunt, Diary, April 13, 1829.

17. Garretson Hageman, Diary, August 16, 1871, Sp. Cols., RUL.

18. Hageman, ibid., April 16, 1875.

19. Vermilye, "Funeral Discourse," 7; T. De Witt Talmage, *Around the Tea-table* (Philadelphia, 1875), 493–494.

20. *CI,* December 5, 1835; and John C. Cruickshank, "No Intermediate Place: A Sermon . . . in the Reformed Dutch Church of Hyde Park [N.Y.], September 9, 1838" (Poughkeepsie, N.Y., 1839), 8, 15, 16.

21. *CI,* January 4, 1845.

22. Ibid.; *CI,* April 17, 1845.

23. Vermilye, "Funeral Discourse," 8, 11.

24. *CI,* June 2, 1870.

25. *CI,* September 5, 1840; How Papers, June 1, 1836, Sp. Cols., RUL.

26. *CI,* December 18, 1845.

27. Abbott, *Child at Home*, p. 137; American Sunday School Union, *The Paradise of Children* (Philadelphia, 1838), 32–33, 37. The quatrain is found on p. 45.

28. American Sunday School Union (hereafter ASSU), *Paradise*, 46–66 passim.

29. William C. Brownlee, *Lights and Shadows of Christian Life: Designed for the Instruction of the Young* (New York, 1837), 370–371.

30. Cruickshank, "No Intermediate Place," 14, 15, 18.

31. ASSU, *Paradise*, 69–70

32. William C. Brownlee, *The Christian Father at Home* (New York, 1837), 131.

33. John Scudder, *A Voice from the East to the Youth, in a Series of Letters to the Children of the Reformed Protestant Dutch Church of North America* (New York, 1859), 59–61 passim.

34. For this and the next paragraph, Hoagland Family Papers, Sp. Cols., RUL, Folder 8. This eleven-page document is dated September 25, 1858.

35. For this and the following paragraphs, Alice S. White, Memoir, Schenck Family Papers, Sp. Cols., RUL, Ac. 2071, Envelope 10, 16, 17, 19, 39ff., 58, 66–67.

36. S.L.B. Baldwin, "Extracts from Entries in the Diary of the Founder and First Editor of the *Somerset Whig*," as published in the *Unionist Gazette* (Somerville, N.J., 1897), April 28, May 5, and May 12, 1887, Sp. Cols., RUL.

37. A. Th. Van Deursen, *Private Lives in a Golden Age: Popular Culture, Religion, and Society in Seventeenth-Century Holland*, trans. Maarten Ultee (Cambridge, 1991), 244.

38. William B. Sprague, "An Address Delivered in the Middle Dutch Church, Albany, at the Funeral of Mrs. Jane Wyckoff, Wife of the Rev. I. N. Wyckoff, D.D., Monday, January 31, 1847" (Albany, N.Y., 1848), 4.

39. *CI,* July 9, 1831; *CI,* April 11, 1850.

40. *CI,* May 17, 1855.

41. For this and the next paragraph, *The Little Drummer Boy* (New York, 1861), 111–112, 132.

42. *Frank Moore's Antiquities of Long Island*, 1838, reprinted in the *CI,* February 25, 1875.

43. *CI,* June 14, 1855.

44. Cherry Hill Papers, Series 2, Subseries .3, Box 9, Folder 1, April 24, 1852, New York State Library, Albany, N.Y. For the comparison, see H.F.K. Van Nierop, *The Nobility*

*of Holland from Knights to Regents, 1500–1650,* trans. Maarten Ultee (Cambridge, 1992).

45. Baldwin, Diary, March 2, 1838; *CI,* June 6, 1835.
46. *CI,* April 20, 1876.
47. Lou Taylor, *Mourning Dress: A Costume and Social History* (London, 1983), 88. I am grateful to David William Voorhees for the Farmer reference, which can be found in *New York Wills,* Liber 40, 96ff.
48. *Moore's Antiquities,* 1838, as reprinted in the *CI,* February 25, 1875; Elizabeth L. Gebhard, *The Parsonage between Two Manors[:] Annals of Clover-Reach* (Hudson, N.Y., 1909), 265.
49. William Clinton Armstrong, *A Genealogical Record of the Descendants of Nathan Armstrong* (n.p., 1895).
50. Taylor, *Mourning Dress,* 22.
51. Address at consecration ceremonies at the Albany Rural Cemetery, October 7, 1846, 25; hereafter Albany Consecration.
52. C. R. Jones, "The Rural Cemetery in New York," *Heritage* (the Magazine of the New York State Historical Association), 11 (Autumn 1994):7. See also Stanley French, "The Cemetery as Cultural Institution: The Establishment of Mount Auburn and the 'Rural Cemetery' Movement," in *Death in America,* ed. Stannard; and David Charles Sloane, *The Last Great Necessity: Cemeteries in American History* (Baltimore and London, 1991).
53. Albany Consecration, 29 and 30.
54. Ibid., 27–28. Among the original subscribers were Bogart, Brinckerhoff, De Witt, Dey, Gansevoort, Lansing, Pruyn, Schoonhaven, Staats, Ten Broeck, Ten Eyck, Van Alstyne, Van Benthuysen, Van Buren, Van Heusen, Van Ness, Van Rensselaer, Van Schaick, Van Vechten, Vosburgh, Wendell, and Westerlo.
55. Ibid., 31–32.
56. Ibid., 28–29.
57. Ibid., 35–36.
58. *CI,* October 28, 1854.

CHAPTER 10    *"A New American Thing," 1850–1876*

1. Bound typescript, *Memoirs of an Emigrant: The Journal of Alexander Coventry, MD . . . 1766–1831,* 2 vols. (Albany, N.Y., 1978), vol. 2, 2153, 2152, 2344, 2345, 2347, 2554, New York State Library, Albany, N.Y.
2. Washington Irving, Journal, Mss. Room, New York Public Library.
3. S.L.B. Baldwin, Diary, reprinted in the *Unionist Gazette* (Somerville, N.J.), 1897. (The diary itself has been lost.) Special Collections, Alexander Library, Rutgers University; hereafter Sp. Cols., RUL. Entries for Sunday, December 4, 1836; January 14, 1838; May 25, 1842.
4. *The Christian Intelligencer,* August 28, July 22, 1845; hereafter *CI.*
5. *CI,* January 5, 1865. Diaries of Catherine Gansevoort, Box 255, Gansevoort-Lansing Collection, Mss. Room, New York Public Library; hereafter G-L Coll.
6. Calling cards folders, Box 155, G-L Coll.; Maria Melville to Catherine G. Lansing, Box 216, G-L Coll., January 2, 1868. *Olekoeks* or *olykoks* were also called *olicooks* or *olibollen* (oily balls in Bergen County). Kevin Wright, "A Jersey Dutch Christmas at Historic New Bridge Landing," *Early American Life,* December 1993.

7. "Blyth in Holland," *CI,* December 20, 1855.

8. [Guy La Turette], *A North Jersey Jaunt* (n.p., 1873), 84–85.

9. Adrian C. Leiby, *The Dutch and Swedish Settlers of New Jersey* (Princeton, N.J., 1964), 118, 120; Franklin Burdge, "A Notice of John Haring: A Patriotic Statesman of the Revolution," Budke Collection 55, New York Public Library, unpaged. See also Van Cleaf Bachman, Alice P. Kenney, and Lawrence G. Van Loon, "'Het Poelmeisie': An Introduction to the Hudson Valley Dutch Dialect," *New York History* (April 1980), 161–171, for a discussion of *Lag Duits* (Low Dutch), which Van Loon learned to speak from his grandfather, Walter Hill (and which is usually described as of the Mohawk, not the Hudson Valley). An extensive grammar and vocabulary of *Lag Duits,* compiled by Walter Hill beginning in 1869, when the dialect was still in common use in the Mohawk Valley, is in the collections of the New York State Historical Association in Cooperstown, N.Y.

10. James D. Bratt, *Dutch Calvinism in Modern America: A History of a Conservative Subculture* (Grand Rapids, Mich., 1984), 57.

11. [Thomas De Witt], *Memorials of Rev. Thomas De Witt, D.D.* (New York, 1875), 104, 105, 99; Bratt, *Dutch Calvinism,* 41–44.

12. The strictest Calvinists among them came to consider the doctrinal and liturgical purity of the American churches to be too severely compromised to allow of permanent union, and they eventually formed their own denomination, the Christian Reformed Church, to "return to the standpoint of the fathers." Bratt, *Dutch Calvinism,* 39.

13. William O. Van Eyck, *The Union of 1850: A Collection of Papers . . . on the Union of the Classis of Holland [Michigan], with the Reformed Church in America, in June, 1850,* selected and edited by the Permanent Committee on History and Research of the General Synod of the Reformed Church in America (Grand Rapids, Mich., 1950), 96.

14. T. De Witt Talmage, *Around the Tea-table* (Philadelphia, 1875), 414–418.

15. The gap, and the misunderstandings, between the most Calvinistic of the new Dutch from the Netherlands and their American brethren widened over time, as a feisty series of letters to the *Intelligencer* that appeared in 1876 under the headlines "Americanizing the Hollanders" and "Hollandizing the Americans" makes clear. One writer pointed out that even when Americanized, all nationalities retain remnants of their native cultures, and the native-born American continues to regard them as foreign. Thus, wrote "Mont Blanc," there is "no greater question before the nation today than . . . how to amalgamate all the valuable material in these various [foreign] elements, and form out of them [through education] the American nation of the future. . . . Whether our Reformed Church is finally to be classed among what may be called the American churches, or is to be permanently placed among the exotic denominations, depends [on whether the Hollanders] advance as Americans." *CI,* September 7, 1876.

16. The North Dutch Reformed Church was built in 1769 and was the first in which English was used for preaching. News of the meeting had reached as far as Macao, off the south coast of China, in a matter of months. Letter of the Rev. Samuel Bonney, Cherry Hill Papers, Series 3, subseries .1, Box 20, Folder 2, June 10, 1858, New York State Library, Albany, N.Y.

17. *CI,* November 21, 1850. Of the eleven Collegiate churches in the city in the mid-nineteenth century, the most famous were the South Dutch Church at Garden Street, the Middle Dutch Church, which was located over the years in at least three places, the North Dutch Church at Fulton and William streets, the Marble Collegiate Church

at Fifth Avenue and 29th Street, and the West End Collegiate Church on West End Avenue and 77th Street today. The Collegiate churches (called so because their ministers and their consistories were colleagues in every sense of the word) were able with their resources and status to attract the most illustrious clergymen in the denomination, and outside of it. Until 1871, the ministers preached in rotation among the various pulpits under the Collegiate umbrella. Even today, the churches share finances through a corporate structure established by royal charter in 1696, just as they share one large consistory. The archives of the Collegiate churches are at 45 John Street, New York, N.Y.

18. *CI,* September 26, 1860.
19. *CI,* October 4, 1860.
20. Talbot W. Chambers, ed., *Hours of Prayer in the Noon Prayer-Meeting, Fulton Street, New York* (New York, 1871), 28–29.
21. *CI,* June 21, 1860.
22. *CI,* August 23, 1860.
23. *CI,* October 4, 1860; *CI,* June 9, 1870.
24. Talmage, *Around the Tea-table,* 401–402, 404.
25. *CI,* October 28, 1875; *CI,* November 4, 1875.
26. *CI,* January 6, January 20, January 27, 1876. New Yorkers referred to St. Nicholas as the Protestant Cathedral not only because of its proximity to St. Patrick's Roman Catholic Cathedral, but because of its exquisite architecture in the style of the Gothic cathedrals of Europe. It was demolished in 1950 to make room for a commercial building.
27. *CI,* February 17, 1876; Firth Haring Fabend, "Life On and Off the Farm: Diaries of Helen Verbryck Clark, 1876 and 1877," *South of the Mountain* (Historical Society of Rockland County), 36 (October–December 1992):3–12.
28. *CI,* February 3, 1876.
29. *CI,* February 17, 1876.
30. Elbert S. Porter, "The Literature of the Church during the Last Hundred Years," in *Centennial Discourses. A Series of Sermons Delivered in the Year 1876. By the Order of the General Synod of the Reformed (Dutch) Church in America,* 2d ed. (New York, 1877), 10. See H. Richard Niebuhr, *The Social Sources of Denominationalism* (New York, 1929), 6, for an indictment of denominationalism as an "unacknowledged hypocrisy" in the church, a compromise between Christianity and the world, and the accommodation of Christianity to the "caste-system of human society."
31. *CI,* August 26, 1875.
32. *CI,* August 19, August 26, October 14, October 21, and October 28, 1875; May 4, July 27, August 3, August 10, August 17, August 24, and August 31, 1876.
33. *CI,* March 11, 1875.
34. Gerald F. De Jong, in "The Controversy over Dropping the Word Dutch from the Name of the Reformed Church," *Reformed Review* 34 (Spring 1981), noted that the struggle was "frequently bitter and seriously disturbed the peace and harmony of the church."
35. Isaac Ferris, "Ecclesiastical Characteristics of the Reformed Dutch Church," 1848, in *Writings* (bound sermons, addresses, and discourses), Sage Library, New Brunswick Theological Seminary, 40.
36. New Jersey Broadsides, 1854, Sp. Cols., RUL.
37. Parts I and III of the Constitution of 1793 and its revisions can be found in Edward T. Corwin, *A Digest of Constitutional and Synodical Legislation of the Reformed*

*Church in America* (New York, 1906). The three-part Constitution includes a full liturgy (Part II) equal in importance to the doctrines of the church (Part I) and to the rules of government (Part III). The liturgy can be found in the two works by Daniel J. Meeter cited in notes 39 and 42.

38. A recent translation of the full text of the Canons of Dort and the Refutations of the Arminian errors can be found in *Ecumenical Creeds and Reformed Confessions* (Grand Rapids, Mich., 1987) and in the Psalter Hymnal of the Christian Reformed Church, copyright 1987. Both of these are published by CRC Publications, 2850 Kalamazoo SE., Grand Rapids, Michigan 49560.

39. Daniel J. Meeter, "The 'North American Liturgy': A Critical Edition of the Liturgy of the Reformed Dutch Church in North America, 1793" (diss., Drew University, 1989). Before its adjournment, Meeter writes, the Synod appointed an editorial committee to review the records of the Synod and to publish an official version of the Canons and the Post-Acta, as well as new editions of the Heidelberg Catechism, the Belgic Confession, and the Liturgy. "But of all the items on the committee's agenda, the texts of the Catechism and Liturgy were the least controversial and pressing, and the assignment was never completed," 50–51.

40. Eugene Heideman, "It Made Us Who We Are," *Church Herald*, December 1992, 8–9. Further, in language stating that "the unerring Word of God remaining the only standard of the Faith and Worship of his people, they can never incur the charge of presumption, in openly declaring what to them appears to be the mind and will of their Divine Lord and Savior," the Constitution officially maintained the doctrines of Dort. But, as Heideman has written in another context, "local ministers and consistories were left free to follow the leading of the Spirit of God." Eugene Heideman, "Theology," in *Piety and Patriotism: Bicentennial Studies of the Reformed Church in America, 1776–1976*, ed. James Van Hoeven (Grand Rapids, Mich., 1976), 99, 101–102. See also James Van Hoeven, "Dort and Albany," in *Word and World: Reformed Theology in America*, ed. James Van Hoeven (Grand Rapids, Mich., 1986).

41. John W. Coakley, "John Henry Livingston and the Liberty of the Conscience," *Reformed Review* 46 (Winter 1992):119–135.

42. Daniel J. Meeter, *Meeting Each Other in Doctrine, Liturgy, and Government: The Bicentennial of the Celebration of the Constitution of the Reformed Church in America* (Grand Rapids, Mich., 1993), 145–149, and chap. 5, "The Constitution, Text and Commentary," 46–144 passim.

43. General Synod Papers, Box 4, Classical Reports 1854, Sage Library, New Brunswick Theological Seminary; *Acts and Proceedings of the General Synod of the Reformed Protestant Dutch Church in North America* (New York, 1854), 494.

44. "Dr. Vermilye's Discourse," *Quarter-Millennial Anniversary of the Protestant Reformed Dutch Church* (New York, 1878), 23–24.

45. Gansevoort Memoir, 239, G-L Coll.

46. Gordon S. Wood, reviewing Jill Lepore, *The Name of War: King Philip's War and the Origins of American Identity*, in the *New York Review of Books,* 45 (Spring 1998):44.

# A NOTE ON SOURCES

The printed primary sources consulted in the writing of this book are cited in the notes, and they are not repeated here. They fall into several broad categories: the invaluable documents and records of the Reformed Church in America itself, including individual church histories; the *Christian Intelligencer,* the denomination's weekly newspaper; the prescriptive literature aimed at parents, especially mothers; teachers' and students' Sabbath school guides; juvenilia; and sermons.

Secondary sources indispensable to an understanding of the era and the Reformed Church's role in it include, first, works in The Historical Series of the Reformed Church in America, of which there are at this writing thirty-one. Of these, which are all published by William B. Eerdmans in Grand Rapids, Michigan, the most important are, in chronological order, James W. Van Hoeven, ed., *Piety and Patriotism: Bicentennial Studies of the Reformed Church in America, 1776–1976* (1976); Gerald F. De Jong, *The Dutch Reformed Church in the American Colonies* (1978); John W. Beardslee III, ed., *Vision from the Hill* (1984); Howard G. Hageman, *Two Centuries Plus: The Story of New Brunswick Seminary* (1984); James W. Van Hoeven, ed., *Word and World: Reformed Theology in America* (1986); Daniel J. Meeter, *Meeting Each Other in Doctrine, Liturgy, and Government: The Bicentennial of the Celebration of the Constitution of the Reformed Church in America* (1993); Elton J. Bruins, *The Americanization of a Congregation,* revised edition (1995); and Renée S. House and John W. Coakley, eds., *Patterns and Portraits: Women in the History of the Reformed Church in America* (1999). Important works about the Reformed Church that are not in the Historical Series are also extremely useful, especially James D. Bratt, *Dutch Calvinism in Modern America: A History of a Conservative Subculture* (Grand Rapids, Mich., 1984); M. Eugene Osterhaven,

*The Faith of the Church: A Reformed Perspective on Its Historical Development* (Grand Rapids, Mich., 1982); and James R. Tanis, *Dutch Calvinistic Pietism in the Middle Colonies: A Study of the Life and Theology of Theodorus J. Frelinghuysen* (The Hague, 1967).

For American religion in general, and for both the Great Awakening in the eighteenth century, and the Second Great Awakening and the so-called age of revivals in the nineteenth, secondary works that inform and enrich *Zion on the Hudson*, whether cited in the text or not, are those (listed here alphabetically by author) by Patricia U. Bonomi, *Under the Cope of Heaven: Religion, Science, and Politics in Colonial America* (New York, 1986); Jon Butler, *Awash in a Sea of Faith: Christianizing the American People* (Cambridge, Mass., 1990); Paul Boyer, *Urban Masses and Moral Order in America, 1820–1920* (Cambridge, Mass., 1978); Joseph A. Conforti, *Samuel Hopkins and the New Divinity Movement: Calvinism, the Congregational Ministry, and Reform in New England between the Great Awakenings* (Grand Rapids, Mich., 1981); and Whitney R. Cross, *The Burned-Over District: The Social and Intellectual History of Enthusiastic Religion in Western New York, 1800–1850* (Ithaca, N.Y., 1950). Also, Charles I. Foster, *An Errand of Mercy: The Evangelical United Front, 1790–1837* (Chapel Hill, N.C., 1960); Charles E. Hambrick-Stowe, *Charles G. Finney and the Spirit of American Evangelicalism* (Grand Rapids, Mich., 1996); Nathan Hatch, *Democratization of American Christianity* (New Haven, Conn., 1989); Curtis D. Johnson, *Islands of Holiness: Rural Religion in Upstate New York, 1790–1860* (Ithaca, N.Y., 1989); Paul E. Johnson, *Shopkeeper's Millennium: Society and Revivals in Rochester, New York, 1815–1837* (New York, 1978); George M. Marsden, *The Evangelical Mind and the New School Presbyterian Experience: A Case Study of Thought* (New Haven, Conn., 1970); George M. Marsden, *Theology in Nineteenth-Century America* (New Haven, Conn., 1970); George M. Marsden, *Religion and American Culture* (New York, 1990); William G. McLouglin, *Revivals, Awakenings, and Reform: An Essay on Religion and Social Change in America, 1607–1977* (Chicago, 1978); Timothy L. Smith, *Revivalism and Social Reform: American Protestantism on the Eve of the Civil War* (Baltimore, 1957); Leonard I. Sweet, *The Minister's Wife: Her Role in Nineteenth-Century American Evangelicalism* (Philadelphia, 1983); Leonard I. Sweet, ed., *The Evangelical Tradition in America* (Macon, Ga., 1984); William Warren Sweet, *Revivalism in America: Its Origin, Growth and Decline* (New York, 1944); and Bernard A. Weisberger, *They Gathered at the River: The Story of the Great Revivalists and Their Impact upon Religion in America* (Boston, 1958). The many works on the connections between religion and ethnicity by John Higham, Martin E. Marty, Timothy L. Smith, Harry S.

Stout, and others were also invaluable to an appreciation of that important relationship. I might add here that, in spite of its unique experience of and contributions to the events and ideas of the evangelical age, neither the Reformed Dutch Church nor its many influential nineteenth-century clergymen are given any attention in any of the excellent works cited in this paragraph.

Rather than go into these printed sources in detail, I will instead briefly describe here the unprinted sources and the printed ephemera that allowed the fleshing out of this portrait of Dutch New York and New Jersey in the middle five decades of the nineteenth century, and how I identified them.

The material I sought consisted of diaries, letters, and family papers that might shed light on the connection between the Reformed Dutch religion and the persistence of Dutchness in nineteenth-century New York and New Jersey. As I conceived of this work as a view not only into the pew but also out of it, I looked as well for personal descriptions of social and family life, trends in education, marrying patterns, attitudes toward ecumenical, moral reform, and benevolent activities, and information about the culture of death and dying that would bolster the context I was trying to reconstitute of the evangelical era and an evangelical people.

The collections holding this material are in the libraries cited in the Acknowledgments, and I used a rather primitive method for locating what I sought. I asked to see, from the printed guides to the collections, or in the card catalogs, as it depended, those particular items that belonged to persons with Dutch-sounding last names. I also asked to see the papers of known Reformed Dutch clergy. This rudimentary approach proved surprisingly fruitful. I located in this way the papers of the Beekman, Bogert, Chamberlain, Frelinghuysen, Gansevoort, Hageman, Hardenbergh, How, Kiersted, Knox, Lansing, Lloyd, Nevius, Pohlman, Pruyn, Schenck, Schureman, Stryker, Ten Eyck, Van Brunt, Van Cleef, Van Dyke, Van Rensselaer, Van Schaick, Vanderveer, Van Deventer, Van Olinda, Van Vorst, Vermeule, Vredenburg, Wortendyke, Wyckoff, and Zabriskie families and individuals, among others.

Sometimes, of course, the Dutch-sounding name turned out to be associated with a Presbyterian or an Episcopalian church, and sometimes a request yielded only one nugget of information or, disappointingly, nothing at all. But often I hit upon a gold mine of social history unbelievably rich, as in the case of the Hageman diaries and the Schenck and related family papers at Rutgers, the Fred Bogert Collection at the Bergen County Historical Archives, the Maria Ferdon diaries at the Bergen County Historical Society—all of which opened up to me the life of the times and the people I was trying to recapture.

Another primitive but effective technique I used to get at the era and Reformed evangelicals' part in it was to browse through the imprint catalogs and broadsides files of libraries and collections. In this way I found the forgotten documents of an era also much forgotten: sermons and learned disquisitions to be sure, but also Sabbath school classroom plans, calling cards and graduation exercises, Fourth of July programs, notices of revival meetings and strawberry festivals and Sunday school picnics, golden wedding invitations, funeral programs, prayer meetings, singing schools, and sleigh rides—a blend of sacred and secular images that perfectly reflected the era's intertwining of the religious and the secular.

Together, all of this material—printed and scholarly, unprinted and personal, printed and public—has yielded, I hope, a picture of the religious culture of the Second Great Awakening and its aftermath in New York and New Jersey, a portrait also of the earnest people who attempted so strenuously to make their world a better place, while also having a very good time, and an explanation for the long persistence of Dutchness in the area once known as New Netherland.

# INDEX

Page numbers in italics refer to illustrations or their captions.

# ABOUT THE AUTHOR

Firth Haring Fabend holds a doctorate in American Studies from New York University. She is the author of *A Dutch Family in the Middle Colonies, 1660–1800* (Rutgers University Press, 1991), winner of the New York State Historical Association Annual Book Award and the Hendricks Prize of the New Netherland Project. A Fellow of both the Holland Society of New York and of the New Netherland Project, she is also the author of five novels published between 1968 and 1985, numerous articles, and a historical poem, *A Cutch of Grandmothers* (New York, 2000).